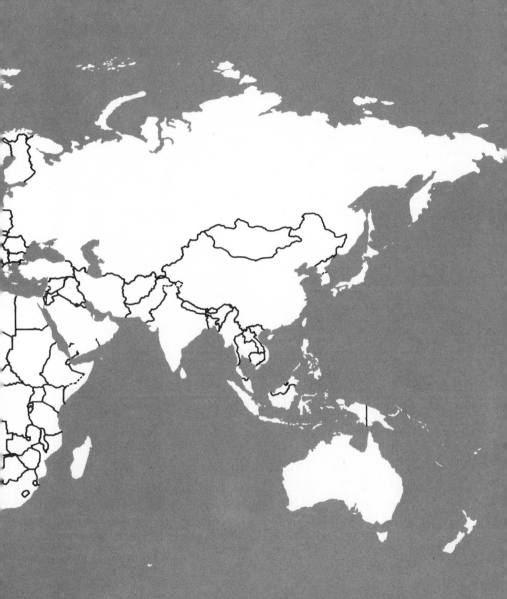

Thailand
a country study

Federal Research Division
Library of Congress
Edited by
Barbara Leitch LePoer
Research Completed
September 1987

On the cover: Wat Phra Keo (Temple of the Emerald
Buddha) on the grounds of the Grand Palace in Bangkok;
illustration by Teresa Kamp

#18 90 7877

Sixth Edition, First Printing, 1989.

Library of Congress Cataloging-in-Publication Data

Thailand: A Country Study

(Area handbook series) (DA Pam; 550-53)
Research completed November 1987.
Bibliography: pp. 313–346.
Includes index.
Supt. of Docs. no.: D 101.22:550-53/987
1. Thailand. I. LePoer, Barbara Leitch, 1941-   .
II. Library of Congress. Federal Research Division. III. Series.
IV. Series: DA Pam; 550-53.

DS563.5.T4563   1989   959.3   88-600485

Headquarters, Department of the Army
DA Pam 550-53

For sale by the Superintendent of Documents, U.S. Government Printing Office
Washington, D.C. 20402

Foreword

This volume is one in a continuing series of books now being prepared by the Federal Research Division of the Library of Congress under the Country Studies—Area Handbook Program. The last page of this book lists the other published studies.

Most books in the series deal with a particular foreign country, describing and analyzing its political, economic, social, and national security systems and institutions, and examining the interrelationships of those systems and the ways they are shaped by cultural factors. Each study is written by a multidisciplinary team of social scientists. The authors seek to provide a basic understanding of the observed society, striving for a dynamic rather than a static portrayal. Particular attention is devoted to the people who make up the society, their origins, dominant beliefs and values, their common interests and the issues on which they are divided, the nature and extent of their involvement with national institutions, and their attitudes toward each other and toward their social system and political order.

The books represent the analysis of the authors and should not be construed as an expression of an official United States government position, policy, or decision. The authors have sought to adhere to accepted standards of scholarly objectivity. Corrections, additions, and suggestions for changes from readers will be welcomed for use in future editions.

Louis R. Mortimer
Acting Chief
Federal Research Division
Library of Congress
Washington, D.C. 20540

Acknowledgments

The editor and authors are grateful to numerous individuals in the international community, in various agencies of the United States government, and in private organizations who gave of their time, research materials, and special knowledge to provide data and perspective for this study.

The authors also wish to express their appreciation to staff members of the Federal Research Division, Library of Congress, whose high standards and dedication helped shape this volume. These include Martha E. Hopkins, who managed editing and book production, as well as editing portions of the text, Marilyn L. Majeska, who edited parts of the manuscript and the accompanying figures and tables, and editorial assistants Barbara Edgerton and Izella Watson. David P. Cabitto and Kimberly A. Lord prepared the book's graphics, Susan M. Lender reviewed the maps, and Arvies J. Staton contributed to the charts on military rank and insignia.

The following individuals are gratefully acknowledged as well: Ruth Nieland, Vincent Ercolano, and Mary Ann Saour for editing various chapters; Catherine Schwartzstein for the final prepublication editorial review; Shirley Kessell of Communicators Connection for preparing the index; and Malinda B. Neale of the Printing and Processing Section, Library of Congress, for phototypesetting, under the direction of Peggy Pixley. Special thanks go to Teresa E. Kamp, who designed the illustrations for the cover of the volume and the title pages of the chapters. The inclusion of photographs in this book was made possible by the generosity of various individuals and public and private agencies.

Finally, the editor and authors wish to thank Federal Research Division staff members Mervin J. Shello and Ly H. Burnham for sharing their expertise in telecommunications and demography; Tracy M. Henry for her assistance in word processing; Meridel M. Jackson for her economic insights and computer expertise; and Russell R. Ross, Robert L. Worden, and Richard F. Nyrop for reviewing all parts of the book.

Contents

List of Figures

Preface

The *Area Handbook for Thailand*, first published in 1971, was revised in 1981 as *Thailand: A Country Study*. This volume, a revision of the 1981 edition, recounts developments in Thailand during the 1980s, a period of relative political stability and respectable economic growth. Recently Thailand's attention has focused increasingly on regional concerns as, in concert with other members of the Association of Southeast Asian Nations (ASEAN), it has attempted to deal with the problem of the Vietnamese occupation of Cambodia.

Like its predecessors, this study is an attempt to present an objective and concise account of the dominant social, economic, political, and national security concerns of contemporary Thailand, as well as to provide a historical framework for this overview. The 1981 edition, which this volume replaces, was prepared by a team composed of Robert Rinehart, Irving Kaplan, Donald P. Whitaker, Rinn-Sup Shinn, and Harold D. Nelson and led by Frederica M. Bunge.

The current *Thailand: A Country Study* results from the combined efforts of a multidisciplinary team. The authors obtained information from a variety of sources, including scholarly studies, official reports of government and international organizations, and foreign and domestic newspapers and periodicals. Brief commentary on some of the more useful and readily accessible English-language sources appears at the end of each chapter. Full references to these and other sources used by the authors are listed in the Bibliography.

The authors have tried to limit the use of foreign and technical terms, which are defined when they first appear in the study. Readers are also referred to the Glossary at the back of the book. In general, Thai personal names conform to the system of romanization followed by the Library of Congress. Certain exceptions have been made, including names of the monarchs of the Chakkri Dynasty (see table 2, Appendix) and those of certain other persons more familiar to Western readers in variant forms. Some religious and social terms are given in Thai; others are in Sanskrit, following usage in *Webster's Third New International Dictionary* (unabridged edition), or in Pali, the language of Theravada Buddhist scriptures. Contemporary place-names used in this study are those approved by the United States Board on Geographic Names. All measurements are given in the metric system (see table 1, Appendix).

Country Profile

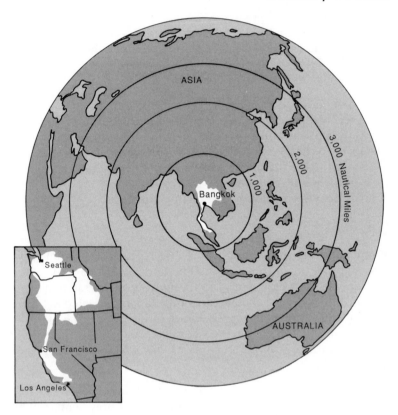

Country

Formal Name: Kingdom of Thailand.

Short Form: Thailand (formerly Siam).

Term for Citizens: Thai.

Capital: Bangkok.

Geography

Size: Approximately 514,000 square kilometers.

Topography: Chief topographic features include central plain dominated by Mae Nam (river) Chao Phraya and its tributaries. To northeast rises dry, undulating Khorat Plateau bordered on east by Mekong River. Mountains along northern and western borders with Burma extend south into narrow, largely rain-forested Malay Peninsula. Network of rivers and canals associated with northern mountains and central plain drain, via Chao Phraya, into Gulf of Thailand. Mae Nam Mun and other northeastern streams drain via Mekong into South China Sea. Soils vary. Topography and drainage define four regions: North, Northeast, Center, and South.

Climate: Tropical monsoon climate. Southwest monsoons arriving between May and July signal start of rainy season lasting until October. Cycle reverses with northeast monsoon in November and December, ushering in dry season. Cooler temperatures give way to extremely hot, dry weather March through May. In general, rainfall heaviest in South, lightest in Northeast.

Society

Population: About 53 million in 1987; 1.9 percent annual growth rate in 1986, down from 3.1 in 1960 and 2.5 in late 1970s. Level of urbanization 17 percent in 1987, mostly concentrated in capital region. Bangkok metropolitan area population estimated at 5.5 million in 1987; ten next largest cities range between 80,000 and 110,000 in population. Overall density 100.5 persons per square kilometer in 1987, varying from 62 in Chiang Mai Province to 3,292 in Bangkok.

Languages: More than 85 percent of population speak dialect of Thai (a member of Tai language family); most prevalent are Thai-Lao, spoken in Northeast, and Central Thai, which is official language taught in schools and used in government. Other languages spoken by members of ethnic minorities include Chinese (chiefly Teochiu), Malay, Karen, and Khmer. Smaller groups speak Tai languages such as Shan, Lua, and Phutai. Many minority peoples, especially Chinese, also speak Thai.

Ethnic and Regional Groups: Four regional categories make up core Thai population: Central Thai (32 percent); Thai-Lao (30 percent); Northern Thai (17 percent); and Southern Thai (5 percent). Largest minority consists of Chinese (11 percent), followed by Malay (3–4 percent), and Khmer (1 percent). Remaining minority groups, including numerous hill tribes, together constituted no more than 2 percent of the population.

Religion: Almost all core Thai, some other Tai speakers, Khmer, and Mon practice Theravada Buddhism. Islam represented chiefly among Malay. Christians found among hill peoples and Vietnamese.

Education: Government supports universal free primary education. Most children attend school several years at least, and more than 85 percent of population literate. Fewer than three out of ten children continue beyond elementary level. More than a dozen universities and specialized postsecondary institutions provide higher education for about 3 percent of youth.

Health: Access to modern medical care and trained physicians chiefly in Bangkok and provincial towns, although government developing rural health centers. Unavailability of potable water for most of rural population contributes to disease. In 1986 life expectancy at birth sixty-one years for men, sixty-five years for women.

Economy

Salient Features: Mixed economy includes both strong private sector and state enterprises; government assumes responsibility for general infrastructure development. Basically capitalist, committed to free trade. Rapid economic development of 1960s and 1970s slowed by worldwide recession of early 1980s. Strong recovery by 1987. Bangkok metropolitan area faced problems of rapid modernization, including housing shortages and pressure on such basic services as water, sewage, and health care.

Agriculture: Food surpluses produced by dominant agricultural sector of enterprising, independent smallholders. About 69 percent of labor force engaged in sector, and nearly 80 percent of population dependent on it for livelihood in the mid-1980s. Agricultural commodities accounted for some 60 percent of export values in late 1980s. Major crops included rice, maize, cassava, rubber, sugarcane, coconuts, cotton, kenaf, and tobacco. Forest cover decreased from more than 50 percent in 1961 to less than 30 percent in 1987. Fisheries important for food supply and foreign exchange earnings.

Industry: Modern enterprises mainly concentrated in Bangkok and surrounding provinces. Majority Thai owned, but joint foreign ventures numerous; state enterprises form important segment. In late 1980s, sector accounted for roughly 20 percent of gross domestic product (GDP) and 30 percent of total exports. Main categories of manufacturing included food and beverages, textiles and apparel, and wood and mineral products. Mineral resources contributed about 2 percent to gross national product (GNP) and included tin, tungsten, fluorite, antimony, and precious stones, all significant foreign exchange earners.

Energy Sources: Exploited domestic resources include small oil fields, large lignite deposits, natural gas in Gulf of Thailand, and hydroelectric power. Extensive, largely unevaluated oil shale deposits also identified, but exploitation economically infeasible in 1980s. Thermal (oil, natural gas, and lignite) power generation accounted for about 70 percent of total 7,570 megawatt installed generating capacity in 1986; hydropower, which remained largely unexploited, supplied about 30 percent. Electricity generally available in Bangkok metropolitan area and in about 43,000 of nation's some 48,000 villages (mostly near Bangkok). Rural program under way for electrification of remaining villages by late 1990s.

Foreign Trade: Major exports primary and processed agricultural products, tin, clothing, and other manufactured consumer goods. Major imports capital goods, intermediate products, and raw materials; petroleum products largest single import by monetary value since mid-1970s. Largest trading partners Japan and United States; trade with Japan characterized by large deficit.

Transportation and Communications

Railroads: Main lines (4,000 kilometers of track) originating in Bangkok run to national borders with Malaysia in south, Cambodia in east, and Laos in northeast; a northern line goes to Chiang Mai. Railroads remained important in 1987 for transport of bulk commodities and passengers despite heavy inroads by truck and bus transport.

Roads: Primary network of national highways (20,000 kilometers), more than 90 percent paved. Secondary system of provincial roads (more than 24,000 kilometers)—many impassable in rainy season—tie provincial towns and population centers to national highway system. Village roads, tracks, and footpaths totaled between 40,000 and 60,000 kilometers. Motor vehicles registered in 1984 included 688,000 automobiles (most in Bangkok metropolitan area), 600,000 commercial vehicles, and nearly 2 million motorcycles.

Inland Waterways: Extensive network of waterways formed by rivers and canals of central plain and Chao Phraya Delta carry passengers and extensive quantities of rice and other freight. Navigable by barge to Uttaradit in rainy season and to Nakhon Sawan in dry season.

Maritime Shipping: Bangkok, preeminent port, handled about 98 percent of imports, 65 percent of exports, and about 40 percent of coastal traffic in the mid-1980s. Some thirty small ports along Gulf of Thailand and Andaman Sea. Merchant fleet in international service in 1985 totaled about 100 freighters, tankers, and bulk carriers. Unknown number of small coastal craft supported trade with Malaysia and Singapore.

Civil Aviation: Domestic air service to about twenty cities and towns throughout country and also flights to Penang, Vientiane, and Hanoi in late 1980s. International service provided by Thai Airways International (THAI) from Bangkok and Chiang Mai to Asia, Middle East, Europe, North America, and Australia. About forty international airlines also served Thailand. Bangkok main air traffic center for Asia-Europe flights.

Telecommunications: By mid-1980s about 560,000 telephones (70 percent located in Bangkok), 275 radio stations, nearly 8 million radio receivers, 9 television stations (all color), and more than 3 million television sets.

Government and Politics

Party and Government: Constitutional monarchy established 1932. King Bhumibol Adulyadej (1946–) formally reigns over highly centralized unitary state, but real decision making in affairs of state rests with prime minister, in late 1987 General Prem Tinsulanonda. Prime minister need not be elected member of National Assembly, the national legislature; can assume position solely by assertion of leadership, with his role subsequently legitimized through pro forma royal appointment. Governmental system based on Constitution promulgated in December 1978 and divided into executive, bicameral legislature (House of Representatives and Senate), and judiciary. Multiparty system with sixteen parties participating in 1986 election; partisan politics gaining in importance but still largely a function of personalities. Practical politics confined mostly to members of military-bureaucratic elites and their supporters.

Administrative Divisions: Country divided into seventy-three provinces (*changwat*); subdivisions include districts (*amphoe*), subdistricts (*king amphoe*), communes (*tambon*), villages (*muban*), and municipalities (*tesaban*).

Judicial System: Judiciary consists of Supreme Court, Court of Appeal, magistrates' courts, labor and juvenile courts, and courts of first instance. Judges appointed and removed only with approval of Judicial Service Commission, which exercises jurisdiction over courts. Ministry of Justice appoints and supervises administrative personnel and determines matters of judicial procedure.

Foreign Affairs: Strong interest shown in development of multilateral relations with neighboring countries through Association of Southeast Asian Nations (ASEAN); in early 1987, major concern of Thailand and ASEAN was continuing presence of Vietnamese troops in Cambodia.

National Security

Armed Forces: Total personnel strength about 273,000 in mid-1987; components were Royal Thai Army (190,000), Royal Thai Navy (40,000, including 20,000 marines), and Royal Thai Air Force (43,000). Conscription law required 2 years' military service by male citizens between ages of 21 and 30, except those granted exemptions for variety of reasons; about 30,000 inducted annually. Reserves totaled approximately 500,000, most having served in army.

Combat Units and Major Equipment: Army organized into seven infantry divisions (including five tank battalions), one armored division, one cavalry division (with an armor capability), eight independent infantry battalions, two special forces divisions, one field artillery division, and one air defense artillery division. Naval combat forces included Royal Fleet of some 150 vessels and brigade of Royal Thai Marine Corps composed of one artillery battalion, six infantry battalions, and one amphibious assault battalion. Air force consisted of one forward ground attack squadron, two fighter-interceptor squadrons, one armed reconnaissance squadron, three transport squadrons, one utility squadron, two helicopter squadrons, one training squadron, seven counterinsurgency squadrons, and four battalions of airfield defense troops. Equipment inventory included about 150 combat and 100 support aircraft. Combat aircraft included thirty-eight F–5E and F–5F fighter-bombers; twelve F–16 fighters scheduled for delivery in 1988. In 1987 bulk of armored fighting vehicles, artillery, missiles, aircraft, and naval vessels provided by United States; additional sources included Britain, Italy, Israel, Canada, France, Indonesia, Japan, and New Zealand. Domestic arms industry growing rapidly.

Military Budget: In the mid-1980s, outlays for national defense, including internal security costs, averaged about 30 percent of total annual government expenditures and about 4.2 percent of GNP.

Police Agencies and Paramilitary Forces: Thailand National Police Department total personnel strength about 110,000 in 1987; major operational components included Provincial Police, Metropolitan Police, Border Patrol Police (BPP), and Central

Investigation Bureau. Paramilitary forces included BPP and civilian militia-like Volunteer Defense Corps; both used in suppressing armed insurgency supported by Communist Party of Thailand.

Foreign Military Alliances: United States remained committed to Thai security under Rusk-Thanat agreement of 1962 between United States and Thailand.

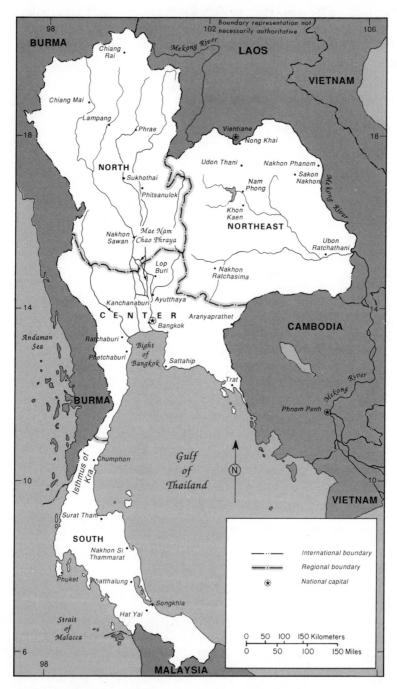

Figure 1. Thailand, 1987

Introduction

A STABLE AND PROSPERING NATION located in the heart of mainland Southeast Asia, Thailand faced the 1990s with abundant resources, not the least of which was its people. Thai society was characterized by a rich blend of cultural traits, an openness to new ideas, and a high degree of adaptability to new situations. Despite a certain amount of diversity, Thai society, according to many observers, was bound together by three basic tenets: Theravada Buddhism, support for the Thai monarchy, and pride of citizenship in the only nation in Southeast Asia to have maintained its independence throughout its history, including the colonial era (see fig. 1).

Centuries of migration of various peoples into the region centered on the valley of the Mae Nam (river) Chao Phraya, followed by decades of conscious nation building by the rulers of the Chakkri Dynasty, had resulted in a relatively homogeneous society based on a wide range of cultural influences. The majority of the populace could trace its lineage over the centuries to the Tai peoples (see Glossary) who inhabited southern China in the first millennium A.D. Forced southward by the pressure of an expanding Chinese empire, bands of Tai filtered into Southeast Asia interacting with other ethnic groups that had preceded them. By the late thirteenth century, the Tai states of Sukhothai and Lan Na had been founded in regions previously ruled by the Khmer and the Mon, respectively. Through interaction with these two peoples, the Tai were exposed to the culture, religion, arts, and languages of India. The Hindu-Buddhist traditions of neighboring Mon and Khmer kingdoms strongly influenced the development of the Tai concept of kingship.

Following the fourteenth-century relocation of the Sukhothai capital southward to Ayutthaya on the floodplain of the Chao Phraya, Theravada Buddhism was made the state religion. The Ayutthaya kings gradually extended their suzerainty southward into the Malay Peninsula in the fifteenth century, where their expansion was stopped by the Muslim state of Malacca. To the east, Ayutthaya established intermittent control over the old Khmer Empire. The sixteenth to eighteenth centuries were marked by frequent wars with the Burmese kingdoms to the northwest, culminating in the destruction of the capital of Ayutthaya by the Burmese in 1767. Out of the ashes of Ayutthaya arose a new Tai kingdom centered at Thon Buri on the Chao Phraya Delta. In the following century the rulers of the Chakkri Dynasty, having moved the capital across the river to Bangkok, expanded their control over neighboring Tai principalities centered at Chiang Mai to the north and Vientiane and Luang Prabang to the east. The new kingdom, known as Siam, also established a tributary relationship over the Khmers of Cambodia. Trade with China and India was greatly expanded, and Siamese control was established over many of the trade depots of the Malay Peninsula.

The economy of Siam, as that of its predecessers, Ayutthaya and Sukhothai, was based on wet-rice agriculture. The peasantry, who worked not only their own rice fields but also performed service for a lord or patron under a system known as *sakdi na* (see Glossary), made up the vast majority of the population. Rice production was greatly increased in the second half of the nineteenth century as new lands were cultivated by an expanding peasantry. By the end of the century, Siam was a major rice-exporting country, with most exports going to India and China. Jobs associated with the rice trade—merchants, millers, and stevedores—were filled by Chinese immigrants, who increasingly flooded into the region from southeastern China after 1850. Many Chinese also entered the lower echelons of the Siamese civil service at that time.

The international side of Siam's rice trade was largely handled by Western merchants. European traders and missionaries had made their way to the Tai court at Ayutthaya as early as the sixteenth century. Substantial Western impact on Siam, however, began with the reign of King Mongkut (Rama IV, 1851–68). Prior to his accession to the throne, Mongkut had had extensive contact with Western missionaries and had studied European languages, science, and mathematics. Determined that his kingdom should not fall under Western colonial rule, as had neighboring Burma, Mongkut established diplomatic and trade relations with Britain, France, the United States, and other Western powers during his reign. As a result, Siam became a part of the international economic community. Under Mongkut's son and successor, Chulalongkorn (Rama V, 1868–1910), major reforms and Westernization of the bureaucracy and society were adopted. At the same time, the central government tightened its control over outlying territories in the North and Northeast geographical regions that had previously been rather loosely governed through local princes and chiefs. By the early twentieth century, however, Siam had been forced to give up its suzerainty over Laos and western Cambodia to the French and its control over four Muslim states on the Malay Peninsula to the British. In return for these losses, Siam became a protected buffer state between French Indochina and British Malaya and Burma.

Reform and modernization supported by Mongkut and Chulalongkorn led to the rise of a Westernized military and political elite who increasingly agitated for a liberalizing of the political process. The Chakkri kings of the early twentieth century and their close advisers were somewhat less concerned with modernization of their rule and resisted efforts at establishing a constitutional monarchy. In 1932 a small group of Westernized military leaders and top bureaucrats organized a bloodless coup, forcing a constitutional monarchy on King Prajadhipok (Rama VII, 1925–35). Divisiveness within the coup leadership, however, resulted in several decades of new constitutions and repeated coups, led by various military-bureaucratic factions.

In 1939 the highly nationalistic regime of Prime Minister Luang Plaek Phibunsongkhram changed the name of the country to Muang Thai (Land of the Free), or Thailand. Negotiation and compromise by Phibun (as he was known) and his colleagues in government enabled the Thai to avoid the whole weight of a Japanese occupation force during World War II. Although officially the Thai government had declared war on the Allies, its declaration was never delivered or accepted in the United States, which became a gathering point for Thai resistance efforts. Following the war, the Thai military continued its ascendancy in national life, and a growing communist insurgency in the 1950s prompted a buildup of Thai military strength. The United States government provided aid in the form of weapons and training for the Royal Thai Armed Forces. As United States involvement in Southeast Asia steadily increased during the Second Indochina War (1954–75), Thailand gave permission for the stationing of United States troops at a number of Thai naval and air bases, which were expanded and modernized. Following the end of the war and the détente between Beijing and Washington, Thailand established its own détente with China, which agreed not to support the Communist Party of Thailand. Thereafter, the government applied a combined military-economic approach to defeat the communist insurgents, who had dwindled to a handful by the mid-1980s.

Student-led demonstrations in the 1970s had resulted in the liberalization of government policies and a brief, but unsuccessful, experiment with democratic government. By the late 1970s, the Thai military-bureaucratic elites were again firmly in charge. Although the 1978 Constitution called for an elected House of Representatives in the nation's bicameral legislature, the National Assembly, the prime minister continued to be selected by a small group of top-ranking military and bureaucratic leaders with the official approval of the king. There was no constitutional requirement that the prime minister be an elected official, and not since 1976 had the position been filled by an elected member of parliament. The members of the Senate, largely drawn from the armed forces and police, were nominated by the prime minister and approved by the king (see The Central Government, ch. 4).

As a constitutional monarch, King Bhumibol Adulyadej (Rama IX, 1946–) had endeavored to maintain a low political profile throughout his reign, and he appeared to be dedicated to the expansion of the democratic process in Thailand. Bhumibol's devotion to the welfare of his people was widely recognized. His particular interests included agricultural research and water resource management, and he had initiated some 4,600 development projects in these areas. A working monarch, the king (as well as his family) spent many months of the year visiting all corners of the realm, acquainting himself with the problems and needs of the people. Bhumibol's rare assertions of political influence had been employed chiefly to maintain stability; in 1981 and again in 1985 he refused to support a military coup attempt, instead backing the legitimately elected government and the Constitution. Although the Thai government had been changed by an endless succession of coups and countercoups following the 1932 revolt, there had not been a successful coup since 1977. In 1987 Prime Minister Prem Tinsulanonda had served seven years in the post, despite the two attempted coups. The country's political stability in the 1980s had provided a favorable setting for Thailand's expanding economy.

By 1987 the Thai economy was continuing to rebound from the worldwide recession that had resulted from the rising oil prices of the mid-1970s (see Economic and Financial Development, ch. 3). The economy grew by more than 6 percent in 1987 and was expected to increase by at least that much in 1988. The manufacturing sector increased by more than 8 percent in 1987, reflecting a growing trend in the structure of the Thai economy toward light industry. Although food processing and other agro-industries continued to be important, expansion was taking place in many industries, such as textiles, where production was up nearly 50 percent in 1987 over the previous year. Exports of manufactures that grew rapidly in 1987 included plastic parts (up 187 percent), computer parts (up 111 percent), footwear (up 100 percent), and ball bearings (up 70 percent). In 1987 manufacturing accounted for about 22 percent of the gross domestic product (GDP—see Glossary). Providing sufficient energy for its fast-growing industrial base, however, was a serious problem. Efforts were ongoing to find a cost-effective way to tap the country's limited petroleum and natural gas potential. Despite energy shortages, Thailand in the late 1980s was moving assuredly into the category of newly industrialized country (NIC), to join the ranks of its Asian neighbors Singapore, Taiwan, the Republic of Korea (South Korea), and Hong Kong.

Agriculture, for centuries the cornerstone of the Thai economy, continued to be of major importance. The chief exports were rice, rubber, cassava, maize, and sugar (see Agriculture, ch. 3). Agriculture's share of GDP, however, had declined from 22 percent in 1982 to less than 17 percent in 1987. Part of the slowdown in the growth of agriculture was a result of the unavailability of new arable land. Moreover, most of the new land that had been opened in the 1960s and 1970s had been turned to agriculture at the expense of Thailand's forests, which had dwindled from more than 50 percent of the country in 1961 to less than 30 percent by 1987. Although processing of agricultural commodities remained important, Thailand's growing manufacturing sector was increasingly becoming based on such products as integrated circuits, motorcycles, textiles, jewelry, electrical appliances, and plastics.

In the late 1980s, there was some disagreement among policy planners over which sector of manufacturing should be most strongly supported and emphasized. Some felt that support for agricultural processing would best benefit the poorer northeastern and southern regions. A project particularly designed to help the region east of Bangkok was the Eastern Seaboard Development Program. Under this plan a new deep-water seaport was being built at Sattahip, both to relieve the pressure on Bangkok's overcrowded Khlong Toei port and to encourage development of the eastern region. Included among the projects were fertilizer and petrochemical plants. Also being developed was a new railroad line from Sattahip eastward to Rayong. Aside from the energy shortage, the inadequacy of the infrastructure—ports, railroads, and highways—was the country's most serious economic problem. Its greatest economic asset was its highly adaptable, increasingly skilled work force.

Thai society, taken as a whole, was reasonably homogenous. The Tai ethnic stock, Tai language family, and Theravada Buddhism were common denominators for about 85 percent of the population. The presence of other ethnic, linguistic, and religious groups created some tensions in Thai society. Even among these groups, however, most members thought of themselves as Thai citizens owing allegiance to the Thai king and state. Among Thai citizens who were both ethnically and linguistically Tai, there were important differences. The dialect spoken by the Central Thai was considered the standard for the country and was used in government and schools. There were, however, nearly as many speakers of Thai-Lao, the dialect of much of the Northeast and parts of the North. The Southern Thai spoke yet another dialect. All of these dialects were mutually intelligible, but with some difficulty. Most Tai speakers were also Theravada Buddhists (see Religion, ch. 2). Among the non-Thai minorities, the Chinese were the largest, amounting to about 11 percent of the population. Most Chinese spoke Central Thai, at least as a second language. The Chinese varied in their degree of assimilation into Thai society, assimilation often depending on the length of time their families had been in the country.

The next largest minority group was religious rather than ethnic. Thai Muslims included ethnic Malay, Thai, Cham, and South Asians. The majority of Muslims, however, were Malay who lived in the four southern provinces on the Malay Peninsula, a traditionally disadvantaged part of the country. Several Muslim separatist insurgent groups in the provinces near the Malaysian border continued in late 1987 to be a thorn in the side of the Thai military. Each of the other minority groups numbered less than 1 percent of the population. Among these were various hill tribes, who were part of larger groups living in Laos, China, or Burma. Largely assimilated were the Mon and the Cham peoples, most of whose ancestors had been in the region for centuries. The Khmer were also fairly well integrated for the same reason, with the exception of several hundred thousand Khmer refugees driven into Thailand since the 1970s by the continuing war in Cambodia. Other refugee groups included the Hmong from Laos.

Since the 1960s, the Thai central government had taken a more enlightened view toward its minority peoples than in the past, when its policies vacillated between suppression, neglect, and forced assimilation. Partly as a result of King Bhumibol's interest in the various minorities, increasing government assistance was being given to these groups in the form of improved health and social services and agricultural assistance.

Although Thai society as a whole was enjoying the benefits of modernization—improved health care and sanitation, education, and modern tools and conveniences—it also faced the usual problems associated with too rapid modernization. Bangkok, particularly, endured problems of overcrowding, pollution, traffic, housing shortages, unemployment, and the social ills of crime, drug abuse, and prostitution.

As the national leadership looked ahead to the 1990s, its major concerns were the continued stabilization of the polity, encouragement of economic growth, and resolution of the security problems of the country. By the late 1980s, internal security was largely under control, with communist insurgents dwindling to a small number and Muslim separatist groups mainly a nuisance factor in the South (see Insurgency, ch. 5). External security was more problematic. Vietnam, which had invaded Cambodia in late 1978, continued to occupy the country, causing a steady stream of Khmer refugees into Thailand. Relations between Bangkok and Beijing grew increasingly cordial during the 1980s as a result of the Vietnamese occupation of Cambodia. This issue also brought a growing solidarity among the membership of the Association of Southeast Asian Nations (ASEAN). Although resolutions and endless rounds of talks were sponsored by the regional organization, by late 1987 the ASEAN nations seemed no closer to being able to induce Vietnam to withdraw from Cambodia either through negotiation or through the pressure of regional and world opinion.

*   *   *

After the manuscript for this book was completed in the autumn of 1987, there were a number of important developments affecting Thailand both domestically and internationally. On April 29, 1988, King Bhumibol decreed the dissolution of the House of Representatives at the request of Prime Minister Prem, who had been faced with increasing disunity in the political parties that made up the ruling coalition. New elections were scheduled for July 24, 1988, amid calls from student and labor groups for a prime minister who was an elected member of parliament. On election day, the Thai voters gave 87 seats in the 357-seat House of Representatives to the Chart Thai (Thai Nation) Party, which formed a 215-member coalition government with four other parties: Social Action (Kit Sangkhom) Party, Democrat (Prachathipat) Party, Rassadorn (People) Party, and United Democracy (Saha Prachathipatai) Party. All but the United Democracy Party had been partners in the previous government. In a surprise move, Prem refused an invitation by the ruling coalition to head the new government, saying he was responding to the people's call for an elected prime minister. The coalition then selected Chatichai Choonhaven, leader of the Chart Thai and deputy prime minister under Prem, to take the number one spot, thus giving Thailand its first elected prime minister in twelve years. Chatichai, who left the military in 1958 to serve as a diplomat and cabinet official, was considered to be probusiness and not likely to change Prem's economic policies significantly.

The Thai economy continued to boom in the first half of 1988. Exports were projected to total US$12 billion for the year, up 20 percent for the second year in a row. Foreign investment in Thailand increased 30 percent in 1987 to US$210 million, with applications for investment up 140 percent to 1,057. Investor confidence was expected to continue under the new government. Tourism, the country's largest foreign exchange earner, was up 23.6 percent in 1987, which had been billed as "Visit Thailand Year." Visitor arrivals during the first half of 1988 signaled an even bigger year, and more than 3.5 million tourists were expected.

Particular attractions for visitors in 1987 and 1988 were two grand national celebrations accompanied by elaborate pomp and pageantry. On December 5, 1987, the country celebrated King Bhumibol's sixtieth birthday; and July 2, 1988, marked the forty-second year and twenty-third day of Bhumibol's reign. Passing the mark set by his grandfather, Chulalongkorn, he thus became the longest ruler of the 200-year-old Chakkri Dynasty. Both occasions were marked by an outpouring of the tremendous love and respect of the Thai people for their monarch.

The first half of 1988 was also marked by regional developments important to Thailand's sense of national security. While on a visit to Moscow in May, Prime Minister Prem was informed by the Soviets of Vietnam's pledge to withdraw 50,000 troops from Cambodia in 1988. Hanoi already had withdrawn 20,000 troops in December 1987 and, according to its own projections, would be down to 50,000 troops by the end of 1988. These forces it promised to withdraw by its previously stated timetable of the end of 1990. Thailand at first reacted cautiously to the news. By mid-June, however, with its usual flexibility in foreign affairs, Bangkok was rolling out the red carpet for visiting Vietnamese foreign minister Nguyen Co Thach. The following month, the Vietnamese-controlled government in Cambodia freed the first group of an estimated 120 Thai prisoners it had promised to release in order to improve relations with Thailand.

Bangkok's response to the new developments in Cambodia was also expressed in concert with the other ASEAN nations. In July the regional organization sponsored informal peace talks in Jakarta between the four warring Cambodian factions and other interested parties, including Vietnam, Laos, and the ASEAN countries. Little that was concrete came out of the Jakarta Informal Meeting other than an agreement to hold another meeting in 1989 at the senior official level. The Jakarta meeting did mark, however, the first time the various Cambodian factions had all sat down together to talk.

In any event, more progress had been made in 1988 toward alleviating Thailand's most serious security concern than had been made in the previous decade.

August 24, 1988   Barbara Leitch LePoer

Chapter 1. Historical Setting

Stone Wheel of Law, Dvaravati Period (sixth to ninth centuries A.D.), found at Phra Pathom Chedi, Nakhon Pathom Province

LITTLE IS KNOWN of the earliest inhabitants of what is now Thailand, but 5,000-year-old archaeological sites in the northeastern part of the country are believed to contain the oldest evidence of rice cultivation and bronze casting in Asia and perhaps in the world. In early historical times, a succession of tribal groups controlled what is now Thailand. The Mon and Khmer peoples established powerful kingdoms that included large areas of the country. They absorbed from contact with South Asian peoples religious, social, political, and cultural ideas and institutions that later influenced the development of Thailand's culture and national identity.

The Tai, a people who originally lived in southwestern China, migrated into mainland Southeast Asia over a period of many centuries. The first mention of their existence in the region is a twelfth-century A.D. inscription at the Khmer temple complex of Angkor Wat in Cambodia, which refers to *syam,* or "dark brown" people (the origin of the term *Siam*) as vassals of the Khmer monarch. In 1238 a Tai chieftain declared his independence from the Khmer and established a kingdom at Sukhothai in the broad valley of the Mae Nam (river) Chao Phraya, at the center of modern Thailand. Sukhothai was succeeded in the fourteenth century by the kingdom of Ayutthaya. The Burmese invaded Ayutthaya and in 1767 destroyed the capital, but two national heroes, Taksin and Chakkri, soon expelled the invaders and reunified the country under the Chakkri Dynasty.

Over the centuries Thai national identity evolved around a common language and religion and the institution of the monarchy. Although the inhabitants of Thailand are a mixture of Tai, Mon, Khmer, and other ethnic groups, most speak a language of the Tai family. A Tai language alphabet, based on Indian and Khmer scripts, developed early in the fourteenth century. Later in the century a famous monarch, Ramathibodi, made Theravada Buddhism the official religion of his kingdom, and Buddhism continued into the twentieth century as a dominant factor in the nation's social, cultural, and political life. Finally, the monarchy, buttressed ideologically by Hindu and Buddhist mythology, was a focus for popular loyalties for more than seven centuries. In the late twentieth century the monarchy remained central to national unity.

During the nineteenth century, European expansionism, rather than Thailand's traditional enemies, posed the greatest threat to the kingdom's survival. Thai success in preserving the country's independence (it was the only Southeast Asian country to do so) was in part a result of the desire of Britain and France for a stable buffer state separating their dominions in Burma, Malaya, and Indochina. More important, however, was the willingness of Thailand's monarchs, Mongkut (Rama IV, 1851–68) and Chulalongkorn (Rama V, 1868–1910), to negotiate openly with the European powers and to adopt European-style reforms that modernized the country and won it sovereign status among the world's nations. Thailand (then known as Siam) paid a high price for its independence, however: loss of suzerainty over Cambodia and Laos to France and cession of the northern states of the Malay Peninsula to Britain. By 1910 the area under Thai control was a fraction of what it had been a century earlier.

In the early decades of the twentieth century, Thailand's political system, armed forces, schools, and economy underwent drastic changes. Many Thai studied overseas, and a small, Western-educated elite with less traditional ideas emerged. In 1932 a bloodless coup d'état by military officers and civil servants ended the absolute monarchy and inaugurated Thailand's constitutional era. Progress toward a stable, democratic political system since that time, however, has been erratic. Politics has been dominated by rival military-bureaucratic cliques headed by powerful generals. These cliques have initiated repeated coups d'état and have imposed prolonged periods of martial law. Parliamentary institutions, as defined by Thailand's fourteen constitutions between 1932 and 1987, and competition among civilian politicians have generally been facades for military governments.

Early History

Over the course of millennia, migrations from southern China peopled Southeast Asia, including the area of contemporary Thailand (see fig. 2). Archaeological evidence indicates a thriving Paleolithic culture in the region and continuous human habitation for at least 20,000 years.

The pace of economic and social development was uneven and conditioned by climate and geography. The dense forests of the Chao Phraya Valley in the central part of Thailand and the Malay Peninsula in the south produced such an abundance of food that for a long time there was no need to move beyond a hunting-and-gathering economy. In contrast, rice cultivation appeared early in the highlands of the far north and hastened the development of a more communal social and political organization.

Excavations at Ban Chiang, a small village on the Khorat Plateau in northeastern Thailand, have revealed evidence of prehistoric inhabitants who may have forged bronze implements as early as 3000 B.C. and cultivated rice around the fourth millennium B.C. If so, the Khorat Plateau would be the oldest rice-producing area in Asia because the inhabitants of China at that time still consumed millet. Archaeologists have assembled evidence that the bronze implements found at the Thai sites were forged in the area and not transported from elsewhere. They supported this claim by pointing out that both copper and tin deposits (components of bronze) are found in close proximity to the Ban Chiang sites. If these claims are correct, Thai bronze forgers would have predated the "Bronze Age," which archaeologists had traditionally believed began in the Middle East around 2800 B.C. and in China about a thousand years later.

Before the end of the first millennium B.C., tribal territories had begun to coalesce into protohistorical kingdoms whose names survive in Chinese dynastic annals of the period. Funan, a state of substantial proportions, emerged in the second century B.C. as the earliest and most significant power in Southeast Asia (see fig. 3). Its Hindu ruling class controlled all of present-day Cambodia and extended its power to the center of modern Thailand. The Funan economy was based on maritime trade and a well-developed agricultural system; Funan maintained close commercial contact with India and served as a base for the Brahman merchant-missionaries who brought Hindu culture to Southeast Asia.

On the narrow isthmus to the southwest of Funan, Malay city-states controlled the portage routes that were traversed by traders and travelers journeying between India and Indochina. By the tenth century A.D. the strongest of them, Tambralinga (present-day Nakhon Si Thammarat), had gained control of all routes across the isthmus. Along with other city-states on the Malay Peninsula and Sumatra, it had become part of the Srivijaya Empire, a maritime confederation that between the seventh and thirteenth centuries dominated trade on the South China Sea and exacted tolls from all traffic through the Strait of Malacca. Tambralinga adopted Buddhism, but farther south many of the Malay city-states converted to Islam, and by the fifteenth century an enduring religious boundary had been established on the isthmus between Buddhist mainland Southeast Asia and Muslim Malaya.

Although the Thai conquered the states of the isthmus in the thirteenth century and continued to control them in the modern period, the Malay of the peninsula were never culturally absorbed into the mainstream of Thai society. The differences in religion, language, and ethnic origin caused strains in social and political relations between the central government and the southern

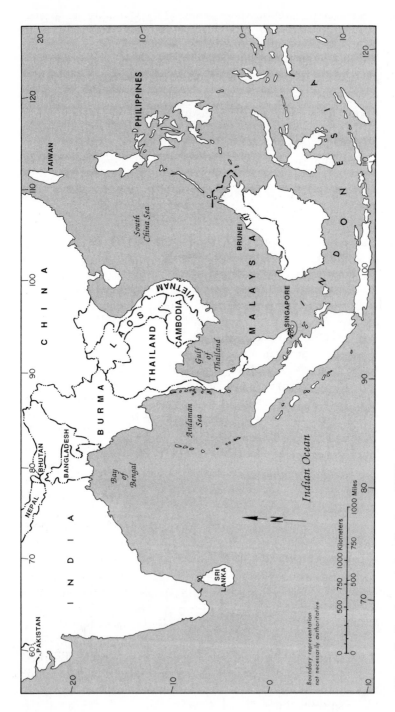

Figure 2. Southeast Asian Region, 1987

provinces into the late twentieth century (see Ethnicity, Regionalism, and Language, ch. 2).

The Mon and the Khmer

The closely related Mon and Khmer peoples entered Southeast Asia along migration routes from southern China in the ninth century B.C. The Khmer settled in the Mekong River Valley, while the Mon occupied the central plain and northern highlands of modern Thailand and large parts of Burma. Taking advantage of Funan's decline in the sixth century A.D., the Mon began to establish independent kingdoms, among them Dvaravati in the northern part of the area formerly controlled by Funan and farther north at Haripunjaya. Meanwhile the Khmer laid the foundation for their great empire of the ninth to fifteenth centuries A.D. This empire would be centered at Angkor (near modern Siem Reap) in Cambodia.

The Mon were receptive to the art and literature of India, and for centuries they were the agents for diffusing Hindu cultural values in the region. The frequent occurrence of Sanskrit place-names in modern Thailand is one result of the long and pervasive Indian influence.

In the eighth century, missionaries from Ceylon (present-day Sri Lanka) introduced the Mon to Theravada Buddhism. The Mon embraced Buddhism enthusiastically and conveyed it to the Khmer and the Malay of Tambralinga (see Religion, ch. 2). The two Indian religious systems—Hindu and Buddhist—existed side by side without conflict. Hinduism continued to provide the cultural setting in which Buddhist religious values and ethical standards were articulated. Although Buddhism was the official religion of the Mon and the Khmer, in popular practice it incorporated many local cults.

In spite of cultural dominance in the region, the Mon were repeatedly subdued by their Burmese and Khmer neighbors. In the tenth century Dvaravati and the whole of the Chao Phraya Valley came under the control of Angkor. The Khmer maintained the Hindu-Buddhist culture received from the Mon but placed added emphasis on the Hindu concept of sacred kingship. The history of Angkor can be read in the magnificent structures built to glorify its monarchy. Ultimately, however, obsession with palaces and temples led the Khmer rulers to divert too much manpower to their construction and to neglect the elaborate agricultural system—part of Angkor's heritage from Funan—that was the empire's most important economic asset.

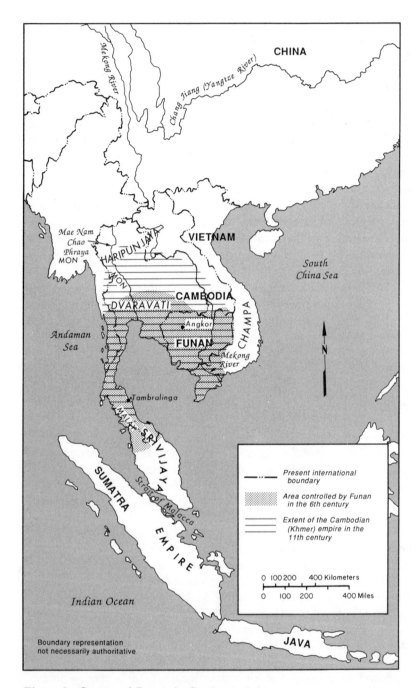

Figure 3. Centers of Power in Southeast Asia,
    Second to Thirteenth Centuries

The Tai People: Origins and Migrations

The forebears of the modern Thai were Tai-speaking people living south of the Chang Jiang (Yangtze River) on the mountainous plateau of what is now the Chinese province of Yunnan (see The Thai and Other Tai-Speaking Peoples, ch. 2). Early Chinese records (the first recorded Chinese reference to the Tai is dated sixth century B.C.) document the Tai cultivating wetland rice in valley and lowland areas. During the first millennium A.D., before the emergence of formal states governed by Tai-speaking elites, these people lived in scattered villages drawn together into *muang,* or principalities. Each *muang* was governed by a *chao,* or lord, who ruled by virtue of personal qualities and a network of patron-client relationships. Often the constituent villages of a *muang* would band together to defend their lands from more powerful neighboring peoples, such as the Chinese and Vietnamese.

The state of Nanchao played a key role in Tai development. In the mid-seventh century A.D., the Chinese Tang Dynasty, threatened by powerful western neighbors like Tibet, sought to secure its southwestern borders by fostering the growth of a friendly state formed by the people they called *man* (southern barbarians) in the Yunnan region. This state was known as Nanchao. Originally an ally, Nanchao became a powerful foe of the Chinese in subsequent centuries and extended its domain into what is now Burma and northern Vietnam. In 1253 the armies of Kublai Khan conquered Nanchao and incorporated it into the Yuan (Mongol) Chinese empire.

Nanchao's significance for the Tai people was twofold. First, it blocked Chinese influence from the north for many centuries. Had Nanchao not existed, the Tai, like most of the originally non-Chinese peoples south of the Chang Jiang, might have been completely assimilated into the Chinese cultural sphere. Second, Nanchao stimulated Tai migration and expansion. Over several centuries, bands of Tai from Yunnan moved steadily into Southeast Asia, and by the thirteenth century they had reached as far west as Assam (in present-day India). Once settled, they became identified in Burma as the Shan and in the upper Mekong region as the Lao. In Tonkin and Annam, the northern and central portions of present-day Vietnam, the Tai formed distinct tribal groupings: Tai Dam (Black Tai), Tai Deng (Red Tai), Tai Khao (White Tai), and Nung. However, most of the Tai settled on the northern and western fringes of the Khmer Empire.

The Thai have traditionally regarded the founding of the kingdom of Sukhothai as marking their emergence as a distinct nation.

Tradition sets 1238 as the date when Tai chieftains overthrew the Khmer at Sukhothai, capital of Angkor's outlying northwestern province, and established a Tai kingdom. A flood of migration resulting from Kublai Khan's conquest of Nanchao furthered the consolidation of independent Tai states. Tai warriors, fleeing the Mongol invaders, reinforced Sukhothai against the Khmer, ensuring its supremacy in the central plain. In the north, other Tai war parties conquered the old Mon state of Haripunjaya and in 1296 founded the kingdom of Lan Na with its capital at Chiang Mai (see fig. 4).

Sukhothai

Situated on the banks of the Mae Nam Yom some 375 kilometers north of present-day Bangkok, Sukhothai was the cradle of Thai civilization, the place where its institutions and culture first developed. Indeed, it was there in the late thirteenth century that the people of the central plain, lately freed from Khmer rule, took the name *Thai,* meaning ''free,'' to set themselves apart from other Tai speakers still under foreign rule.

The first ruler of Sukhothai for whom historical records survive was Ramkhamhaeng (Rama the Great, 1277–1317). He was a famous warrior who claimed to be ''sovereign lord of all the Tai'' and financed his court with war booty and tribute from vassal states in Burma, Laos, and the Malay Peninsula. During his reign, the Thai established diplomatic relations with China and acknowledged the Chinese emperor as nominal overlord of the Thai kingdom. Ramkhamhaeng brought Chinese artisans to Sukhothai to develop the ceramics industry that was a mainstay of the Thai economy for 500 years. He also devised the Thai alphabet by adapting a Khmer script derived from the Indian Devanagari script.

Sukhothai declined rapidly after Ramkhamhaeng's death, as vassal states broke away from the suzerainty of his weak successors. Despite the reputation of its later kings for wisdom and piety, the politically weakened Sukhothai was forced to submit in 1378 to the Thai kingdom of Ayutthaya.

The Ayutthaya Era, 1350–1767

The kingdom of Ayutthaya was founded by U Thong, an adventurer allegedly descended from a rich Chinese merchant family who married royalty. In 1350, to escape the threat of an epidemic, he moved his court south into the rich floodplain of the Chao Phraya. On an island in the river he founded a new capital, which he called Ayutthaya, after Ayodhya in northern India, the city of the hero Rama in the Hindu epic *Ramayana*. U Thong assumed the royal name of Ramathibodi (1350–60).

Ramathibodi tried to unify his kingdom. In 1360 he declared Theravada Buddhism the official religion of Ayutthaya and brought members of a *sangha,* a Buddhist monastic community, from Ceylon to establish new religious orders and spread the faith among his subjects. He also compiled a legal code, based on the Indian *Dharmashastra* (a Hindu legal text) and Thai custom, which became the basis of royal legislation. Composed in Pali—an Indo-Aryan language closely related to Sanskrit and the language of the Theravada Buddhist scriptures—it had the force of divine injunction. Supplemented by royal decrees, Ramathibodi's legal code remained generally in force until the late nineteenth century.

By the end of the fourteenth century, Ayutthaya was regarded as the strongest power in Southeast Asia, but it lacked the manpower to dominate the region. In the last year of his reign, Ramathibodi had seized Angkor during what was to be the first of many successful Thai assaults on the Khmer capital. Thai policy was aimed at securing Ayutthaya's eastern frontier by preempting Vietnamese designs on Khmer territory. The weakened Khmer periodically submitted to Thai suzerainty, but efforts by Ayutthaya to maintain control over Angkor were repeatedly frustrated. Thai troops were frequently diverted to suppress rebellions in Sukhothai or to campaign against Chiang Mai, where Ayutthaya's expansion was tenaciously resisted. Eventually Ayutthaya subdued the territory that had belonged to Sukhothai, and the year after Ramathibodi died, his kingdom was recognized by the emperor of China's newly established Ming Dynasty as Sukhothai's rightful successor.

The Thai kingdom was not a single, unified state but rather a patchwork of self-governing principalities and tributary provinces owing allegiance to the king of Ayutthaya. These states were ruled by members of the royal family of Ayutthaya who had their own armies and warred among themselves. The king had to be vigilant to prevent royal princes from combining against him or allying with Ayutthaya's enemies. Whenever the succession was in dispute, princely governors gathered their forces and moved on the capital to press their claims.

During much of the fifteenth century Ayutthaya's energies were directed toward the Malay Peninsula, where the great trading port of Malacca contested Thai claims to sovereignty. Malacca and other Malay states south of Tambralinga had become Muslim early in the century, and thereafter Islam served as a symbol of Malay solidarity against the Thai. Although the Thai failed to make a

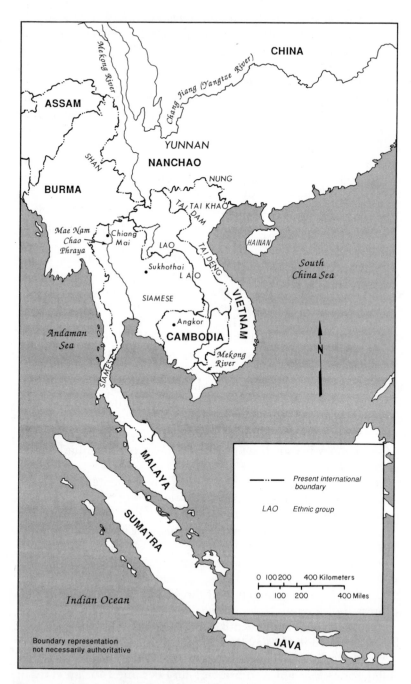

Figure 4. Origin and Range of the Tai Peoples in Southeast Asia, Thirteenth Century

vassal state of Malacca, Ayutthaya continued to control the lucrative trade on the isthmus, which attracted Chinese traders of specialty goods for the luxury markets of China.

Thai Kingship

Thai rulers were absolute monarchs whose office was partly religious in nature. They derived their authority from the ideal qualities they were believed to possess. The king was the moral model, who personified the virtue of his people, and his country lived at peace and prospered because of his meritorious actions. At Sukhothai, where Ramkhamhaeng was said to hear the petition of any subject who rang the bell at the palace gate to summon him, the king was revered as a father by his people. But the paternal aspects of kingship disappeared at Ayutthaya, where, under Khmer influence, the monarchy withdrew behind a wall of taboos and rituals. The king was considered *chakkraphat,* the Sanskrit-Pali term for the "wheel-rolling" universal prince who through his adherence to the law made all the world revolve around him. As the Hindu god Shiva was "lord of the universe," the Thai king also became by analogy "lord of the land," distinguished in his appearance and bearing from his subjects. According to the elaborate court etiquette, even a special language, Phasa Ratchasap, was used to communicate with or about royalty.

As *devaraja* (Sanskrit for "divine king"), the king ultimately came to be recognized as the earthly incarnation of Shiva and became the object of a politico-religious cult officiated over by a corps of royal Brahmans who were part of the Buddhist court retinue. In the Buddhist context, the *devaraja* was a bodhisattva (an enlightened being who, out of compassion, foregoes nirvana in order to aid others). The belief in divine kingship prevailed into the eighteenth century, although by that time its religious implications had limited impact.

One of the numerous institutional innovations of King Trailok (1448–88) was to create the position of *uparaja,* or heir apparent, usually held by the king's senior son or full brother, in an attempt to regularize the succession to the throne—a particularly difficult feat for a polygamous dynasty. In practice, there was inherent conflict between king and *uparaja* and frequent disputed successions.

Social and Political Development

The king stood at the apex of a highly stratified social and political hierarchy that extended throughout the society. In Ayutthayan society the basic unit of social organization was the village community composed of extended family households. Generally the elected headmen provided leadership for communal projects. Title to land resided with the headman, who held it in the name of the community, although peasant proprietors enjoyed the use of land as long as they cultivated it.

With ample reserves of land available for cultivation, the viability of the state depended on the acquisition and control of adequate manpower for farm labor and defense. The dramatic rise of Ayutthaya had entailed constant warfare and, as none of the parties in the region possessed a technological advantage, the outcome of battles was usually determined by the size of the armies. After each victorious campaign, Ayutthaya carried away a number of conquered people to its own territory, where they were assimilated and added to the labor force.

Every freeman had to be registered as a servant, or *phrai* (see Glossary), with the local lord, or *nai* (see Glossary), for military service and corvée labor on public works and on the land of the official to whom he was assigned. The *phrai* could also meet his labor obligation by paying a tax. If he found the forced labor under his *nai* repugnant, he could sell himself into slavery to a more attractive *nai*, who then paid a fee to the government in compensation for the loss of corvée labor. As much as one-third of the manpower supply into the nineteenth century was composed of *phrai*.

Wealth, status, and political influence were interrelated. The king allotted rice fields to governors, military commanders, and court officials in payment for their services to the crown, according to the *sakdi na* (see Glossary) system. The size of each official's allotment was determined by the number of persons he could command to work it. The amount of manpower a particular *nai* could command determined his status relative to others in the hierarchy and his wealth. At the apex of the hierarchy, the king, who was the realm's largest landholder, also commanded the services of the largest number of *phrai*, called *phrai luang* (royal servants), who paid taxes, served in the royal army, and worked on the crown lands. King Trailok established definite allotments of land and *phrai* for the royal officials at each rung in the hierarchy, thus determining the country's social structure until the introduction of salaries for government officials in the nineteenth century.

The Chinese alone stood outside this social structure. They were not obliged to register for corvée duty, so they were free to move about the kingdom at will and engage in commerce. By the sixteenth century, the Chinese controlled Ayutthaya's internal trade and had found important places in the civil and military service. Most of these men took Thai wives because few women left China to accompany the men.

The sixteenth century witnessed the rise of Burma, which, under an aggressive dynasty, had overrun Chiang Mai and Laos and made war on the Thai. In 1569 Burmese forces, joined by Thai rebels, captured the city of Ayutthaya and carried off the royal family to Burma. Dhammaraja (1569–90), a Thai governor who had aided the Burmese, was installed as vassal king at Ayutthaya. Thai independence was restored by his son, King Naresuan (1590–1605), who turned on the Burmese and by 1600 had driven them from the country (see fig. 5).

Determined to prevent another treason like his father's, Naresuan set about unifying the country's administration directly under the royal court at Ayutthaya. He ended the practice of nominating royal princes to govern Ayutthaya's provinces, assigning instead court officials who were expected to execute policies handed down by the king. Thereafter royal princes were confined to the capital. Their power struggles continued, but at court under the king's watchful eye.

In order to ensure his control over the new class of governors, Naresuan decreed that all freemen subject to *phrai* service had become *phrai luang,* bound directly to the king, who distributed the use of their services to his officials. This measure gave the king a theoretical monopoly on all manpower, and the idea developed that since the king owned the services of all the people, he also possessed all the land. Ministerial offices and governorships—and the *sakdi na* that went with them—were usually inherited positions dominated by a few families often connected to the king by marriage. Indeed, marriage was frequently used by Thai kings to cement alliances between themselves and powerful families, a custom prevailing through the nineteenth century. As a result of this policy, the king's wives usually numbered in the dozens.

Even with Naresuan's reforms, the effectiveness of the royal government over the next 150 years should not be overestimated. Royal power outside the crown lands—although in theory absolute—was in practice limited by the looseness of the civil administration. The influence of central government ministers was not extensive beyond the capital until the late nineteenth century.

Economic Development

The Thai never lacked a rich food supply. Peasants planted rice for their own consumption and to pay taxes. Whatever remained was used to support religious institutions. From the thirteenth to the fifteenth century, however, a remarkable transformation took place in Thai rice cultivation. In the highlands, where rainfall had to be supplemented by a system of irrigation that controlled the

Figure 5. Centers of Power, Thirteenth to Eighteenth Centuries

water level in flooded paddies, the Thai sowed the glutinous rice that is still the staple in the geographical regions of the North and Northeast. But in the floodplain of the Chao Phraya, farmers turned to a different variety of rice—the so-called floating rice, a slender, nonglutinous grain introduced from Bengal—that would grow fast enough to keep pace with the rise of the water level in the lowland fields (see Crops, ch. 3).

The new strain grew easily and abundantly, producing a surplus that could be sold cheaply abroad. Ayutthaya, situated at the southern extremity of the floodplain, thus became the hub of economic activity. Under royal patronage, corvée labor dug canals on which rice was brought from the fields to the king's ships for export to China. In the process, the Chao Phraya Delta—mud flats between the sea and firm land hitherto considered unsuitable for habitation—was reclaimed and placed under cultivation.

Contacts with the West

In 1511 Ayutthaya received a diplomatic mission from the Portuguese, who earlier that year had conquered Malacca. These were probably the first Europeans to visit the country. Five years after that initial contact, Ayutthaya and Portugal concluded a treaty granting the Portuguese permission to trade in the kingdom. A similar treaty in 1592 gave the Dutch a privileged position in the rice trade.

Foreigners were cordially welcomed at the court of Narai (1657–88), a ruler with a cosmopolitan outlook who was nonetheless wary of outside influence. Important commercial ties were forged with Japan. Dutch and English trading companies were allowed to establish factories, and Thai diplomatic missions were sent to Paris and The Hague. By maintaining all these ties, the Thai court skillfully played off the Dutch against the English and the French against the Dutch in order to avoid the excessive influence of a single power.

In 1664, however, the Dutch used force to exact a treaty granting them extraterritorial rights as well as freer access to trade. At the urging of his foreign minister, the Greek adventurer Constantine Phaulkon, Narai turned to France for assistance. French engineers constructed fortifications for the Thai and built a new palace at Lop Buri for Narai. In addition, French missionaries engaged in education and medicine and brought the first printing press into the country. Louis XIV's personal interest was aroused by reports from missionaries suggesting that Narai might be converted to Christianity.

The French presence encouraged by Phaulkon, however, stirred the resentment and suspicions of the Thai nobles and Buddhist clergy. When word spread that Narai was dying, a general, Phra Phetracha, killed the designated heir, a Christian, and had Phaulkon put to death along with a number of missionaries. The arrival of English warships provoked a massacre of more Europeans. Phetracha (reigned 1688–93) seized the throne, expelled the remaining foreigners, and ushered in a 150-year period during which the Thai consciously isolated themselves from contacts with the West.

Ayutthaya: The Final Phase

After a bloody period of dynastic struggle, Ayutthaya entered into what has been called its golden age, a relatively peaceful episode in the second quarter of the eighteenth century when art, literature, and learning flourished. Ayutthaya continued to compete with Vietnam for control of Cambodia, but a greater threat came from Burma, where a new dynasty had subdued the Shan states.

In 1765 Thai territory was invaded by three Burmese armies that converged on Ayutthaya. After a lengthy siege, the city capitulated and was burned in 1767. Ayutthaya's art treasures, the libraries containing its literature, and the archives housing its historic records were almost totally destroyed, and the city was left in ruins.

The country was reduced to chaos. Provinces were proclaimed independent states under military leaders, rogue monks, and cadet members of the royal family. The Thai were saved from Burmese subjugation, however, by an opportune Chinese invasion of Burma and by the leadership of a Thai military commander, Phraya Taksin.

The Bangkok Period, 1767–1932

As they had in the sixteenth century, the Thai made a rapid recovery under a brilliant military leader. Taksin (1767–82) had slipped away from besieged Ayutthaya and, starting with a handful of followers who quickly grew into an army, organized a resistance to the Burmese invaders, driving them out after a long and arduous war. Assuming the royal title, he abandoned the ruined Ayutthaya and founded a new capital farther south in the delta at Thon Buri, a fortress town across the river from modern Bangkok. By 1776 Taksin had reunited the Thai kingdom, which had fragmented into small states after the fall of the old capital, and had annexed Chiang Mai. Taksin, who eventually developed delusions of his own divinity, was deposed and executed by his ministers, invoking the interests of the state. His manifold accomplishments, however, won Taksin a secure place among Thailand's national heroes.

The Chakkri Dynasty

With the death of Taksin, the Thai throne fell to Chakkri, a general who had played a leading role with Taksin in the struggle against the Burmese. As King Yot Fa (Rama I, 1782–1809), he founded the present Thai ruling house and moved the court to Bangkok, the modern capital (see table 2, Appendix). During an energetic reign, he revived the country's economy and restored what remained of the great artistic heritage lost in the destruction of Ayutthaya. The king is credited with composing a new edition of the *Ramakian* (the Thai version of the *Ramayana*) to replace manuscripts of the Thai national epic that were lost in the conflagration.

In the following years Thai influence grew until challenged by Western powers. In 1795 the Thai seized the provinces of Battambang and Siem Reap in Cambodia, where throughout the first half of the next century Chakkri kings would resist Vietnamese incursions. The conflict between the Thai and the Vietnamese was resolved finally by a compromise providing for the establishment of a joint protectorate over Cambodia. The Thai also pressed their claim to suzerainty in the Malay state of Kedah in the face of growing British interest in the peninsula. As a result of the Anglo-Burmese War (1824–26), Britain annexed territory in the region that had been contested by the Thai and the Burmese for centuries. This move led to the signing of the Burney Treaty in 1826, an Anglo-Thai agreement that allowed British merchants modest trade concessions in the kingdom. In 1833 the Thai reached a similar understanding with the United States.

Chakkri expansionism had been halted in all directions by the end of the reign of Nang Klao (Rama III, 1824–51) as tributary provinces began to slip away from Bangkok's control and Western influence grew. In 1850 Nang Klao spurned British and American requests for more generous trading privileges similar to those that Western powers had exacted by force from China. Succeeding Thai monarchs, however, were less successful in controlling Western economic influence in their country.

The first three Chakkri kings, by succeeding each other without bloodshed, had brought the kingdom a degree of political stability that had been lacking in the Ayutthaya period. There was, however, no rule providing for automatic succession to the throne. If there was no *uparaja* at the time of the king's death—and this was frequently the case—the choice of a new monarch drawn from the royal family was left to the Senabodi, the council of senior officials, princes, and Buddhist prelates that assembled at the death of a king. It was such a council that chose Nang Klao's successor.

Mongkut's Opening to the West

Nang Klao died in 1851 and was succeeded by his forty-seven-year-old half brother, Mongkut (Rama IV, 1851-68). Mongkut's father, Loet La (Rama II, 1809-24), had placed him in a Buddhist monastery in 1824 to prevent a bloody succession struggle between factions loyal to Mongkut and those supporting Nang Klao (although Nang Klao was older than Mongkut, his mother was a concubine, whereas Mongkut's mother was a royal queen). As a Buddhist monk, Mongkut won distinction as an authority on the Pali Buddhist scriptures and became head of a reformed order of the Siamese *sangha*. Thai Buddhism had become heavily overlain with superstitions through the centuries, and Mongkut attempted to purge the religion of these accretions and restore to it the spirit of Buddha's original teachings (see Religion, ch. 2).

Mongkut's twenty-seven years as a Buddhist monk not only made him a religious figure of some consequence but also exposed him to a wide array of foreign influences. Blessed with an inquiring mind and great curiosity about the outside world, he cultivated contacts with French Roman Catholic and United States Protestant missionaries. He studied Western languages (Latin and English), science, and mathematics. His lengthy conversations with the missionaries gave him a broad perspective that greatly influenced his policies when he became king in 1851. He was more knowledgeable of, and at ease with, Western ways than any previous Thai monarch.

Mongkut was convinced that his realm must have full relations with the Western countries in order to survive as an independent nation and avoid the humiliations China and Burma had suffered in wars with Britain. Against the advice of his court, he abolished the old royal trade monopoly in commodities and in 1855 signed the Treaty of Friendship and Commerce with Britain. (This treaty, commonly known as the Bowring Treaty, was signed on Britain's behalf by Sir John Bowring, governor of Hong Kong.) Under the terms of the treaty, British merchants were permitted to buy and sell in Siam without intermediaries, a consulate was established, and British subjects were granted extraterritorial rights. Similar treaties were negotiated the next year with the United States and France, and over the next fifteen years with a number of other European countries. These agreements not only provided for free trade but also limited the Siamese government's authority to tax foreign enterprises. The elimination of these barriers led to an enormous increase in commerce with the West. This expansion of trade in turn revolutionized the Thai economy and connected it to the world monetary system.

The demand for extraterritorial privileges also convinced the king that unless Siam's legal and administrative systems were reformed, the country would never be treated as an equal by the Western powers. Although little in the way of substantive modernization was accomplished during his reign, Mongkut eliminated some of the ancient mystique of the monarch's divinity by allowing commoners to gaze on his face, published a royal gazette of the country's laws, and hired a number of Western experts as consultants, teachers, and technicians. Long-standing institutions such as slavery remained basically untouched, however, and the political system continued to be dominated by the great families. Conservatives at court remained strong, and the king's death from malaria in 1868 postponed pending reform projects.

Chulalongkorn's Reforms

When Mongkut died, his eldest son, Chulalongkorn (Rama V, 1868–1910), a minor at the time, succeeded him. Under his father's direction, Chulalongkorn had received a thorough education by European tutors. During the regency that preceded his coming of age, the young king visited Java and India in order to witness European colonial administration. Thus he was the first Chakkri monarch to leave the country. At his coronation in 1873, he announced the abolition of the ancient practice of prostrating before the monarch, which he regarded as unsuitable for a modern nation. A number of reform decrees followed, designed to modernize the judiciary, state finances, and political structure. The reforms, however, provoked a revolt by conservatives under Prince Wichaichan in December 1874. Although the revolt was suppressed, it obliged Chulalongkorn to abandon "radicalism" and proceed more carefully with reforms. It was more than a decade before the king and his associates were in a position to enact more significant changes.

One of the most far-reaching of the later reforms was the abolition of slavery and the *phrai* corvée. Slavery was eliminated gradually, allowing considerable time for social and economic adaptation, and only disappeared in 1905. As a result of the introduction of a head tax paid in currency and a regular army manned by conscription, the corvée lost most of its function, and wage labor, often provided by Chinese immigrants, proved more efficient for public works projects. Likewise, the introduction of salaries for public

21

officials eliminated the need for the *sakdi na.* These reforms wrought profound changes in Thai society.

In 1887 the king asked one of his princes, Devawongse, to initiate a study of European forms of government and how European institutions might be fruitfully adopted. The following year, the prince returned with a proposal for a cabinet government consisting of twelve functionally differentiated ministries. The king approved the plan, though several years passed before it could be fully implemented. In 1893 Prince Damrong Rajanubhab, acting as minister of interior, began an overhaul of Siam's antiquated provincial administration. The old semifeudal system in the outer provinces was gradually replaced by a centralized state administration. Under Damrong, the Ministry of Interior became immensely powerful and played a central role in national unification.

Like his father, Chulalongkorn fully appreciated the importance of education. He founded three schools on European lines for children of the royal family and government officials, including one for girls. Specialized schools were attached to government departments for the training of civil servants. Study abroad was encouraged, and promising civil servants and military officers were sent to Europe for further education. In 1891 Prince Damrong went to Europe to study modern systems of education. Upon his return he became head of the new Ministry of Public Instruction, though he was obliged to assume the Ministry of Interior post a year later.

The country's first railroads were built during Chulalongkorn's reign, and a line was completed between Bangkok and Ayutthaya in 1897. This was extended farther north to Lop Buri in 1901 and to Sawankhalok in 1909. A rail line built south to Phetchaburi by 1903 was eventually linked with British rail lines in peninsular Malaya.

The Crisis of 1893

The steady encroachment of the two most aggressive European powers in the region, Britain and France, gravely threatened Siam during the last years of the nineteenth century. To the west, Britain completed its conquest of Burma in 1885 with the annexation of Upper Burma and the involuntary abdication of Burma's last king, Thibaw. To the south, the British were firmly established in the major Muslim states of the Malay Peninsula.

Even more than Britain, France posed a serious danger to Siamese independence. The French occupied Cochinchina (southern Vietnam, around the Mekong Delta) in 1863. From there they extended their influence into Cambodia, over which Vietnam and Siam had long been struggling for control. Assuming Vietnam's traditional interests, France obliged the Cambodian king, Norodom, to accept a French protectorate. Siam formally relinquished its claim to Cambodia four years later, in return for French recognition of Siamese sovereignty over the Cambodian provinces of Siem Reap and Battambang.

The French dreamed of outflanking their British rivals by developing a trade route to the supposed riches of southwestern China through the Mekong Valley. This seemed possible once France had assumed complete control over Vietnam in the 1880s. The small Laotian kingdoms, under Siamese suzerainty, were the keys to this dream. The French claimed these territories, arguing that areas previously under Vietnamese control should now come under the French, the new rulers of Vietnam.

Auguste Pavie, French vice consul in Luang Prabang in 1886, was the chief agent in furthering French interests in Laos. His intrigues, which took advantage of Siamese weakness in the region and periodic invasions by Chinese rebels from Yunnan Province, increased tensions between Bangkok and Paris. When fighting broke out between French and Siamese forces in Laos in April 1893, the French sent gunboats to blockade Bangkok. At gunpoint, the Siamese agreed to the cession of Laos. Britain's acquiescence in French expansionism was evident in a treaty signed by the two countries in 1896 recognizing a border between French territory in Laos and British territory in Upper Burma.

French pressure on Siam continued, however, and in 1907 Chulalongkorn was forced to surrender Battambang and Siem Reap to French-occupied Cambodia. Two years later, Siam relinquished its claims to the northern Malay states of Kelantan, Trengganu, Kedah, and Perlis to the British in exchange for legal jurisdiction over British subjects on its soil and a large loan for railroad construction. In terms of territory under its control, Siam was now much diminished. Its independence, however, had been preserved as a useful and generally stable buffer state between French and British territories. (see fig. 6).

Chulalongkorn's son and successor, Vajiravudh (Rama VI, 1910–25), had received his education in Britain. As much as the theme of modernization had typified the policies of his father, Vajiravudh's reign was characterized by support of nationalism. The king wrote extensively on nationalist themes. He also organized and financed a military auxiliary, the Wild Tiger Corps, which he looked on as a means of spreading nationalist fervor.

Thai nationalist attitudes at all levels of society were colored by anti-Chinese sentiment. For centuries members of the Chinese community had dominated domestic commerce and had been employed

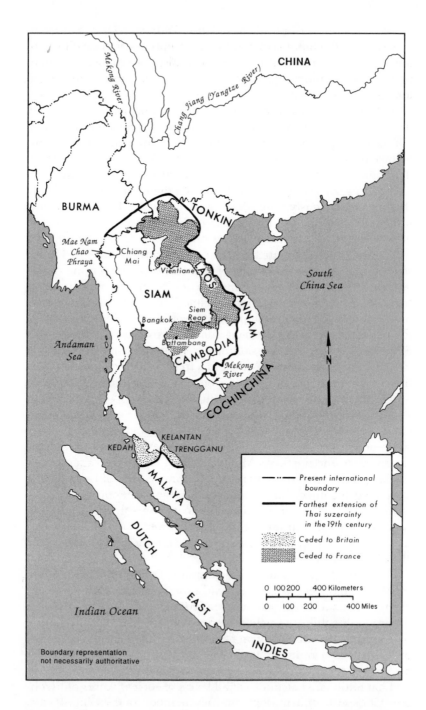

Figure 6. Siam in the Late Nineteenth and Early Twentieth Centuries

as agents for the royal trade monopoly. With the rise of European economic influence many Chinese entrepreneurs had shifted to opium traffic and tax collecting, both despised occupations. In addition, Chinese millers and middlemen in the rice trade were blamed for the economic recession that gripped Siam for nearly a decade after 1905. Accusations of bribery of high officials, wars between the Chinese secret societies, and use of oppressive practices to extract taxes also served to inflame Thai opinion against the Chinese community at a time when it was expanding rapidly as a result of increased immigration from China. By 1910 nearly 10 percent of Thailand's population was Chinese. Whereas earlier immigrants had intermarried with the Thai, the new arrivals frequently came with families and resisted assimilation into Thai society. Chinese nationalism, encouraged by Sun Yat-sen, the leader of the Chinese revolution, had also begun to develop, parallel with Thai nationalism. The Chinese community even supported a separate school system for its children. Legislation in 1909 requiring adoption of surnames was in large part directed against the Chinese community, whose members would be faced with the choice of forsaking their Chinese identity or accepting the status of foreigners. Many of them made the accommodation and opted to become Thai—if in name only. Those who did not became even more alienated from the rest of Thai society (see The Non-Tai Minorities, ch. 2).

To the consternation of his advisers, who still smarted from Siam's territorial losses to France, Vajiravudh declared war on Germany and took Siam into World War I on the side of the Allies, sending a token expeditionary force to the Western front. This limited participation, however, won Siam favorable amendments to its treaties with France and Britain at the end of the war and also gained a windfall in impounded German shipping for its merchant marine. Siam took part in the Versailles peace conference in 1919 and was a founding member of the League of Nations.

Beginning of the Constitutional Era

Early in his reign, King Prajadhipok (Rama VII, 1925–35) showed a tendency to share responsibility for political decision making with his ministers. He also appointed an advisory council to study the possibility of providing the country with a constitution, but its royalist members advised against such a measure. The civil bureaucracy, by contrast, considered the time ripe for such a move. Siam faced severe economic problems because of the world depression, which had caused a sharp drop in the price of rice. Discontent among the political elite grew in reaction to retrenchment in government spending, which necessitated severe cutbacks in the numbers of civil servants and military personnel, the demotion in rank of others, and the cancellation of government programs.

1932 Coup

The long era of absolute monarchy was brought to a sudden end on June 24, 1932, by a bloodless coup d'état engineered by a group of civil servants and army officers with the support of army units in the Bangkok area. The action was specifically directed against ministers of the conservative royal government and not against the person of the king. Three days after the coup a military junta put into effect a provisional constitution drawn up by a young law professor, Pridi Phanomyong. Prajadhipok reluctantly accepted the new situation that had stripped him of his political power but in principle had left the prestige of the monarchy unimpaired.

The coup leaders, who were known as the ''promoters,'' were representative of the younger generation of Western-oriented political elite that had been educated to be instruments of an absolute monarchy—an institution they now viewed as archaic and inadequate to the task of modern government. The principals in the coup identified themselves as nationalists, and none questioned the institution of the monarchy. Their numbers included the major figures in Thai politics for the next three decades. Pridi, one of the country's leading intellectuals, was the most influential civilian promoter. His chief rival among the other promoters was Phibun, or Luang Plaek Phibunsongkhram, an ambitious junior army officer who later attained the rank of field marshal. Phahon, or Phraya Phahonphonphayuhasena, the senior member of the group, represented old-line military officers dissatisfied with cuts in appropriations for the armed forces. These three exercised power as members of a cabinet, the Commissariat of the People, chosen by the National Assembly that had been summoned by the promoters soon after the coup. To assuage conservative opinion, a retired jurist, Phraya Manopakorn, was selected as prime minister.

A permanent constitution was promulgated before the end of 1932. It provided for a quasi-parliamentary regime in which executive power was vested in a unicameral legislature, the National Assembly, of which half of the members were elected by limited suffrage and half appointed by the government in power. The constitution provided that the entire legislature would be elected when half of the electorate had received four years of schooling or after ten years had elapsed, whichever came first. The National Assembly was responsible for the budget and could override a royal veto. Real power resided with the promoters, however, and was exercised with army backing through their political organization, the People's Party.

A rift soon developed within the ranks of the promoters between civilian technicians and military officers. As finance minister, Pridi proposed a radical economic plan in 1933, calling for the nationalization of natural resources. This plan was unacceptable to Manopakorn and the more conservative military members in the cabinet. The prime minister closed the National Assembly, in which Pridi had support, and ruled by decree. Accused of being a communist, Pridi fled into exile, but army officers opposing the civilian prime minister's move staged a coup in June 1933 that turned out Manopakorn, restored the National Assembly, and set up a new government headed by Phahon. With sentiment running in his favor, Pridi was permitted to return to Bangkok and was subsequently cleared of the charges against him.

In addition to factionalism within the cabinet, the government was also confronted with a serious royalist revolt in October 1933. The revolt was led by the king's cousin, Prince Boworadet, who had been defense minister during the old regime. Although the king gave no support to the prince, relations between Prajadhipok and the political leaders deteriorated thereafter.

The first parliamentary elections in the country's history were held in November 1933. Although fewer than 10 percent of the eligible voters cast their ballots, they confirmed Pridi's popularity. Pridi and his supporters in the civilian left wing of the People's Party were countered by a military faction that rallied around his rival, Phibun. In 1934 Phibun was named defense minister and proceeded to use his ministerial powers to build his political constituency within the army. Campaigning for a stronger military establishment in order to keep the country out of foreign hands, he took every opportunity to assert the superior efficiency of the military administration over the civilian bureaucracy, which looked to Pridi for leadership. Prime Minister Phahon had to maintain a precarious balance between the Pridi and Phibun factions in the government.

The civilian conservatives had been discredited during the Manopakorn regime and by the support some had given to the royalist revolt. Their loss of influence deprived the king of effective political allies in the government. In March 1935, Prajadhipok abdicated without naming a successor, charging the Phahon government with abuse of power in curtailing the royal veto. He went into retirement in Britain. His ten-year-old nephew, Ananda Mahidol (Rama VIII, 1935–46), who was attending school in Switzerland, was named king to succeed him, and a regency council, which included Pridi, was appointed to carry out those functions of the monarchy retained under the constitution. The new king did not return to his country until 1945.

Phibun and the Nationalist Regime

The promoters, both civilian and military, had given their political movement a nationalist label, but unanimity among them went no further than acceptance of the official ideology. Although it was essential for the stability of any cabinet that they work together, relations between the civilian and military factions steadily deteriorated as more civil offices went to military personnel. Sensing a tendency toward military rule that he could no longer contain, Phahon retired in December 1938. Phibun took office as prime minister, with his rival, Pridi, as finance minister.

The Phibun regime sold nationalism to the public by using propaganda methods borrowed from authoritarian regimes in Europe, and nationalism was equated with Westernization. To make clear to the world—in Phibun's words—that the country belonged to the Thai, in 1939 the name of the country was officially changed to Muang Thai (Land of the Free), or Thailand. That same year Pridi introduced his "Thailand for the Thai" economic plan, which levied heavy taxes on foreign-owned businesses, the majority of them Chinese, while offering state subsidies to Thai-owned enterprises. The government encouraged the Thai to emulate European fashions, decreeing, for example, that shoes and hats be worn in public. Betel chewing was prohibited, and opium addicts were prosecuted and, if Chinese, deported.

Although nationalism was equated with Westernization, it was not pro-Western, either politically or culturally. Thai Christians, especially those in government service, as well as Muslims, suffered official discrimination. The clear inference of government statements was that only Buddhists could be Thai patriots. At its source Thai nationalism was anti-Chinese in character. Regulations were enacted to check Chinese immigration and to reserve for the Thai numerous occupations that had formerly been held predominantly by Chinese.

Phibun's nationalist regime also revived irredentist claims, stirring up anti-French sentiment and supporting restoration of former Thai territories in Cambodia and Laos. Seeking support against France, Phibun cultivated closer relations with Japan. The Thai nationalists looked to Japan as the model of an Asian country that had used Western methods and technology to achieve rapid modernization. As Thailand confronted the French in Indochina, the Thai looked to Japan as the only Asian country to challenge the European

Ruins of Thai capital at Ayutthaya
Courtesy Tourism Authority of Thailand

powers successfully. Although the Thai were united in their demand for the return of the lost provinces, Phibun's enthusiasm for the Japanese was markedly greater than that of Pridi, and many old conservatives as well viewed the course of the prime minister's foreign policy with misgivings.

World War II

Thailand responded pragmatically to the military and political pressures of World War II. When sporadic fighting broke out between Thai and French forces along Thailand's eastern frontier in late 1940 and early 1941, Japan used its influence with the Vichy regime in France to obtain concessions for Thailand. As a result, France agreed in March 1941 to cede 54,000 square kilometers of Laotian territory west of the Mekong and most of the Cambodian province of Battambang to Thailand. The recovery of this lost territory and the regime's apparent victory over a European colonial power greatly enhanced Phibun's reputation.

Then, on December 8, 1941, after several hours of fighting between Thai and Japanese troops at Chumphon, Thailand had to accede to Japanese demands for access through the country for Japanese forces invading Burma and Malaya. Phibun assured the country that the Japanese action was prearranged with a sympathetic Thai government. Later in the month Phibun signed

29

a mutual defense pact with Japan. Pridi resigned from the cabinet in protest but subsequently accepted the nonpolitical position of regent for the absent Ananda Mahidol.

Under pressure from Japan, the Phibun regime declared war on Britain and the United States in January 1942, but the Thai ambassador in Washington, Seni Pramoj, refused to deliver the declaration to the United States government. Accordingly, the United States refrained from declaring war on Thailand. With American assistance Seni, a conservative aristocrat whose anti-Japanese credentials were well established, organized the Free Thai Movement, recruiting Thai students in the United States to work with the United States Office of Strategic Services (OSS). The OSS trained Thai personnel for underground activities, and units were readied to infiltrate Thailand. From the office of the regent in Thailand, Pridi ran a clandestine movement that by the end of the war had with Allied aid armed more than 50,000 Thai to resist the Japanese.

Thailand was rewarded for Phibun's close cooperation with Japan during the early years of war with the return of further territory that had once been under Bangkok's control, including portions of the Shan states in Burma and the four northernmost Malay states. Japan meanwhile had stationed 150,000 troops on Thai soil and built the infamous ''death railway'' through Thailand using Allied prisoners of war.

As the war dragged on, however, the Japanese presence grew more irksome. Trade came to a halt, and Japanese military personnel requisitioning supplies increasingly dealt with Thailand as a conquered territory rather than as an ally. Allied bombing raids damaged Bangkok and other targets and caused several thousand casualties. Public opinion and, even more important, the sympathies of the civilian political elite, moved perceptibly against the Phibun regime and the military. In June 1944, Phibun was forced from office and replaced by the first predominantly civilian government since the 1932 coup.

Pridi and the Civilian Regime, 1944–47

The new government was headed by Khuang Aphaiwong, a civilian linked politically with conservatives like Seni. The most influential figure in the regime, however, was Pridi, whose anti-Japanese views were increasingly attractive to the Thai. In the last year of the war, Allied agents were tacitly given free access by Bangkok. As the war came to an end, Thailand repudiated its wartime agreements with Japan.

The civilian leaders, however, were unable to achieve unity. After a falling-out with Pridi, Khuang was replaced as prime minister by the regent's nominee, Seni, who had returned to Thailand from his post in Washington. The scramble for power among factions in late 1945 created political divisions in the ranks of the civilian leaders that destroyed their potential for making a common stand against the resurgent political force of the military in the postwar years.

Postwar accommodations with the Allies also weakened the civilian government. As a result of the contributions made to the Allied war efforts by the Free Thai Movement, the United States, which unlike the other Allies had never officially been at war with Thailand, refrained from dealing with Thailand as an enemy country in postwar peace negotiations. Before signing a peace treaty, however, Britain demanded war reparations in the form of rice for shipment to Malaya, and France refused to permit admission of Thailand to the United Nations (UN) until Indochinese territories annexed during the war were returned. The Soviet Union insisted on the repeal of anticommunist legislation.

The government set up an agency to manage the delivery of rice as part of Thai war reparations. These reparations were initially to total 1.5 million tons, or approximately 10 percent of the annual yield, but the figure was adjusted downward, and the reparations were paid off within two years. However, the government retained the policy of regulating the rice trade as an income-producing device.

The Seni government survived only until the peace treaty with Britain was signed in January 1946. Public discontent grew—the result of inflation, the reparation payments to the British, the surrender of territorial gains that many Thai considered to have been legitimate, and mismanagement at every level of government. Pridi restored Khuang to office for a time but in March 1946 was obliged to assume the prime ministership himself in an effort to restore confidence in the civilian regime.

Pridi, who argued that the strength of any civilian regime depended on a functioning parliament, worked with his cabinet to draft a new constitution that established parliamentary structures. The constitution, promulgated in May 1946, called for a bicameral legislature. The lower house, the House of Representatives, was elected by popular vote; the upper house, the Senate, was elected by the lower house. This constitution was tailor made for Pridi's purposes, ensuring him a parliamentary majority that would support his programs.

The 1946 election, which had in fact preceded enactment of the constitution, was the first in which political parties participated. Two coalition parties—Pridi's own party, the Constitutional Front, and the Cooperation Party—won a large majority of seats in the lower house and, in turn, sent a pro-Pridi majority to the upper house. Parliamentary opposition was led by the Democrat (Prachathipat) Party, headed by Seni and Khuang.

Pridi's prestige suffered permanent damage two weeks after the election of the upper house, however, when Ananda Mahidol, who had returned from Switzerland a few months earlier, was found dead in his bed at the palace, a bullet wound through his head. Although the official account attributed the king's death to an accident, there was widespread doubt because few facts were made public. Rumors implicated Pridi. Two months later, in August, Pridi resigned on grounds of ill health and went abroad, leaving Luang Thamrongnawasawat as prime minister.

The late king's younger brother, nineteen-year-old Bhumibol Adulyadej (Rama IX, 1946–), was chosen as successor to the throne. The new king had been born in the United States, had spent his childhood in Switzerland, and had gone to Thailand for the first time in 1945 with his brother. He returned to Switzerland to complete his schooling and did not return to Bangkok to take up his duties until 1951.

Return of Phibun and the Military

As a result of Pridi's fall from grace and the manner in which the civilian government that succeeded him handled the investigation of the king's death, Phibun's military faction regained some of the stature that it had lost through its wartime association with the Japanese. Reviving the nationalistic theme of its years in power, Phibun's group played on intense public resentment of the war reparations Thailand had to pay and the economic dislocation the payments were believed to have caused. Army officers also blamed the civilian government for a humiliation the military suffered in 1946 when their units, facing expatriated Chinese Guomindang (Kuomintang—KMT) forces in the north, were ordered to disband in the field and were left without supplies or transport. They also criticized the civilian government's conciliatory policy toward minorities—Chinese, Muslims, and hill tribes.

Phibun had been arrested as a war criminal in 1945 but was released by the courts soon afterward. Always an efficient leader and known as a staunch anticommunist, Phibun had retained his constituency of supporters in the officer corps. Even the civilian elite, dismayed at the economic disorder and frightened at the rise of communist insurgencies in neighboring countries, regarded him as an attractive candidate for office. Some observers contended that his rehabilitation had been due to United States influence.

November 1947 Coup

In November 1947, the so-called Coup d'Etat Group, led by two retired generals and backed by Phibun, seized power from the civilian government. Pridi, who had recently returned from his world tour, fled the country again and eventually took refuge in China. The coup leaders appointed an interim government headed by Khuang and promised a new constitution. General elections held in January 1948 confirmed support for the junta, particularly the Phibun faction. In order to placate conservative civilian supporters, Khuang was retained as prime minister until he proved too independent in his policies. In April 1948, Phibun—by then a field marshal—forcibly removed Khuang from office and took over as prime minister.

For the next three years Phibun struggled to maintain his government against numerous attempted coups by rival military factions. To build support, he allowed disaffected political groups, including Khuang's conservative Democrat Party, to participate in drafting a new constitution, which was promulgated in 1949. When leaders of an anti-Phibun army group were arrested in October 1948, supporters of former prime ministers Pridi and Khuang in the navy and the marines were not seized. In February 1949, a revolt allegedly sponsored by Pridi supporters in the marines and navy was suppressed after three days of fighting. In June 1951, marine and navy troops again rebelled and abducted Phibun. The revolt, which was put down by loyal army and air force units, resulted in a serious cutback of navy strength and a purge of senior naval officers.

Phibun's policies during his second government (1948–57) were similar to those he had initiated in the late 1930s. He restored the use of the name *Thailand* in 1949. (In reaction to extreme nationalism, there had been a reversion to the name *Siam* in 1946.) Legislation to make Thai social behavior conform to Western standards—begun by Phibun before the war—was reintroduced. Secondary education was improved, and military appropriations were substantially increased. The Phibun regime was also characterized by harassment of Chinese and the tendency to regard them as disloyal and, after 1949, as communists.

Phibun's anticommunist position had great influence on his foreign policy. Thailand refused to recognize the People's Republic of China, supported UN action in Korea in 1950, and backed the

French against communist insurgents in Indochina. Phibun's Thailand was regarded as the most loyal supporter of United States foreign policy in mainland Southeast Asia.

November 1951 Coup

By 1951 Phibun had begun to share political power with two associates who had participated with him in the 1947 coup that overthrew the civilian regime. One of these was General Phao Siyanon, director general of police and a close associate of Phibun since the original coup of 1932. The other, more junior, partner was General Sarit Thanarat, commander of the Bangkok garrison. As time passed, Phibun's stock within the military declined as a result of the plots against him. Phao and Sarit grew more powerful than Phibun, who was able to retain the prime ministership only because of their rivalry for the succession.

In November 1951, military and police officers announced in a radio broadcast that the 1949 constitution was suspended by the government and that the 1932 constitution was in force. The reason given for restoring a unicameral parliament with half its membership appointed by the government was the danger of communist aggression. Shortly after the government-engineered coup, King Bhumibol Adulyadej was called back to Thailand, and for the first time since 1935 an adult monarch resided in the palace in Bangkok. A revised constitution was promulgated in February 1952, and an election was held for seats in the new, single-house legislature, half of the members of which were to be appointed. Nearly all the appointed parliamentary members were army officers.

The Phibun-Phao-Sarit triumvirate continued to operate along the policy lines of the previous five years. In November 1952, the police announced the discovery of a communist plot against the government and began a series of arrests of Chinese. Many Chinese schools were closed and Chinese associations banned. The campaign against communists, with its anti-Chinese emphasis, gathered momentum throughout 1953.

In 1954 Thailand participated in the Manila meeting that resulted in the Southeast Asia Collective Defense Treaty, of which the Southeast Asia Treaty Organization (SEATO) was the operative arm (see Foreign Affairs, ch. 4). The next year SEATO, which made its headquarters at Bangkok, was offered the use of military bases in Thailand. Relations with the United States continued to be cordial during this period, and substantial amounts of American economic, technical, and military aid were provided.

In 1955 the Thai government had imposed a restrictive export tax on rice—the controversial rice premium—and required that

Tanks in the streets of Bangkok following 1932 coup
Courtesy New York Times *Paris Collection, National Archives*

traders purchase rice export licenses. The ultimate goal of this tax was to nurture Thailand's developing industries and to discourage rice production. The government hoped the tax on tonnage of rice exported would drive the price of Thai rice in the world market beyond a competitive level, thus discouraging exports. The government then purchased the rice that could not be sold abroad to create a public rice reserve and sold it on the domestic market at artificially low prices.

By providing low-cost rice, the government hoped to hold down the cost of living in urban areas and prevent demands for higher wages, thereby making Thai industrial production more competitive on world markets. It also argued that the rice policy would encourage diversification in the agricultural sector as traditional rice farmers in the central plain turned to other cash crops—maize, sugarcane, and pineapple. Export controls had no effect however, on rice farmers in the North and Northeast, who produced glutinous rice for local consumption only. Introduction of the rice premium fundamentally altered the liberal policy toward free trade that had been in place since the Bowring Treaty, and it cast the Thai government in an activist economic role, such as that advocated by the nationalists since 1932 (see Mongkut's Opening to the West, this ch.).

Opponents of the rice policy charged that the rice premium was an excessive tax that ultimately placed the heaviest burden on small farmers in the central plain engaged in growing rice for export, who were deprived of an increase in real income and were prevented from sharing in the benefits of Thailand's economic boom in the 1960s. Lacking incentive to increase their production, farmers planted less and refrained from introducing improved seeds or using costly fertilizers. Government officials, however, predicted that as rice production increased abroad, world and domestic prices would come together and end the need for the rice premium.

Phibun's Experiment with "Democracy"

The struggle for control of the Thai government continued, meanwhile, and Phibun attempted to offset Sarit's advantage among the military by generating popular support for himself. In 1955 he toured the United States and Britain and, on his return to Thailand, articulated a policy of *prachathipatai* ("democracy"), which he stated he was giving to the country as a gift. Encouraging the public to feel free to criticize his "open regime," he set aside a portion of a central park near the royal palace in Bangkok for public debate, in emulation of Hyde Park in London, and gave the press free rein in covering the dissent expressed there. Criticism, especially as it appeared in the press, was outspoken and often extreme in its attacks on the government. In addition to encouraging criticism, Phibun halted the anti-Chinese campaign, made plans to increase the responsibilities of local government, and again permitted political parties to register. Phibun intended more to convey the appearance of democracy, however, than to allow for its functional development.

Phao and Phibun devoted much effort to ensuring a government victory in the general election scheduled for February 1957. Phao headed a newly founded government party, the Seri Manangkhasila, which was the largest and best funded of the twenty-five parties that had sprung up in response to *prachathipatai*. Sarit, on the other hand, kept out of the campaign and, after the election, dissociated himself from the disappointing results, which gave the Seri Manangkhasila a bare majority but saw half of the incumbent party members defeated. Sarit and others questioned even these returns and accused the government party of stuffing ballot boxes. When university students came out in great numbers to protest the government's handling of the elections, Phibun declared a state of emergency and shelved *prachathipatai*.

Sarit and Thanom

Phibun had failed to win the popular support that he had sought, and the effort cost him what remained of his standing among the military faction. As a result of the election, Phibun formed a new government in March 1957, appointing Phao as interior minister with responsibility for internal security. However, it was Sarit, whose prestige had not been at stake in the election, who as newly named armed forces commander in chief emerged as the strongest member of the ruling group. In September he openly broke with his colleagues, ordered tanks into the streets, and displaced Phibun and Phao in a bloodless coup d'état. He suspended the constitution and dissolved parliament. The king approved Sarit's action; the royal family had opposed Phibun since the 1930s.

New elections were held in December under an interim civilian government headed by Pote Sarasin, the secretary general of SEATO. No single party won a parliamentary majority, but Sarit organized a government party, the National Socialist Party, to contain the loose coalition of parties and individuals backing his regime. Because of poor health Sarit did not attempt to form a government but turned over responsibility to his deputy in the armed forces, Thanom Kittikachorn. Intraparty wrangling over political and economic spoils plagued Thanom's government. The situation was further aggravated by the inclusion in the government party of left-wing politicians who opposed its pro-Western foreign policy.

Sarit's Return

In October 1958, Sarit, recently returned from the United States where he had undergone extensive medical treatment, took over personal control of the government with the consent of Thanom, who resigned as prime minister. Sarit, who spoke of instilling "national discipline" in the country, justified his action on the grounds that Thailand's various constitutional experiments had not succeeded in providing the stability needed for economic development. He outlawed political parties and jailed critics of the regime—teachers, students, labor leaders, journalists, and liberal parliamentarians. A dozen or more newspapers were closed.

In January 1960, Sarit decreed an interim constitution that provided for an appointed assembly to draft a new constitution, Thailand's eighth since 1932. Work on the document continued throughout the 1960s. Sarit assumed the office of prime minister provided for in the interim constitution, but his regime was clearly that of a military dictatorship.

Whatever else might be said about its political shortcomings, Sarit's government was more dynamic than the previous regimes of the constitutional era. Sarit gave ministers in his cabinet considerable independence in the affairs of their own ministries. At the same time he made all major decisions and kept members of the government responsible solely to his office.

Despite recurring scandals involving official corruption, in the early 1960s Sarit seemed to have succeeded in achieving political stability and economic growth. In 1961 the government instituted the first in a series of economic development schemes that were intended to foster employment and expand production. Although military officers were frequently appointed as directors of state and quasi-governmental economic enterprises, civilian personnel gradually assumed a greater share in implementing government policies. Sarit welcomed foreign investment and assured investors of government protection. Major electrification and irrigation projects began, with aid from the United States and international agencies. In addition, Sarit initiated a cleanup campaign to improve sanitation in the cities.

Sarit revived the motto ''Nation-Religion-King'' as a fighting political slogan for his regime, which he characterized as combining the paternalism of the ancient Thai state and the benevolent ideals of Buddhism. He spoke of his intention to ''restore'' the king, a retiring man, to active participation in national life, and he urged Bhumibol Adulyadej and his consort, Queen Sirikit, to have more contact with the Thai public, which had a strong affection for the monarchy. Royal tours were also scheduled for the king and queen to represent Thailand abroad. Sarit likewise played on the religious attachments of the people. In 1962 he centralized administration of monastic institutions under a superior patriarchate friendly to the regime, and he mobilized monks, especially in the North and Northeast, to support government programs. Critics protested that Sarit had demeaned religion by using it for political ends and had compromised the monarchy by using it to legitimize a military dictatorship. They asserted that the regime's policies, rather than restoring these institutions, had contributed to the growth of materialism and secularism and to the erosion of religious belief in the country.

Under Sarit's guidance, Thailand's anticommunist policy continued, and steps were taken to deal militarily with the growing threat of insurgency posed by communist-inspired activities in neighboring countries. Sarit sought closer ties with Thailand's anticommunist neighbors and with the United States, and in 1961 Thailand and another SEATO member, the Philippines, joined

Prince Bhumibol Adulyadej (left) and King Ananda Mahidol (right)
as schoolboys in Switzerland in 1940
Courtesy New York Times *Paris Collection, National Archives*

with newly independent Malaya (since 1963, Malaysia) to form the Association of Southeast Asia (ASA). The Pathet Lao (as the leftist Lao People's Liberation Army was known until 1965) moved into northwestern Laos in March 1962. United States secretary of state Dean Rusk and Thai foreign minister Thanat Khoman agreed that their countries would interpret the Southeast Asia Collective Defense Treaty of 1954 as a bilateral as well as multilateral pact binding the United States to come to the aid of Thailand in time of need, with or without the agreement of the other signers of the pact. Two months after the foreign ministers' agreement, President John F. Kennedy stationed United States troops in Thailand in response to the deteriorating situation in Laos. The arrival of the troops in May 1962 was seen by the Thai government as evidence of the United States commitment to preserving Thailand's independence and integrity against communist expansion. Despite United States pressure, however, Sarit refused to entertain ideas of democratic reform.

Thai Politics and Foreign Policy, 1963–71

In December 1963 Sarit died in office. His deputy, Thanom, peacefully succeeded to the prime ministership and pursued without major modifications the foreign and domestic policies of his

39

predecessor. Retaining the cabinet that he inherited from Sarit, Thanom focused his efforts on seeking to maintain political stability; promoting economic development, especially in security-sensitive areas; raising the standard of living; and safeguarding the country from the communist threat at home and abroad.

A notable departure from Sarit's policies, however, was the Thanom government's decision to shorten the timetable for the country's transition from the military-dominated leadership structure to a popularly elected government. The prime minister urged the Constituent Assembly, appointed in 1959, to finish drafting a constitution as soon as practicable. The new leadership also relaxed stringent official controls on the press, an attempt that the authorities said was aimed at creating a new, relatively liberalized, political climate.

Although the leaders agreed on the desirability of establishing what they described as a more democratic political system in tune with the country's heritage, there were indications that they disagreed on the pace of the projected change. Some leading officials thought that an early resumption of political activities would broaden the base of politics and strengthen popular identification with the government, the monarchy, and Buddhism. Others argued that the restoration of party politics at a time when the country was confronted with serious internal problems was likely to aid the communists in their efforts to infiltrate civic, labor, student, and political organizations.

The constitution was finally proclaimed in June 1968, but martial law, which had been imposed in 1958, remained in effect. Party politics were legalized and resumed shortly after mid-1968, and general elections for the new National Assembly were held in February 1969. Thanom's United Thai People's Party returned 75 members to the 219-seat lower house, giving them the largest representation of the 13 parties, while the second-running Democrat Party won 57 seats.

Thailand's annual economic growth rate in the 1960s and early 1970s averaged a booming 8 percent, much of it attributable to United States military expenditures there during the years of its involvement in Vietnam. An increased flow of foreign exchange resulted from United States and multilateral aid loans as well as from foreign investment, which came primarily from Japan, the United States, and Taiwan.

Foreign policy concerns focused on neighboring Laos, where it was believed a Pathet Lao victory would destabilize the North and Northeast and open Thailand to a direct attack by communist forces. Thailand allied itself closely with the United States position in the Republic of Vietnam (South Vietnam), permitting bases in Thailand to be used for raids on both the Democratic Republic of Vietnam (North Vietnam) and Cambodia. Although more than 45,000 United States troops and 500 combat aircraft were stationed in the country by 1968, their mission was not officially acknowledged for fear of possible communist retaliation against Thailand. Sarit also committed a division of Thai army troops to the war in South Vietnam.

President Lyndon B. Johnson's March 1968 announcement that the United States would halt bombing in North Vietnam and seek a negotiated settlement came as a blow to the Thai government, which had not been consulted on the change in policy. Although the defense of Thailand clearly remained essential to the security of Southeast Asia in United States strategic thinking, no provision was made for Laos, whose security the Thai saw as essential to their own defense.

While remaining loyal to its commitments, Thailand thereafter determined to restore flexibility to its foreign policy by moving away from one-sided dependence on the United States. The military, however, was anxious to continue Thailand's active involvement in South Vietnam and in Laos, where several thousand Thai "volunteers" were engaged against the Pathet Lao. Thanom urged United States backing for the Lon Nol regime in Cambodia in 1970 and proposed a formal alliance linking Thailand with Laos, Cambodia, and South Vietnam that would give the conflict in Southeast Asia the appearance of a war being fought by Asian anticommunists for Asian security. The plan failed to get United States support.

Communist activities in Laos and Malaya had already begun to affect the domestic situation in the South and the Northeast in the 1950s, and by the 1960s they presented a problem of increasing magnitude. Communist guerrillas, mostly ethnic Chinese, operated in jungle areas north of the Thai-Malayan border, where they had taken refuge from Commonwealth of Nations security forces during the 1948–60 Emergency in Malaya. A more serious threat in same region were the Muslim insurgents of the Pattani National Liberation Front, a Thai separatist group composed of ethnic Malays. Meanwhile, in the northern provinces dissident Meo tribesmen reportedly had begun receiving training and arms from the Pathet Lao by 1950. In the Northeast, underground leftist parties took advantage of grievances over relatively poor economic and social conditions to rally opposition to the government. Faced with the problems in the South, North, and Northeast, the Bangkok government frequently identified regional unrest and protest against ethnic and economic policies with the genuine communist-based insurgencies that overlapped and often benefited from it. Opposition groups and critics of the regime in Bangkok were also generally labeled as communists.

November 1971 Coup

In November 1971, Prime Minister Thanom executed a coup against his own government, thereby ending the three-year experiment with what had passed for parliamentary democracy. The 1968 constitution was suspended, political parties banned, and undisguised military rule imposed on the country. Under the new regime, executive and legislative authority was held by a military junta, the National Executive Council. Heading the council was a triumvirate that included Thanom, who retained the office of prime minister; Field Marshal Praphat Charusathian, his deputy prime minister; and Thanom's son (also Praphat's son-in-law), Narong Kittikachorn, an army colonel.

Despite stern moves to suppress opposition, popular dissatisfaction with the dictatorial regime mounted in the universities and labor organizations as well as among rival military factions. The discontent focused on United States support for Thanom, the growth of Japanese economic influence, and the official corruption that the regime made no effort to conceal. The civilian political elite joined students and workers in opposing Thanom's apparent aim to perpetuate a political dynasty through his son, Narong, whose rise the officer corps particularly resented. Thanom's aggrandizement of his family was at odds with the image he tried to project and the standards of the "civic religion" with its call for veneration of "Nation-Religion-King." The triumvirate also ignored the king, who had moderated his earlier enthusiasm for Thanom, and opponents charged that the junta disregarded religion. Some critics detected signs of republicanism in the regime and feared another Thanom-sponsored coup to overthrow the monarchy.

Thailand in Transition

In December 1972, Thanom announced a new interim constitution that provided for a totally appointed legislative assembly, two-thirds of the members of which would be drawn from the military and police. This move provoked widespread protest, however, especially among students and led to Thanom's eventual removal. In May and June 1973, students and workers rallied in the streets to demand a more democratic constitution and genuine parliamentary elections. By early October, there was renewed violence, protesting the detention of eleven students arrested for handing out

*Prime Minister Phibunsongkhram meeting with
President Dwight D. Eisenhower and other United States
government officials
Courtesy National Archives*

antigovernment pamphlets. The demonstrations grew in size and scope as students demanded an end to the military dictatorship. On October 13, more than 250,000 people rallied in Bangkok before the Democracy Memorial, in the largest demonstration of its kind in Thai history, to press their grievances against the government.

The next day troops opened fire on the demonstrators, killing seventy-five, and occupied the campus of Thammasat University. King Bhumibol, who had been seeking Thanom's ouster, took a direct role in dealing with the crisis in order to prevent further bloodshed and called Thanom and his cabinet to Chitralada Palace for talks. In the evening, the king went on television and radio to announce a compromise solution: Thanom had resigned as prime minister but would remain as supreme commander of the armed forces. In consultation with student leaders, the king appointed Sanya Dharmasakti (Sanya Thammasak) as interim prime minister, with instructions to draft a new constitution. Sanya, a civilian conservative, was the rector of Thammasat University and known to be sympathetic to the students' position. On October 15, Thanom, Praphat, and Narong—dubbed Thailand's "three most hated men"—were allowed to leave the country in secret, the king overruling student militants who wanted to put them on trial. Their departure was announced to the public only after they had left the country, Praphat and Narong for Taiwan and Thanom initially for the United States.

The student demonstrations of 1973 had not been intended as a prelude to a revolution. They resulted, at least in part, from the frustration of large numbers of students who were unable to fulfill professional expectations after graduation, partly because university enrollment had increased dramatically in the 1960s and early 1970s (see Education and the Arts, ch. 2). Students were careful, however, to legitimize their actions against the military dictatorship by an appeal to religion and the monarchy, displaying in the streets the symbols of the ''civic religion''—figures of Buddha, pictures of the king, and the national flag.

Prime Minister Sanya gave full credit to the student movement for bringing down the military dictatorship. At the state ceremony honoring those who had been killed during the 1973 demonstrations, he pledged, ''Their death has brought us democracy which we will preserve forever.'' However, political change in Thailand did not bring the shift to the left that had been hoped for by some and feared by many. Student militants, who already felt betrayed by the king's complicity in Thanom's escape, were not satisfied with the direction taken by the new government, which seemed to have been preempted by the professional politicians.

The new constitution, which went into effect in October 1974, called for a popularly elected House of Representatives and elections within 120 days. Political parties proliferated following the passage in 1974 of legislation permitting their registration. As a result, the January 1975 parliamentary elections were inconclusive. With forty-two officially sanctioned parties in the field, none won a parliamentary majority. The parties for the most part had been organized around familiar political personalities, and few had offered any ideological base or even specific programs. Only 47 percent of eligible voters cast ballots; public cynicism about politicians and improper management of voter registration were blamed for the relatively low turnout. According to observers, however, the election was not openly corrupt.

The election put a large bloc of right-wing and centrist parties in control of nearly 90 percent of the seats. None could be described as reformist, and, to a degree, all represented the status quo. On the left, a small and inexperienced but idealistic group advocated land redistribution and favored neutrality in foreign affairs. Seni Pramoj, whose Democrat Party was the largest in the right-wing bloc, formed a shaky government that could depend on only 91 of the 269 votes in the House of Representatives. It fell within a month, after failing to win a vote of confidence. In March Seni's brother, Kukrit Pramoj, leader of the small, right-wing Social Action (Kit Sangkhom) Party, was able to put together a more stable centrist coalition. During his year in office, Kukrit proposed such reforms as decentralizing economic planning to put development in the hands of locally elected committees, but measures of this nature were repeatedly defeated as members of the National Assembly rallied to protect their vested interests.

The overthrow of the Thanom regime had brought on a more vocal questioning of ties with the United States. Nationalist sentiment, which was frequently expressed in terms of anti-Americanism, ran high among students, who protested alleged American involvement in domestic Thai affairs and called for the speedy withdrawal of United States forces. Moreover, the changed geopolitical situation in Southeast Asia refocused the issue of the United States presence. Many Thai concluded that the country could not be reconciled with its communist neighbors as long as United States personnel were stationed on Thai soil.

The pullout of the 27,000 United States military personnel in Thailand began in March 1975 and was completed in mid-1976 (see Foreign Security Assistance, ch. 5). The Thai government stressed the need for continued United States military commitment in Southeast Asia, but from Bangkok's standpoint, the emphasis in relations between the two allies clearly shifted from one of military cooperation to economic and technical cooperation. United States-Thai relations were dealt a setback, however, by the Mayaguez incident in May 1975, when the United States used the airfield at Ban U Taphao without Thai consent as a staging base for the rescue of an American freighter detained by the Khmer Rouge. The incident was seen as a blow to Thai sovereignty and touched off anti-American demonstrations in Bangkok.

When South Vietnam, Laos, and Cambodia came under communist control in the spring of 1975, the Thai government's initial reaction was to seek an accommodation with the victors, but feelers extended to Hanoi met with a chilly reception. In July, however, Thailand established diplomatic relations with China, after two years of negotiations. That same year, Thailand became active in regional technical and economic cooperation as part of the Association of Southeast Asian Nations (ASEAN), of which it had been a member since the organization's founding in 1967 (see Foreign Affairs, ch. 4).

In addition to political changes, both in its own government and in its relationship with other powers, Thailand also experienced economic shifts. Kukrit's government was plagued by labor unrest and rising prices. The economic boom that had spurred employment and produced an apparent prosperity in the 1960s fizzled with the phasing out of United States military expenditures in Thailand. Furthermore, the impressive economic growth was insufficient to keep pace with the growth of the population, which had increased from 26 million in 1960 to 34 million in 1970. Although agricultural yield per hectare remained static, agricultural production kept up with population growth during the 1960s and 1970s because the amount of land under cultivation doubled during that period. Arable land reserves were being used up by the mid-1970s, however, except in the southern peninsula. Moreover, although increasing rice production had indeed brought together world and domestic rice prices, as government leaders of the 1960s had predicted, the premium nevertheless remained in effect. Its purpose now was to augment government revenues. More than US$40 million was derived from the rice premium in 1975, much of it earmarked, according to government sources, for agricultural development schemes as a form of income distribution.

The low incomes imposed by the rice premium and the lack of available credit adversely affected small owner-operated farms in the central plain's rice bowl that produced for the export market. Farmers left the land either to become wage laborers on large farms or to secure industrial and service jobs in the cities. This migration to the cities was evident in the dramatic growth of the Bangkok-Thon Buri metropolitan area, where population exploded by 250 percent in the 1960s and 1970s to exceed 4.5 million in 1980.

Maintaining order was the most pressing problem facing the parliamentary regime and the most difficult one to resolve. For one thing, the communist-inspired insurgency persisted and generated a mistrust of all dissidents (see Insurgency, ch. 5). The radicalization of the student movement was attributed to communist influence, and student leaders were regularly accused of being agents for Beijing and Hanoi. Particularly after the fall of South Vietnam, Laos, and Cambodia, all dissidents were likely to be labeled communists by the military and by right-wing politicians. Even in moderate government circles, misgivings were expressed about continued student activism and the growth of militancy against the monarchy. In April 1975, fourteen labor organizers and student leaders were arrested under anticommunist legislation used for the first time since Thanom's overthrow.

Adding to these political tensions were the plethora of new newspapers that came into existence after censorship and restrictions on the press were lifted in 1973. Although most were too small to be economically viable, they gave a voice to political factions

Ruins of Khmer city of Phimai (thirteenth century)
in northeastern Thailand
Courtesy Tourism Authority of Thailand

of every persuasion and produced a cacophony with which many
had difficulty coping. News reporting was a low priority for many
newspapers, some of which operated solely as rumor mills engaging in extortion and blackmail. Government officials admitted that
they were intimidated by the press.

Political murders and bombing became commonplace as open
warfare broke out between leftist students and workers and rightist
paramilitary groups, the latter openly supported by the police. In
August 1975, police in Bangkok, striking to protest government
weakness toward leftist students, went on a rampage through the
Thammasat University campus. Several senior military officers and
civilian conservatives formed the ultranationalist Nawa Phon (New
Force) movement to defend ''Nation-Religion-King'' against the
students, and by mid-1975 it claimed 50,000 members. A group
of paramilitary vigilantes, the Red Gaurs (Red Bulls), recruited
25,000 members, largely unemployed vocational graduates and technical students, to disrupt student rallies and break strikes. The group
was believed to have been organized by the police as an unofficial
auxiliary. Another right-wing group with similar origins was the
Village Scouts (Luk Sua Chaoban; literally, ''village tiger cubs'').

Right-wing power grew early in 1976, as pressure from the military forced Kukrit to resign after he had pressed corruption charges

47

against army officers. Violence during the parliamentary election campaign the following April left more than thirty dead, including Socialist Party leader Bunsanong Bunyothanyan, and the new alignment in the House of Representatives brought back Seni as prime minister at the head of a four-party, right-wing coalition.

In August Praphat reappeared in Thailand and was received by the king. Although Seni asserted that he could not legally deport him, the former dictator's presence provoked widespread demonstrations that forced his return to Taiwan. The next month, however, Thanom was back in Thailand, garbed in a monk's robe and expressing his intention to enter a monastery. Despite renewed protests, the demoralized government allowed him to stay.

Political tensions between leftist and rightist forces reached a bloody climax in October 1976. On October 5, right-wing newspapers in the capital published a photograph of student demonstrators at Thammasat University reenacting the strangling and hanging of two student protestors by police the previous month. The photograph, which was later found to have been altered, showed one of the students as being made up to resemble the king's son, Crown Prince Vajiralongkorn. The right wing perceived the demonstration as a damning act of lèse-majesté. That evening police surrounded the campus of Thammasat University, where 2,000 students were holding a sit-in. Fighting between students and police (including contingents of the paramilitary Border Patrol Police) broke out. The following day, groups of Nawa Phon, Red Gaurs, and Village Scouts "shock troops" surged onto the campus and launched a bloody assault in which hundreds of students were killed and wounded and more than 1,000 arrested. That evening the military seized power, established the National Administrative Reform Council (NARC), and ended that phase of Thailand's intermittent experimentation with democracy.

Military Rule and Limited Parliamentary Government, 1976–83

With the support of the king and the military membership of NARC, a new government was formed under the prime ministership of Thanin Kraivichien, a former Supreme Court justice who had a reputation for honesty and integrity. Though a civilian, Thanin was a passionate anticommunist and established a regime that was in many ways more repressive than those of earlier military strongmen. He imposed strict censorship, placed unions under tight controls, and carried out anticommunist purges of the civil service and education institutions. Student leaders, driven underground by the October 1976 violence, left urban areas to join the communist insurgency in the provinces. As a result of his harsh rule and a growing feeling within the political elite that university students, themselves members of the privileged classes, had been poorly treated, Thanin was replaced in October 1977 by General Kriangsak Chomanand.

Kriangsak was more conciliatory than his civilian predecessor and promised a new constitution and elections by 1979. He courted moderate union leaders, raising the minimum daily wage in the Bangkok area in 1978 and again in 1979. He allowed limited press freedom, and he gave verbal support to the idea of land reform,. though no action in this area was forthcoming. In September 1978, he issued an amnesty for the ''Bangkok 18'' dissidents who had been arrested in the October 1976 violence and tried by military courts.

A new constitution was promulgated in December 1978. The 1978 Constitution established a bicameral legislature, the National Assembly, consisting of the popularly elected House of Representatives (301 members) and the appointed Senate (225 members). The military controlled appointment to the Senate, and it could block House of Representatives initiatives in important areas such as national security, the economy, the budget, and votes of no confidence. The 1978 document also stipulated that the prime minister and cabinet ministers did not have to be popularly elected. When elections were held on schedule in April 1979, moderate rightist parties—the Social Action Party, the Thai Citizens' Party, and the Chart Thai (Thai Nation) Party—won the largest number of seats, whereas the Democrats lost most of their seats.

Further changes came during 1979 and 1980, however, as economic conditions deteriorated in the wake of the second oil crisis. Uncontrolled inflation caused the standard of living to fall in urban areas, especially Bangkok, while government dilatoriness and corruption in the villages stalled policies designed to help the farmers. In February 1980, the Kriangsak government announced sudden increases in the prices of oil, gas, and electricity. This action provoked opposition from elected politicians and demonstrations similar to those of 1973 by students and workers. As opposition grew, Kriangsak resigned. In March 1980, General Prem Tinsulanonda, who had been army commander in chief and defense minister, became prime minister with the support of younger officers of the armed forces and civilian political leaders.

Prem in Power

Although a military figure, Thailand's new prime minister sought to give civilians a greater role in government and promote more stable and democratic political institutions. He enlisted the support of the Democrat Party and the Social Action Party in the House of Representatives and, in contrast to Kriangsak, appointed mostly civilians to his cabinet. He benefited immensely from the support given him by the royal family, as was especially evident in April 1981 when "Young Turk" officers launched a coup attempt in the capital region. These officers established a "Revolutionary Council," disbanded the National Assembly, and promised sweeping social changes, including land reform. Prem rushed to Khorat, where the royal family was in residence. When it became clear to regional military commanders that Prem enjoyed the king's backing in the present crisis, they offered him their support. On April 3, 1981, loyalist military units secured Bangkok and rounded up the rebellious officers with minimal fighting and casualties.

The monarch's role in politics was low key, but still pivotal. He had played a major part in the 1973 transition from military dictatorship to democracy. During the 1973–76 period, however, the king became increasingly apprehensive about the kinds of changes that were emerging because of a more liberalized political system. Communism seemed a genuine threat not only to political stability but also to the continuity of the royal family. This danger explains the king's support for extremist groups such as the Village Scouts, his controversial decision to visit ex-strongman Thanom in a Buddhist monastery on the eve of the October 1976 violence, and his backing of Thanin's repressive anticommunist regime. Bhumibol's support of Prem after 1980, however, suggests that although his basically conservative perspective was unchanged, the king was also concerned with promoting the development of stable parliamentary institutions in which the military would have a limited, and institutionalized, role.

Prem, however, faced serious problems. A major figure in the suppression of the April 1981 coup attempt was General Arthit Kamlangek, deputy commander of the Second Army Region. After Bangkok was retaken, Arthit was rewarded for his loyalty with the post of commander of the First Army Region, which encompassed the capital. In October 1982, he was appointed army commander in chief. Arthit thus seemed poised to succeed, or push aside, Prem as Thailand's prime minister. Prem's government had been severely weakened by the coup attempt and by continual dissension among the civilian members of the government. Moreover, economic problems focused popular dissatisfaction on Prem in both urban and rural areas. Students became politically more active, though the leftist extremism of the 1973–76 period was not evident. Students and workers combined forces to protest an increase in bus fares in 1982, obliging the government to rescind the increase. Demonstrations by farmers to raise the price of rice also occurred during this year with the backing of civilian politicians.

By early 1983, however, Prem had the distinction of being the longest serving prime minister since the fall of Thanom in 1973. Although the military had remained the most powerful political force in the early 1980s, civilian political institutions had shown surprising vitality. One reason for their strength was that the political parties had some success in mobilizing popular support behind economic and social issues. On a more basic level, there was evidence that the population, especially in the urban areas, had grown tired of military strongmen and wanted stable and more open political institutions.

Elections were scheduled for April 1983. A major obstacle to be overcome before the polling, however, was resolution of the heated dispute over "transitory" clauses in the 1978 Constitution. These clauses, which had ensured military control over the political system, were to become inoperative on April 21, 1983. Unless a constitutional amendment was passed to sustain the clauses, the appointed upper house, the Senate, would no longer be able to sit in joint session with the lower house and thus would lose a substantial measure of power. Also, government officials, including military officers, would no longer be allowed to serve in the cabinet. Finally, the structure of election constituencies would be radically altered. Small, single-member constituencies would be replaced by large constituencies covering entire provinces. The first two changes were naturally unpopular with the military elite, while the third alienated the members of the smaller political parties, who believed the creation of "winner take all" province-level constituencies would deprive them of parliamentary representation.

These groups supported constitutional amendments to make the transitory clauses permanent and preserve the conservative aspects of the 1978 Constitution. The amendment proposals, however, were narrowly defeated when the Chart Thai voted against them in the legislature (see The Central Government, ch. 4). Prem deftly engineered a compromise by declaring that elections would be held before the transitory clauses (and the small constituency system) expired on April 21. The April 18 balloting, however, resulted in gains for the major parties. A coalition of the Social Action Party, Democrat Party, and National Democracy (Chart Prachathipatai) Party was stitched together and had a small majority in the lower house (the Chart Thai was excluded from the government because it lacked military backing). As a result of his continued military backing and image as a leader above party politics, Prem was reappointed prime minister.

Foreign Relations, 1977–83

Beginning in 1977, the Thai government under Prime Minister Kriangsak had sought a rapprochement with Indochina's new communist states. Trade agreements and a transit accord were signed with Laos in 1978. In September of that year, Pham Van Dong, premier of Vietnam, visited Bangkok and gave assurances that his government would not support a communist insurgency within Thailand. Troubles on the Thai-Cambodian border, including assaults on Thai border villages by Cambodian forces, however, continued to disrupt relations with Democratic Kampuchea.

Vietnam's invasion of Democratic Kampuchea in December 1978 initiated a new crisis. Vietnamese forces captured Phnom Penh in January 1979 and proclaimed the People's Republic of Kampuchea—a virtual satellite of Vietnam—a few days later. This action altered Cambodia's position as a buffer between Thailand and Vietnam. Thai and Vietnamese forces now faced each other over a common border, and there were repeated Vietnamese incursions into Thai territory (see State of National Security, ch. 5). Moreover, a flood of refugees from Cambodia placed great strains on Thai resources despite the donation of emergency aid by outside nations (see The Indochinese Refugee Question, ch. 2).

As a frontline state in the Cambodian crisis, Thailand joined the other members of ASEAN, the United States, and China in demanding a Vietnamese withdrawal from Cambodia. In June 1982, the Thai government extended support to the anti-Vietnamese coalition formed by Prince Norodom Sihanouk, the Khmer Rouge's Khieu Samphan, and noncommunist Cambodian leader Son Sann. One unforeseen benefit of the Cambodian crisis was greatly improved relations between Thailand and China, as both countries found themselves in confrontation with Vietnam. By 1983 China had drastically reduced aid and support for the Thai and other Southeast Asian communist insurgencies as part of its new policy of improved relations within the region (see Foreign Affairs, ch. 4).

*　*　*

David K. Wyatt's *Thailand: A Short History* is the best general survey in English and covers the history of the country from the earliest recorded appearance of the Tai peoples to events in the early 1980s. D.G.E. Hall's classic *A History of South-East Asia* presents a well-written general survey within the regional context, ending in the 1950s. On the earlier phases of Thai history, Georges Coedès's *The Making of South East Asia* is most helpful. In *Thailand: Buddhist Kingdom as Modern Nation-State,* Charles F. Keyes presents a general historical survey within the context of the Thai social and cultural setting. John L. S. Girling's *Thailand: Society and Politics* provides an interesting interpretation of recent political, social, and economic developments. Periodicals such as the *Journal of Asian Studies, Pacific Affairs,* and the *Journal of Southeast Asian Studies* publish articles of historical interest, and *Asian Survey* and the *Far Eastern Economic Review Asia Year Book* provide good accounts of contemporary events. (For further information and complete citations, see Bibliography.)

Chapter 2. The Society and Its Environment

Ayutthayan-style bronze Buddha in royal attire, Pencamapabitra (Monastery of the Fifth King), Bangkok

NEITHER A STATIC nor a revolutionary society, Thailand has always been able to harness the talents of its people, make effective use of its natural environment, and progress at an evolutionary pace. The tendency of the Central Thai—for centuries the controlling group in Thai society—to eliminate or suppress ethnic or religious differences was tempered by the Chakkri Dynasty, which had, for the most part, fostered toleration since assuming the monarchy in 1782.

Although Thai society appeared homogeneous, it actually represented a compromise among various groups, which, in order to preserve their own identity, accepted certain aspects of general Thai identity, or Ekkalak Thai. As in the past, in modern Thailand the basic social and communal structure was controlled by a power elite system comprising the monarchy, the military, and upper level bureaucrats. These groups had a symbiotic relationship with the economic and business community that strongly influenced decision making. As a result of modern education and international influences, however, the composition of all parts of the elite system was changing in the late 1980s.

As Thailand became more active in world trade and the international community in general, the traditional practice of measuring status by the extent of landholdings became less meaningful. Although the Buddhist *sangha* (monastic community) and the royal family remained the largest landholders, they were no longer the richest elements in society. Their wealth was often surpassed by that of members of the business community and the bureaucracy (including the military), who derived their growing affluence from diverse sources.

Commerce and other economic endeavors had always had a place in Thai society, but it was only in the late twentieth century that income derived by means other than landholding became socially acceptable. In modern Thailand, entrepreneurs, educated civil servants, and career military officers were all accepted into the elite ranks. This expansion of the ruling elite was reflected in the growing influence of elected members of the National Assembly. More kinds of people had the opportunity to participate in the shaping of Thai society after 1973; however, the gap continued to widen between rich and poor.

As it made the transition from less developed country to industrialized state, Thailand often was cited as one of the success stories of the Third World. Although Thailand benefited from modernization, being a rapidly developing nation was not without problems and costs. One problem related to increased urbanization and a growing market economy was the heightened desire for more consumer products at the expense of locally made goods, services, and recreational activities. The growing incidence of violent crime, divorce, prostitution, and drug addiction also could be attributed in part to increased urbanization. Modernization was also changing the traditional ways by which individual Thai improved their economic and social condition. A university education, for example, used to virtually guarantee financial betterment; by the late 1980s, however, large numbers of liberal arts graduates were either unemployed or underemployed. Modernization also hurt the rural Thai. Previously, their access to housing, forests, and usable water sources had been a given. By the 1980s, however, environmental destruction and a growing scarcity of arable land made it increasingly difficult for the rural Thai to be relatively independent of the government.

Another cost of modernization was loss of security by some, including the elderly and Thailand's Buddhist monks, who previously had had an assured place in Thai society. Care of and respect for the elderly had once been the responsibility of the immediate or extended family, but by the 1980s Thailand was beginning to build public and private senior citizen centers. Before World War II, the local monks and the *sangha* had been the main source of advice and information; in the 1980s, civil servants were often better equipped to attend to the needs of the people in an increasingly urban society.

One of the greatest changes in society following World War II was the emergence of a middle group that included affluent bureaucrats, medium-scale entrepreneurs, educated professionals, and small shopkeepers. The lower class included steadily employed wage workers and unskilled laborers who worked intermittently, if at all. Those in the middle and lower groups had not traditionally constituted self-conscious classes; those categories were relatively new and just beginning to develop common interests. Labor unions, for example, hopelessly divided over political differences in the past, made active attempts to unite on a number of issues, such as basic health and social benefits, in their negotiations with the government and the private sector.

The peasants still comprised the majority of the population. They were, however, much more differentiated than in the past. The peasantry could be defined in terms of its desire for or ownership of land or other agricultural resources, such as teak forests. The

issue of landlessness in the central plain arose in the early twentieth century but was soon resolved by the opening of previously untilled areas in the northern part of the country. As a result of rapid population growth in the 1960s and 1970s, international competition in a number of Thailand's traditional agro-economic industries, and migration to the city, landlessness was again on the rise in the 1980s. The number of rural Thai remained large and continued to increase. As Thailand's economy continued to grow in the service areas of banking and tourism, more young adults were attracted to city jobs, thus reducing the ability of families to continue labor-intensive rice farming. At the same time, land increased in value, and absentee landlords bought up small family farms because there were no legally enforceable limits on the amount of land that could be acquired.

Cutting across rural and national strata was the system of patron-client relationships that tied specific households or individuals together as long as both patron and client saw benefits in the arrangement. In many respects, the dynamics of political and economic life were comprehensible only in terms of patron-client relations.

Another traditional system of complex values and behaviors that the majority of Thai shared through the 1980s was Theravada Buddhism. Complementing the religion were beliefs and practices assuming the existence of several types of spirits (*phi*—see Glossary) whose behavior was supposed to affect human welfare. The Buddhism of the Thai villagers, and even of poorly educated monks, often differed substantially from the canonical religion.

Physical Setting

Thailand's 514,000 square kilometers lie in the middle of mainland Southeast Asia. The nation's axial position influenced many aspects of Thailand's society and culture. The earliest speakers of the Tai (see Glossary) language migrated from what is now China, following rivers into northern Thailand and southward to the Mae Nam (river) Chao Phraya Valley. The fertile floodplain and tropical monsoon climate, ideally suited to wet-rice (*thamna*) cultivation, attracted settlers to this central area rather than to the marginal uplands and mountains of the northern region or the Khorat Plateau to the northeast. By the twelfth century, a number of loosely connected rice-growing and trading states flourished in the upper Chao Phraya Valley. Starting in the middle of the fourteenth century, these central chiefdoms gradually came under the control of the kingdom of Ayutthaya at the southern extremity of the floodplain. Successive capitals, built at various points along the river, became centers of great Thai kingdoms based on rice cultivation and foreign commerce. Unlike the neighboring Khmer and Burmese, the Thai continued to look outward across the Gulf of Thailand and the Andaman Sea toward foreign ports of trade. When European imperialism brought a new phase in Southeast Asian commerce in the late 1800s, Thailand (known then as Siam—see Glossary) was able to maintain its independence as a buffer zone between British-controlled Burma to the west and French-dominated Indochina to the east (see The Bangkok Period, 1767–1932, ch. 1).

Boundaries

Thailand in the late 1980s shared boundaries with Burma, Malaysia, Laos, and Cambodia. Although neither China nor Vietnam bordered Thailand, the territory of both countries came within 100 kilometers of Thai territory (see fig. 2). Many parts of Thailand's boundaries followed natural features, such as the Mekong River. Most borders had been stabilized and demarcated in the late nineteenth and early twentieth centuries in accordance with treaties forced on Thailand and its neighbors by Britain and France. In some areas, however, exact boundaries, especially along Thailand's eastern borders with Laos and Cambodia, were still in dispute in the late 1980s.

Disputes with Cambodia after 1950 arose in part from ill-defined boundaries; the most notable case was a dispute over the Preah Vihear Temple area submitted to the International Court of Justice, which ruled in favor of Cambodia in 1962. During the years that the Cambodian capital, Phnom Penh, was controlled by the Khmer Rouge regime of Pol Pot (1975–79), the border disputes continued. In the early 1980s, the People's Republic of Kampuchea and its mentor, Vietnam, made an issue of boundaries in Prachin Buri Province in eastern Thailand. In contrast to these incidents, which attracted international attention, boundary disputes with Malaysia and Burma were usually handled more cooperatively. Continuing mineral exploration and fishing in the Gulf of Thailand, however, were sources of potential conflict with both neighbors. Adding to general border tensions were the activities of communist-led insurgents, whose operations had been of paramount concern to the Thai government and its security forces for several decades. The problem of communist insurgency was compounded by the activity of what the Thai government labeled "antistate elements." Often the real source of border problems was ordinary criminals or local merchants involved in illegal mining, logging, smuggling, and narcotics production and trade (see State of National Security, ch. 5).

Topography and Drainage

The most conspicuous features of Thailand's terrain are high mountains, a central plain, and an upland plateau (see fig. 7). Mountains cover much of northern Thailand and extend along the Burmese border down through the Malay Peninsula. The central plain is a lowland area drained by the Chao Phraya and its tributaries, the country's principal river system, which feeds into the delta at the head of the Bight of Bangkok. The Chao Phraya system drains about one-third of the nation's territory. In the northeastern part of the country the Khorat Plateau, a region of gently rolling low hills and shallow lakes, drains into the Mekong River through the Mae Nam Mun. The Mekong system empties into the South China Sea and includes a series of canals and dams.

Together, the Chao Phraya and Mekong systems sustain Thailand's agricultural economy by supporting wet-rice cultivation and providing waterways for the transport of goods and people. In contrast, the distinguishing natural features of peninsular Thailand are long coastlines, offshore islands, and diminishing mangrove swamps.

Regions

Landforms and drainage divide the country more or less into four natural regions—the North, the Northeast, the Center, and the South. Although Bangkok geographically is part of the central plain, as the capital and largest city this metropolitan area may be considered in other respects a separate region. Each of the four geographical regions differs from the others in population, basic resources, natural features, and level of social and economic development. The diversity of the regions is in fact the most pronounced attribute of Thailand's physical setting.

During the winter months, in the mountainous North the temperature is cool enough for the cultivation of fruits such as lychees and strawberries. These high mountains are incised by steep river valleys and upland areas that border the central plain. A series of rivers, including the Nan, Ping, Wang, and Yom, unite in the lowlands to form the Chao Phraya watershed. Traditionally, these natural features made possible several different types of agriculture, including wet-rice farming in the valleys and shifting cultivation (see Glossary) in the uplands. The forested mountains also promoted a spirit of regional independence. Forests, including stands of teak and other economically useful hardwoods that once dominated the North and parts of the Northeast, had diminished by the 1980s to 13 million hectares. In 1961 they covered 56 percent of the country, but by the mid-1980s forestland had been reduced to less than 30 percent of Thailand's total area.

The Northeast, with its poor soils, is not favored agriculturally. The region consists mainly of the dry Khorat Plateau and a few low hills. The short monsoon season brings heavy flooding in the river valleys. Unlike the more fertile areas of Thailand, the Northeast has a long dry season, and much of the land is covered by sparse grasses. Mountains ring the plateau on the west and the south, and the Mekong delineates much of the eastern rim.

The "heartland" of the Central Thai, the Center is a natural self-contained basin often termed "the rice bowl of Asia." The complex irrigation system developed for wet-rice agriculture in this region provided the necessary economic support to sustain the development of the Thai state from the thirteenth-century kingdom of Sukhothai to contemporary Bangkok. Here the rather flat unchanging landscape facilitated inland water and road transport. The fertile area was able to sustain a dense population, 422 persons per square kilometer in 1987, compared with an average of 98 for the country as a whole. The terrain of the region is dominated by the Chao Phraya and its tributaries and by the cultivated paddy fields.

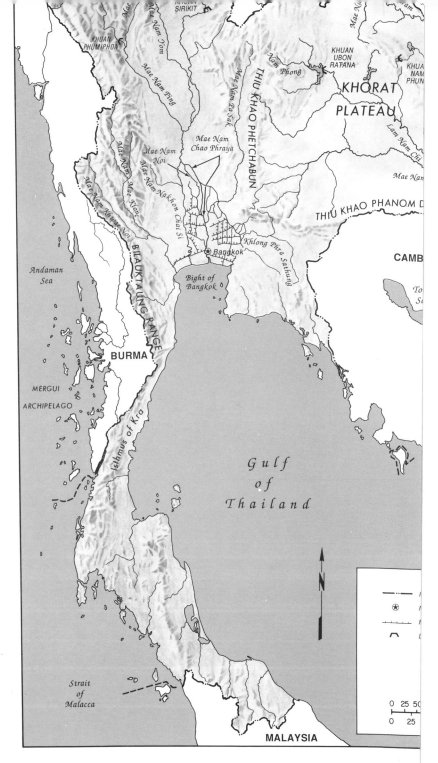

Figure 7. Topography and Drainage

Metropolitan Bangkok, the focal point of trade, transport, and industrial activity, is situated on the southern edge of the region at the head of the Gulf of Thailand and includes part of the delta of the Chao Phraya system.

The South, a narrow peninsula, is distinctive in climate, terrain, and resources. Its economy is based on rice cultivation for subsistence and rubber production for industry. Other sources of income include coconut plantations, tin mining, and tourism, which is particularly lucrative on Phuket Island. Rolling and mountainous terrain and the absence of large rivers are conspicuous features of the South. North-south mountain barriers and impenetrable tropical forest caused the early isolation and separate political development of this region. International access through the Andaman Sea and the Gulf of Thailand made the South a crossroads for both Theravada Buddhism, centered at Nakhon Si Thammarat, and Islam, especially in the former sultanate of Pattani on the border with Malaysia.

Thailand's regions are further divided into a total of seventy-three provinces (see fig. 8). The country's provinces have the same names as their respective capitals.

Climate

Thailand has a tropical monsoon climate; temperatures normally range from an average annual high of 38°C to a low of 19°C. Southwest monsoons that arrive between May and July (except in the South) signal the advent of the rainy season (*ridu fon*), which lasts into October. November and December mark the onset of the dry season. Temperatures begin to climb in January, and a hot sun parches the landscape. The dry season is shortest in the South because of the proximity of the sea to all parts of the Malay Peninsula. With only minor exceptions, every area of the country receives adequate rainfall, but the duration of the rainy season and the amount of rain vary substantially from region to region and with altitude. The Northeast experiences a long dry season, and its red, porous (laterite) soils retain water poorly, which limits their agricultural potential.

Population

Since 1911 Thailand has taken frequent national censuses, and its National Statistical Office, working closely with a number of international agencies, was in the 1980s one of the most extensive sources of statistical information in Asia. One of the 20 most populous nations in the world, Thailand had in 1987 about 53 million people. This total was divided about equally between males

esentation not
horitative   106

VIETNAM

18

17   18

25   27

A S T
        28
26

29

36   37

14

CAMBODIA

Mekong River

Phnom Penh ⊛

10

VIETNAM

⋯⋯ International boundary
⋯⋯ Regional boundary
⎯⎯ Provincial boundary
⊛   National capital

50 100 150 Kilometers
    50   100   150 Miles

and females. The regional breakdown was approximately 16.7 million in the Center (which included the Bangkok metropolitan area), 17.8 million in the Northeast, 11.3 million in the North, and 6.8 million in the South. As in most Southeast Asian nations, the population was youthful and agrarian; approximately 37 percent of the population was between the ages of 15 and 29. In the decades after World War II, however, the percentage of agricultural population declined; it decreased from 79.3 percent to 72.3 percent of the population between 1970 and 1980, for example.

The shrinking of the rural population resulted in part from internal migration to the capital and provincial centers. In 1987 about 10 percent of the population lived in Bangkok, which had 3,292 persons per square kilometer. The 9 largest cities after Bangkok ranged in population from 80,000 to 110,000. They were Khon Kaen, Hat Yai, Chiang Mai, Ubon Ratchathani, Nakhon Sawan, Nakhon Ratchasima, Krabi, Udon Thani, and Songkhla (see fig. 9).

Bangkok, with 1,537 square kilometers, represented the combining of the royal capital of the Chakkri Dynasty with Thon Buri, the capital of King Taksin (see The Bangkok Period, 1767–1932, ch. 1). In the late 1980s, this urban area was made up of 24 districts (*khet*), with a combined population of 5.5 million. In spite of massive construction and changes in the economy, many of the districts retained their unique identities. For example, Dusit District, where the royal family had its principal residence, was also home to many of the city's military officers and civil servants.

Rapid urbanization in the 1980s was changing not only where the Thai lived but also how they lived. Separate private houses were located in high-density areas or out in new sprawling suburbs. The Thai were also moving into townhouses and condominiums; by 1984 sixty-nine residential condominium communities had been built or were in the final phase of construction. A family compound along a tree-shaded *khlong* (canal) was a rare sight. Although ferries continued to ply the Chao Phraya, the boat was no longer the main mode of transportation. Bangkok had about 900,000 registered motor vehicles and a new superhighway system partially completed in the late 1980s; massive traffic jams, noise, and air pollution had become part of everyday life. Most of the canals in the "Venice of the East" had been replaced with roads; this replacement was in part causing the city to sink. Annual flooding in the city and growing slums such as Khlong Toei often made city services rather than politics the key issue in metropolitan elections. Bangkok had 10 percent of the national population, but the capital required a

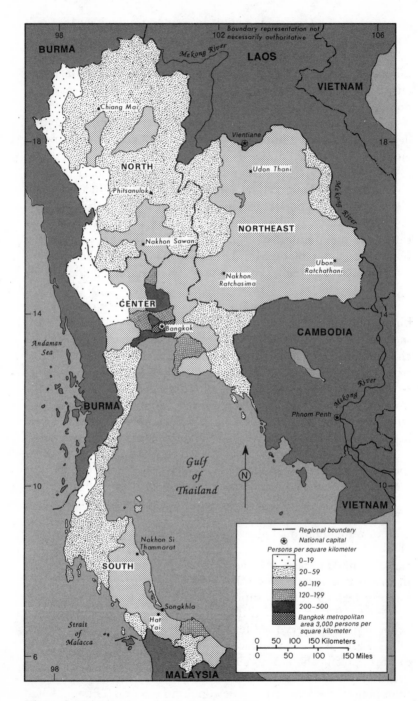

Figure 9. Distribution of Population, 1980

disproportionate percentage of the national budget to maintain basic city services.

Thailand's rush both to develop and to satisfy the demand for consumer products had several side effects, including dwindling agricultural land, the destruction of forests, and damage to watersheds. These consequences prompted the central government, with support from international agencies, to make a concerted effort to limit population growth. In 1968 the cabinet sanctioned a family-planning service, and by March 1970 a national population policy was announced. The official slogan "Many Children Make You Poor" and the economic arguments for keeping the number of children at two per family found acceptance among both city and rural populations. Successful programs were undertaken by the Planned Parenthood Association of Thailand and the Family Planning Services. By 1974 an estimated 25 percent of all married couples of childbearing age were using modern contraceptives, one of the highest percentages for developing countries. The population growth rate, 3.4 percent per annum in the 1960s, had been reduced to 1.9 percent per annum by 1986. The goal for the late 1980s was a growth rate of 1.5 percent (see table 3, Appendix).

Ethnicity, Regionalism, and Language

Although the population was relatively homogeneous in the 1980s—an estimated 85 percent or more spoke a language of the Tai family and shared other cultural features, such as adherence to Theravada Buddhism—regionalism and ethnic differences were socially and politically significant. Moreover, these differences affected the access of specific groups and regions to economic and other resources, which in turn heightened ethnic or regional consciousness.

Perhaps the principal fact of regional and ethnic relations was the social, linguistic, and political dominance of the Central Thai, who were descendants of the subjects of the premodern kingdoms of the Chao Phraya floodplain. The Central Thai were defined as those who considered central Thailand their birthplace or the Central Thai (Standard Thai) dialect their first language. With the advent of increased migration, modern communication, and education, however, it was becoming increasingly difficult to use language to determine place of origin.

The Central Thai constituted but one of the regionally defined categories that made up the majority of Thai—the core Thai. The number of persons belonging to groups other than the core Thai was difficult to specify precisely, whether membership in those groups was defined by language, by other features of culture, or by an individual's self-identification. Part of the problem was the Thai government's policy of promoting assimilation but not encouraging the active collection of data on Thai ethnicity. Government statistics on aliens, tribal minorities, and refugees were more readily available, although sometimes disputed by both scholars and the groups in question.

Despite the inadequacy of the data, it was possible to make some rough estimates of the ethnic composition of the minority sector of the Thai population in 1987. Among the largest minority groups, Chinese constituted about 11 percent of the population, Malay about 3 percent, and long-term resident (as opposed to refugee) Khmer less than 1 percent. The remaining minority groups ranged in number from a few hundred to more than 100,000. Of these, the largest group was the Karen, estimated at about 250,000 in the 1980s. Some of the minority groups spoke languages of the Tai family but differed in several ways from the core Thai.

The Thai and Other Tai-Speaking Peoples

The core Thai—the Central Thai, the Northeastern Thai (Thai-Lao), the Northern Thai, and the Southern Thai—spoke dialects of one of the languages of the Tai language family. The peoples who spoke those languages—generically also referred to as Tai—originated in southern China, but they were dispersed throughout mainland Southeast Asia from Burma to Vietnam (see Early History, ch. 1). It was conventional in the 1980s to refer to Tai-speaking peoples in Thailand as Thai (same pronunciation) with a regional or other qualifier, e.g., Central Thai. There were, however, groups in Thailand in the late twentieth century who spoke a language of the Tai family but who were not part of the core population.

Although the four major Tai-speaking groups taken together clearly constituted the overwhelming majority of Thailand's population, it was not entirely clear what proportion of the core Thai fell into each of the regional categories. Among the reasons for the uncertainty were the movements of many who were not Central Thai in origin into the Bangkok area and its environs and the movement of Central Thai, perhaps in smaller numbers, into other regions as administrators, educators, technicians, bureaucrats, soldiers, and sometimes as settlers. The Central Thai, of generally higher status than the general populace, tended to retain their identities wherever they lived, whereas those from other regions migrating to the central plain might seek to take on Central Thai speech, customs, and identity.

Although politically, socially, and culturally dominant, the Central Thai did not constitute a majority of the population and barely exceeded the Thai-Lao in numbers, according to a mid-1960s estimate. At that time, the Central Thai made up roughly 32 percent of the population, with the Thai-Lao a close second at about 30 percent. The Thai-Lao were essentially the same ethnic group that constituted the dominant population of Laos, although they far outnumbered the population of that country (see Ethnic and Regional Relations, this ch.).

A number of linguistic scholars mark the reign of King Narai (1657–88) as the point when the Central Thai (or Ayutthaya Thai) dialect was established as the standard to which other forms or dialects were compared. Central Thai was the required form used in modern Thailand for official, business, academic, and other daily transactions. From Ayutthayan times, Central Thai borrowed words from Khmer, Pali, and Sanskrit. Thailand still maintained a court language called Phasa Ratchasap, although King Bhumibol Adulyadej (Rama IX, 1946–) encouraged the use of Central Thai. Similarly, Pali, the religious language, although still used, gradually was being replaced by Central Thai for many ceremonies and writings. Although the Thai Royal Academy was the final arbiter of new words added to the language, post-World War II Thai has been influenced heavily by American English, especially in the area of science and technology.

Increasingly, Central Thai was spoken with varied fluency all over the country as the education system reached larger numbers of children (see Education and the Arts, this ch.). Nevertheless, regional dialects (or their local variants) remained the language of the home and of the local community. Learning Central Thai is not a simple matter. The dialects of the four regional components of the core population are only mutually intelligible with difficulty. There are lexical and syntactic differences as well as differences in pronunciation.

Differences in dialect were sometimes an irritant in relations between those whose native tongue was Central Thai and persons from other regions. On the one hand, if persons migrating from other regions to Bangkok spoke their own dialect, they might be treated with contempt by the Central Thai. If, on the other hand, such persons failed to speak Central Thai with sufficient fluency and a proper accent, that, too, could lead to their being treated disrespectfully.

Generally, before the trend toward homogenization of dress, language, and forms of entertainment fostered by modern communication, there were regional differences in costume, folklore, and other aspects of culture among the Thai people. The continuing retention of these differences into the 1980s seemed to be a function of relative remoteness from Bangkok and other urban areas. Of some importance, according to observers, was the tendency to cling to, and even accentuate, these regional differences as symbols of a sense of grievance.

In the past, some Thai governments put great pressure on the various Thai peoples to forsake regional customs and dialects for "modern" Central Thai culture. In the 1980s, however, there was a rebirth of the study and teaching of local languages, especially Lanna Thai in the North and also the Southern Thai dialect. Efforts were also made to expose all Thai to the different cultures and traditions of the various regions through regional translation and art programs. At the same time, Central Thai became more readily accepted as a second language. The success of the national identity programs could be explained in part by the Thai literacy rate, one of the highest in Asia.

The Tai-speaking peoples of the Northeast, known as Thai-Lao or Isan, live on the Khorat Plateau. Once the weakest in Thailand, the Northeast's economy started to improve somewhat in the 1970s because of irrigation and energy projects, such as the construction of the Khuan Ubon Ratana (Nam Phong Dam). Moreover, because the Northeast was the location of several United States military bases during the Second Indochina War (1954–75), the region had one of the best transportation systems in Asia, which facilitated internal migration as well as communication with Bangkok. Historically, this area relied heavily on border trade with Laos and Cambodia; in 1987 the Thai government permitted increased Laotian border commerce and lifted a ban on the export of all but 61 of 273 "strategic" items previously barred from leaving Thailand. Also, traditional handicrafts, e.g., silk weavings and mats, increasingly were being sold outside the region to produce extra income. Still, approximately 82 percent of the region's labor force was involved in agriculture.

In terms of language and culture, both the Northeastern Thai and the Northern Thai were closer to the peoples of Laos than to the Central Thai. Speakers of the Tai language of Kham Mu'ang (known as Yuan in its written form) made up the majority of the population of the 9 northernmost provinces from the Burmese-Lao border down through the province of Uttaradit, an area of about 102,000 square kilometers. Highly independent, the Northern Thai lived mainly in small river valleys where they grew glutinous rice as their staple food. The Chakkri Dynasty continued to maintain a court in Chiang Mai, the largest city of the North, which the Thai people looked to as a major religious and cultural center.

Lisu tribespeople in northern Thailand
Courtesy United Nations

The fourteen provinces of the South made up the poorest region of Thailand. Primarily rural, the South had an urban population of only 12.2 percent of its total inhabitants. Although rice was the staple food, the South's economy was not based on wet-rice agriculture. Never directly colonized, the southern provinces, with their dependence on rubber and tin production and fishing, had nonetheless long been vulnerable to international economic forces. As world market prices for rubber and tin declined in the 1970s, more southerners went to work in the Middle East; and as neighboring countries established 200-mile limits on their territorial waters, an increasing number of Thai fishing vessels could be found as far away as the coast of Australia.

In 1985 there were more than 6 million Southern Thai. Malay vocabulary was used in the Southern Thai dialect, and Malay in Jawi (Arabic) script remained in many instances the medium of written communication. Like the other regions of Thailand, the South at times opposed the central government. Following the closer incorporation of the Pattani region into the Thai kingdom as the result of the provincial administrative reform of 1902, reactions in the form of rebellions, underground movements, and violent uprisings were common. For many years, any type of antistate behavior or banditry reported by the government or press was usually attributed either to Muslim insurgents or the Communist Party of Thailand. By the mid-1980s, the press and government had become more objective in reporting and recognizing problems caused by environmental factors, other groups, and government policies. Moreover, the Muslim leadership, together with progressive political and military forces in the Thai government, had begun addressing some of the problems of the South, which led to increased national tranquillity.

Of the more than 85 percent of the country's population that spoke a language of the Tai family, only a small fraction constituted the membership of the half-dozen or so ethnic groups outside the core Thai. These groups lived in the North or Northeast and were often closely related to ethnic groups in neighboring countries. In Thailand, the largest of these Tai-speaking minorities were the Phutai (or Phuthai) of the far Northeast, who numbered about 100,000 in the mid-1960s. There were also many Phutai in neighboring Laos. The Phuan and the Saek, also in the Northeast and with kin in Laos, were similar but much smaller groups. Whereas all other Tai languages spoken in Thailand belonged to the southwestern branch of the family, that spoken by the Saek belonged to the northern branch, suggesting a more recent arrival from China. The Khorat Thai were not considered Central Thai, despite their close resemblance in language and dress, because they and others tended to identify them as a separate group. The Khorat Thai were said to be descendants of Thai soldiers and Khmer women. The Shan (a Burmese term) in the North were part of a much larger group, the majority of whom lived in Burma, while others lived in China. Different groups of the Shan called themselves by names in which the term *Tai* was modified by a word meaning ''great'' or something similar. The Thai called them Thai Ngio or Thai Yai. Also in the North were a people called the Lue, estimated in the mid-1960s to number less than 50,000. Like the Shan, they resided in greater numbers elsewhere, particularly in southern China.

The Non-Tai Minorities

Besides the Tai-speaking minorities, there were a number of peoples speaking languages of other families (although increasing numbers were acquainted with a Thai dialect, especially Central Thai, if they acquired the language in school). Some—such as the Khmer in the eastern portion of the country, the Karen in the northern and western parts of Thailand, and the Malay in the South—found themselves within the boundaries of Thailand as a consequence of conflict and shifting borders. Others, such as many of the hill peoples, were relatively recent migrants from China and the

Indochinese Peninsula. They found their way to the peripheries of Thailand either in search of land or to escape political turmoil. Groups entering Thailand that had been minorities in their countries of origin, as hill peoples typically were, became more or less permanent residents of Thailand, although still largely unassimilated. Others, particularly the Mon, who lived in the central region, became substantially integrated. The groups of Vietnamese who had arrived for various reasons from the nineteenth through the mid-twentieth centuries varied in the extent to which they were rooted in Thailand. Some groups of Khmer, refugees from political turmoil in their own country since 1975, were also recent arrivals in Thailand. Finally, there were the Chinese. Of the estimated 6 million in Thailand in 1987, most could be differentiated by the region of China from which they came, when they had arrived, and the extent to which they had been assimilated into Thai society.

The Highland, or Hill, Peoples

Commonly included among the highland people were the ethnic groups living in the mountains of northern and northwestern Thailand in the area known, because of its illegal opium production, as the "Golden Triangle." Until the 1970s, the Thai central government tended to regard these groups chiefly as opium cultivators engaged in illegal activities. Since that time the highland minorities, through their own efforts and government-organized crop substitution projects, have become involved in the legal market economy of the country.

Among the larger groups of highland people were the Karen (Kariang, Yang), Hmong (Meo, Miao), Mien (Yao), Lahu (Mussur), Akha (Kaw), and Lisu, or Lisaw (see fig. 10). Some of the smaller groups preceded the Tai-speaking peoples in the area, but many were relative latecomers. Through natural increase and immigration, the population of the highlands increased from approximately 100,000 in 1948 to about 700,000 in the late 1980s, according to Ministry of Interior estimates. This population growth led to a significant increase in the number of landless people in the highlands. As a result, many of the landless began cultivating forest reserves, thereby accelerating the depletion of the country's forestland.

The varying estimates for specific groups in some cases reflected the tendency of estimators to include only those still living in relatively isolated mountain communities, whereas other observers might include some or all of those who had come down from the mountains and were at various points in the process of becoming Thai. Observers noted that for some groups, more individuals were

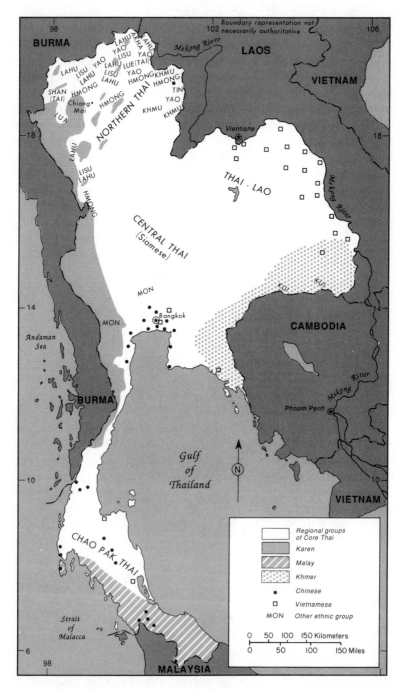

Figure 10. Distribution of Selected Ethnolinguistic and Regional Groups

in the process of assimilation than remained in the mountain communities that were their traditional homes. The languages spoken by the hill peoples fell into three broad categories: Tibeto-Burman (a subfamily of the larger Sino-Tibetan language family), Mon-Khmer (a subfamily of the Austro-Asiatic language family), and the small Miao-Yao language family. The language of the most numerous of these hill peoples, the Karen, was generally considered Sino-Tibetan, but some authorities included it in the subset Tibeto-Burman, or placed it in a category of its own. The other languages included in the Tibeto-Burman category—Akha, Lisu, Lahu, and Jinghpaw (Kachin)—have been estimated as ranging from a few hundred speakers (Jinghpaw) to about 25,000 speakers (Akha).

The category of Mon-Khmer included a number of highland groups: the Kui (called Soai by the Thai), which totaled between 100,000 and 150,000 in the mid-1960s; the Tin, about 20,000; and several smaller groups, including the Lua (also called Lawa), about 9,000; the Khmu, about 7,600; and the Chaobon, about 2,000. The Kui were said to be largely assimilated into Thai society. The figure for the Khmu pertained only to those presumably living in the highlands in a more or less traditional setting. Substantial numbers were said to be pursuing a Thai way of life.

The Miao-Yao languages were spoken by two peoples, the Hmong and Mien, both originally from China (the terms *Miao* and *Yao* are Chinese). There were Hmong and Mien still living in China as well as other Southeast Asian countries. Called Meo by the Thai, the Hmong began to arrive in Thailand in the late nineteenth century, and some continued to migrate directly from China or other neighboring states, particularly Laos. Numbering about 50,000 in 1970, the Hmong were one of the largest groups of hill peoples. An additional 40,000 Hmong fled from Laos to Thailand in 1975, but by the late 1980s many of these had migrated elsewhere, some going to the United States. The Mien were even more recent arrivals, most of them having come from Laos after 1945. Their numbers were estimated at 30,000 in the 1980s. These two groups, particularly the Hmong, were among those affected by the security operations of the Thai government that began in the mid-1960s. These actions occurred in part because the Hmong, like other mountain groups, were said to be destroying forests in the course of practicing their traditional shifting cultivation, and in part because their chief cash crop was the opium poppy (see State of National Security, ch. 5).

The Khmer

Two groups of Khmer could also be distinguished—long-time inhabitants of Thailand and more recent arrivals. By the mid-fifteenth century, much of the western region of the Khmer Empire had come under the control of Ayutthaya. Many of the Khmer peoples remained in the area that had come under Thai domination. Five centuries later the protracted civil conflict in Cambodia, which began with the overthrow of the Lon Nol regime in 1975 and included the Vietnam-supported overthrow of the Pol Pot regime in 1979, led to the arrival at the Thai-Cambodian border of additional hundreds of thousands of Khmer. Some Khmer had crossed over into Thailand; many others might be expected to do so if several political obstacles were overcome (see The Indochinese Refugee Question, this ch.; Potential External Threats, ch. 5).

Theravada Buddhists and wet-rice cultivators, the Khmer spoke a language of the Mon-Khmer group and were heirs to a long and complex political and cultural tradition. If long-term resident Khmer and Khmer refugees were both included, there were perhaps as many as 600,000 to 800,000 Khmer living in Thailand in the 1980s. Many of the long-resident Khmer were said to speak Thai, sometimes as a first language, and religious and other similarities contributed over time to Thai-Khmer intermarriage and to Khmer assimilation into Thai society. Newly arrived Khmer, however, were not yet assimilated.

The Mon

Perhaps the first Theravada Buddhists in Southeast Asia, and the founders in the seventh century of the kingdom of Haripunjaya near present-day Chiang Mai, the Mon greatly influenced the development of Thai culture. Mon architecture dotted the North, where a number of temples were still inhabited by Mon monks in the 1980s. The Mon, also known as Raman or Tailaing, migrated from Burma during the sixteenth to eighteenth centuries. They were welcomed by the Chakkri rulers, and their religious discipline helped inspire the reforms made by King Mongkut (Rama IV, reigned 1851–68). The Mon who settled chiefly in the North and the central plain, e.g., at Nonthaburi, Ayutthaya, Lop Buri, Uthai Thani, and Ratchaburi, generally were wet-rice farmers who also had specialized skills such as pottery-making. They maintained a social organization similar to that of the Thai and other lowland cultures. Their villages were governed by Mon headmen, who in turn were responsible to district and provincial officers of Mon ancestry. Although their language was related to Khmer, the Mon incorporated a large number of Thai words into their vocabulary. Moreover, language differences became less important as Mon children, educated in Thai schools, learned Central Thai. In the 1980s, some Mon still used their own language in certain contexts, but few did not know Thai. In general, the Mon were more integrated into Thai society than any other non-Thai group.

The Vietnamese

In the mid-1970s, the number of Vietnamese in Thailand was estimated at between 60,000 and 70,000, most of them in the Northeast. Three broad categories of Vietnamese were in the country. The first were the descendants of persons who fled from political upheaval and persecution during the precolonial era in the late eighteenth century and through much of the nineteenth century. Most of them settled either in Bangkok or in the area southeast of it, and many of their descendants were absorbed into Thai society, although some still lived in villages that were identifiably Vietnamese. Many who came in the nineteenth century were refugees from anti-Catholic persecution by rulers in Cochinchina (southern Vietnam, around the Mekong Delta) before the French established political control over that area. The second category consisted of persons who opposed the establishment of French domination over all Vietnam in 1884 and presumably expected their stay in Thailand to be short. With some exceptions, however, their descendants and those of other Vietnamese who came to Thailand in the first decades of the twentieth century remained. The earliest arrivals in this category, like their predecessors, mostly came to southeast Thailand. Later immigrants tended to go to the Northeast. The third category included those who fled from Vietnam between the end of World War II in 1945 and the consolidation of North Vietnamese rule over all of Vietnam in 1975. For those who came after the Second Indochina War had ended, Thailand was simply a way station en route to somewhere else, usually the United States.

Most of the 40,000 to 50,000 Vietnamese who came in 1946 and shortly thereafter were driven from Laos by the French, who were then reimposing their rule over all of Indochina. More Vietnamese came later, and, like those who came in the 1920s and 1930s, they expected to return to Vietnam. Between 1958 and 1964 (when the intensification of the war in Vietnam inhibited their return), arrangements were made for the repatriation of Vietnamese to the Democratic Republic of Vietnam (North Vietnam), and an estimated 40,000 left Thailand. Over the years a few families went to the Republic of Vietnam (South Vietnam). The movements of this period, both voluntary and involuntary, left between 60,000 and 70,000 Vietnamese in Thailand, an undetermined portion of which were post-World War II migrants who could not or would not return to their homeland.

The Chinese

The largest number of non-Tai peoples were the Chinese. In 1987 an estimated 11 percent of the total Thai population, or about 6 million people, were of Chinese origin, which meant that Thailand had the largest Chinese population in Southeast Asia. Assimilation of the various Chinese communities was a continuing process. Chinese were encouraged to become Thai citizens, and in 1970 it was estimated that more than 90 percent of the Chinese born in Thailand had done so. When diplomatic relations were established with China in the 1970s, resident Chinese not born in Thailand had the option of becoming Thai citizens; the remaining permanent Chinese alien population was estimated at fewer than 200,000.

Given their historic role as middlemen, Chinese were found everywhere in Thailand, particularly in the towns. There was, however, a major concentration in the Bangkok metropolitan area and another in the central part of peninsular Thailand, where many Chinese were engaged in several capacities in the tin mines and on the rubber plantations. Although many Chinese played an important part in the ownership and management of economic enterprises and in the professions, a substantial portion had less lucrative and significant occupations (see National and Urban Structures: Class and Status, this ch.).

Except for a minority, the Chinese not only were Thai nationals but also had, in some respects at least, assimilated into Thai society; many spoke Thai as well as they spoke Chinese. Most of the descendants of pretwentieth-century immigrants and those people of mixed Chinese-Thai ancestry (the so-called Sino-Thai—see Glossary) were so fully integrated into Thai society that they were not included in the Chinese population estimates.

The accommodation between Thai and Chinese historically depended in part on the changing economic and political interests and perspectives of the Thai monarchs and others in the ruling group. Also relevant were the roles assigned to the Chinese at various times, e.g., in the nineteenth century, that of tax farmers. Under the tax farming system, private individuals were sold the right to collect taxes at a price below the actual value of the taxes. The barriers between Thai and Chinese became more rigid in the early twentieth century with the emergence of Thai and Chinese nationalism and also the increased tendency of Chinese females to accompany male immigrants, which reduced the amount of inter-marriage. Consequently, despite a level of Chinese integration in the host society surpassing that found elsewhere in Southeast Asia, the Chinese remained a separate ethnic community, although the boundaries became less defined in the more mobile post-World War II society. The Chinese spoke a number of southern Chinese dialects, the most important being Teochiu, which was used by most Chinese as a commercial lingua franca.

The South Asians

In 1979 the Ministry of Interior estimated that there were 60,000 Hindus and Sikhs in Thailand (0.13 percent of the total population). Small South Asian trading communities in southern Thailand were noted in a ninth-century Tamil inscription. In addition to being trade centers, these early Indian communities served as a conduit for Indian culture and political theory, especially during the Ayutthayan period. The modern South Asian community, however, was largely apolitical and attempted to blend into Thai society, its members working as tailors, night watchmen, and textile merchants.

Ethnic and Regional Relations

In the past, the government took the position that all Tai people should be accorded all the rights, privileges, and opportunities that went with being a citizen. In the 1980s, members of non-Tai minority groups were being afforded similar rights, and efforts were being made to incorporate them into the Ekkalak Thai. The higher a person's aspirations, however, the more thoroughly he or she needed to assimilate into Central Thai culture. Thus, most of the representatives of the government were either from Central Thailand or had absorbed the perspective of that region.

By law the Central Thai dialect was taught in all government schools, and all who aspired to government positions, from village headman on up, were expected to master Central Thai. Nonetheless, because local dialects remained the medium of communication in schools, markets, and provincial government offices, differences between the Central Thai and other dialects survived. The Central Thai tended to see other Thai as both different and inferior. In turn, the latter saw the Central Thai as exploiters. Inevitably, many non-Central Thai sometimes felt inferior to the Central Thai, who represented progress, prestige, wealth, and national power.

In the past, the government had often ignored the needs of the outlying regions. Neglect, corrupt administration, and heavy taxation perhaps affected the Thai-Lao more than others. Until King Mongkut established central control through administrators in the nineteenth century, the Thai-Lao region was governed by local Lao princes who were really vassals of the Thai monarch. Corvée (forced) labor and oppressive taxation supported a rapidly expanding Thai court, bureaucracy, and military. Peasant revolts erupted and were suppressed. Real social and economic changes did not began until the reign of King Bhumibol, who in the early 1960s was assisted in these efforts by Prime Minister Sarit Thanarat, a northeasterner. In the 1960s, programs of community and agricultural development were coupled with counterinsurgency measures; these efforts continued into the 1980s with mixed results (see Insurgency, ch. 5).

The problems had accumulated over time, and solutions were difficult. Whether the tensions and the potential for conflict between the central government and the Thai-Lao could be understood solely or even largely in ethnic terms was questionable. Besides ethnicity and regionalism, a number of other factors required consideration, including the inadequacy of most economic reform measures and the insensitivity or repressiveness of administrators. The Central Thai lack of understanding of social forms and practices different from their own contributed to the mishandling of local situations and the imposition of so-called reforms without full consideration of the effects of these changes on the local people. The Thai-Lao had a close cultural and linguistic relationship with the people of Laos that was further strengthened by trade and kinship. Laos was viewed by many northeasterners as their home country.

In the South the language, religion, and culture of the Malay or Thai Muslims were markedly different from those of other Thai. Although Islamic religious and cultural practices accentuated the differences, more divisive and destabilizing were economic and political factors. In the past, Central Thai administrators from the national government assigned to the South often spent their time amassing personal fortunes rather than attending to the welfare of the people of the region. Government provision of health, education, and welfare services was inadequate or nonexistent; schools were established only in the cities, for the benefit of children of Central Thai officials. In the 1980s, King Bhumibol and government leaders, especially those from the South, were deeply involved in rectifying those inequalities, but resentment and suspicion hampered development.

Substantial numbers of Malay were loyalists who saw no point in making impossible demands. They were prepared to work within the system toward amelioration of their economic, educational, and

Laboratory technician at Rubber Research Center
in southern Thailand
Courtesy United Nations

administrative situation. Those Malay were not prepared to become Thai culturally, but they saw government programs, including secular education in Thai-language schools, as a means to social mobility and to an expansion of their administrative and economic roles.

Because of severe restrictions on Chinese immigration that were put into effect in the early 1950s, the great majority of Thailand's Chinese in the late 1980s had been born in Thailand. Not only did most Chinese speak Thai, many also acquired Thai names (in addition to their Chinese ones) and were Mahayana Buddhists (one of the major schools of Buddhism, active in China, Japan, Korea, and Nepal). Although many Thai resented the significant role the Chinese played in commerce and envied their wealth, the Thai also admired Chinese industriousness and business acumen, a pattern common elsewhere in Southeast Asia.

The Social System

The rural areas, where most Thai live, have been affected by change for many decades, especially since the mid-nineteenth century, when the impact of European economic and political activity was first felt. The full effects of change started to become manifest in the 1930s. Among the factors reflecting and creating change in local social patterns was the coup of 1932, which brought military and bureaucratic elites into power and extended the power of the central government more effectively than before into rural areas. More important in its cumulative effect, however, was the rapid growth of the population and the consequent shortage of land, which led to the development of occupations outside agriculture and the emergence of a rural and small-town bourgeoisie.

At the national level, society was stratified at the beginning of the twentieth century into three classes—kin of the reigning king and his immediate predecessors, government officials (often nobles granted their particular status by the king), and, by far the largest group, the peasantry. These classes comprised a social system in which those who had political power and status also had prestige and access to wealth. Buddhist monks had a special status outside this system. Also outside the system were the Chinese, who were largely laborers and small traders in the early twentieth century.

As the twentieth century progressed, the government bureaucracy proliferated. A growing number in the higher ranks had their origins outside the hereditary nobility, as did the upper ranks of the expanding armed forces. By the 1960s, the military and the bureaucracy included persons from several levels of the social and economic hierarchy. Directly or indirectly, the military and bureaucratic elites disposed of power and economic resources, the latter often in combination with those Chinese who controlled the major business enterprises of Thailand. Hereditary nobles retained high status, but they no longer wielded power and did not match some of the members of the military oligarchy in wealth. Monkhood remained a source of special status and was an avenue of social mobility for persons of rural origin with talent and a willingness to give part or all of their lives to the *sangha,* but monkhood was less and less attractive to urbanites or to those who had access to other avenues to power, wealth, and status. After World War II, an incipient urban middle class and an urban proletariat also emerged, particularly in Bangkok, partly in response to a commercial and tourist boom generated by the presence of large numbers of foreigners, particularly Americans.

Still outside the social system, in the sense that their direct access to political power was restricted and that their sense of a worthwhile career differed from that of most Thai, were the Chinese. Members of other non-Thai ethnic groups could occasionally make a place for themselves in the middle or upper reaches of Thai society by assimilating Thai culture. The Chinese were less able to do so until the 1960s and 1970s, when they began to move into the upper bureaucracy in larger numbers.

More significant in the daily life of many Thai than differences in status was the relationship between patron and client. This link between two specific persons required the client to render services and other kinds of support in return for protection, the use of the patron's influence on the client's behalf, and occasional favors or financial aid. The basic pattern was old, but the relationship had evolved from a social one with economic overtones to one in which economic transactions and political support were more important.

Rural Social Patterns

Certain basic rural social patterns were discernable in modern Thai society. According to United States anthropologist Jack M. Potter, "The spatially defined rural village, which receives the allegiance of its members, furnishes an important part of their social identity, manages its own affairs and communal property, and has its own temple and school, is present in all parts of Thailand as an ideal cultural model, although in many cases the actual form of community life only approximates it."

Affecting the degree to which specific communities approached the model were "ecological, economic and demographic circumstances and the nature of rural administration," Potter writes. In the densely settled central plain, villages were often spatially indistinct, although boundaries defined by patterns of marriage, *wat* (Buddhist religious complex) attendance, and other social factors might be discerned. In other cases, some of the important features of a functioning community were lacking. Thus, if the proportion of nonlandholders was high and if landowners were absentee and did not provide the social or political leadership typically supplied by wealthy local peasants, community structure was weak.

The *wat* in the 1980s remained the center of the rural community in many respects, although some of its functions, e.g., as an educational center, were lost, and it was increasingly difficult to retain monks. Most rural communities built and maintained a *wat* because, as Potter states, the Thai consider it "necessary for a civilized social existence." The *wat* included the special quarters and facilities reserved for monks, a building for public worship and religious ceremony, and a community meeting place. Typically, the *wat* was run by a temple committee that consisted of prominent laymen as well as monks who had left the *sangha* without prejudice. Abbots and senior monks often enjoyed considerable prestige. In times of personal crisis, people often sought their advice.

The *wat* was first of all a center for religious ceremony, much of which was regularly carried out according to a ritual calendar.

These scheduled rites involved the community as a whole, even if their ultimate purpose was the acquisition of merit by individuals. Other irregularly held rites also took place in the *wat* and almost always included the community or a significant segment of it. The temple was also the locus for astrological and other quasi-magical activities. Although such rites were outside the canon of Buddhism, they were important to the community and were often carried out by monks. Thus, a person would go to a monk versed in these matters to learn the propitious day for certain undertakings (for example, a wedding) or to be cured of certain illnesses by the application of holy water. A large *wat* usually had a crematorium; almost all dead were cremated.

The temple committee often administered a loan fund from which the poor of the community might borrow in emergencies. The *wat* was also the repository of mats, dishes, and other housewares that could be borrowed by members of the community. If an aged person had nowhere else to go, the *wat* was a refuge. The *wat* was not reserved solely for serious matters; entertainment and dances open to the community were also held there.

Within the village in the 1980s, the basic organizational unit was the family, which changed its character in the course of a developmental cycle. A nuclear family became, in time, a larger unit, but the death of the older generation once again left a nuclear family. Typically, a man went to live with the parents of the woman he married. Such residence was temporary except in the case of the youngest daughter. She and her husband (and their unmarried children) remained with her parents, taking care of them in their old age and inheriting the house when they died. Thus, at some point in the cycle, the household included what has been referred to as a matrilineal extended stem family: the aging parents, their youngest daughter and her husband, and the younger couple's children.

Emerging from this developmental cycle was a cluster of related and cooperating households consisting of the extended stem family household and the households of those daughters who had settled nearby with their husbands. That pattern was predicated on the continuing control over land and other resources by the senior couple. The closeness of these related households and the extent of their cooperation in a range of domestic activities varied considerably. With a growing shortage of arable land in parts of the country and the aggregation of substantial holdings by a limited number of landowners, the pattern was no longer as common as it had been. The senior couple may have had little or no land to allocate to their older daughters, and the daughters and their husbands may have had to move elsewhere. In the case of wholly landless agricultural workers, even the extended stem family might not be possible.

Most villages were divided into local units or neighborhoods. In the North, neighborhoods were often the entities that on a weekly basis collectively provided food for the monks in the local *wat,* but these neighborhoods also engaged in other forms of cooperation. Inasmuch as the nucleus of a neighborhood, perhaps all of it, often consisted of related households, activities such as house-raisings might be undertaken in response to either territorial or kinship requirements. If the community was the result of relatively recent pioneering by landless families from other communities, the neighborhood was important, and those living in the same area might come to address each other in kinship terms.

The labor exchange system was initially based on villagers' relative parity in landholding and their participation in subsistence agriculture. Typically, those involved in an exchange system were kin or neighbors, but the system sometimes extended beyond these categories. Each household arranged with others to provide labor at various stages in the agricultural cycle; in return, the same number of units of labor would be provided to those who had worked for it. Besides a labor exchange, the system provided opportunities for socializing and feasting. Although the arrangements were made by a single household with other specific households, the regularity with which representatives of households worked together gave the households a grouplike character.

The growing commercialization of agriculture in certain parts of the country and increasing landlessness and tenancy in the 1980s diminished the ubiquity of reciprocal work arrangements. Wealthy peasants hired labor; those who had no land or too little to subsist on worked for wages. Commercialization alone, however, did not prevent the use of a labor exchange system if those in it held roughly equivalent amounts of land. In some cases, a household would hire labor for one task and engage in the exchange system for others.

Peasants could be categorized on the basis of the nature of their land rights and the quantity of the land they held. The holdings that made a peasant family rich in one part of Thailand might not make it rich elsewhere. A rich rural family was one with substantial landholdings, some of which it might rent out. Moreover, if a family had the capital to hire agricultural labor and the implements necessary to cultivate additional land, it might rent plots from others. In any case, such a family would rely almost exclusively on hired labor rather than on the system of labor exchange, and it was likely to invest in other local enterprises, such as rice mills, thereby acquiring additional sources of income. The category of rich peasants could be subdivided into those with very large quantities of land and those with smaller but still substantial amounts. Usually that distinction would correlate with the magnitude of their nonfarming enterprises and the extent to which they had money to lend to others. In any case, rich peasants tended to be creditors, while other peasants were often debtors.

At the other end of the scale were the agricultural laborers, who held no land as owners or tenants except, perhaps, for the small plot on which their houses stood. To the extent that opportunities were available, they supported themselves as hired farm workers. Life was so precarious for some families, however, that they had to resort to hunting and gathering. Between the wealthy peasants and agricultural workers were two other categories. The families in the first group had sufficient land (some of it rented) to meet their own rice needs. If there were a crop surplus, it would be sold, but the families in this category did not produce primarily for the market, as the rich peasants did. They might also acquire cash through wage labor from time to time if opportunities were available. The families in the second category owned less land and had to rent additional parcels. Owned and rented holdings combined, however, did not always provide the means for subsistence, so these families frequently had to resort to wage labor. Not all tenants were poor. In some cases, tenants did well in good crop and market years, particularly in central Thailand. In general, however, the tenant farmer's situation was precarious. Rents, whether in cash or in kind, tended to be fixed without regard for the size of the harvest, and in a bad year tenant farmer families were likely to go into debt. Tenants and agricultural laborers had little or nothing of their own to pass on to their children.

In some areas, particularly in central Thailand, the land was controlled by absentee landlords who lived in Bangkok or in provincial towns and for whom landownership was another form of investment. They could have direct or indirect effect on the social and political lives of their tenants, and some occasionally acted as patrons to their tenants. At the local level, however, it was the rich peasant who wielded political power and was granted deference by others in the community. Differences in wealth were consistent with the Thai villager's understanding of the Buddhist concept of merit (see Religion, this ch.). According to this view, the accumulation of merit led not to nirvana but to a better personal situation in this world, preferably in this life. Wealth signified that one had merit. One might, therefore, demonstrate one's merit by striving and succeeding. Villagers at the lower end of the social scale, however, sometimes questioned the doctrine of merit

Central Thailand's vast network of waterways
serves as a means of transportation and irrigation
Courtesy United Nations

if they perceived the behavior of those at the upper end as un-righteous.

Most observers agreed that the patron-client relationship was pervasive in Thai society, not only at the village level but throughout the military and the bureaucracy. There was less agreement on its links to a class system and the degree to which the relationship was typically marked by social ties of affection and concern as opposed to a clearly calculated assessment of relative economic or political advantage. At the village level, it was not necessary to be rich to have a client, although a wealthy family was likely to have more than one client. It was possible for an ordinary peasant (although not a landless one) to provide limited benefits to some-one less fortunate in return for certain services. Often such a rela-tionship was arranged between kin. In the modern era, however, it was the wealthy villager who could provide benefits and expect, even demand, certain services from his client.

In principle, a patron-client relationship lasted only so long as both parties gained something from it, and the relationship could be broken at the option of either. Often, however, the client had few alternatives and would remain in the relationship in the hope of eliciting more benefits than had hitherto been forthcoming. To the extent, however, that prestige and power accrued to the person (or family) who had and could retain a large number of clients, the patron was motivated to provide benefits to those dependent on him.

The patron-client relationship also linked villagers and persons at other levels of the social, political, and economic orders: leading figures in the village, themselves patrons of others in the rural community, became clients of officials, politicians, or traders at the district or provincial levels. In such cases, clientship might reinforce the status of the rich villager who could, at least occasionally, call on his patron at a higher level for benefits that he might in turn use to bind his own clients to him. Just the fact that the rich villager was known to have a powerful patron outside the village could enhance his status.

National and Urban Structures: Class and Status

Although in the 1980s the hierarchy of social status or prestige and the hierarchy of political and economic power in the rural community overlapped, a disjunction of sorts existed between them at the national level. A rich villager—other things being equal—wielded political and economic power and had prestige. In the national system, the hierarchy of status began with the hereditary nobility—the royal family and the holders of royal titles. None of these people were poor; the royal family owned much land and some of its members had political influence. The royal family was not part of the ruling class, however, nor did it control the economy. The ruling class consisted of several levels, the uppermost of which comprised the military and, to a lesser extent, the bureaucratic elite.

In general, the Thai accorded high status to those who wielded power, and the prestige accorded the highest bureaucrats was consistent with a historical pattern, even if in modern times these bureaucrats were rarely members of the royal family. Whether the position of the military was fully legitimated in the eyes of most Thai was uncertain. The military was given deference, but it was not clear that its members were freely accorded esteem.

Below the military and bureaucratic elites were those in high government posts who performed the tasks requiring considerable knowledge, technical competence, or simply experience in the ways of bureaucracy. Like the bureaucratic elites, these upper middle-level bureaucrats were well educated, often holding undergraduate or graduate degrees from foreign universities. From the point of view of the Thai, such officeholders had much prestige even if they were not the primary wielders of power.

Positions at the highest levels of the military and the bureaucracy brought very good incomes to those holding them. Often these
positions provided access to other sources of income, including large
landholdings and other real estate, or participation in the actual
ownership of businesses, often in conjunction with Chinese businessmen. With some exceptions, the latter exercised day-to-day control of financial, commercial, and industrial organizations and
institutions.

The social status of the Chinese economic elite was not clear.
After World War II, a limited number of Chinese business families, who had begun as middlemen financing aspects of agricultural production and marketing, became bankers and industrial
and commercial entrepreneurs. These families had considerable
economic power, and they clearly influenced some political decisions through the Thai military and bureaucrats with whom they
had connections. Whether the Thai in general granted them the
prestige ordinarily given to those holding high posts in government
was another matter.

These Chinese businessmen should be distinguished from the
many Thai in the military and the civil bureaucracy who had
Chinese ancestry. In many cases, this Chinese ancestry was several
generations removed. In any case, such individuals were considered
Thai, operated chiefly in a Thai social and cultural milieu, and
were evaluated on the same social scale as other Thai.

Until the 1970s, persons who were fully Chinese entered the
bureaucracy only at the middle levels or, if higher, as technical
staff. This was in part a matter of Thai policy, in part a matter
of Chinese orientation. The Chinese were not indifferent to political power or administrative skill as desirable qualities or as sources
of prestige, but they adapted to the limits imposed by their minority
status. Within the Chinese community there was a hierarchy of
political influence, and there were organizations (ranging from
chambers of commerce to community groups and mutual aid
societies) in which Chinese had the opportunity to exercise their
power and skills. Even there, however, political power and prestige flowed to those who had been successful as entrepreneurs,
whereas among the Thai, achievement in the military or the
bureaucracy preceded access to significant economic opportunities
or resources. Chinese in the economic elite who moved into important positions in Chinese-centered organizations or, occasionally, other organizations, not only gained prestige within the
Chinese community but also became the links between that community and Thai elites, particularly with respect to the establishment of economic ties.

By the early 1970s, significant numbers of Chinese had been admitted to the higher bureaucracy. According to one analyst, they held roughly 30 percent of the posts in the special grades (upper ranks) at that time. Presumably they were the sons and daughters of wealthy entrepreneurs and had acquired the higher education necessary for admission to the bureaucracy's upper ranks.

Below the hereditary nobility and the ruling class was a socially and occupationally heterogeneous middle class that emerged in the years after World War II, especially after 1960. Its members were diverse with respect to their control over wealth, their social status, and their access to power. The simplest distinction within this amorphous category was based partially on income and partially on occupation, but subcategories thus drawn were rather mixed. The wealthier segment of this middle class (for convenience, the upper middle class) consisted of bureaucrats and military men at middle levels (including higher provincial officials), salaried administrative and managerial workers in private enterprise, middle-level businessmen, provincial notables and landlords living in provincial towns, and professionals. A much larger group, the petty bourgeoisie, comprised those who provided a range of services, largely in Bangkok, to the ruling class, the upper middle class, and to tourists and other foreigners. Often this petty bourgeoisie consisted of small-scale independent businessmen, some of them shop owners, others furnishing their services contractually. Some were salaried clerical staff. Both upper and lower segments of this middle category include many Chinese as well as Thai.

In the Thai scale of values, higher prestige tended to be accorded to those in government employment and perhaps to those in the professions. The private sector as a source of substantial income was a relatively new idea to the Thai, however, and their scale of values might change as an entrepreneurial bourgeoisie began seeking to have its status validated. In any case, the elements in the upper segment of this middle category could be said to share the same outlook and values or the same political status implied in the notion of class. The position of bureaucrats and notables (middle-level businessmen and landowners) who lived in provincial towns was of particular interest. On their home ground they exercised considerable power, formally and informally, but they owed this power at least in part to their connections, usually as clients to patrons in Bangkok, although they in turn had clients at lower levels.

There was also a lower urban stratum, but this too was heterogeneous. On the one hand, there were the more or less steady wage workers in commercial and industrial enterprises, mainly in Bangkok (and in mining outside Bangkok). On the other hand, there were large numbers of persons, like the wage workers, often from rural areas, who had no steady work and sought to eke out a living by offering their services as unskilled labor.

There were two other urban groups that were not part of the status hierarchy. Just as the monks of a village *wat* were outside the local rural system of stratification but enjoyed a special status, so too was the hierarchy of the *sangha,* the highest elements of which were located in Bangkok. Within the monkhood, the supreme patriarch and the Council of Elders exercised considerable authority, and they were given a great deal of deference by laymen, even those in the royal family and the ruling class. They did not have significant power outside the *sangha,* although some monks have had a substantial impact on politics.

Also outside the urban status hierarchy—but sometimes with higher incomes than those in the upper middle class and themselves requiring the services of those in the lower middle category—were the many men and women engaged in illegal activities that were nonetheless countenanced or protected. Among them were prostitutes, pimps, and narcotics dealers. In the mid-1980s, the number of women in Bangkok estimated to be engaged in prostitution or in related services ranged from 100,000 to 1 million. Some observers noted that prostitution was firmly entrenched in modern Thailand as a result of historical, economic, and social factors. The majority of Bangkok prostitutes were rural migrants providing economic support to relatives back in the country, which was expected of Thai daughters within the extended stem family system. In other words, Thai prostitutes were not fleeing from a family background or rural society that oppressed women in conventional ways but were engaging in an entrepreneurial move designed to sustain the family units of the rural economy, which had come under increasing pressure. Since these women usually did not reveal the source of their remittances back to the village, their families could retain or gain status based upon their earnings.

Class Consciousness

Of the categories or strata discernible in Thai society, only one—the royal family and the hereditary nobility—constituted a self-conscious group. It was not clear that class consciousness had developed among the power elites or upper middle-level bureaucrats by the 1980s, in spite of their shared views and aspirations. Nevertheless, as social mobility diminished, which it had begun to do in the early 1980s, and as each category or section increasingly generated its own replacements, distinct status groups might emerge. Outwardly there were many indications of a conscious middle class, consumer-oriented, cosmopolitan way of life. For example, golf, tennis, delicatessens, fast-food restaurants, boutiques, and shopping malls were very popular among the Thai residents of Bangkok in the late 1980s.

Militating against solidarity, particularly at the upper and middle levels, was the continuing competition for political power and the access to economic opportunities and resources that flowed from such power. People competing for high-level positions in the military, the bureaucracy, or within the economy were engaged in a complex and shifting pattern of patron-client relationships. In this system, all but the individuals at the highest and lowest ends of a chain of such relationships were simultaneously patrons to one or more others and clients to someone above them. A developing career was likely to put a person at different places in the chain at various stages.

Given the fluctuations in the fortunes of individuals (to which the patron-client system contributed), patrons and clients, particularly at the higher levels, had to make judgments as to the benefits accruing to them from their relationship. Moreover, a client had to assess present and potential sources of power and the extent to which his support and services would be reciprocated by the current or alternative patrons. It was not uncommon in this system for both patrons and clients to shift allegiances. Patrons often had several clients, but there were no real bonds between the clients of a single patron.

Social Mobility

The expansion of the bureaucracy and the military and the movement of the Thai into a rapidly growing private sector created opportunities for social mobility, although the major part of the population remained rural workers or moved into low-level occupations in the urban labor force. Associated with upward mobility, given the Thai orientation toward bureaucratic careers, was the availability of education. Expansion of education facilities beyond the secondary level occurred in the early 1970s. In 1961, for example, about 42,000 full-time and part-time students were enrolled in 6 higher education institutions, but by 1972 there were roughly 72,000 in more than a dozen institutions. The oldest and most prestigious universities, such as Chulalongkorn, Thammasat, and Mahidol, were in Bangkok. Many students attended universities outside Thailand, but these were more likely to be the children of Thai or Chinese who had already attained a fairly high socioeconomic position.

Homeless people living under bridge in Bangkok
Courtesy United Nations

Education was necessary for entry into the bureaucracy, but other capabilities or characteristics, including political reliability and involvement in the patron-client system, also played a part in upward mobility within the bureaucracy. In the military, the system played perhaps a greater role than education. Military expertise as such did not seem to be an important consideration.

The *sangha* offered a special avenue of social mobility to some of the sons of the peasants at the base of Thailand's socioeconomic pyramid. Positions in the upper tiers were filled by examination, and monks were offered higher education at two Buddhist universities (Mahachulalongkorn and Mahamongkut), which by the 1960s included significant secular components in their curricula. The Buddhist education system provided support for its talented students through the highest level; access to these opportunities by villagers might reflect the declining interest among the urban classes and the provincial middle group in a career in the *sangha*. The social mobility achieved through the *sangha* was not necessarily limited to those who were lifetime monks. Monks who left the *sangha* in their thirties and forties could legitimately enter other careers, and their education and experience in the *sangha* were helpful.

By the mid-1970s, the number of aspirants to the bureaucracy with undergraduate and even graduate degrees had begun to exceed the number of openings. Moreover, the economy was no longer expanding as it had in the 1960s and early 1970s (see Economic and Financial Development, ch. 3). Opportunities for upward mobility had lessened in the early 1980s, and children of families already established in the upper or middle reaches of the socioeconomic system were able to maintain their head start in a system that was no longer growing so rapidly.

Religion

Theravada Buddhism, the form of Buddhism practiced in Sri Lanka, Burma, Cambodia, and Laos, was the religion of more than 80 percent of the Thai people in the 1980s. These coreligionists included not only the core Thai, but most other Tai speakers, as well as the Khmer, the Mon, and some members of other minorities, among them the Chinese. Relatively few Thai were adherents of Mahayana Buddhism or other religions, including Hinduism, Christianity, Taoism, animism, and Islam. Of these only Islam, largely identified with but not restricted to Southern Thai of Malay origin, was a dominant religion in a specific geographic area.

Theravada Buddhism was the established religion, in that there were formal organizational and ideological links between it and the state. Thai rulers (the king formerly, and the military and bureaucratic oligarchy subsequently) sought or—if they thought it necessary—commanded the support of the Buddhist clergy or *sangha,* who usually acquiesced to (if not welcomed) the state's support and protection. A Thai religious writer pointed out that Thailand was the only country in the world where the king was constitutionally required to be a Buddhist and upholder of the faith.

Buddhism's place in Thai society was by no means defined solely by its relation to the state. The role of religious belief and institutions in Thai life had changed, and, with increasing commercialism and urbanization, some observers questioned the prevalence of Thai piety and good works. However, the peasant's or villager's view of the world remained at least partly defined by an understanding of Buddhist doctrine, and significant events in his or her life and community were marked by rituals performed or at least supervised by Buddhist clergy. Often, the villager's city-dwelling siblings would return to the home village for significant events such as weddings and funerals. Additionally, much of Thai village life— social, political, economic, and religious—centered on the local *wat.*

As is often the case when a scripturally based religion becomes dominant in a largely agrarian society, the religious beliefs and behavior of most Thai were compounded of elements derived from both formal doctrine and other sources. The latter either developed

during the long history of Buddhism or derived from religious systems indigenous to the area. Implementation of the same Buddhist
rite and tradition often varied from region to region. In Central
Thailand, for example, praiseworthy priests were selected and honored by the king, whereas in the Northeast this recognition was
bestowed by the people.

Historical Background

Thai Buddhism was based on the religious movement founded
in the sixth century B.C. by Siddhartha Gautama Sakyamuni, later
known as the Buddha, who urged the world to relinquish the
extremes of sensuality and self-mortification and follow the enlightened Middle Way. The focus was on man, not gods; the assumption was that life was pain or suffering, which was a consequence
of craving, and that suffering could end only if desire ceased. The
end of suffering was the achievement of nirvana (in Theravada Buddhist scriptures, *nibbana*), often defined negatively as the absence
of craving and therefore of suffering, sometimes as enlightenment
or bliss.

By the third century B.C., Buddhism had spread widely in Asia,
and divergent interpretations of the Buddha's teachings had led
to the establishment of several sects. The teachings that reached
Ceylon (present-day Sri Lanka) were given in a final written form
in Pali (an Indo-Aryan language closely related to Sanskrit) to
religious centers there in the first century A.D. and provided the
Tipitaka (the scriptures or ''three baskets''; in Sanskrit, Tripitaka)
of Theravada Buddhism. This form of Buddhism reached what is
now Thailand around the sixth century A.D. Theravada Buddhism
was made the state religion only with the establishment of the Thai
kingdom of Sukhothai in the thirteenth century A.D. (see Early
History, ch. 1).

The details of the history of Buddhism in Thailand from the thirteenth to the nineteenth century are obscure, in part because few
historical records or religious texts survived the Burmese destruction of Ayutthaya, the capital city of the kingdom, in 1767. The
anthropologist-historian S.J. Tambiah, however, has suggested a
general pattern for that era, at least with respect to the relations
between Buddhism and the *sangha* on the one hand and the king
on the other hand. In Thailand, as in other Theravada Buddhist
kingdoms, the king was in principle thought of as patron and protector of the religion (*sasana*) and the *sangha,* while *sasana* and the
sangha were considered in turn the treasures of the polity and the
signs of its legitimacy. Religion and polity, however, remained

separate domains, and in ordinary times the organizational links between the *sangha* and the king were not close.

Among the chief characteristics of Thai kingdoms and principalities in the centuries before 1800 were the tendency to expand and contract, problems of succession, and the changing scope of the king's authority. In effect, some Thai kings had greater power over larger territories, others less, and almost invariably a king who sought successfully to expand his power also exercised greater control over the *sangha*. That control was coupled with greater support and patronage of the ecclesiastical hierarchy. When a king was weak, however, protection and supervision of the *sangha* also weakened, and the *sangha* declined. This fluctuating pattern appears to have continued until the emergence of the Chakkri Dynasty in the last quarter of the eighteenth century.

By the nineteenth century, and especially with the coming to power in 1851 of King Mongkut, who had been a monk himself for twenty-seven years, the *sangha,* like the kingdom, became steadily more centralized and hierarchical in nature and its links to the state more institutionalized. As a monk, Mongkut was a distinguished scholar of Pali Buddhist scripture. Moreover, at that time the immigration of numbers of Mon from Burma was introducing the more rigorous discipline characteristic of the Mon *sangha.* Influenced by the Mon and guided by his own understanding of the Tipitaka, Mongkut began a reform movement that later became the basis for the Dhammayuttika order of monks. Under the reform, all practices having no authority other than custom were to be abandoned, canonical regulations were to be followed not mechanically but in spirit, and acts intended to improve an individual's standing on the road to nirvana but having no social value were rejected. This more rigorous discipline was adopted in its entirety by only a small minority of monasteries and monks. The Mahanikaya order, perhaps somewhat influenced by Mongkut's reforms but with a less exacting discipline than the Dhammayuttika order, comprised about 95 percent of all monks in 1970 and probably about the same percentage in the late 1980s. In any case, Mongkut was in a position to regularize and tighten the relations between monarchy and *sangha* at a time when the monarchy was expanding its control over the country in general and developing the kind of bureaucracy necessary to such control. The administrative and *sangha* reforms that Mongkut started were continued by his successor. In 1902 King Chulalongkorn (Rama V, 1868–1910) made the new *sangha* hierarchy formal and permanent through the Sangha Law of 1902, which remained the foundation of *sangha* administration in modern Thailand.

Procession of decorated rockets for Fire Festival
Courtesy Tourism Authority of Thailand

Buddhist Doctrine and Popular Religion

The doctrine of Theravada Buddhism can be found in the three-part Tipitaka. The first of the three baskets (or sections) sets forth the discipline governing the monastic order. The second presents the sermons or discourses of the Buddha and contains the dharma (literally, doctrine). The third comprises the commentaries and explications produced by learned monks in the centuries after the death of the Buddha. It is here that significant differences exist between Theravada and Mahayana Buddhism.

In the first basket, and central to the structure of Buddhist belief, are the doctrines of karma, the sum and the consequences of an individual's actions during the successive phases of his existence, and *samsara,* the eternal cycle of birth, death, and rebirth. Both doctrines were derived from the Indian thought of the Buddha's time, although he invested the concept of karma with very strong ethical implications. Broadly, these ideas taken together assert that evil acts have evil consequences for those committing them, and good acts yield good consequences, not necessarily in any one life-time, but over the inevitable cycle of births and deaths. A concomitant to the belief in karma and *samsara* is the view that all forms of life are related because every form originated in a previous one. In the canonical view, but not in the popular one, the entity that undergoes reincarnation is not the soul (although the idea of soul exists) but a complex of attributes—actions and their consequences—that taken together are said to constitute the karma of an individual. It is karma in this sense that survives in another form.

The second basket, containing the dharma, provides the essentials that define the way to nirvana. The foundation of the system lies in the Four Noble Truths: suffering exists, it is caused by craving or desire, it can be made to cease, and it can be brought to an end by following the Noble Eightfold Path. The last Noble Truth contains the eight precepts to be followed by Buddhists: right view, or having an understanding of the Four Noble Truths; right thought—freedom from lust, ill will, and cruelty; right speech, which means abstention from lying, gossiping, harsh language, and vain talk; right action, by which killing, stealing, and sexual misconduct are proscribed; right livelihood, which requires an individual's sustenance be earned in a way that is not harmful to living things; right effort, by which good thoughts are encouraged and bad thoughts are avoided or overcome; right mindfulness, or close attention to all states of the body, feeling, and mind; and right concentration, that is, concentration on a single object to bring about a special state of consciousness in meditation. Following the Noble Eightfold Path conscientiously is necessary if a person aspires to become an *arhat* (usually translated as saint), ready for nirvana.

Virtually from the beginning, however, the Buddha acknowledged that it would be difficult for a layperson to follow all aspects of the Noble Eightfold Path singlemindedly. The conditions appropriate to such pursuit are available only to mendicant monks. The demands on the layperson are therefore less rigorous, and most interpret the doctrine as requiring acts gaining merit so that the layperson may achieve a condition in the next life that will allow stricter attention to the requirements of the path.

The acts that bring merit are, in principle, those that conform as closely as possible to the ethical demands of the Noble Eightfold Path. Acts that support the brotherhood of monks are also included. Consequently, providing material support, e.g., food, to the members of the *sangha,* showing them deference, underwriting and participating in certain ceremonies, and supporting the construction and maintenance of the *wat* have come to be the chief methods of gaining merit. The powerful ethical content of the Noble Eightfold Path is reduced to five precepts or injunctions. The laity are expected to refrain from the following: taking life, stealing, lying, engaging in illicit sexual relations, and drinking intoxicating liquors. Thai Buddhists—like many followers of other religions—select only a few of the Buddha's teachings to guide them. Many Buddhist principles, while not actually practiced, are venerated as ideals.

According to some observers, most Thai place little emphasis on the achievement of nirvana, whether as a final state after many rebirths or as an interior condition. What is hoped for is an improved condition in this life or the next. In Thai thinking, the ideas of merit and demerit so essential to the doctrine of karma are linked linguistically to those of good and evil; good and merit are both *bun;* evil and the absence of merit are *bap.* The Theravada idea of karma (and the Thai peasant's understanding of it) charges the individual with responsibility for good and evil acts and their consequences. Thai do not rely solely on the accumulation of merit, however gained, to bring that improved state into being. Other forms of causality, ranging from astrology to the action of spirits of various kinds, are also part of their outlook.

The world of the Thai villager (and that of many city folk as well) is inhabited by a host of spirits of greater or lesser relevance to an individual's well-being. Although many of these are not sanctioned by Buddhist scripture or even by Buddhist tradition, many monks, themselves of rural origin and essentially tied to the village, are as likely as the peasant to accept the beliefs and rituals associated with spirits.

Most important are the spirits included in the rather heterogeneous category of *phi,* thought to have power over human beings. The category includes spirits believed to have a permanent existence and others that are reincarnations of deceased human beings. *Phi* exist virtually everywhere—in trees, hills, water, animals, the earth, and so on. Some are malevolent, others beneficial.

The ghosts of persons who died violently under mysterious circumstances or whose funeral rites were improperly performed constitute another class of *phi;* almost all of these spirits are malevolent. In contrast, the ghosts of notable people are said to reside in small shrines along the roads and are referred to as "spirit lords." They are often petitioned in prayers and can enter and possess the bodies of mediums to give oracles. Among the more important of the spirits and ghosts is the evil *phi pop* (ghoul spirit), which, at the instigation of witches, can enter human beings and consume their internal organs.

Another category consists of the *chao* (guardian spirits), of which perhaps the most important is the *chao thi,* or guardian of the house compound (an alternative name is *phra phum*). Fixed on a post in the compound of most houses in Thailand's central region is a small spirit dwelling. Food offerings are made to the *chao thi* on the anniversary of the spirit's installation in the house, on New Year's

Day, and on other special days. The spirit is told of the arrival of guests who are to stay any length of time, of projected journeys by members of the family, and of births and deaths. The spirit's intercession is also sought during illness and misfortune.

Other spirits protect gardens, the rice fields, and the *wat.* The spirit of the rice field is worshiped only once a year, at the beginning of the rice planting; the Rice Goddess receives offerings when the seedbed is to be prepared and when the harvest is ready. The Mother Earth Goddess often receives offerings at transplanting time.

In addition to the rites dedicated to an assortment of spirits either regularly or as the occasion demands, other rites intended to maximize merit for the participants are practiced. The Buddha prescribed no ceremonies for birth, death, and marriage, but the Hindu rites, which were adopted by the Thai people, entail the participation of Buddhist monks. The ceremonies, which are held at home rather than in the *wat,* have no scriptural sanction. The monks limit their participation to chanting the appropriate Buddhist scriptural texts or to providing holy water.

The propitiation of an individual's *khwan* (body spirit or life soul) remains a basic feature of Thai family rites. Any ceremony undertaken to benefit a person, animal, or plant is referred to as the making of *khwan.* On important occasions, such as birth, ordination into the priesthood, marriage, a return from a long journey, or the reception of an honored guest, a *khwan* ceremony is performed.

Of all the life cycle and family ceremonies, funeral rites are the most elaborate. When a person is dying, he or she should fix his or her mind on the Buddhist scriptures or repeat some of the names of the Buddha. If the last thoughts of the dying person are directed toward the Buddha and his precepts, the fruits of this meritorious behavior will be repaid to the deceased in the next incarnation. After his or her death, other meritorious acts are performed for the benefit of the deceased, such as attendance at the wake and provision of food to the officiating monks. Every effort is made to banish sorrow, loneliness, and fear of the spirits by means of music and fellowship.

Ceremonies in the *wat* consist of those that benefit the entire community and those that primarily affect the *sangha.* The first kind include the rites held on such occasions as Mahka Bucha (an important February holiday that marks the beginning of the season for making pilgrimages to Phra Phuttabaht, the Buddha's Footprint Shrine), Wisakha Bucha (a festival commemorating the Buddha's birth, enlightenment, and death), Khao Phansa (the holiday marking the beginning of the three-month Buddhist holy season, July to October), and Thot Kathin (a festival during which robes and other items are given to the monks by the laity). Ceremonies that primarily concern the *sangha* include ordination, confession, recitation of the 227 monastic rules, and distribution of new robes after Thot Kathin.

Of all the ceremonies affecting the *sangha,* ordination is the one in which the laity are most involved, both physically and spiritually. Frequently, before a young man makes his initial entry into the *sangha,* a ceremony is held in the home of the aspirant to prepare him for ordination. His *khwan* is invited to enter the *sangha* with him; otherwise, evil and illness might befall him. He is informed of his parents' happiness with his decision, of the sacrifices they have made for him, and of the life of austerity and discipline he is to begin. In Thailand, it is a popular belief that by becoming a monk great merit is gained, merit which also accrues to persons or parents who sponsor the ordination.

The Sangha

The *sangha* comprises two sects or schools, the Mahanikaya and the Dhammayuttika. The first has far more members than the second, but the Dhammayuttika—exercising a more rigorous discipline, having a reputation for scholarship in the doctrine, and having a close connection to royalty—continues to wield influence beyond its numbers among intellectuals and in *sangha* administration. Both schools are included in the same ecclesiastical hierarchy, which is very closely tied to the government. The strengthening of those ties began in the nineteenth century, ostensibly to deal with problems of internal disorganization in the *sangha* but also so that the *sangha* could be used to help integrate a government that was just beginning to extend and strengthen its administrative control over the North and Northeast. Each of these regions in effect had had its own *sangha,* and the unification of the *sangha* was seen as an important step toward the unification of Thailand. The pattern of legislative and other steps culminating in the Sangha Act of 1963 tended to tighten government control of the *sangha;* there was no significant resistance to this control from the monks. Conflicts existed between the two schools, however, over issues such as position in the hierarchy.

In spite of a long tradition of monkhood in Thailand, the great majority of males did not become monks. Those who did usually entered in their early twenties but did not necessarily remain monks for a long time. During the three-month holy season (Khao Phansa), sometimes referred to as the Buddhist Lent, monks go into retreat, and more attention than usual is given to the study of dharma. In the mid-1980s, Thai male civil servants were given three months' leave with full pay if they spent the Lenten period as monks. It has been estimated that the proportion of temporary monks during this period varies between 25 and 40 percent of the total. The motivation for monkhood of such short duration is complex, but even the temporary status, for those who are unable or unwilling to commit themselves to the discipline for life, brings merit, not only to the monk but also to his parents, particularly to his mother. (Some Buddhist women live as nuns, but they enjoy lower status than monks do.) Whether temporary or permanent, a monk in principle is subject to the 227 rules of conduct embodied in that portion (basket) of the Tipitaka devoted to the *sangha.*

Aside from the religious motivation of those who enter and remain in the *sangha,* another inducement for many is the chance to pursue the contemplative life within the monastic community. Other reasons in modern Thailand include the opportunity for education at one of the two Buddhist universities and the chance, particularly for monks of rural origin, to gain social status.

Thai villagers expect monks to be pious and to adhere to the rules. Beyond that, monks are expected to provide services to individual members of the laity and local communities by performing various ceremonies and chanting appropriate passages from the Buddhist scriptures on important occasions. The presence of monks is believed to result in the accrual of merit to lay participants.

Thai Buddhists generally do not expect monks to be directly involved in the working world; the monks' sustenance is provided by the members of the community in which the monks live. Their contribution to community life, besides their religious and ceremonial functions, is primarily educational. Beginning in the late 1960s, the government encouraged monks to engage in missionary activity in the remote, less developed provinces, particularly among the hill peoples, as part of the effort to integrate these groups into the polity. Leaders at the Buddhist universities have taken the stand that monks owe something to society in return for the support given them and that, in addition to the advanced study of Buddhism, the universities ought to include secular subjects conducive to the enrichment of the nation.

Buddhism, Politics, and Values

The organizational links between the *sangha* and the government are an indication of their interdependence, although the fine points of that relationship may have changed over time. The traditional interdependence was between religion and the monarchy. The king was, in theory, a righteous ruler, a bodhisattva (an enlightened being who, out of compassion, foregoes nirvana in order to aid

Right: King Bhumibol during his period of service as a Buddhist monk
Courtesy Royal Thai Embassy

Below: King Bhumibol performing a ceremony with members of the sangha
Courtesy Royal Thai Embassy

others), and the protector of the religion. Because succession to the throne was problematic and the position of any king in many respects unstable, each ruler sought legitimation from the *sangha*. In return, he offered the religion his support.

After the king became a constitutional monarch in 1932, actual power lay in the hands of the elites, primarily the military but also the higher levels of the bureaucracy. Regardless of the political complexion of the specific persons in power (who, more often than not, had rightist views), the significance of Buddhism to the nation was never attacked. In the late 1980s, the king remained an important symbol, and public ideology insisted that religion, king, and nation were inextricably intertwined (see The Central Government, ch. 4). Opposition groups have rarely attacked this set of related symbols. Some observers have argued that the acceptance of religion, king, and nation as ultimate symbols of Thai political values was misleading in that the great bulk of the population—the Thai villagers—although attached to Buddhism and respectful of the king, often resented the particular manifestations of government in local communities and situations. It seemed, however, that whatever discontent there was with the political, social, and economic orders, most Thai remained at least passively committed to a national identity symbolized by the king and Buddhism.

Puey Ungphakorn, a former rector of Thammasat University and human rights advocate, viewed the ethical precepts of Buddhism as insurance against oppressive national development. Although the fundamental role of development was to improve the welfare of the villagers, in a number of nations without the protection of religion the rights of the villager were often abused. In Thailand, according to Puey, the peasant, like the urban dweller, has an individual identity protected by the shared belief in Buddhism.

The support given the king (and whatever political regime was in power) by the *sangha* was coupled with a prohibition on the direct intervention of monks in politics, particularly in party, political, and ideological conflicts. It was taken for granted that members of the *sangha* would oppose a communist regime, and available evidence suggested that virtually all Thai monks found Marxist thought alien, although monks elsewhere in Southeast Asia have been influenced by socialist, if not explicitly communist, ideas. Historically, monks occasionally have been involved in politics, but this involvement was not the norm. In the second half of the twentieth century, however, monks became aware of the political and ideological ferment in Southeast Asia and in a few cases engaged in political propaganda, if not in direct action. A few were accused of doing so from a position on the left, but the most explicit instance of political propaganda in the 1970s was that of a highly influential monk, Kittivuddha Bikkhu, who preached that it was meritorious to kill communists. Although not supported by the religious and political establishments, he provided right-wing militants with a Buddhist ideological justification for their extremist activities.

Religious Minorities

Defining Thai minority religions was as complex as defining Thai ethnic minorities. This problem was further compounded by the number of Thai whose Buddhism was a combination of differing beliefs. In the 1980s, the religious affiliation of the Chinese minority was particularly difficult to identify. Some adopted the Theravada beliefs of the Thai, and many participated in the activities of the local *wat*. Most Chinese, however, consciously retained the mixture of Confucian social ethics, formal veneration of ancestors, Mahayana Buddhist doctrine, and Taoist supernaturalism that was characteristic of the popular religious tradition in China. To the Chinese community as a whole, neither organized religion nor theological speculation had strong appeal. There were some Chinese members of the *sangha,* and most large Chinese temples had active lay associations attached to them. It was estimated in the 1980s that there were about twenty-one Chinese monasteries and thirteen major Vietnamese monasteries in Thailand.

The practice of Islam in the 1980s was concentrated in Thailand's southernmost provinces, where the vast majority of the country's Muslims, predominantly Malay in origin, were found. The remaining Muslims were Pakistani immigrants in the urban centers, ethnic Thai in the rural areas of the Center, and a few Chinese Muslims in the far north. Education and maintenance of their own cultural traditions were vital interests of these groups.

Except in the small circle of theologically trained believers, the Islamic faith in Thailand, like Buddhism, had become integrated with many beliefs and practices not integral to Islam. It would be difficult to draw a line between animistic practices indigenous to Malay culture that were used to drive off evil spirits and local Islamic ceremonies because each contained aspects of the other. In the mid-1980s, the country had more than 2,000 mosques in 38 Thai provinces, with the largest number (434) in Narathiwat Province. All but a very small number of the mosques were associated with the Sunni branch of Islam; the remainder were of the Shia branch. Each mosque had an imam (prayer leader), a muezzin (who issued the call to prayer), and perhaps other functionaries. Although the majority of the country's Muslims were ethnically Malay, the

Muslim community also included the Thai Muslims, who were either hereditary Muslims, Muslims by intermarriage, or recent converts; Cham Muslims originally from Cambodia; West Asians, including both Sunnis and Shias; South Asians, including Tamils, Punjabis and Bengalis; Indonesians, especially Javanese and Minangkabau; Thai-Malay or people of Malay ethnicity who have accepted many aspects of Thai language and culture, except Buddhism, and have intermarried with Thai; and Chinese Muslims, who were mostly Haw living in the North.

The National Council for Muslims, consisting of at least five persons (all Muslims) and appointed by royal proclamation, advised the ministries of education and interior on Islamic matters. Its presiding officer, the state counselor for Muslim affairs, was appointed by the king and held the office of division chief in the Department of Religious Affairs in the Ministry of Education. Provincial councils for Muslim affairs existed in the provinces that had substantial Muslim minorities, and there were other links between the government and the Muslim community, including government financial assistance to Islamic education institutions, assistance with construction of some of the larger mosques, and the funding of pilgrimages by Thai Muslims to Mecca. Thailand also maintained several hundred Islamic schools at the primary and secondary levels.

During the sixteenth and seventeenth centuries, Portuguese and Spanish Dominicans and other missionaries introduced Christianity to Siam. Christian missions have had only modest success in winning converts among the Thai, and the Christian community, estimated at 260,000 in the 1980s, was proportionately the smallest in any Asian country. The missions played an important role, however, as agents for the transmission of Western ideas to the Thai. Missionaries opened hospitals, introduced Western medical knowledge, and sponsored some excellent private elementary and secondary schools. Many of the Thai urban elite who planned to have their children complete their studies in European or North American universities sent them first to the mission-sponsored schools.

A high percentage of the Christian community was Chinese, although there were several Lao and Vietnamese Roman Catholic communities, the latter in southeastern Thailand. About half the total Christian population lived in the Center. The remainder were located in almost equal numbers in the North and Northeast. More than half the total Christian community in Thailand was Roman Catholic. Some of the Protestant groups had banded together in the mid-1930s to form the Church of Christ in Thailand,

and nearly half of the more than 300 Protestant congregations in the country were part of that association.

Other religions represented in Thailand included Hinduism and Sikhism, both associated with small ethnic groups of Indian origin. Most of the Hindus and Sikhs lived in Bangkok.

Education and the Arts

In the late eighteenth and early nineteenth centuries, United States and British missionaries introduced formal European education, primarily in the palaces. Up to that time, scholarly pursuits had been confined largely to Buddhist temples, where monastic instruction, much of it entailing the memorization of scriptures, was provided to boys and young men. Like his father Mongkut, King Chulalongkorn (Rama V, 1868–1910) wanted to integrate monastic instruction with Western education. Unsuccessful in this effort, he appointed his half brother, Prince Damrong Rajanubhab, to design a new system of education. Western teachers were engaged to provide assistance, and in 1921 a compulsory education law was enacted. In 1917 the first university in the country, Chulalongkorn University, was established.

Emphasis on education grew after the 1932 coup as a result of the new constitutional requirement for a literate populace able to participate in electoral politics. Government efforts focused on primary education; private schools, concentrated in Bangkok and a few provincial centers, supported a major share of educational activity, especially at the secondary level. Despite ambitious planning, little was accomplished. Even after World War II, the educated segment of Thai society continued to consist mainly of a small elite in Bangkok. The postwar years showed the influence of American education. By the mid-1980s, perhaps as many as 100,000 Thai students had studied in the United States, and tens of thousands had benefited from Peace Corps and other United States government educational assistance projects.

Only 4 million children were enrolled in government schools in the 1960s, but by the late 1980s nearly 80 percent of the population above the age of 11 had some formal education. This dramatic change reflected government interest in accelerating the pace of social development through education, especially in less secure areas of the country, as a means of promoting political stability. By 1983 an estimated 99.4 percent of the children between the ages of 7 and 12 attended primary school. (Compulsory schooling lasted only until grade six.) Adult literacy reportedly was more than 85.5 percent in the mid-1980s, compared with about 50 percent in the 1950s. Substantial public investment and foreign assistance made significant gains possible in literacy and school enrollments (see table 4, Appendix).

The government operated schools in all parts of the country, but there were many private schools as well, chiefly in Bangkok, sponsored principally by missionaries or Chinese communal organizations. Several universities ran what were effectively their own preparatory academies. In the late 1970s, the schools were reorganized into a six-three-three pattern that comprised six years of primary schooling, three years of lower secondary education, and three years at the upper secondary level.

Students in the upper secondary program could choose either academic or vocational courses. A core curriculum was common to both tracks, but the academic program focused on preparation for university entrance, whereas the vocational program emphasized skilled trades and agriculture. Only a small percentage of students continued their education beyond secondary school. Some who would have chosen to do so failed to qualify for university acceptance. Secondary-school graduates often had difficulty finding suitable employment. Even vocational graduates in rural areas frequently found their industrial skills poorly fitted to the agro-economic job market.

Access to education and the quality of education varied significantly by region. At the primary level, rural schools, administered since 1963 by the Ministry of Interior, tended to have the least qualified teachers and the most serious shortage of teaching materials. In an effort to increase the number of teachers, other ministries, including the Ministry of Defense, offered teacher-training programs. Although more students gained access to education, this arrangement led to a duplication of resources. Competition began to replace cooperation among some of the teachers' colleges and universities. Opportunities for secondary education were concentrated in major towns and in the Center. In the mid-1970s, Bangkok, with 10 percent of the country's population, had 45 percent of the secondary-school population, while the North and the Northeast combined, with 55 percent of the nation's population, had only 26 percent of these students. The government has since attempted to rectify these inequities by improving administrative structure, making education more relevant to socioeconomic development, and adding qualitative and quantitative support to both public and private systems. Nevertheless, in the late 1980s the underlying problem of inequitable distribution of funds between the Center and the outlying provinces remained.

The Office of University Affairs administered higher education at government universities (except for teachers' colleges, military

Bangkok schoolchildren participating in
Boy Scouts and Girl Guides program
Courtesy United Nations

academies, and the two Buddhist universities) and supervised higher education in private colleges. By the late 1980s, the country had 13 public universities, 3 institutes, and about 10 private colleges, the latter accounting for only about 7 percent of total university enrollment. A Western education was highly valued, and those who could afford to study abroad often did. Chulalongkorn University was the leading domestic university. Until the establishment of Ramkhamhaeng University in 1971, Chulalongkorn had the largest student body (18,000 full-time and part-time students in 1987). Thammasat University (11,000 student population in 1987) ranked next in academic quality. Operations at Thammasat suffered somewhat from punitive measures imposed after the massive student disorders of October 1973 (see Thailand in Transition, ch. 1). Thereafter, Mahidol University (formerly the University of Medical Sciences), which had nearly 9,000 students in 1987, began to overtake Thammasat University as Thailand's second-best university. Another respected academic institution was the agricultural university, Kasetsart University, which in 1987 had 11,000 students. All the major universities were located in Bangkok. The various provincial universities, which were established in the 1960s and the 1970s, and a number of specialized academies, some of them in Bangkok, mostly had small student populations. Chiang

Mai University, founded in 1964, however, had 13,000 students by 1987.

Pressure from a society that increasingly valued career-oriented education was in part responsible for the government's establishment of two "open universities," beginning in 1971. Both open universities were established for those who could not be accommodated by the older institutions of higher learning, and each admitted secondary school graduates without any competitive examination. Ramkhamhaeng University conducted classes, whereas Sukhothai Thammathirat University offered its courses via national radio and television broadcasts and by correspondence. In 1987 Ramkhamhaeng had more than 400,000 students enrolled and Sukhothai Thammathirat more than 150,000.

To maintain its own language and script, Thailand constantly promoted reading through both formal and informal education. Thailand had one of the highest levels of functional literacy in Asia as well as one of the largest publishing rates per person of any developing nation. In 1982 there were 5,645 titles published, more than 7 million radio receivers, 830,000 televisions, 69 daily newspapers, and 175 periodicals. Thai-language paperbacks, often translations of English-language best-sellers or "how to" books, had a wide audience. The publishing house of Kled Thai, with 60 percent of the national market, distributed between 80,000 and 120,000 volumes monthly.

Thailand had a long history of written literature dating back to the thirteenth century, when much of the literature written in poetic style was religious or related to the monarchy. Examples include the *Maha Chat Kham Luang,* an epic adapted from the Buddhist Jataka tales, and *Kotmai Tra Sam Duang,* a legal work on Buddhist ethics. Beginning with the Chakkri Dynasty in the late eighteenth century, writing for both the court and the public flourished. New trends in literary style included *Phra Aphai Mani,* by Thailand's greatest poet Sunthon Phu (1786–1855), the written version of the popular epic romance poem called *Khun Chang Khun Phaen,* and *Sang Thong,* attributed to King Loet La (Rama II, 1809–24). Dynastic chronicles and poetry usually were dominant until the twentieth century, when King Vajiravudh (Rama VI, 1910–25) helped foster the birth of the modern Thai novel. Modern life was the theme of books such as *Phudi* (The Genteel) by Dotmai Sot (1905–63) or *Songkhram Chiwit* (The War of Life) by social realist Si Burapha (1905–74). Specific social ills, such as inadequate education, were documented in Khammaan Khonkhai's *Khru Ban Nok,* translated by Genhan Wijeyeaardene as *The Teachers of Mad Dog*

Swamp, or in the revolutionary writings of Chit Phumisak and the progressive poetry of Naovarat Pongpaiboon.

The modern period in Thai art began with the breakdown of the traditional patterns of society following the 1932 coup. A strong artistic influence in the modern period was exerted by the work of Silpa Bhirasri, an Italian-born professor. American culture also influenced modern Thai art forms both through Thai artists studying in the United States and through the popularity of Hollywood movies. Modern artists such as Kamol Tassananchalee have integrated American ideas into Thai art, just as centuries before the artists of Sukhothai and Ayutthaya applied Indian or Khmer concepts to Thai design.

The Thai motion picture industry's first film was made by a younger brother of King Chulalongkorn in 1900. By the late 1980s, some 3,000 feature films had been produced and a National Film Archives established. Although a few of these films, such as *Tong Pha Luang* (Yellow Sky, 1980) and *Sut Thon Nun* (End of the Road, 1985), were well known outside Thailand, the language barrier rather than their quality or relevance limited their distribution internationally.

In theater in the 1980s, Thailand produced *khon* (classical masked drama) based on epics such as the Indian *Ramayana* (*Ramakian* in Thai), as well as more modern plays. Drama, like books, movies, and art, has moved out of the royal palaces within the last century to be enjoyed by a wider audience in a less controlled form, which incorporates Western elements. The Thai people accepted Westernization in all areas, including the arts, on their own terms as a pragmatic necessity and not as something imposed by foreigners. For example, modern techniques in set and costume designs, makeup, lighting, sound systems, and theater construction were combined with traditional drama such as the *khon*. Thai monarchs beginning with King Mongkut initiated and led this modernization. King Bhumibol not only continued this movement but also widened its scope in an effort to make regional art forms an integral part of the Thai national identity.

Health and Welfare

By Asian standards, the level of public health in Thailand was relatively good. In 1986 the life expectancy for men was 61 years; for women it was 65 years. In 1960 for both sexes life expectancy had been only 51 years. In 1984 deaths among children under age 4 averaged 4 per 1,000, while infant mortality for the same year was 47.7 per 1,000. The crude death rate for the population as a whole declined fairly consistently between 1920 and 1984, from

113

31.3 to 7.7 per 1,000. Much of the decline was a reflection of the successful struggle against malaria, which once had been the single greatest cause of illness and death. The expansion of the public health system in general, however, was also an undeniable factor in the improved health picture.

Health and related social welfare services received an allocation of 10.3 percent of the total 1984 budget. Of this amount, about 50 percent was assigned to public health activities; the remainder went to social security and welfare, housing, and community services. Although a disproportionate number of health care facilities were concentrated in the Bangkok area, Western-style medical treatment was provided throughout the country by a network of hospitals, regional health centers, and other clinics. In 1981 there were 359 hospitals, with 1 bed per 734 people and 1 physician per 6,951 people. In the same year, the nation registered 1,142 dentists and more than 50,000 nurses and midwives.

Despite progress in lengthening life expectancy, combating disease, and building public health facilities, Thailand in the late 1980s faced a bleak public health situation. One of the most critical national health problems was the water supply. In the mid-1970s, little more than 20 percent of the population, most of that portion being urban dwellers, was reported to have access to safe water. Even in Bangkok, where the proportion with such access was highest, only about 60 percent of the population had access to potable public water. In the countryside, inhabitants depended on shallow wells, roof drainage, rivers, and canals.

Throughout Thailand, but especially in Bangkok, the traditional skyline with its Buddhist temples was becoming overshadowed by Western-style buildings and skyscrapers. Construction was done mostly by laborers who usually lived on site with their families. In 1980 there were more than 373,000 construction workers (79 percent of whom had once been farmers) living in temporary housing, which typically measured only 3 to 4 meters square and had a door but no windows. Workers' compensation and paid sick leave were almost nonexistent, and illness and inadequate sanitation were common in these shantytowns. Although public and private agencies were becoming aware of the seriousness of the problem from both a health and a legal point of view, the transient nature of the burgeoning construction community made this population difficult to serve. In the urban areas, modern development and outward prosperity often masked deficiencies in basic infrastructure that arose from rapid and unplanned growth. Urban planners were confronted with traffic congestion, housing shortages, and air, water, and noise pollution.

The development of an international consumer economy brought new challenges and Western diseases, particularly for urban dwellers. Prostitution and narcotics use, which had been part of Thai culture for centuries, took on new dimensions as health hazards. With the worldwide spread of acquired immune deficiency syndrome (AIDS) and new strains of venereal diseases, Thailand became concerned about the welfare of its female citizens and the effects on tourism. By mid-1987 eleven people in Thailand were reported to have AIDS and about another eighty to be AIDS carriers. The government had begun to take such action as testing homosexuals and drug addicts for AIDS, testing donated blood supplies, sponsoring public information campaigns, and funding the development of an inexpensive AIDS testing kit by Mahidol University.

In the mid-nineteenth century, narcotics were seen as a domestic problem, but one limited mostly to the Chinese. By the 1960s, drug use was considered a security or a foreign affairs issue. Only by the late 1970s did Thailand recognize drugs as a growing domestic problem. By that time, in addition to organic narcotic production, there was a dramatic rise in the production and use of synthetic drugs. Narcotics-related crimes ranked third among all types of criminal activity in 1983. In that year, there were 28,992 convictions for drug offenses nationally and 11,777 in Bangkok, which resulted in the overcrowding of prisons and detention centers. To combat the problem, the government instituted both public information campaigns and drug treatment centers. The national media began to make daily announcements about the social effects of drug use, and even in small provincial cities billboards were used to carry the message. Some traditional social systems were also employed in an innovative fashion. For example, Wat Tam Krabok, in Sara Buri Province, became one of the most important centers for the treatment of opiate addiction. Moreover, the government responded to the increase in health-related problems by placing new emphasis on meeting basic social needs in its economic and social development planning.

The Indochinese Refugee Question

The forced migrations of Indochinese to Thailand for political or economic reasons had been a common occurrence throughout the 200 years of the Chakkri Dynasty. The most recent refugee influx began in 1975 with the fall of the Lon Nol regime in Cambodia, then the collapse of the South Vietnamese government in April, followed by the change of leadership in Laos in December. According to official Thai figures, 228,200 refugees, mostly from

Laos, entered Thailand between 1975 and 1978. Included were Lao, Khmer, Tai Dam, Tai Nung, and Hmong, who came overland, and Vietnamese, who came by boat. Fifteen camps and four detention centers were established and jointly funded and operated by the Thai government, the United Nations High Commissioner for Refugees (UNHCR), and various international relief agencies. Most of the camps were along the border with Laos and Cambodia or at ports on the Gulf of Thailand. Until October 1977, Thai authorities generally accepted incoming Indochinese on the assumption that they would stay only until repatriated or relocated elsewhere.

After the coup of October 1977, the new Kriangsak Chomanand government reviewed Thai refugee policy. As a result of the growing refugee burden, the Thai government made it clear that greater international recognition of the refugee problem was needed, as well as financial and technical support for Thailand's relief program. Citing population pressures, land shortages, and potential economic friction between Thai and refugees, the Thai government refused to permit permanent resettlement of large numbers of refugees. Thus, in November 1977 the government banned new arrivals from Laos (termed "illegals") on the basis of the determination that these refugees were economically rather than politically motivated.

The actual number of Lao in Thailand continued to be impossible to determine; in 1987 Thai authorities claimed that up to 10,000 arrived daily, adding to an estimated 84,000 Lao refugees and illegals already in the Mekong Valley and border camps. Of the 42,000 inhabitants of Ban Vanai camp, between 3,000 and 6,000 were illegals. These numbers were subject to rapid change because of government-enforced repatriation, resettlement, and voluntary returns. In 1987 Amnesty International expressed concern over the fate of 155 Hmong who presumably were forcibly repatriated from Thailand; they were then arrested and detained without charge or trial by Lao authorities. This alleged incident may have led to resettlement requests by at least 5,000 Hmong (there were 56,000 in Thai camps) at the time. There was also a steady flow of persons returning to Laos on their own.

Laotians were not the only refugees caught in the Thai repatriation policy, which vacillated between national interest and humanitarian concerns. In 1979 tens of thousands of people, mostly ethnic Chinese, began to leave Vietnam by sea; hostilities between China and Vietnam directly or indirectly encouraged this migration by boat. Ships of the Royal Thai Navy sometimes discouraged Vietnamese refugee craft from attempting landings; some of Thailand's

Cambodian refugee children in Thailand
Courtesy CARE, Inc.

neighbors had been even more strict about turning away "boat people." Despite its relatively lenient position, Thailand was judged harshly by the international community as a result of reported acts of piracy by Thai vessels. However, because of increased vigilance and improvement in training of Thai maritime police in the 1980s, convictions for piracy increased significantly, and Thai fishermen began to provide greater assistance to the boat people. Nonetheless, the international press continued to report acts of piracy by Thai citizens.

In January 1979, Cambodia's Pol Pot regime was overthrown in fighting between Vietnamese and Khmer Rouge forces, and hundreds of thousands of destitute Cambodian civilians fled westward to the provinces of their country adjacent to the Thai border. Tensions built quickly along the ill-defined and disputed Thai-Cambodian border. It was extremely difficult for Thai police to mount effective patrols against illegal entry or illicit trade activities. Smuggling by Thai citizens and foraging raids into Thailand by Khmer Rouge troops soon became a major source of concern. In June 1979, Thailand began forced repatriation of more than 40,000 Cambodians, who were loaded into buses with a week's supply of food each and taken back across the border.

In July representatives of fifty nations concerned about this forced repatriation met in Geneva, where they pledged increased aid and permanent asylum for more refugees. Under international pressure, Thailand revised its refugee policy in October 1979; although still considered illegal entrants, Cambodians would not automatically be intercepted but would be given every assistance possible as a matter of compassion. In November 1979, camps were opened near the border with Cambodia, and within 2 months 156,000 illegal immigrants were housed in them. The Thai military had assumed responsibility for another 149,000 Cambodians; there were also 113,000 at Khao-I-Dang and 28,400 at Sa Kaeo. The Ministry of Interior was responsible for the illegal immigrants in other camps.

Increased armed warfare along the Thai-Cambodian border disrupted the lives of the Thai citizens as well as Cambodian civilians. Hence, Thai military officials became more closely involved in refugee affairs and at times overruled or interfered with civilian government policies. Supporters of the People's Republic of Kampuchea occasionally staged border attacks on refugee holding centers. In March 1984, Cambodian civilians encamped directly across from the Thai province of Sisaket were attacked; because of such activities, about 10,000 Cambodian civilians fled into Thailand. Between 1975 and February 1987, some 211,000 Cambodians were resettled abroad; this left about 22,000 in Khao-I-Dang, near the southeastern border city of Aranyaprathet in Prachin Buri Province, since all other camps for Cambodians had been officially closed. More than 100,000 remained at various sites along the border, however. The possibilities for resettlement remained unclear.

As refugees in East Africa and Central America began to receive more international attention in the 1980s, Thailand became increasingly concerned that the large number of Indochinese people, especially Cambodians, would become solely a Thai problem instead of an international one. In 1987 the Thai government officially closed the Khao-I-Dang holding center, in part to refocus international attention on the issue of Indochinese refugees. In announcing the closing of Khao-I-Dang, Prasong Soonsiri, secretary general to Thailand's prime minister, stated, among other reasons, that these camps in Thailand had created a "pull factor" that had encouraged more Cambodians to cross the border. Asked about the border people's fate, a high official of a Cambodian resistance group answered in December 1986 that "the camps [are] closed but not closed."

The Thai government stated that as of February 1986 there were still 127,817 Indochinese refugees in Thai holding and processing centers, while some 500,000 refugees had been resettled in third countries. After 1981 the rate of resettlement declined sharply; for example, only 33,090 people were resettled in 1982, a drop of about two-thirds from the 102,564 resettled in 1981. Thai authorities had become concerned not only that international attention had decreased but also that the decline in third-country resettlement would continue because of more selective criteria and more stringent procedures for screening and accepting candidates for resettlement. People had always moved across natural and artificially imposed borders in Indochina for economic and political reasons, but between 1975 and 1980 about 1.3 million people were displaced by the Second Indochina War and its aftermath. Because of its common borders with Laos and Cambodia, Thailand had shouldered the burden of a great number of these refugees who sought first asylum there. The flow of refugees after 1980 decreased little, but the numbers who found permanent homes did. In the late 1980s, the Indochinese refugee crisis remained both unsolved and a factor of growing importance in understanding late twentieth-century Thai society.

The burden of sheltering, even temporarily, several hundred thousand refugees placed stresses on social services already stretched thin by rapid urbanization. The more serious prospect of having permanently to assimilate large numbers of refugees was an even greater worry for Thai officials and the society as a whole. It was not a new problem, however, for a nation composed as Thailand was of many ethnic groups whose ancestors down through the centuries had sought refuge in the region of the Chao Phraya Valley.

* * *

American, British, Thai, and other scholars have carried out research on Thailand's rural communities since the late 1940s. These studies are marked by varying perspectives and different, sometimes contradictory, emphases. From the end of World War II until the 1970s, Americans were the leaders in Thai studies. This dominance has ended, however, because of the dramatic improvement in education in Thailand and the increased involvement of the scholars of other countries, such as Australia. In the late 1980s, excellent studies in both English and Thai were being produced by Thammasat University's Thai Khadi Research Institute and Chulalongkorn University's Institute of Asian Studies. *The Study of Thailand*, edited by Eliezer B. Ayal, presents a historical review of works relating to Thai studies.

Thailand in the 80s, published by the National Identity Office of the Office of the Prime Minister of Thailand, presents a comprehensive overview of Thailand with an economic and social orientation. An examination of changes in Thai society, polity, and culture since World War II is presented in Charles F. Keyes's *Thailand: Buddhist Kingdom as Modern Nation-State*. A more historical approach is presented in David K. Wyatt's *Thailand: A Short History*. The Thai political framework is addressed by John L.S. Girling in *Thailand: Society and Politics*. Several texts have been written on Thailand's physical setting and population; the most comprehensive of those was Wolf Donner's *The Five Faces of Thailand*. In the Thai context, it is best to accept the melding of society and religion; true to this blending is Japanese scholar Yoneo Ishii's *Sangha, State, and Society*. Wyatt's *The Politics of Reform in Thailand* still stands as the preeminent work on Thai education, but a number of new works on Thai literature have been published. Most recently, Herbert P. Phillips's *Modern Thai Literature* and Wibha Senanan's *The Genesis of the Novel in Thailand* provide a good overview of twentieth-century thought through the medium of literature. For a wider perspective on Thai art and culture, *Facets of Thai Cultural Life*, published by the Office of the Prime Minister in 1984, is useful. (For further information and complete citations, see Bibliography.)

Chapter 3. The Economy

Floating market scene along a bustling khlong *(canal) in the old capital city of Thon Buri, across the river from Bangkok*

THE THAI ECONOMY of the 1980s continued to function much along the open market lines that had traditionally characterized it. It remained capitalist in orientation, largely operated by the private sector with supportive infrastructure furnished by the government, which had some participation in production and commerce through a limited number of state-owned enterprises. Commitment to the existing economic system appeared general—none of the numerous Thai governments of the post-World War II years had advocated significant changes.

In the 1960s and 1970s, Thailand was among the fastest growing and most successful developing countries in the world. Rapid growth in production, accompanied by progress in alleviating poverty, was impressive, especially in the 1970s. By the early 1980s, however, Thailand's economic performance had slowed, partly as a result of the worldwide recession. Although its annual growth rate remained higher than the average for middle-income countries, earlier expectations had not been met. The targets of the Fifth Economic Development Plan (1982–86) had not been achieved, and serious macroeconomic imbalances persisted.

The government sought balanced economic growth and the closing of the income gap, along with improvement of the inequitable distribution of social services. Social and economic trends included increasing urbanization, expansion of industrial activities at a faster rate than agriculture, and growth of income in the service industries. These trends, often associated with modernization, produced problems with which the government tried to cope. Bangkok continued to face serious housing shortages and severe pressure on such basic services as water, sewerage, energy, and transport facilities. Although agriculture had been the most important economic activity of the country with most of the population living in the rural areas, the area of land under cultivation was unlikely to increase. Rather, it was projected that any increase in income would have to be gained through higher productivity of the labor and land now in use and by the development and diversification of industrial production. Accordingly, the government promoted enterprises that produced agricultural products, chemicals, and mechanical and electronic equipment and those that were labor intensive or export oriented.

Because foreign trade and investment were an important part of the economy, external conditions greatly influenced the country's economic performance. Thailand's harvests exceeded domestic consumption, enabling the country to export large quantities of food each year. The major agricultural exports were rice, cassava products, rubber, maize, and sugar; the major nonagricultural exports were textiles, electronics, and tin. Imports included more than half the country's national petroleum consumption. Although Thailand was a member of the Association of Southeast Asian Nations (ASEAN) with preferential trading arrangements, its principal trading partners were Japan, the United States, countries of the European Economic Community (EEC), and Australia.

Long-term prospects depended greatly on the effects of international economic conditions on the Thai economy. In the late 1970s and early 1980s, rising interest rates, declining demand and prices for Thai exports, and rising petroleum prices had caused a serious economic slump. Further growth of the economy depended, in part, on the success of the Thai government in improving economic efficiency and increasing domestic savings through development planning.

Economic and Financial Development

In the 1960s and 1970s, the country's abundant natural resources, an enterprising and competitive private sector, and cautious and pragmatic economic management resulted in the emergence of one of the fastest growing and most successful economies among the developing countries. Between 1960 and 1970, the country's average annual growth rate of gross domestic product (GDP—see Glossary) was 8.4 percent, compared with 5.8 percent for all middle-income, oil-importing countries. Between 1970 and 1980, the GDP rate of growth was 7.2 percent, compared with 5.6 percent for the middle-income oil-importing countries. The world slowdown by the late 1970s was mainly caused by the rise in oil prices. The Thai GDP in 1982 was US$36.7 billion. It rose to US$42 billion in 1985 (see table 5, Appendix). The projected rate of growth for GDP during the early 1980s was around 4.3 percent as a result of falling demand and prices for Thai exports despite a drop in oil price. It was apparent that in the 1980s Thailand had lost its momentum; its Fifth Economic Development Plan targets had not been met because of serious macroeconomic imbalances, such as decreasing savings and investment rates, increasing budget deficits, and increasing debt and debt-servicing obligations. Whether Thailand could regain its former momentum depended on the success of its Sixth Economic Development Plan (1987–91).

Between 1970 and 1980, investment represented on the average 25.2 percent of GDP, compared with 24.7 percent by the mid-1980s. This proportion was one of the lowest investment rates in Southeast Asia. The national savings rate had fallen even more, from an average of 22 percent during the 1970s to around 17.8 percent by the mid-1980s. Hence, the average current-account deficit of 7 percent of GDP during the early 1980s had been caused by a declining savings rate rather than by an increase in investment rate. This imbalance was more serious than one caused by rising investment because rising investment could pay for itself with increased output and, possibly, increased savings so that debt could be repaid. With falling savings, foreign borrowing was used not to raise investment but merely to fill the investment-savings gap, which was mirrored in the external debt ratio of 39 percent of GDP and 146 percent of exports by the mid-1980s. The total debt service ratio went up from 17.3 percent in 1980 to more than 25 percent by the mid-1980s. The increase was an important factor in the decision of the government to sharply reduce authorization for new commitments of public debt.

Public Finance

By the mid-1980s, government revenues averaged around 14 percent of GDP and consumption averaged around 13 percent, leaving a public savings net of interest payments of 1 percent of GDP. This was low compared with an average savings of 7 percent for the lower middle-income countries and 10 percent for the upper middle-income countries.

The financing of public expenditures caused a major imbalance because of high deficit and low public savings. Although not a new problem, increases in public expenditure needed to be matched by increases in revenues. Efforts were made to tackle the problem, and the public capital expenditures annual growth rate had dropped from 64.7 percent in 1980 to 8.5 percent in 1982 and 7.4 percent by the mid-1980s. The problem remained serious, however, because of political unwillingness to raise public revenue to the required level. In fact, the central government managed to finance only its public current expenditures with its revenues. Almost all capital expenditures, which averaged around 3.5 percent of GDP by the mid-1980s, were financed with borrowed funds, and often even some of the current expenditures had been financed with borrowed funds, thus increasing the debt-servicing burden.

Total revenue averaged around 13 percent of GDP in the 1970s and remained at the same level in the mid-1980s. In view of the disappointing revenue level, a new tax package was instituted in 1984–85 to raise revenues, including an increase in the tax rates on interest earnings from 10 percent to 12.5 percent, a reduction in the standard deduction for self-employed persons, the introduction of an estate tax, the abolition of preferential rates for companies listed on the stock exchange, the abolition of tax exemptions for selected state enterprises, streamlined exemptions and deductions for business taxes, and other measures. The resulting gains in revenue were, however, partially offset by measures to simplify the personal and corporate tax system. No effort had been made to reduce legal exemptions and illegal evasions. The net revenue effect of the package was therefore negligible.

Some experts concluded that a broader tax base, less complicated tax structure, and lower tax rates needed to be considered in the tax reform. Also, contributions and taxes paid by the state-owned enterprises should be increased because they had dropped from 41 percent of profit in the late 1970s to only 23 percent by the mid-1980s.

The Ministry of Finance required state enterprises to make specific improvements in their financial condition as a prerequisite for obtaining guarantees for borrowing. The measures included financing 25 percent of new investment from the state enterprises' own resources, forwarding at least 30 percent of their profits to the treasury, privatizing commercial enterprises, introducing corporate-planning systems, and limiting debt financing. Such measures did not lessen the burden of state enterprises on the budget, and their capital expenditure financed by the government had stayed at the same average annual rate of 3.5 percent of GDP in the 1970s and mid-1980s. It was noteworthy, however, that their performance had improved, with savings rising from 0.2 percent of GDP during the Fourth Economic Development Plan period (1977–81) to 1.4 percent of GDP by the mid-1980s.

With approximately 68 state-owned enterprises, Thailand had fewer than the average in other Southeast Asian countries, such as the Philippines, with 264. Nevertheless, the government was very concerned with their performance. The largest ones in terms of assets were in public utilities, transport and communication, financial institutions, and petroleum. The smaller ones were in manufacturing, agriculture, commerce, and services. The state enterprises did not represent the entire extent of public ownership in the economy; in the mid-1980s, the government received 75 percent of the shares of 24 troubled finance companies in order to rescue them from bankruptcy. In addition, the Ministry of Finance held minority shares in eighty-eight other private firms. All state enterprises were attached to a parent ministry or to the Office of the Prime Minister, and there were five core agencies and two committees to supervise their activities. Some experts suggested that,

in order to improve the efficiency of state enterprises, the enterprises needed to be more decentralized and exposed to free market competition.

The government spent approximately US$16 billion during the period from 1982 to 1985 (see table 6, Appendix). In real terms, this represented an increase of about 52 percent over public expenditures from 1977 to 1981, the fourth plan period. Because an increasing percentage of the budget was devoted to recurring obligations, fewer funds were available for capital investment. Close to 70 percent of current expenditure was used for wages, salaries, interest costs, and defense. Investment in energy, transport, and communication had taken nearly 64 percent of total capital expenditure by the mid-1980s. Agriculture received a fairly constant proportion of about 15 percent of total public capital expenditure, and industry dropped from 1.3 percent to 0.9 percent between the end of the 1970s and the mid-1980s. Education, health, and welfare together continued to receive about 12 percent throughout the same period.

Money and Banking

Thailand's performance in managing its money and banking affairs through successful development and diversification of its financial institutions was impressive in the 1960s and 1970s.

However, economic imbalances in the early 1980s and the rising tendency of governmental intervention put the financial sector under stress, thus reducing its efficiency in resource mobilization and allocation. Efforts to remedy the economic imbalances in the Fifth Economic Development Plan included restructuring monetary, exchange rate, and interest rate policies; strengthening the open securities market; and encouraging competition among financial institutions.

Financial Institutions

Thailand had many types of financial institutions, subject to different laws and regulated by different agencies. Most of them were privately owned, but some were state owned. The primary state-owned facility was the Bank of Thailand, which had responsibility and authority for monetary control in its role as the central bank. It served as the fiscal agent and the financier of the government; regulated the money supply, foreign exchange, and the banking system; and also served as the lender of last resort to the banks. Other state-owned facilities included the Government Savings Bank, the Bank for Agriculture and Agricultural Cooperatives, the Industrial Finance Corporation of Thailand, the Government Housing Bank, and the Small Industry Finance Corporation of Thailand.

By the mid-1980s, the 30 commercial banks had 1,526 branches handling the majority of all financial transactions in Thailand. The 16 largest banks accounted for over 90 percent of assets, deposits, and loans of the commercial banks, indicating a high concentration and little competition in the banking industry. Moreover, despite the impressive growth of banks, entrance by new banks was limited.

Finance and security companies comprised the second largest group of financial institutions with assets equaling nearly 22 percent of those of commercial banks. Concentration also existed in the securities industry, the 5 largest companies (out of 112) holding 19 percent of all finance and security assets. The finance companies were created by many domestic and foreign banks to overcome banking restrictions. Although they were intended to increase competition with commercial banks, the objective was not met because many banks used the companies as an extension of their own activities.

Money and Capital Markets

The money and capital markets were still underdeveloped in the mid-1980s. One striking fact was that the money market was very rudimentary and there was practically no open market for

short-term securities; the only investors in treasury bills and government bonds were commercial banks and a few other financial
institutions, which had to hold them until maturity. Certificates
of deposits did not exist, and, for all intents and purposes, promis-
sory notes issued by the finance companies were nonnegotiable.
In order to increase the liquidity aspect of government bonds, in
April 1979 the Bank of Thailand established the government bond
repurchase market. In reality this was only a brokerage window
at the central bank for institutional investors and, therefore, did
not help to achieve the desired objective of open-market operation.
Thus, Thai interest rates were determined, to a significant degree,
by international forces rather than central bank sales and purchases
of government securities.

The Security Exchange of Thailand (SET) had combined the
functions of securities market and securities commission, providing the legal framework for underwriting and trading of corporation shares of common stocks and bonds as well as government
securities. In 1974 the SET assumed the functions of the Bangkok
Stock Exchange, which never had been very active. In 1976 the
SET had an upsurge because of expansionary monetary policy.
In 1978 the SET collapsed, however, because of massive speculation, easy margin finance of up to 70 percent of a transaction, unpre-
paredness and inexperience of the brokers as well as the investors,
and inadequate regulation and supervision of the market and such
activities as inside trading and manipulation. The government created at that time two special public funds to purchase securities in
order to limit the negative effects of price swings in the SET. Many
investors, however, held on to their investments that had declined
in value in order to wait for a better price, thus decreasing normal
stock market activity. The hesitation to trade in the market created
a surplus problem for the SET, further damaging investor confidence. Some economists suggested that more specific regulations
and supervisory systems were needed in order to revive the SET
and restore public confidence.

Rural Finance

Beginning in the late 1960s, the government gave top priority
to increasing credit availability to the agricultural sector despite
the fact that agricultural performance had been excellent during
the previous two decades. The emphasis was on providing credit
to agriculture at below market interest rates and channeling credit
to poor farmers. In 1975 the central bank imposed a mandatory
credit allocation system, under which a required minimum of 5
percent of all outstanding bank loans were allocated to agriculture.

This quota was increased to 7 percent, then 9 percent, and finally to 13 percent by the mid-1980s. Moreover, all new rural and provincial branches of banks were required to lend 60 percent of their local deposits in the area served by the branch, with one-third of that amount reserved for farmers.

In 1966 the government established the Bank for Agriculture and Agriculture Cooperatives to supply credit for the development of the agricultural sector. In the 1980s, it became the most important single source of credit for farmers, and it had a wide coverage of 62 branches and 514 field units located throughout the country; more than 2 million farm families were reached directly and indirectly via the cooperatives and farmers associations. Noninstitutional sources, such as agriculture and savings cooperatives, supplied 50 percent of agricultural credit, and commercial banks and the agricultural banks each supplied 25 percent. Finance for nonagricultural activities in the rural sector, which provided 50 percent of rural income, was largely neglected.

Industrial Finance

The government did not use a mandatory allocation system or interest controls to affect the distribution of credit among industrial subsectors or regions or classes of industrial borrowers. The interest rate ceiling, however, did limit credit availability to small and medium industrial firms. Therefore, most credit went to the larger firms, which were mainly engaged in import substitution and were concentrated in the Bangkok metropolitan area.

Commercial banks, finance companies, and the Industrial Finance Corporation of Thailand (IFCT) were the main suppliers of credit to the industrial sector. Commercial banks accounted for nearly 70 percent of the total credit granted to the manufacturing sector by the mid-1980s, the finance companies 24 percent, and IFCT the rest. Although the share of the IFCT was modest, it was the only one that offered extensive term-financing on a project basis. It was a private institution, but its mandate was to grant loans for projects having a low financial rate of return, which were unacceptable to commercial banks but were important to the economy as a whole. Such loans were possible because of the government guaranty for liquidity assistance to small borrowers and soft-term loans. The activities of the IFCT were hampered, however, by its being limited to fixed assets financing and by the lengthy project-evaluation procedure.

Finance companies tended to deal with smaller borrowers than did commercial banks in their lending to manufacturing firms because they were allowed to charge higher rates to offset the higher

Umbrella-painting cottage industry in Chiang Mai
Courtesy United Nations

risk associated with smaller borrowers. Yet, because of the limited regional spread of their branch networks and their limited resources, they could not fill all the gaps left by commercial banks, such as the supply of long-term loans.

Commercial banks provided the widest range of services. Besides credit, they offered checking services, short-term trade credits, guarantees for third-party borrowing, foreign exchange services, and letters of credit. The breakdown of bank loan portfolios showed 19 percent for discount of trade bills, 58 percent for overdrafts, and 23 percent for loans. Because discounting and overdrafts were short-term activities, the 23-percent share for loans meant that long-term financing was scarce relative to short-term financing. Because fixed assets such as land and buildings represented the preferred collateral for banks, smaller borrowers with fewer fixed assets tended to be limited in their access to loans. Once a borrower had pledged its assets to banks for short-term financing, it could not use the assets for collateral with another institution, such as the IFCT, for long-term loans.

Monetary Policies

Monetary policy was traditionally passive. Control over the rate of credit extension was the primary means for supporting growth, maintaining price stability, and monitoring the balance of payments. Interest rates were allowed to adjust to the rate of credit expansion and were very much affected by international rates as a result of the Thai open economy. Low returns tended to discourage private savings and encourage high demand for consumer goods.

Domestic prices also were largely determined by world price movements as a result of the country's open economy and minimal domestic price controls. In fact the oil price increases in the early 1970s caused inflation to rise from 4.8 percent in 1972 to 24.3 percent in 1974. The deceleration of world prices in the early 1980s caused domestic inflation to decline from 13 percent in 1981 to 5 percent in 1982. Measuring by the price indexes, with 1972 as a base of 100, price increase was less for agricultural products, going from 130.2 in 1973 to 227.7 in 1983 compared with 115.7 to 276.3 for nonagricultural products. The highest increase among agricultural goods was for forest products, which went from 122.9 to 403.2 during the same period. Among nonagricultural goods, mining and quarrying showed the highest increases. The consumer price index, taking 1976 as the base of 100, showed the highest increase in transportation prices with 231.2 in 1982, while the rest of the consumption basket had an increase of about 180 between 1976 and 1982. The Bangkok metropolitan area had the highest increase with 194 in 1983, compared with 188.4 for the Northeast region, 181.6 for the Center, 180 for the North, and 178.4 for the South (these being Thailand's four geographic regions).

Employment and Wages

The average annual rate of employment growth in the 1970s was 2.7 percent, compared with 2.9 percent in labor force growth caused by rapid population growth in the 1950s and 1960s. As a result, unemployment reached 1.7 million in 1985, which corresponded to an unemployment rate of around 6.3 percent. Agriculture was the major employer with about 69 percent of total employment in the mid-1980s, a decline from 84 percent in 1960. Between 1970 and 1983 manufacturing increased its share of the total employed labor force from 4.1 percent to 7.4 percent. Commerce increased from 1.6 percent to 8.7 percent, and services from 7 percent to 10 percent during the same period.

The work force had gone through some structural changes in terms of age and sex. The fastest growing age-group in the 1960s was eleven- to fourteen-year-olds. In the 1980s, that age-group dropped as a result of a falling birth rate in the early 1970s and increasing primary and secondary school enrollment. By the mid-1980s, the fastest growing group in the work force was aged between twenty and thirty, with increasing participation by females. The proportion of women employed went from 66 percent in 1971 to around 70 percent by the mid-1980s. Female employment was highest in commerce with 54 percent in 1979, followed by 50 percent in agriculture, 43 percent in industries, and 36 percent in services.

In terms of regional distribution, the North had the lowest rate of labor force growth, with 3 percent between 1971 and 1985, followed by the Northeast, with 3.3 percent as a result of limited job opportunities and migration. Bangkok had the highest labor force growth with 6.9 percent. Regional growth of the labor force depended partly on the level of education. An increasing (although still small) number of new entrants in the work force had received a higher education. In 1971 the percentage of the total labor force that had an elementary education was 90.2. This figure declined to 72.6 percent in 1985. For people with lower and upper secondary education, the share went from 4.8 percent to 10.4 percent during the same period. The percentage of the labor force with vocational training jumped from 1.9 percent to 10.4 percent between 1971 and 1985. Yet unemployment in Thailand for those with a college or vocational education rose from 8.4 to 9 percent by the mid-1980s, mostly because of an average increase of 13.7 percent per year in the educated work force between 1977 and 1985.

The real wage rate between 1978 and 1985 remained the same for most of the country, but in some regions, such as the North, it dropped from B1.81 per hour to B1.66 (for value of the baht—B—see Glossary). Only in Bangkok did wages increase—from B3.64 to B4.20—during the period. Real wages were stagnant because minimum wage adjustments were not always closely linked to inflation rates, and compliance with the minimum wage laws was not observed by the various sectors of the economy and regions of the country. Minimum wage laws were first introduced in April 1973 after the legalization of unions in 1972. At the outset, the laws covered only Bangkok. They were subsequently applied to the entire country, which was divided into three regions with three different scales for various types of activities; agriculture and government administration were exempted. By 1982 minimum wages in Bangkok had been raised by 100 percent; those in other regions had been raised by 50 to 70 percent.

International Trade and Finance

International Trade

Thailand sustained a trade balance deficit from the early 1970s to the mid-1980s. Although the trade balance had improved during the first part of the 1970s, it worsened after the oil shocks of 1973 and 1979. In fact the net value of oil imports went from US$52.5 million in 1970 to US$684.7 million in 1982, with dependence on foreign oil reaching 75 percent in 1980 and declining to 50 percent by 1985. Although there was a general decline in the export performance of developing countries in the early 1980s, Thailand's recovery from the oil shock was further delayed by a loss in export competitiveness, a slowdown in the economies of major trading partners, and a growing debt service obligation resulting in part from rising interest rates. The current account balance deficits were not as severe as the trade deficits as a result of improving service balances. By 1986 the balance of payments had moved into surplus on current account (see table 7, Appendix). The major contribution to the service balance surplus was tourism, which increased from 630,000 tourists in 1970 to 2.6 million in 1986. Tourism was the top foreign exchange earner from 1981 to 1986. The trade deficit was caused in part by a decreasing growth rate of exports between 1980 and 1983, which improved slightly by 1985. The growth rate of imports also declined, but at a slower rate. Despite an increase in tourism, the trade deficit reached a peak in 1983 of US$3.9 billion. In 1985 exports totaled US$7.1 billion and imports US$9.2 billion, leaving an unfavorable trade balance of US$2.1 billion. By 1986 the deficit had decreased even further, with some of the reduction a result of the lower cost of imported oil.

The composition or structure of merchandise exports changed substantially between 1965 and 1985. Primary commodities accounted for 95 percent of Thailand's exports in 1965, and manufactured exports accounted for only 4 percent. By 1986 manufactured products comprised 55 percent of total exports, with textile products increasing from less than 1 percent in 1965 to 13 percent by 1986 (see table 8, Appendix). Other major manufacturing exports in the mid-1980s included rubber products, processed foods, integrated circuits, metal products, jewelry, footwear, and furniture. Although agricultural exports as a percentage of total exports declined during this period, rice and other agricultural exports remained important for the Thai economy. By the mid-1980s, rice took the highest share of total agricultural exports. Cassava products, maize, sugar, rubber, fruit, and marine products were the other main exports in this category.

Between 1965 and 1985, the destinations of merchandise exports shifted from 54 percent of 1965 exports destined for developing countries to 56 percent of 1985 exports going to industrialized countries. This increase in the percentage of exports to industrialized countries, in combination with the changing structure of merchandise exports from predominantly agricultural to manufactured products, has fueled Thailand's economic growth (see table 9, Appendix). Thailand's major industrialized trading partners included the EEC, the United States, Japan, and the Netherlands. Furthermore, Thailand has developed significant trade relations with the newly industrializing countries (NICs) of Singapore, Hong Kong, the Republic of Korea (South Korea), and Taiwan. Additionally, Thailand has developed trade relations with Malaysia, the Philippines, Indonesia, and China (see table 10, Appendix).

Tariff barriers on imports from the developing countries had dropped with the implementation of the Tokyo Round (1973–79) of the General Agreement on Tariffs and Trade (GATT—see Glossary). Rising nontariff barriers, resulting from domestic and international economic conditions in industrial countries, had more than offset the tariff reductions. In the United States the proportion of imports subject to such barriers more than doubled, and in the other industrial countries it rose by as much as 40 percent. Examples of nontariff barriers were quotas, voluntary exports restraints, the Multifiber Arrangements, sanitation rules, and subsidies.

Thai rice exports encountered the stiffest barriers in Japan, where the tariff rate was 15 percent and a global quota was in force. In the United States, tariff on rice was only 2.6 percent, and no explicit nontariff barriers existed except for stringent controls by the United States Food and Drug Administration. In the other industrialized countries, Thai rice exports faced varying levies. Thai agricultural exports to the developing countries met with stiff competition from subsidized United States cereal exports. Thailand entered into a voluntary export restraint with France for its cassava exports because of strong resistance to imports from the French producers of cereal-based animal feed. Rubber did not face major barriers except for quotas imposed by Japan. Maize exports did relatively poorly because of subsidized production and high tariffs in the industrialized countries. Sugar exports also faced subsidy problems in Western Europe and a 50 percent quota reduction by the United States. Despite nontariff barriers, Thai agricultural and manufactured exports faced less protectionism than the NICs in the early 1980s.

Of Thailand's manufactured exports, textiles were most affected by barriers because Thailand had to enter into bilateral agreements with industrial countries, which were similar to the voluntary export restraints under the Multifiber Arrangements. In addition, tariffs escalated with the degree of processing. For example, in the United States the average tariff for cotton fabrics was 9.6 percent, whereas

135

Phuket, a popular tourist destination in southern Thailand
Courtesy Thai Airways International

it was 18 percent for garments. The United States imposed coun-
tervailing duties on Thai textile exports in protest against Thai
government subsidies to textile exporters in the form of export pack-
ing credits, rediscount facilities for industrial bills, electricity dis-
counts, and tax certificates.

Tariffs in Thailand before the 1970s were primarily used to generate revenues rather than to influence domestic production. The rates
ranged from 15 to 30 percent, with higher rates applied to finished
consumer goods imports. In the 1970s, however, tariff rates on
finished consumer goods imports increased 30 to 50 percent. Rising protectionism continued in the late 1970s and early 1980s, with
high tariff rates and the application of surcharges, quantitative
restrictions, price controls, and domestic contents requirements (see
table 11, Appendix).

External Debt

The Thai total long-term public and private debt grew from
US$728 million in 1970 to US$13.3 billion in 1985. The external
debt was increasing at a faster rate during this period than the growing gross national product (GNP—see Glossary). In 1970 the
external debt was 11.1 percent of GNP, increasing to 36 percent
of GNP by 1985. The ratio of debt payments or debt service to
the total export of goods and services, one indicator of Thailand's
ability to meet debt payments, increased from 14 percent in 1970
to 25.4 percent in 1985. The growth of external indebtedness averaged 25.2 percent between 1970 and 1980, compared with an average of 21 percent for Southeast and East Asian middle-income
oil-importer countries. Public debt as a percentage of exports went
from 47.9 percent to 75.9 percent between 1980 and 1983, but the
proportion of public borrowing from foreign sources dropped from
52 percent to 42 percent during the same period. This was indica-
tive of the growing concern of the public sector with the enlarged
foreign debt and hence a higher reliance on domestic borrowing,
which went from 48 percent to 55 percent during the same period.
In the early 1980s, Thailand was characterized by high competition between the government and the private sector for scarce
domestic savings, which forced private firms to rely more on external borrowing.

The composition of Thai indebtedness in terms of interest rates,
maturity, and currency structure appeared to be better than that
in most other developing countries. Because of its high credit rat-
ing, Thailand could borrow at about 8.4 percent in late 1983, compared with an average rate of 10.1 percent for other middle-income
oil-importer countries. It had also the longest loan average maturity, 17.2 years compared with 12.2 years.

In terms of currency denomination, the Thai external debt consisted mostly of two currencies: the United States dollar and the Japanese yen, with increasing reliance on the yen because of the willingness of Japanese banks to lend at a lower spread than the other banks. Thailand was exposed to the risk of yen appreciation in the early 1980s because Japan received only 14 percent of Thai exports while accounting for 26 percent of imports. Meanwhile, the value of the yen had appreciated substantially relative to the baht. The baht was pegged to the United States dollar until 1984 when it had a fixed exchange rate of B23 per US$1. Thereafter, the baht was pegged to a basket of currencies and devalued by 14.8 percent against the dollar. According to some observers, Thailand needed to revise its external debt portfolio as well as limit its reliance on external debt.

Industry

The industrial sector in Thailand contributed considerably to economic growth during the 1970s and 1980s. As a percentage of GDP, industry accounted for an average of 25.7 percent in the 1970s and about 29 percent in the mid-1980s. The average annual growth rate was 9.3 percent for the 1970s, with a slowdown to 6.7 percent in 1985, which was still very respectable by international standards. Manufacturing constituted the most important industrial subsector, providing an average of 17.9 percent of GDP in the 1970s and about 19.8 percent in the mid-1980s. Construction accounted for an average of 4.8 percent of GDP during the 1970s and rose to 5.1 by the mid-1980s. Mining and quarrying represented an average of 1.8 percent of GDP in the 1970s and remained fairly constant. The annual growth rate was the highest for the public utilities industrial subsector in the 1970s and mid-1980s, 13.1 percent and 8.8 percent, respectively. The annual growth rate for manufacturing dropped from an average of 10.1 percent in the 1970s to 7.3 percent in 1985. A decline in the growth rate of mining and construction occurred during the same period.

Manufacturing

Manufacturing was the most important industrial subsector in Thailand, comprising on average 25 percent of each addition to GDP (incremental GDP), or 70 percent of all industrial value added during the 1970s and mid-1980s. Manufacturing was characterized by a high reliance on agricultural products, including rubber products, textile products, food processing, beverages, and tobacco. Thailand's food and agriculture share of manufacturing value added was about 36 percent by the mid-1980s, compared with 20 percent for South Korea and 22 percent for Malaysia. The next most important area of manufacturing was textiles, clothing, and leather products, produced mainly for export, with 23 percent of manufacturing value added. Machinery and transport equipment, which consisted mostly of repair and assembly of motor vehicles, accounted for 11 percent, and chemicals accounted for 7 percent. The remaining 23 percent included processed minerals, wood, rubber, carpets, batteries, rope, gunnysacks, plastic goods, tires, footwear, and an expanding domestic small arms production.

The composition of Thai foreign trade reflected the manufacturing sector of the Thai economy. Exports of processed food, leather, wood, rubber, and basic metals represented a considerable share of manufacturing output. The capital and intermediate goods industries were less developed, however, necessitating high levels of imports of those products. Exports of manufactured goods grew from 5.5 percent of total exports in the 1970s to about 30 percent by the mid-1980s. Textiles and garments were the most important contributors in the 1970s, accounting for almost half of the total manufactured exports, but by the mid-1980s they had dropped to about 13 percent because of rising foreign protectionism of textiles. Exports of manufactured goods that grew rapidly during this period were wood products, nonmetallic minerals, electronics, electrical machinery, jewelry, and precious stones.

Employment in the manufacturing subsector accounted for 7.9 percent of total employment by the mid-1980s and had absorbed over 16 percent of labor force growth during the 1970s. Textile, apparel, and leather firms had the highest share of manufacturing employment, with 25.8 percent in the early 1980s, followed by processed food, beverage, and tobacco firms, which accounted for 19.9 percent. Furniture and other wood products firms accounted for 15.8 percent of manufacturing employment; minerals, metals, and metal products, 12.6 percent; transportation equipment, 8.5 percent; and other manufacturing firms accounted for the remaining 17.4 percent. The growth in manufacturing employment resulted both from the absolute growth of the subsector itself and from the labor intensiveness of such industries as textiles. Small-scale firms with fewer than 10 workers employed 50 percent more workers at the beginning of the 1980s than all larger firms. However, both groups had the same average annual growth rate of around 10 percent in the 1970s.

Manufacturing was heavily concentrated in the Bangkok metropolitan area, as indicated by its share of 35.3 percent of total manufacturing employment. The next highest area of concentration was in the Center. Industries outside Bangkok were based primarily on the processing of agricultural products, such as rubber, sugar, cassava, and rice, or on the repair of agricultural implements. Bangkok's role as the manufacturing center resulted from its position as the leading port, the largest market, and the transportation, communications, and financial center of the country.

State-owned manufacturing firms produced tobacco, playing cards, liquor, marble, jute, sugar, paper, textiles, leather goods, glass, batteries, and pharmaceutical products. Each state enterprise was required to submit an annual operational and investment budget to be approved by its board of directors, its parent ministry, the Bureau of the Budget, and the National Economic and Social Development Board under the Office of the Prime Minister. Each firm had on its board of directors between nine and eleven members, all of whom were appointed by the parent ministry. The board was responsible for setting prices with the approval of the parent ministry. State enterprises were more unionized and more powerful than private firms and often had salaries 50 percent higher than those in the civil service and in some private firms. They also offered higher fringe benefits, bonuses, and overtime pay. Planning for privatization of some unprofitable state-owned manufacturing firms was under way in the mid-1980s, but the government faced labor opposition and other difficulties in selling these firms.

Foreign enterprises accounted for about 30 percent of capital investment in the form of joint ventures with some twenty foreign countries. Japan provided more than one-third of total foreign investment, the United States more than one-seventh, and Taiwan less than one-eighth. The general attitude of the people toward foreign firms was favorable until the early 1970s. At that time, world commodities prices collapsed, causing hardship in the country. This collapse was popularly perceived as resulting from foreign involvement in the economy. Students and liberal elements demanded that contracts with foreign enterprises be reexamined and renegotiated. To placate these groups, the government revoked the extensive offshore concession of the foreign-owned Thailand Exploration and Mining Company (TEMCO).

In the late 1980s, Thailand was considering large-scale industrial development plans, such as the Eastern Seaboard Development Program, which included deep-sea port facilities, a natural gas-based petrochemical complex, a soda ash project, a fertilizer plant, and an integrated steel complex. The petrochemical industries complex was to be developed southeast of Bangkok and was to include a plant to process ethane and propane into ethylene and propylene. It was to be a public and private joint-venture project costing an estimated US$600 million.

The site of the Eastern Seaboard Development Program was to be a major center for industrial development that would extend from east of Bangkok toward the Cambodian border. The site was chosen because of its proximity to Bangkok, access to raw materials and labor supplies from the Northeast, availability of an existing deep-sea port on the Gulf of Thailand, and excellent road and communications infrastructure. One objective of the program was to decentralize economic activities away from Bangkok. The other goals were the development of a wide range of industries, including agro-industries, around Si Racha-Laem Chabang and the development of tourism in and around Pattaya, a popular beach resort area. The total capital requirement for the project was estimated at US$4.5 billion: about 66 percent for heavy industrial development; about 20 percent for infrastructure; 7 percent for housing, industrial estates, and urban services; and the remainder for light industries.

Industrial Policy

The Thai industrial sector was under the supervision of seven governmental agencies. The Ministry of Finance administered taxes and duties and provided tax refunds on exports. It was involved in large-scale industrial projects in the role of deciding on government equity participation, arranging public foreign borrowing to support the project, and extending protection through tariffs. The Board of Investment provided investment incentives, and the Ministry of Commerce controlled prices and international trade. The Ministry of Industry issued factory licenses, drew up industrial regulations, and enforced zoning laws. It also provided technical assistance, management training, and financing for small- and medium-sized enterprises. The Industrial Finance Corporation of Thailand lent long-term funds to medium- and large-scale firms from credit given by the government. The Bank of Thailand provided foreign exchange and rediscount facilities to selected industries and exporters at concessionary terms. Finally, the National Economic and Social Development Board established policy guidelines and targets for the industrial sector. In 1982 the Industrial Restructuring Committee was created to coordinate the various agencies and to formulate detailed policy proposals in line with economic development plans.

Import tariffs were the most important protective measure used for the industrial sector. In the 1960s, the nominal tariff rates were low, ranging from 25 to 30 percent. In the 1970s, the rate went up to a range of 30 to 55 percent for consumer goods. By the end of 1978, nine import categories had tariff rates above 90 percent,

including alcoholic beverages, shoes, perfume, cosmetics, and automobiles. In the early 1980s, the government attempted a more uniform tariff structure and lower protectionism in conformity with the Fifth Economic Development Plan. The adjustments included a reduction in tariffs to 60 percent on 270 categories of imported commodities; a change in tariffs to 30 percent for 1,970 items; and an increase in rate to 5 percent for those nonessential items that had been exempted. Goods considered essential, such as milk for infants or fibers used in textiles, remained exempted.

Other protective measures included price controls, which were quite pervasive in the 1970s but were relaxed at the beginning of the 1980s, except on petroleum products, white sugar, and sweetened condensed milk. Quantitative restrictions on imports were increased in the early 1980s to cover forty-six products. Regulations requiring a certain percentage of domestic content in manufactured imports included 30 to 40 percent for commercial vehicles, 45 percent for automobiles, and 70 percent for motorcycles.

In order to encourage investment, the Board of Investment provided incentives, such as guarantees against nationalization and price controls, tax exemptions of up to 8 years, and tariff surcharges of up to 50 percent to protect against competing imports. The basic objectives of the board were to promote labor-intensive industries, exports, and regional decentralization of industry.

Agriculture

Much of the impressive economic growth recorded by Thailand in the 1970s and the early 1980s was owed to the steady expansion of the agricultural sector. This sector provided adequate food for the rapidly growing population and produced substantial surpluses of some commodities for export.

The Thai farmer's ability to adapt to changing market conditions contributed to the country's agricultural success, but even more important was the availability of large areas of virgin land for cultivation. Between 1950 and 1980, agricultural holdings nearly doubled to an estimated 22 million hectares, of which about three-quarters were farmed annually, and much of the rapidly growing population was absorbed in the expansion. By the early 1980s, however, most of the arable land had been occupied, except in the South, and continued growth of the agricultural sector became increasingly dependent on the acceptance of new technologies and the adoption of more intensive cultivation. Observers feared that without these changes growing domestic demand—both from increasing population and from rising expectations—would seriously affect the nation's balance of payments position through the reduction of exportable surpluses of vital major foreign exchange earners, such as rice and sugar.

Agriculture—crops, livestock, forestry, and fisheries—employed about three-quarters of the labor force, and it was estimated that some four-fifths of the total population was dependent on the sector for its livelihood. During the mid-1980s, agriculture accounted for an average of about 25 percent of GDP, and agricultural commodities accounted annually for over 60 percent of the value of all exports.

The type of agriculture engaged in—whether cash crop, subsistence, or a combination thereof—varied from region to region and within regions. In the central plain, there were farmers whose sole activity was the raising of such cash crops as maize, sugarcane, vegetables, and fruit. In the rice bowl region of the central plain, farmers grew rice for sale as a main crop. Elsewhere, rice was raised basically for subsistence purposes, but many farmers also cultivated secondary crops for the market. In areas without developed access roads and services, such as parts of the upper Northeast, participation in the market economy was limited. Farmers in these areas practiced subsistence cultivation, selling only an occasional surplus locally.

Farmers in Chiang Mai Province, northern Thailand
Courtesy World Bank

Agriculture was dominated by smallholders, most of whom had either outright title to the land or effective possession of it; tenancy was significant only in parts of the central plain. In the early 1980s, the average holding for the whole country was about 5.6 hectares, but considerable size differences existed within different regions and locales that related in part to terrain, soils, rainfall, and other natural factors. In the North, where nearly a quarter of the nation's more than 4.5 million agricultural households were located (1983 estimate), over half the land is mountainous. In the upper part of the region, which is characterized by narrow valleys, average holdings were only about 2.2 hectares. In the parts of this upper area that had controlled irrigation, the typical farm only had slightly more than one hectare. A farm on nonirrigated land consisted of about two hectares, part of which was rain-fed paddy and part upland. The lower part of the region had areas similar to those in the central plain. Farms were considerably larger, the typical one having close to five hectares. Both paddy and upland crops were grown, and maize had become an important secondary cash crop for many farmers (see table 12, Appendix).

In the Northeast, the generally infertile soil required larger holdings to meet subsistence needs. Over half the farms had between 2.4 and 7.2 hectares, and the typical farm had an area of about 4 hectares. In the early 1980s, about 40 percent of the country's agricultural households lived in this region. Holdings in the Center, which contained about 20 percent of the nation's agricultural households, varied considerably. Near Bangkok small farms producing market vegetables might have little more than half a hectare, whereas commercial rice farms outside the city averaged over ten hectares. The typical commercial rice holding on the central plain, however, averaged somewhat over three hectares, and all available land was under cultivation. In the upland to the east of the plain, where maize was grown commercially, the typical farm size was close to 6.5 hectares. Cassava was also grown in this area on somewhat smaller farms, typically of about five hectares. West of the plain, the uplands were devoted in part to sugarcane grown on holdings usually of about three hectares. In the South, the rugged terrain made about two-fifths of the region unsuitable for agriculture. The climate, however, favored the cultivation of rubber trees, and the majority of farms grew rubber as a cash crop along with subsistence rice. A typical household had about three hectares: 1.5 hectares of rubber trees, small areas of coconut or fruit trees, and the rest planted in rice. In the three southernmost provinces holdings were smaller, averaging about two hectares.

Land Use and Soils

Roughly two-fifths of Thailand is covered by mountains and hills, the steepness of which generally precludes cultivation. Nevertheless, perhaps as much as a tenth of this area might also be converted to agricultural purposes once detailed information was obtained through surveys. Estimates in the 1970s of overall land-use suitability classified roughly 58 percent of mountainous and hilly regions as cultivable (compared with 24 percent 2 decades earlier), of which about 19 percent was usable for paddy, 28 percent for upland crops, and 11 percent for both paddy and upland agriculture. Actual holdings of agricultural land—not all of which was under cultivation at any one time—were estimated in the mid-1970s to occupy about 43 percent of the total land area.

Soils throughout most of the country are of low fertility, largely as a result of leaching by heavy rainfall. Differences between the various soil types are the result of differences in parent rock material, variations in the amount of rainfall, length of wet and dry seasons, type of vegetable cover, and other natural factors. In general, stony and shallow soils characterize the hill and mountain terrain of the North.

Large portions of this mountainous area were traditionally used by hill peoples for shifting cultivation (see Glossary). The Lua (also called Lawa) and Karen cultivated for short periods, then permitted the land to lie fallow for long periods, which allowed forest regrowth and restoration of soil fertility (see The Non-Tai Minorities, ch. 2). As a result of population pressures, however, other groups sometimes failed to follow this practice. The principle crop of many hill peoples was upland rice; maize was an important secondary crop. The Hmong, Lisu, and certain other hill peoples cultivated the opium poppy as a cash crop, but this activity had important implications for internal stability as well as major international repercussions (see Criminal Activity and the Narcotics Trade, ch. 5). Thai authorities, with substantial international assistance, increased efforts in the 1980s to redirect these people to other cash crops, including tobacco and coffee.

Many inhabitants of the lowlands in the North also practiced shifting cultivation in hill areas lying not far above the valleys. The valleys usually had better soils, some of fairly high or moderate fertility, which were used mainly to grow irrigated rice. In places where population pressures had developed, the higher areas were often turned to shifting cultivation to supplement lowland production. The principal crop was usually upland rice, although other crops were also grown.

Shallow sandy loams cover a large part of the Khorat Plateau. Their generally low fertility partly explains the lower economic level of the region. Soils along the main rivers are more fertile, and alluvial loams of high fertility are found along the Mekong River. Lowland soils covering about a fifth of the Northeast (some 3.5 million hectares) had been converted to rice paddy.

The central plain rice-growing area and the delta of the Mae Nam (river) Chao Phraya has clayey soils of high to moderate fertility. Low-lying and flat, much of the area is flooded during the rainy season. Higher areas on the edges of the plain are generally well-drained soils of high to moderate fertility that are suitable for intensive cultivation. These lands are used extensively for maize and sugarcane. Among other highly useful soils are the well-drained clayey and loamy soils in parts of the peninsula where rubber is grown.

Land Tenure

Traditionally, the king owned all the land, from which he made grants to nobles, officials, and other free subjects. If left uncultivated for three years, the land could be taken back by the crown, but otherwise it could be passed on to heirs or mortgaged or sold. At the same time, there was abundant unoccupied cultivable land that by tradition and custom could be cleared and used by a farmer, who after three years of continuous cultivation established informal rights. The concept of individual ownership of the land was introduced during the reign of King Chulalongkorn (Rama V, 1868–1910), and beginning in 1901 formal title could be acquired.

The titling of land in the mid-1980s was based on a land code promulgated in 1954. The 1954 code established eight hectares as the maximum permissible holding except where the owner could manage a larger holding by himself. This limitation was generally ignored, however, and was rescinded four years later. A title deed (*chanod tidin*) giving unrestricted ownership rights ordinarily was issued only after a cadastral survey. At least two prior steps were required before the prospective landholder could obtain a full title deed. Application was first made to occupy and cultivate a piece of unused land, and a temporary occupancy permit (*bai chong*— reserve license) that carried no title rights was received. After 75 percent of the land had been cultivated, the landholder could secure an exploitation testimonial (*nor sor*). This gave him the right to occupy the land permanently and to pass the property on to heirs; in effect it was an assurance that a title deed eventually would be forthcoming. Transferring the land through sale, however, was extremely difficult, and the exploitation testimonial was not usually accepted by banks as collateral. In the case of squatters, a special occupancy permit (*sor kor*) could also be obtained, unless the land was in a permanent reserved forest or was intended for public use. Satisfactory development could then lead to the issuance of an exploitation testimonial and ultimately a full title deed.

The issuance of title deeds, which proceeded at a relatively slow pace in the early 1950s, quickened somewhat during the remainder of the decade. By 1960 the total number of title deeds for agricultural land had reached 1 million, although there were 3.4 million agricultural households (this total included an unknown number of tenants' households). The pressure for titles of various kinds increased during the 1960s and 1970s as the number of farm holdings expanded rapidly. In an effort to expedite the processing of title deeds, the Department of Land of the Ministry of Interior resorted in the 1970s to the use of aerial photography in lieu of land surveys.

In the 1980s, a substantial component of the nation's dominant smallholder group nevertheless lacked full title to the land it worked. By 1982 the total number of title deeds was 3.9 million. A 1976 estimate placed the proportion of farm holdings having formal title at about 60 percent. The lack of full title by the remaining 40 percent created not only a sense of insecurity for the landholder but also presented a barrier to securing needed credit.

A major question in the mid-1980s concerned the legalization of farm holdings outside recognized areas for land acquisition. An unknown but substantial number of holdings had been established by squatters—many of them hill people—in the reserve forests, which, according to the central government, were not eligible for titling, although the de facto possession of such holdings was recognized by local authorities. Observers pointed out that in many cases of forest encroachment the occupied land was incorrectly classified and in fact was suitable for cultivation (some reclassification was reported in the late 1970s). It also appeared that in the drafting of the country's land laws there was an underlying assumption that agricultural land meant the lowlands; in other words, the land in mountainous and hill areas was considered nonagricultural. Thus, a large part of the North was not even included in the land registration system, and the hill peoples of the region were therefore unable to acquire legal title to the land they used.

Tenancy and Land Reform

Historically, agricultural tenancy nationwide appeared to have been low except in the commercial rice-growing areas of the central plain and in the North. This situation was the result of land reforms instituted by King Chulalongkorn beginning in 1874, the great availability of free land, the absence of population pressures, and the relatively small amount of funds required by the individual farmer to start cultivating rice. Together with customary practices that tended to limit the amount of cultivable land that could be claimed, these factors resulted in a national pattern of small independent farms. Of great significance to this development was the law that the farmer had to cultivate his own land; if it was more than he or his family could handle, the farmer had to supervise cultivation of the excess. Four hectares were considered the maximum tillable by one family, although with hired help up to about eight hectares could be managed, the amount varying with soil differences and climatic conditions.

Nineteenth-century legislation set a four-hectare limit on freely acquirable agricultural land and acted as a major deterrent to the accumulation of land into large estates. Nevertheless, large holdings did exist as grants to nobles and officials under the *sakdi na* (see Glossary) system (see Social and Political Development, ch. 1). Chulalongkorn's reforms played an important part in the breakup of at least some large estates. In such cases the law provided that the uncultivated land would revert to the state after a period of three years. In the area around the capital, however, where many larger holdings were located, land could be rented out, and the landholdings therefore remained intact.

Statistical data on tenancy in the mid-twentieth century varied considerably. A problem of classification concerning whether the fairly numerous part owner-part tenant arrangements should be included with owners or tenants also led to different conclusions. The part owner-part tenant group consisted largely of farmers who owned small plots but also worked as tenants on other larger farms.

In some areas, 95 percent of the farmers were reported to be deeply in debt. According to the government censuses of agriculture in 1950 and 1963, the rates of full tenancy for the country as a whole were 6.6 percent and 4.1 percent, respectively. Rates varied significantly by region. In 1963 the rate in the Center, the chief agricultural area containing the rice-growing central plain, was 10.7 percent as compared with 1.1 percent in the North. A special 1967–68 survey of the Center determined the full tenancy rate to be 22.5 percent (part owners-part tenants constituted an additional 15.8 percent). A 1973–74 survey of the Center, as well as other regions, showed the full-tenancy rate in the Center to be 12 percent (part owners-part tenants constituted another 28 percent). The remainder were full owners. Tenancy in the Center in areas devoted completely to commercialized agriculture was very high, however, especially in some districts near Bangkok where as many as 75 to 85 percent of the farmers were reported in the mid-1970s to be full tenants. Lower, but still comparatively high, rates of tenancy were also found in certain other districts of the plain.

The unusually high tenancy rates were attributed to several factors, including the proximity to Bangkok of estates that were granted to the ancestors of present-day holders under the *sakdi na* system; large holdings received as remuneration for the digging of canals; and, since the 1950s, acquisition of land as investment by individuals residing mostly in Bangkok. Figures published in 1975 covering 4 provinces in the Bangkok area cited 119 estates ranging in size from 160 hectares to 1,600 hectares and comprising a total of more than 60,000 hectares. Another factor contributing to tenancy in the central plain was the loss of holdings to creditors by farmers unable to repay loans. A large proportion of the small leaseholds was reported to be owned by storekeepers, local craftsmen, and other farmers.

The 1973–74 agricultural survey also provided data on tenancy in other regions. In the North, the survey found that 4 percent of the farmer operators were full tenants, 25 percent were part owners-part tenants, and 69 percent were full owners. The southeastern provinces of the North, where conditions resemble

Rice harvesting
in northern Thailand
Courtesy World Bank

Coffee cultivation
in northern Thailand
Courtesy World Bank

those of the central plain, reportedly had a higher percentage of farmers renting some or all of their land. In the Northeast, full tenants constituted only a negligible proportion; 89 percent of farm operators were full owners, and 8 percent were part owners-part tenants.

In the South, full tenants likewise were only a very small minority; 83 percent were full owners, and 16 percent were part owners-part tenants. One reason given for the development of the part owner-part tenant situation was the effect of Islamic inheritance laws, which in theory divide the land equally among the children. In such cases, the inherited holding might be inadequate to meet family needs, and supplementary land would be rented. The part owned-part rented condition was not in itself detrimental. There appeared to be many cases in which additional land was rented solely because the farmer family believed it would benefit financially by cultivating it.

Unrest among tenants, who constituted a substantial portion of the nation's poorer farmers, began to manifest itself in the early 1970s. Tenant discontent centered chiefly on the amount of rent, but also of great concern was the fact that use of the land was often based on a verbal agreement that rarely exceeded one year and carried no guarantees of renewal. In 1950 a land rent-control act covering part of the central plain was passed but proved generally ineffective. The civilian cabinet that succeeded to power in October 1973 promised rent and land reform. Implementing action was not immediately forthcoming, however, and farmer dissatisfaction mounted, finally erupting in demonstrations in May and June 1974. In December of that year, the government passed a rent reform law known as the Agricultural Land Rent Control Act of 1974, providing for six-year, indefinitely renewable rental contracts. Rents were to be payable once a year only, and procedures for determining the amount were specified. Moreover, if a poor harvest occurred, the rent was to be reduced, and none would be paid if the harvest were less than one-third normal.

Associated with tenancy was the equally serious problem of landless farmers, who by the early 1980s numbered an estimated 500,000 to 700,000. In January 1975, the civilian government, over strong opposition, managed to get through the National Assembly a second reform measure of potentially far-reaching effect. This was the Agricultural Land Reform Act of 1975. The legislation called for the establishment of the Agricultural Land Reform Office in the Ministry of Agriculture and Cooperatives to serve as the implementing agency. Under the act, landless and tenant farmers could be allocated up to eight hectares of land that would be paid for on a long-term installment basis. The land to be allocated was to come from purchases from private holders and from forest and crown lands. Individual landowners were required to make available to the program all but eight hectares of their holding. Under certain circumstances, larger holdings could be retained, but such holdings could be expropriated later if the provisions of the exception were not met. Payment for the private land taken was to be 25 percent in cash and the remainder in government bonds.

Implementation of land reform slowed after the coup of October 1976, which ousted the civilian government, and the act's goals were subsequently shifted. The government of Prime Minister Thanin Kraivichien, installed as head of a military regime in October 1976, announced that a land reform program covering 1.6 million hectares and taking place over a period of four years would be carried out. Prime Minister Kriangsak Chomanand, who succeeded to office in November 1977 after still another military coup, modified this goal to a more realistic one of 1.3 million hectares over five years. By early 1979, almost eighty areas throughout the country had been designated Land Reform Areas under the program. At the same time, although tenancy remained a major issue, a somewhat different concept of reform seemed to have emerged, based on the belief that the most pressing problem was to improve the situation of the large numbers of illegal squatters in the forests. The Land Reform Areas included some areas of high tenancy, but the new goal of helping forest squatters appeared easier to promote than land acquisition by the Agricultural Land Reform Office in the high-tenancy areas of the central plain. There it was strongly opposed by large landowners, including wealthy aristocrats, businessmen, and senior military officers.

The program as projected included furnishing legal titles to squatters and providing them with needed infrastructure and credit. The areas brought under the program were to be organized into self-sufficient cooperatives. Implementation of a given project was expected to take about two years, including about a year and a half to get the basic infrastructure well under way and to provide titles. The latter would permit the landholder to pass on the land to heirs but would not confer the right to sell it to private parties. The title, however, could be used as collateral for credit. According to government sources, by 1978 some 320,000 hectares consisting mainly of public land had been distributed, and another 160,000 hectares were ready to be apportioned.

Irrigation

Thai farmers traditionally relied on rain and flood water for crops, but the amount needed for rice cultivation was not always received. By the mid-1800s, a number of canals had been constructed in the central plain to carry floodwaters from the Chao Phraya, and in the latter half of the century other canals were dug. The canals did not form a controlled irrigation system, however, but simply a distribution net, and whether additional water could be made available depended on the level of the rivers. Records covering almost a hundred years to 1930 showed that in about one-third of the years water from the rivers was insufficient, resulting in considerable crop losses. In 1902 the government contracted with a Dutch expert to develop a controlled irrigation plan for the entire country but failed to take further action. Droughts in 1910 and 1911 led to renewed interest and the hiring of a British irrigation specialist. Nevertheless, the first irrigation project was not completed until 1922.

By 1938 about 440,000 hectares had been irrigated. Supply problems held up projects during World War II, but work resumed with renewed vigor in the late 1940s. By 1950 the irrigated area totaled nearly 650,000 hectares. In 1950 Thailand secured the first of a series of loans from the World Bank (see Glossary) for the construction of the vital Chainant Diversion Dam on the Chao Phraya and a number of major canals. By 1960 over 1.5 million hectares had been irrigated, almost entirely in the Center and in the North.

Systematic development of the irrigation system began with the First Economic Development Plan (1961–66) and was continued in later plans. New assistance from the World Bank included financing of the important multipurpose Phumiphon (Bhumibol) Dam (completed in 1964) on the Mae Nam Ping and the Sirikit Dam (completed in 1973) on the Mae Nam Nan. These dams, both of which have associated hydroelectric power-generating facilities, impound water at two large reservoir locations in the Chao Phraya Basin. Other World Bank-financed projects were also carried out in this basin during the 1970s, and by the end of the decade nearly 1.3 million hectares had controlled water flow in the rainy season, and about 450,000 hectares had it in the dry season.

The Chao Phraya Basin's natural features, as well as its size, made it the most important area for irrigation development. The topography and water systems of the Northeast, by contrast, were not well suited to large-scale irrigation projects (except on the Mekong River, which would involve major resettlement problems). Controlled irrigation potentially could encompass about 10 percent of the Northeast's 3.5 million hectares of paddy. Beginning in the 1960s, the Royal Irrigation Department, founded in 1904 and largely responsible for development and maintenance of the country's main irrigation systems, constructed 6 large and about 200 small dams in the region. The associated irrigation system contained design defects, and in the mid-1970s improvement was undertaken with World Bank assistance. Part of the irrigable area was receiving water in the early 1980s, but completion of necessary additional work was not anticipated before the late 1980s, at which time about 160,000 hectares would have irrigation throughout the year.

Irrigation work also began in the 1960s in the Mae Nam Mae Klong Basin, which contained nearly 400,000 irrigable hectares of paddy. Regulated wet-season irrigation was furnished during the 1970s for roughly 175,000 hectares. A multiple dam completed in the late 1970s and a distribution system under way in the 1980s was expected to provide adequate water for double cropping on over 250,000 hectares. Small irrigation projects also were started in the 1960s in the South, on the east coast where more than 500,000 of the region's 600,000 hectares of paddy were located. About 75,000 hectares had supplementary wet-season water, and work under way in the 1980s in the Mae Nam Pattani Basin was expected eventually to serve about 52,000 hectares.

Crops

Climatic and soil conditions permit the cultivation of a wide range of crops, not only tropical varieties but also many originating in semitropical and temperate zones. Until the late 1950s, however, the major emphasis in agriculture was on rice and, secondarily, on rubber, which together accounted for over half the value of all commodity exports. Other crops regularly grown included maize, cassava, potatoes, yams, beans, sugarcane, fruit, cotton, and various oilseeds, but all were supplementary and intended basically for domestic use. Historically, Thailand's independent status had kept it from being saddled with a colonial plantation economy, in which two or three principal crops were produced for world markets or for the imperial power. Agricultural production, however, had been strongly influenced by the West after the Bowring Treaty of 1855 with Britain, which resulted in crop diversification (see The Bangkok Period, 1767–1932, ch. 1). Accordingly, when new market conditions—increased world demand, higher prices, and developing domestic industry—arose during the 1960s and 1970s, Thailand's independent small farmers responded by expanding substantially the output of many secondary crops. The flexibility of the Thai farmer was evidenced by an unprecedented shift from rice production to other crops by a considerable number of households. In other cases, many farmers continued to produce rice for subsistence purposes while expanding their activities to grow market-oriented upland crops. In the mid-1980s, major export crops included not only rice and rubber but also maize, cassava, sugarcane, mung beans, tobacco, and sorghum. Other important crops in which major production increases also had been made were pineapples, peanuts, cashew nuts, soybeans, bananas, sesame, coconuts, cotton, kapok, and castor beans.

Rice

Rice, the nation's major crop, was grown by about three-quarters of all farm households in the early 1980s. Two main types were cultivated: dry, or upland, rice, grown predominantly in the North and Northeast; and wet rice, grown in irrigated fields throughout the central plain and in the South. About half the 1986 production of 19 million tons was grown in the central plain and major valleys in the North; another two-fifths was produced in the Northeast; and about 6 percent came from the South, which was a rice deficient area. Roughly 8.5 million hectares were devoted to rice production in the early 1980s, about 40 percent more than in the early 1960s. The rice yield was highest in the Center, averaging about 1.9 tons per hectare, which was about a third of the yield per hectare in Taiwan and South Korea.

Low productivity was attributed in part to longstanding government policies aimed at keeping consumer rice prices low. The so-called rice premium (in fact an export tax) and occasional quantitative export controls were claimed by opponents to have discouraged production expansion by reducing profitability. Although perhaps a valid argument for commercial rice farming, the policies probably had a minimal effect on the large number of subsistence farmers in the Northeast and North, who produced small, if any, surpluses and whose dry rice was not usually exported. Perhaps more significant was the apparent loss of paddy fertility in the North and Northeast because of poor soil management and the extension in those regions of the growth of lower yield upland rice.

Rubber

In 1901 British planters introduced rubber trees into the Malay Peninsula, where the soils and climatic conditions were highly suited to rubber cultivation. In Thailand early government restrictions on foreign investment led to development of the industry by local smallholders, usually subsistence rice farmers who were able to start rubber tree stands on the relatively abundant free land in the area. Land under rubber cultivation expanded rapidly in the 1930s, consisting mainly of smallholdings controlled by Chinese, Thai, and Thai Malays rather than large, European-owned plantations, as in other Asian countries. Thailand had about 1.6 million hectares in rubber in the mid-1970s, of which about 10 percent were located in an area along the Gulf of Thailand southeast of Bangkok. Of the 500,000 holdings in the early 1980s, about 150,000 were under 2.5 hectares in size, and another 300,000 were under 10 hectares. The remaining larger holdings were operated more as expanded smallholdings than as plantations. Production was increasing in the early 1980s and had reached about 830,000 tons in 1987. An extensive replanting program, in which old tree stock was replaced with new high-yield varieties, had reportedly been carried out in about half the planted area by the mid-1980s, significantly increasing the potential for expanded production.

Maize

Maize was believed to have been introduced by Spanish or Portuguese traders in the sixteenth century. Export interest and

Smallholder farmer
taps rubber tree
for latex
Courtesy World Bank

Rubber being
processed
for transport
Courtesy World Bank

profitability led to increased maize cultivation after World War II and the introduction of the so-called Guatemala strain in 1951. Output rose rapidly thereafter to almost 600,000 tons in 1961, over 1 million tons in 1965, and 2.3 million tons in 1971. A record 5 million tons were produced in 1985. Fertilizer use was limited, however, and there was concern that yields would gradually decline. The grain was grown throughout Thailand, but the uplands around the central plain were especially suitable. Weather conditions usually permitted commercial growers to produce two crops a year.

Cassava

Cassava, a root crop from which tapioca is made, was introduced in about 1935. The tubers may also be boiled and eaten as a vegetable or ground into flour. An important food in many tropical subsistence economies, cassava had never been significant in Thailand in the past because of the abundance of rice. Cassava developed into an important export item in the 1950s, and production continued through the 1970s and 1980s as external demand increased. Thai output of cassava root in 1984 was more than 19 million tons, second only to Brazil in world production. The main growing areas were Chon Buri and Rayong provinces, southeast of Bangkok, but substantial quantities were also grown in parts of the Northeast. In 1986 Thailand signed a 4-year tapioca trade agreement with the EEC calling for export of 21 million tons of tapioca during the 1987–91 period.

Other Crops

Sugarcane has long been widely grown. Some commercialization was reported by the mid-nineteenth century, but the crop became of major importance only after World War II. In the early 1950s, production averaged 1.6 million tons annually, and in the late 1950s self-sufficiency in sugar was attained. In 1960 Thailand became a net exporter of sugar. Rising world prices led Thailand's market-responsive farmers to expand cropped areas in the 1970s. In 1976 sugarcane production reached a record 26.1 million tons, and sugar output totaled 2.2 million tons, the latter amount being considerably in excess of international and domestic demands. Drought in 1977 greatly reduced output and seriously affected many small growers. Declining world prices after 1975, drought, and lower producer prices in 1978 led many farmers to shift to alternate crops. In 1986 about 24 million tons of sugarcane were produced.

Productivity was low compared with other major sugarcane-growing countries (about fifty-three tons of sugarcane per hectare against Taiwan's seventy tons and Indonesia's eighty tons in the mid-1970s). Introduction of new varieties and improved cultivation and cropping practices were needed to raise output levels. The principal sugarcane-growing areas were in and around Kanchanaburi Province and in Chon Buri Province in the Center. Sugarcane was also grown in the Northeast and in the North around Chiang Mai, Lampang, and Uttaradit.

Kenaf, a coarse fiber similar to jute but of somewhat lesser quality, is native to the country and has long been grown for local use in making sacks, cord, and twine. Commercial cultivation began in the Northeast in the 1950s, and production was largely concentrated in the central and eastern parts of the region in 1980. World shortages created by the Indo-Pakistani War of 1965 temporarily stimulated Thai production of jute, as did shortages resulting from the 1971 civil war in Pakistan. The recovery of jute cultivation in Bangladesh (formerly East Pakistan) and broad swings in producer prices led many Thai farmers in the late 1970s to replace kenaf with cassava, which commanded a higher return. The 1984 kenaf crop was estimated at about 200,000 tons, compared with an average annual output of over 400,000 tons in the previous decade. Increased world demand, however, was expected to encourage a revival in planting.

Tobacco, an important foreign exchange earner, had long been grown by farmers for personal and local use. Virginia flue-cured tobacco had been produced commercially since the 1930s, but export began only in 1956. Some burley and oriental (Turkish) tobacco was also grown. United Nations sanctions against Rhodesia beginning in the mid-1960s opened new markets, and production of Virginia tobacco rose from 13,700 tons in 1967 to more than 50,000 tons in 1981. About half of the commercial tobacco was grown in the North and another quarter in the Northeast. Tobacco growers were licensed, and a large number operated under the aegis of the state-owned Thai Tobacco Monopoly.

Pineapples, exported chiefly as canned fruit and juice in the early 1980s, were grown solely as a supplementary crop for local use until the first pineapple cannery was opened in 1967. A shortage of fruit led several canneries to establish large pineapple plantations (ranging up to more than 3,000 hectares—in sharp contrast to the smallholding character of most Thai agriculture), which supplied about 40 percent of cannery needs in the late 1970s. The industry grew dramatically, and by the early 1980s Thailand was one of the world's largest exporters of pineapples, producing about 1.6 million tons in 1984.

Production and export of coffee expanded rapidly after Thailand became a member of the International Coffee Organization in 1981. Exports of coffee beans, most of which were grown in the South, reached 20,600 tons in 1985.

Livestock and Poultry

Animal husbandry accounted for about 13 percent of the gross value of agricultural production in the early 1980s. Water buffalo and cattle remained the chief draft animals for cultivation, although tractors were playing an increasing role in some areas, as in the maize-growing regions of the central plain. Buffalo, predominantly of the swamp type well suited to paddy culture, were estimated at between 5.5 and 7.2 million. Able to flourish on coarse fodder and roughage indigestible by other livestock, buffalo were found in all farming areas; even very small paddy farmers usually had at least one animal. After maturing, buffalo were used as draft animals for five or six years, or until too old to work, when they were slaughtered and sold for meat. Cattle, numbering between 4.9 and 5.5 million, were used mainly for upland plowing and hauling carts. About 70 percent of all farms had cattle. Although 30 percent of farms had three or more head, there were few herds of more than 10 animals. Cattle also were slaughtered for meat once their usefulness had ended.

Pigs were an important source of meat, and there were about 5 million in the early 1980s. Most farmers raised one or two, and an estimated 150,000 families were engaged in commercial pig raising. Weather conditions were generally unsuitable for using horses except in the North, where the common variety was the so-called Yunnan pony mainly valued as a pack animal. Tame elephants remained important to the forest industry in the 1980s, especially in harvesting teak, where the use of mechanical equipment was economically prohibitive because of the wide dispersal of individual trees.

Livestock reproduction rates were low because most animals were bred only when it did not interfere with work. In addition, debilitating diseases, including foot-and-mouth disease, were endemic to all regions except the South. These diseases retarded expansion of the national herd of livestock, which was reported to be growing at only about 2.5 percent annually in the early 1980s. Shortages of meat in Bangkok in the early 1970s led to student demonstrations and the establishment of export quotas in early 1974 (in early 1979 the quotas were 35,000 head of cattle and 15,000 of buffalo annually). Several commercial dairy herds and smallholder dairy cooperatives furnished some milk for sale. Demand for fresh milk and dairy products had grown, especially in Bangkok.

Almost all smallholders raised some chickens and ducks for eggs and meat. The commercial production of chickens grew dramatically in the 1970s, and nearly 65,000 tons of frozen chickens were exported in 1986, of which 95 percent went to Japan. A considerable number of commercial operations had flocks of over 20,000. Select breeding stock was used, and modern operational practices were followed. Commercial duck farms were almost entirely Chinese operated.

Fisheries

In the 1980s, the fisheries sector was of major importance to the economy as an earner of foreign exchange, marine products accounting for about 10 percent of total exports in 1986. Fish also accounted for about three-fifths of the protein in the national diet and an even higher proportion among the poorer rural population. Until the early 1960s, the country had been a net importer of fish. This situation completely changed with the introduction of trawl fishing, which resulted in a dramatic rise in the marine catch from 146,000 tons in 1960 to 1 million tons in 1968 and 2.1 million tons in 1985. Thailand became the third largest marine fishing nation in Asia after Japan and China. Of Thailand's 40,000 fishing vessels, nearly 20,000 were deep-sea trawlers, many with modern communication and navigation equipment and refrigeration facilities.

By 1980 large-scale fishing operations, based largely in urban areas, were responsible for 88 percent of Thailand's annual catch. The fishing industry was the economic backbone of many Thai coastal cities. The increase in the catch of shrimp was particularly notable, and shrimp exports became a major source of foreign exchange earnings. By about 1972 maximum exploitation of demersal (bottom-dwelling) and pelagic (open-sea) fish appeared to have been reached in the Gulf of Thailand and in the Andaman Sea. In the early 1980s, production remained relatively static, and there was growing concern that these areas were being overfished.

Government control of fishing was limited. The use of certain kinds of fishing gear within three kilometers of the coast was banned, but there appeared to be no restriction on trawl net-mesh size, and undersized commercial food fish were being caught and dumped in with trash fish in the production of fishmeal. Moreover, during the 1970s neighboring Cambodia claimed territorial waters extending to 200 nautical miles from its coast. This reduced the area in the Gulf of Thailand available to Thai fishermen and increased the intensity of fishing off the coast of Thailand. Similar claims by Burma had also restricted Thai fishing in the Andaman Sea.

Inland fisheries, which included both freshwater and brackish water fish, officially reported annual catches of about 160,000 tons in the early 1980s. The actual catch—principally freshwater fish from flooded rice paddies, swamps, irrigation and drainage ditches, canals, reservoirs, rivers, lakes, and ponds—was estimated to be much higher. It was believed, however, to be declining as population growth resulted in overfishing and as increasing water pollution from industrial waste, insecticides, and siltation caused by forest destruction took its toll.

The most promising course for maintenance of fisheries production at the level attained in the 1970s, or for increasing output, was the expansion of aquaculture, including the culture of fish, shrimp, and various mollusks, such as mussels, oysters, and clams. According to the Department of Fisheries, about 4.5 million hectares of inland water areas, mostly rice paddy fields, were suitable for aquaculture. Another 1.3 million hectares, including estuaries, mangrove swamps, and tidal flats, were also usable (see table 13, Appendix).

Forestry

An aerial photographic survey conducted in 1961 showed forests to cover about 54 percent (or if swamp and scrub areas are included, 56 percent) of Thailand. In the succeeding two decades, this area was substantially reduced as a rapidly growing population pushed into the forests seeking new land for agricultural use. Increasing prices for certain upland crops, especially in the 1970s, also acted as a strong incentive for conversion of forests to cultivated lands. By the mid-1980s, the expansion of the cultivated area had resulted in a decrease in the amount of forestland to less than 30 percent.

Except for a few small, privately owned, coastal mangrove areas, all forestland was the property of the state. Roughly 32 percent of the 1961 forest area, largely in the North and Northeast, had been designated permanent reserved forest through the end of the 1960s. Government plans called for additions in subsequent years to raise the total to about 51 percent. Clearing or cutting of timber or settling in such land was possible only with an official permit. Many of the stream valleys in these reserve areas, however, were highly suitable for agricultural use. Traditionally, farmers had been able to occupy unreserved public land on a free basis, restrictions in such cases relating only to the cutting of certain timber tree species, which remained the property of the state. As population growth increased the demand for land, farmers in the 1970s

Fisherman with catch from inland waterway
Courtesy United Nations

also moved into the reserved forests with little or no effective hindrance from government agencies. This situation was generally non-reversible, and observers anticipated that eventually most such holdings suitable for cultivation would be legalized under the agricultural land reform program.

Areas of forest usable for permanent cultivation still existed in the early 1980s, mostly in the South. In other regions there were logged-over areas and scrubland (at times included with forestland), part of which could be used for agriculture. Extant forest areas—minus potentially cultivable land—were still considered sufficient to meet domestic timber and other wood requirements and also to provide a surplus of forest products for export. Foreign and Thai forestry specialists were agreed that for this situation to continue, positive steps would have to be taken, including an adequate program of reforestation, prevention of illicit cutting and the use of steep forest slopes for cultivation purposes, and active promotion of more efficient forest exploitation practices. In the early 1970s, the Food and Agriculture Organization recommended a reforestation program of 1 million hectares. The government later approved a plan to replant 120,000 hectares.

Major exploitation of the highly valuable teak wood for exportation was begun by European interests in the late 1800s, and by 1895 indiscriminate cutting had largely exhausted the more easily workable stands. About this time, the government established a system of control that included leases and cutting cycles (a teak tree takes from 80 to 150 years to mature fully, depending on local soils and weather). By 1909, when controls were further tightened, almost all of the industry was in European hands, mainly British but also Danish and French. During World War II, a Thai company took over all concessions, and although a few were returned to foreign control for a period after the war, the government's long-term goal of full Thai operation was attained in the late 1950s.

Although modern logging equipment was in widespread use, difficult terrain and lack of roads in many areas necessitated the use of elephants in logging operations. In 1982 there were 12,000 working elephants in Thailand, including those trained at the Royal Forestry Department's Young Elephant Training Center.

The exploitation of Thailand's forests was the responsibility of the Royal Forestry Department. Through the Forest Industry Organization, a state-owned enterprise, the government controlled nearly all extraction of mature teak. However, illegal felling of teak continued to be a serious problem in the 1980s, although the extent of the cutting was uncertain. A decade earlier, estimates had placed illegal cutting at from one-third to an amount greater than legal cutting. Some idea of the magnitude of the situation was evident in a 1973 report of the Royal Forestry Department, which cited some 7,600 incidents of illegal teak felling. The department was not only unable to patrol adequately all forest areas but authorities also failed to act against illegal logging operations connected with politically influential individuals and families.

Major damage to permanent forest areas also occurred, especially in the 1970s and 1980s, through occupation of hillside forestland that was not suitable for cultivation. This practice was carried on throughout the country and resulted not only in destruction of forests but also in erosion and damage to watersheds. Notable forest destruction occurred over time in the North because of shifting cultivation practiced mainly by the hill peoples of the region. Of the roughly 70 percent of this region classified as forests, well over a quarter was being used for such cultivation in the late 1960s, according to a government report. The amount grew tremendously during the 1970s as the population of the hill peoples increased. In addition, many landless Thai were reported to have migrated to the area, and others who were farming agricultural land in the valleys also were practicing shifting cultivation on the hills and mountainsides to supplement production. According to some sources, forested lands in the Northeast declined from about 60 percent in 1956 to less than 20 percent two decades later.

Although teak had been a major long-term source of foreign exchange earnings, the output by volume of timber from other commercially valuable species was far greater. Thailand had a large number of such species, of which the most commonly exported one was *yang,* related to the so-called Philippine mahoganies. Others were of great value domestically, supplying the country's general requirements for timber and wood products of various sorts. In the 1980s, however, the forests failed to meet the demand for raw materials for paper and paper products, and these were being imported in growing quantities. Only limited stands of pine existed, and development of a domestic pulp and paper industry appeared to depend on the establishment of suitable forest plantations.

Mining

Thailand's mineral reserves had not been well assessed in the 1980s. Mining and quarrying accounted for only a small share of GDP, in 1986 amounting to about 2 percent of the total in real terms. About thirty minerals were exploited commercially, but many were of minor significance. Tin, tungsten, fluorite, and precious stones were important foreign exchange earners in the early 1980s and so, to a lesser extent, was antimony. Minerals of substantial value to the domestic economy included lignite, gypsum, salt (which was also exported), iron ore, lead, manganese, limestone, and marble.

Tin was the leading mineral. The existence of tin in the area of present-day Thailand was known at least by the thirteenth century, when it was alloyed with copper in casting bronze images of the Buddha. In the 1980s, major workings were located in the southern peninsula, although deposits were also found and worked in several other parts of the country. The ore was obtained from onshore alluvial deposits, weathered and disintegrated formations, river beds, and offshore deposits along the seacoasts.

Production of tin concentrates averaged over 29,000 tons annually in the early 1970s, dropped to about 22,000 tons in the mid-1970s, and then rose to 46,000 tons in 1980. By 1985 tin production had dropped to about 23,000 tons as a result of export controls imposed by the International Tin Council and the indefinite closing of a major offshore mining company. The actual output of concentrates in the 1980s was believed to have been at least 10 percent higher than officially reported. The additional quantity represented tin concentrates smuggled from the country to escape payment of both business taxes and the statutory royalty deducted from the price paid to the seller by the foreign-controlled Thailand Smelting and Refining Company (THAISARCO). The export of tin ore and concentrates was banned by the government after THAISARCO began smelting tin in 1965 at a newly constructed plant on Phuket Island. Most of the smuggled concentrates originally went to Penang, but this trade had been largely halted by the Malaysian authorities; in the 1980s, the illegal ore was sent to Singapore for smelting.

Since the mid-1970s, the tin-mining industry has generated a large amount of political controversy, social unrest, and illegal activity that continued into the mid-1980s. Onshore mining operations were carried on mostly by small miners who were predominantly Thai. Offshore operations included a number of large dredges owned by both Thai enterprises and foreign firms, as well as thousands of suction boats. Both kinds of operations were supposed to be registered with local provincial authorities. The tin fields had attracted large numbers of the unemployed or persons seeking fortunes, however, who mined illegally. Reports of a new tin strike brought thousands of individuals to the area, resulting in such attendant social problems as claim jumping, forged registration certificates, frequent violence, and the like. In 1975 the government-owned Offshore Mining Organization (OMO) was set up to replace large offshore oil concessions owned by foreign corporations and ousted Thai government leaders. A substantial amount of illegal dredging was also reported in the OMO concession area, whose size and restrictions of exploitation to subconcessionaires had created strong resentment among independent small operators, even though the OMO had given concession rights to a considerable number of them. In late 1979, a group of nonconcession-holding small dredgers pressed the provincial authorities of the area to urge the central government to revoke all restrictions on mining in the OMO holdings. The overall magnitude of illegal operations appeared in the early 1980s to be beyond the ability of the local authorities to control. Official action, moreover, was often deterred by public sympathy for the poor person struggling to eke out a living.

Thus, illegal mining was an important source of employment in the southern peninsula and, in conjunction with related illegal operations, created numerous ancillary jobs. From the national viewpoint, however, a great loss of natural wealth occurred because of haphazard and inefficient exploitation. Onshore miners, legal and illegal, tended to take out only the readily accessible richer ore, leaving varying amounts of lower-grade ore that, mined separately, was uneconomic. Large numbers of small dredges sent divers down to find rich spots that were sucked up, avoiding large nearby areas containing ore that was costly to mine. Many of the dredges also had poor separation equipment, and considerable quantities of ore were lost in the tailings. Because of potential political problems, decisive action by the central government (or provincial governments) to resolve this problem did not appear imminent in the late 1980s.

Thailand is a rich source of sapphire, ruby, zircon, garnet, beryl, quartz, and jadeite, and in 1986 gems and jewelry were a large export item in terms of value. Significant deposits of rubies were located in Chanthaburi and Trat provinces in the southern part of the Center, and deposits of sapphire were found in Kanchanaburi Province. Stones were also imported from Sri Lanka, Australia, Africa, and South America for cutting and setting into jewelry. By the mid-1980s, Thailand had become one of the world's major gemcutting centers, and the craftsmanship of Thai gemcutters was widely recognized.

Tungsten, an important source of foreign exchange earnings beginning in the early 1970s, was found in the mountains in the North and in the Bilauktaung Range along the Burmese border. In 1970 a major find of the tungsten mineral wolframite was made in Nakhon Si Thammarat Province in the South. Antimony, also an important export, was found in many parts of the country.

Mining was carried on almost entirely by small operators, but in the mid-1970s cumulative annual production was about 6 percent of total world output. Fluorite, one of Thailand's principal exports, was mined mainly in the North in Chiang Mai and Lamphun provinces, where large reserves existed. Relatively large deposits of rock salt of approximately 97 percent purity underlay areas in the Northeast. Reserves were estimated to be at least 2 billion tons. Although having great future export potential, the lack of an adequate transportation infrastructure posed a major problem for exploitation of the rock salt reserves.

Offering a hopeful promise of a new source of foreign exchange earnings and savings on imports in the 1980s was the long-delayed development of zinc mining and refining. This involved exploitation of a large ore deposit, estimated at 3.5 million tons of 25 percent content, at Mae Sot in Tak Province near the Burmese border. A zinc smelter constructed by a Thai-Belgian consortium began operation in 1984.

Transportation

Thailand's transportation system of inland waterways, railroads, and roads was centered on Bangkok (see fig. 11). Historically, waterways had served to carry agricultural products from the central plain to the capital for export or domestic processing and to transport foreign or locally made goods back to rural areas. In the 1980s, the railroads and roads radiating from the city to all parts of the country served the same purpose. Bangkok's accessibility through the Chao Phraya made it the chief port for foreign ocean-borne trade. Since World War II, Bangkok's strategic location in Southeast Asia has made the city the principal regional center for international air travel.

The existing system of main roads, railroads, and waterways in the late 1980s was considered by foreign experts to be generally adequate for the country's overall transport requirements. Considerable upgrading of provincial roads would be needed in the coming decade to handle growing traffic as commercialization spread through the rural areas. In particular, substantial improvement and development were required for subsidiary roads to provide villages and hamlets access to the main transport arteries.

Inland Waterways

Historically, about 4,000 kilometers of inland waterways consisting of the rivers and canals of the central plain and the Chao Phraya Delta formed the backbone of the transportation system. Although in the twentieth century railroads and roads assumed a

dominant position in the central plain, waterways still carried a sizable portion of the total traffic. Waterborne freight, chiefly consisting of rice, accounted for about 17 percent of total freight transported countrywide in the 1980s. Large numbers of small craft also transported passengers. During the rainy season about 1,600 kilometers of waterways were navigable by barges of up to 80 tons and 1.8-meter draft, which could travel from the Gulf of Thailand to as far north as Uttaradit. Navigation was reduced to about 1,100 kilometers of waterways in the dry season, and traffic could navigate only to Nakhon Sawan, roughly halfway to Uttaradit. Shallow-draft vessels could navigate the interconnected network of canals throughout the year, and Bangkok, Ayutthaya, and other towns had floating markets where a great deal of trading activity took place. Some sections of the Mekong River were also navigable.

Railroads

The state-operated national rail system was started by King Chulalongkorn, and the first section—from Bangkok to Ayutthaya—was inaugurated in 1896. The line was extended to Nakhon Ratchasima in 1910, and during the first decade of the century work had already begun on other lines to the north and south. By 1941 well over four-fifths of the present-day rail system had been opened.

After 1951 control of the railroads was vested by law in the State Railway of Thailand (SRT), an autonomous agency. Through 1979 SRT had received a number of assistance loans from the World Bank, as well as bilateral aid with which the line was first rehabilitated and later modernized, including replacement of steam locomotives by diesel units. In the early 1980s, SRT had about 4,000 kilometers of meter-gauge track, all of it single track except for a 90-kilometer section of double track running north of Bangkok to near Ayutthaya. Four main interconnecting lines originating in Bangkok ran to Chiang Mai (Northern Line), Aranyaprathet (Eastern Line), Nong Khai and Ubon Ratchathani (Northeastern Line), and the Malaysian border (Southern Line). A number of branch lines were also in operation, including a line constructed in the 1980s to link the Lan Krabu oil field in Kamphaeng Phet Province to the Northern Line. Also under construction in the mid-1980s was a link from Bangkok down the eastern seaboard to Rayong, which was completed as far as Sattahip in 1984.

Competition from developing road services had cut heavily into railroad passenger and freight traffic, and the proportional share of freight declined between 1968 and 1976 from 19 percent to 11 percent. In the 1980s, however, the rail lines remained of major

importance in the transport of bulk commodities, such as petroleum products, cement, and rice, over long distances.

Roads

Extensive development of the road network did not start until
after World War II. By the 1980s, however, roads were the most
important part of the transportation system. Before the war the
few existing roads had been intended primarily as feeders to the
railroad system, which had been built largely with foreign funds
that needed to be repaid. Profit from rail transportation was vital,
and the construction of competing roads was deemed uneconomic.
From the mid-1950s to the mid-1960s, however, substantial United
States aid was provided, along with technical assistance, to develop
a national highway system that by 1965 totaled almost 9,500 kilometers. Thereafter, assistance for highway development came
mainly from the World Bank, although in the late 1960s United
States military forces also furnished substantial funds for road construction.

In the 1980s, the primary road system consisted of a net of
national highways that started at Bangkok and extended in all directions to the country's frontiers. They totaled about 20,000 kilometers, of which well over 90 percent were paved. Provincial roads
totaling over 24,000 kilometers formed a secondary system that
tied provincial towns and population centers to the national roads.
About two-fifths were unimproved and often impassable during
rainy weather. In addition to the main and provincial roads, there
were tertiary roads—consisting of village roads, footpaths, tracks,
and the like—variously estimated at from 40,000 to 60,000 kilometers. These roads and trails were important because they
represented in many cases the only link between a village or ham-
let and the provincial system or possibly a railroad stop or inland
waterway point. Several thousand kilometers of tertiary roads had
been improved, but in general they were poorly maintained. Their
administration was spread over a number of government agencies,
in contrast to national and provincial roads, which were administered by the Department of Highways in the Ministry of Communications.

In the early 1980s, no restrictions existed on the importation of
motor vehicles, although taxes and duties on imported vehicles were
higher as a measure to protect the domestic automobile assembly
industry. Under guidelines set in 1986, local automobile assembly
plants were required to use at least 54 percent domestic parts. Motor
vehicles registered in 1984 included 688,000 automobiles, 600,000
commercial vehicles, and nearly 2 million motorcycles. In the 1980s,

about a third of all vehicles registered were in the Bangkok metropolitan area, but this included almost two-thirds of the automobiles. The relatively massive concentration of trucks, buses, and automobiles in the capital area regularly created enormous traffic jams. Construction of an elevated expressway was under way, the first part of which had been completed by the early 1980s.

Ports and Shipping

The country's preeminent port was Bangkok, which in the early 1980s handled 98 percent of imports and 65 percent of exports as well as about 40 percent of coastal traffic. More than 4,000 foreign vessels were reported to have called at Bangkok in 1983, and about 24 million tons of cargo were handled, including coastal cargo. Two other ports of some significance in international trade were Si Racha and Sattahip, both located southeast of Bangkok on the Gulf of Thailand. Both ports were used primarily for exporting agricultural products. Sattahip's deep-water naval facility was also used to handle imports of heavy equipment.

The port of Bangkok had experienced continuous growth since the 1950s, and, through loans from the World Bank, its facilities had been substantially expanded to handle the increased traffic. A major drawback of the port was its limitation on vessel size and draft, which forced ships of more than 10,000 tons or 8.5-meter draft to offload at the mouth of the Chao Phraya, some 27 kilometers downstream. As part of the Eastern Seaboard Development Program, the government in 1986 approved plans to build a new deep-water port at Laem Chabang in Chon Buri Province to supplement Bangkok's Khlong Toei port. An industrial estate was to be built close to the port area for export-oriented industries, such as electronics, and for agro-based industries, such as food processing and rubber products. Under the same program, a new port and industrial park was to be constructed at Mapthaphut to serve the petrochemical, fertilizer, and soda ash industries.

Some thirty smaller ports were found along the Gulf of Thailand and the Andaman Sea. About half were fishing ports, and the remainder served multiple purposes, including coastal services, export and import functions, and fisheries operations. Coastal operations were in general small. In the early 1980s, the government also had under consideration development of deep-water ports at Songkhla on the east coast of the peninsula, through which rubber was exported, and Phuket on the west coast. Phuket served as an outlet for both tin and rubber exports.

In 1985 the Thai merchant fleet consisted of 71 freighters, 2 bulk carriers, and 25 tankers, totaling roughly 700,000 tons. Regular cargo service was provided between Thailand and Japan, and one shipping company made regular calls at West European ports. An unknown number of small coastal vessels conducted trade with Malaysia and Singapore.

Civil Aviation

Domestic air service was furnished by Thai Airways Company (TAC), a government-owned entity established in 1951. There were some 130 airfields of all categories throughout the provinces, 104 of which were in usable condition, in addition to the major airport at Bangkok. In the early 1980s, service was provided to about twenty airports. In addition to domestic service, TAC also flew to Penang in Malaysia, Vientiane in Laos, and Hanoi in Vietnam. The principal Thai-flag international service was provided by Thai Airways International (THAI), founded in 1959 by TAC jointly with the Scandinavian Airlines System (SAS); TAC held 70 percent of the shares and SAS 30 percent. THAI's routes included flights to Asia, the Middle East, Europe, North America, and Australia. Approximately thirty international airlines flew into Thailand. Both TAC and THAI had greatly expanded and upgraded their fleets by the mid-1980s. In 1985 THAI placed orders with the European aircraft manufacturing consortium Airbus Industrie for four A300–600 medium-range jumbo jets, making the airline the third largest Airbus user in the world, with sixteen airplanes. Also in 1985, THAI ordered two more Boeing 747s, making a total of eight, for use on its long-distance routes to Europe, North America, and Australia. In 1987 Prime Minister Prem Tinsulanonda approved the proposed merger of THAI and TAC, which was expected to be carried out by 1989.

The principal international airport was Don Muang outside Bangkok. The airport had long been Southeast Asia's main air traffic center for flights between Asia and Europe (although at the beginning of the 1980s it was experiencing strong competition from Singapore). The airport was used jointly by civilian airlines and the Royal Thai Air Force, resulting in growing congestion as international flights increased. During the mid-1970s, consideration was given to building a new civilian airport, but in 1978 a decision was made to move some military operations to other airports. A two-year expansion program for Don Muang was then initiated, and a new state enterprise, the Airport Authority of Thailand (AAT), was legislated and took over administration of the airport in July 1979. In 1979 the airport at Chiang Mai was upgraded to become an international airport. In 1985 THAI opened a new cargo terminal at Don Muang International Airport as part of its plan to expand its cargo business. That same year a new wide-body aircraft maintenance center was inaugurated at Don Muang as a bid to make Bangkok a regional service center for Airbus and Boeing planes.

Energy

Historically, the population has had adequate supplies of fuel in the form of wood charcoal, which was usually available for the taking from nearby forests and thickets. Until the mid-twentieth century, the chief energy source for the country's limited industry was wood, supplemented by rice husks and bagasse (the dry pulp remaining from sugarcane after the juice is extracted). Even into the 1960s, wood was a major source of fuel for the railroads. Electricity, which was used for power beginning in 1887 with the establishment of the Siam Electric Company, was generated as late as the early 1950s largely by steam produced through burning rice husks. Other natural energy sources existed, although they were underexploited, in the large hydroelectric potential of the Chao Phraya and to a lesser extent of the Mae Klong and other smaller rivers. There were also deposits of lignite, which was used to fuel a number of power plants. Since 1950 small oil deposits have been found and exploited in the North. Oil shales have also been discovered, but exploitation remained economically unfeasible in 1980. The greatest potential for domestic hydrocarbon production in the late 1980s consisted of large natural gas deposits, which had been discovered in the 1970s in the Gulf of Thailand.

Electric Power

As industry revived and began to expand after World War II, the need for electricity grew. The supply was limited and unreliable, and some industrial firms and businesses installed their own generators, mostly fueled by imported oil. In 1958 the Metropolitan Electricity Authority (MEA) was established to generate and supply power to Bangkok and adjacent provinces. A year earlier the government had also set up the Yanhee Electricity Authority (renamed in 1969 the Electricity Generating Authority of Thailand—EGAT) to promote development of hydroelectric power. The first hydroelectric generating facility was the Phumiphon Dam. Completed in 1964 on the Mae Nam Ping, it had an installed capacity of 420 megawatts in 1979 and a potential of 560 megawatts.

Escalating power demand led to construction of a major oil-fired plant, the North Bangkok Power Station, which went into operation in 1961. Installed capacity from 1968 totaled 237 megawatts. The capital area became adequately supplied with the construction of a new oil-fired plant in Bangkok. The South Bangkok Thermal Power Plant started up in late 1970 with a 200-megawatt capacity; by 1977 this was increased to 1,300 megawatts. The country's second major hydroelectric plant, at the Sirikit Dam (potential generating capacity of 500 megawatts) on the Mae Nam Nan, a major tributary of the Chao Phraya, started generation with an installed capacity of 375 megawatts in 1974. A third large hydroelectric facility, part of a multipurpose irrigation, flood control, and power project at Ban Pho on the Mae Nam Mae Klong northwest of Kanchanaburi, was completed in the 1980s with an initial capacity of 360 megawatts and an estimated potential of 720 megawatts.

Generating capacity to other parts of Thailand was on a much smaller and regionally unequal scale. Increased oil prices in the 1970s stimulated a new interest in lignite, and a lignite-fueled plant installed at Mae Mo, the site of a major lignite deposit, was producing 825 megawatts by 1987. Lignite reserves were estimated to be 865 million tons in 1985. In the South a lignite-fired plant at Krabi with an installed capacity of sixty megawatts commenced generation in 1964. A major purpose of this plant was to furnish power for tin mines in the area and the tin smelter on Phuket Island, in addition to meeting local needs. In 1968 additional generating capacity was installed on Phuket through a ten-megawatt-capacity diesel plant, and between 1971 and 1977 three gas turbine units totaling forty-five megawatts were installed on Hat Yai. In the late 1970s, three additional gas turbine units having a combined capacity of forty-five megawatts were also located at Surat Thani.

Development of power facilities in the Northeast received little attention until the mid-1960s, at which time the region had an estimated generating capacity provided by small diesel units of perhaps one megawatt. By the early 1970s, however, four hydroelectric plants had been installed at dams in different parts of the region, with an installed capacity of ninety-five megawatts. New gas turbines furnished an additional thirty megawatts, and diesel units produced an additional four megawatts.

In 1987 the power sector was composed of three government-owned enterprises: EGAT, under the Office of the Prime Minister, was the national power production agency; MEA, under the Ministry of Interior had responsibility for power distribution in Bangkok and the provinces immediately around the city; and the Provincial Electricity Authority (PEA), also under the Ministry of Interior, distributed power throughout the rest of the country. There were also a number of privately held distribution franchises that bought power from PEA or EGAT. Some privately owned

Multipurpose dam on the Pattani River in southern Thailand
Courtesy World Bank

industries also generated their own power. Installed generating capacity in 1986 was 7,570 megawatts, of which 70 percent was thermal and 30 percent hydropower. In 1985 industry used nearly 50 percent of the 20 million megawatt-hours of energy consumed. Residential consumption was 25 percent, commercial establishments used 25 percent, and street lighting and miscellaneous uses accounted for less than 1 percent. By the end of 1986, nearly 43,000 villages of the more than 48,000 throughout the country had been supplied with power. It was projected that 95 percent of all villages would have electricity by 1991 and essentially all villages by 1999.

Petroleum and Natural Gas

Oil was discovered near Fang in the far north of the country in the early 1950s, but by the late 1970s the principal field was reported close to depletion. Onshore deposits were believed to exist in other parts of the country, and several foreign firms had exploration concessions in the 1980s. Exploration in the 1970s in the Gulf of Thailand uncovered oil in limited quantities. Oil shales were found at Mae Sot in Tak Province in the North. Surveys in the mid-1970s indicated a reserve of about 2.5 billion tons. A smaller deposit, estimated at about 15 million tons, existed in Lamphun Province, also in the North. Surveys in the Northeast from the mid-1970s showed the existence of about 2.5 billion tons of oil shale in that region. Although 4 million barrels of petroleum were produced in 1983, extensive commercial exploitation still seemed remote because of comparatively high production costs.

In the early 1980s, petroleum products provided about 68 percent of the annual energy requirement. The country was highly dependent on petroleum imports, and increasing world petroleum prices had a serious impact on the country's balance of payments. In 1980 there were three large, privately operated, oil refineries having a combined design capacity of 165,000 barrels per day (bpd); government sources estimated maximum capacity at 188,000 bpd. The Thailand Oil Refining Company (TORC) started operations in the mid-1960s with a capacity of 42,000 bpd. This was expanded to 65,000 bpd in 1971 under an agreement whereby the entire operation was to become the property of the Thai government in 1981. A second fully integrated plant was government owned but was leased for operation to the private Summit Industrial Corporation; the lease was due to expire in 1990. This plant had a design capacity of 65,000 bpd. A third plant was owned and operated by Esso Standard of Thailand and could handle 35,000 bpd. A very small

1,000 bpd plant was operated in the far north by the Ministry of Defense to refine domestic oil produced in the area.

Natural gas was found by international firms in offshore concessions in the Gulf of Thailand in the mid-1970s, and subsequent explorations determined that large quantities were recoverable, sufficient to alter favorably Thailand's energy position. By 1979 two major gas fields had been generally delineated, one located approximately 425 kilometers south of a proposed pipeline terminal east of Sattahip at the upper end of the gulf, the other 170 kilometers farther south. Proven recoverable reserves in the first field were estimated at nearly 1.6 trillion cubic feet and probable recoverable reserves at 220 billion cubic feet. In the second field, proven recoverable reserves were 1.3 trillion cubic feet and probable reserves 4.5 trillion cubic feet. Two smaller fields about 365 kilometers south of the terminal site were estimated to have about 500 billion cubic feet of recoverable reserves. The country's total proven reserves of natural gas were estimated at 8.5 trillion cubic feet in 1984. Thailand's production of natural gas in 1987 was 162.3 billion cubic feet.

In late 1979, the World Bank approved a loan of US$107 million to the Petroleum Authority of Thailand, a state enterprise, to assist in the first-phase exploitation of the discoveries. A submarine pipeline was built from the terminal near Mapthaphut to a production platform at the major field 425 kilometers south in the gulf. When completed in the early 1980s, it was the world's longest submarine pipeline. Additional pipelines were built to transport the gas overland, initially to the South Bangkok Thermal Power Plant and later to a new thermal power plant at Bang Pakong southeast of Bangkok, built in the early 1980s under EGAT's 1978–85 power generation development plan. Gas was also distributed to industrial users along the pipeline route.

Telecommunications

Two major entities were responsible for the Thai telecommunication and postal services under the supervision of the Ministry of Communications. The Telephone Organization of Thailand (TOT) was responsible for the domestic telephone services; for international telephone services to several neighboring countries, such as Malaysia and Laos; and for leasing circuits for domestic point-to-point transmission of voices, telegraph, radio, and television. The Communication Authority of Thailand (CAT) was responsible for postal service, international telephone service to countries not served by TOT, all telegraph and telex services international lease circuits, domestic radio-telephone links to some isolated areas, and telephotographic and facsimile services. A committee in the Ministry of Communications coordinated the services and investment of TOT and CAT, although the two were state-owned autonomous operations. Numerous government agencies and large private industrial and commercial entities operated their own radio-telephone networks.

By the mid-1980s, Thailand had an average density of one telephone per hundred inhabitants. This density was better than the average of 0.7 for the developing countries in the East Asia region, although it was still lower than Malaysia with 3.3, South Korea with 7.8, Taiwan with 14.6, and Singapore with 26.5. Even Bangkok, which had the most developed telephone service in the country, had only a density of 5.4 telephones per 100 inhabitants. Overall, only 25 percent of the population had access to telephone services. There were about 5,800 local and long-distance pay (coin box) telephones in the capital city and 750 in provincial towns. About 4,500 pay telephones were to be added in Bangkok and 1,500 in provincial towns. About 62 percent of the country's telephone lines were connected to business and government subscribers and the rest to residential subscribers. Business lines accounted for 83 percent of total calls and revenues.

As a rapidly modernizing nation, Thailand in the late 1980s faced many problems related to the growth and expansion of its economy. The development of its industrial base and the continuing need for new cultivable land placed increasing pressure on urban and rural areas alike. However, the abundance of the country's resources, the adaptability of its workforce, and the stability of its polity boded well for Thailand's successful transition to the role of newly industrialized country.

*   *   *

Several studies are available on the Thai economy that furnish background details and analysis of the modern period since about 1850. Particularly valuable is James C. Ingram's *Economic Change in Thailand, 1850-1970*. Further reading should include Larry Sternstein's *Thailand: The Environment of Modernization* and Wolf Donner's *The Five Faces of Thailand*. The period since the late 1960s has been covered in a large number of journal and magazine articles and papers written on particular aspects of the economy. The *Far Eastern Economic Review* is a particularly valuable source. Issues of the Bank of Thailand's *Monthly Bulletin* are also useful. (For further information and complete citations, see Bibliography.)

Chapter 4. Government and Politics

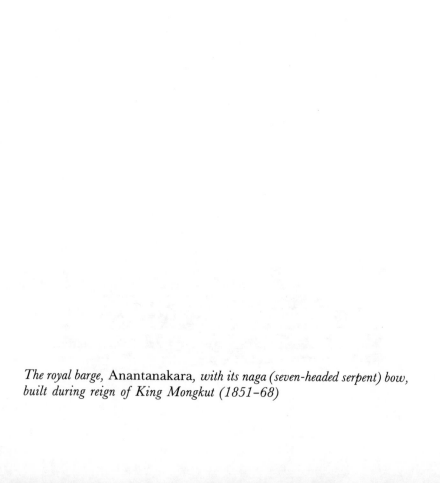

The royal barge, Anantanakara, *with its naga (seven-headed serpent) bow,*
built during reign of King Mongkut (1851–68)

THE RELATIVE STABILITY of the Thai political system in the 1980s may prove to be a political watershed in modern Thai history. This stability, which resulted after several decades of spasmodic experimentation with democracy, could be attributed to the growing support of the monarchy and the traditionally dominant military-bureaucratic elite for parliamentary democracy. Evidently an increasing number of educated Thai had come to believe that a "Thai-style democracy" headed by the king and a parliament representing the people through political parties was preferable to excessively authoritarian rule under military strongmen. The future of parliamentary democracy was not a certainty, however, as many Thai continued to believe that democratic rule was not the most effective option in times of incompetent national leadership, prolonged civil and political disorder, or external threat to independence.

Under the Constitution of 1978, Thailand has a British-style cabinet form of government with King Bhumibol Adulyadej (Rama IX, 1946–) reigning as constitutional monarch and Prime Minister Prem Tinsulanonda heading the government. Unlike the British prime minister, however, Prem was not a leader of or even a member of any political party in the nation's parliament, the National Assembly, nor did he run for election in the July 1986 election that led to the formation of his four-party coalition government. This was his fifth cabinet and seventh year in office—no mean accomplishment in a country that had witnessed numerous coups, countercoups, and attempted coups during its sporadic experiments with parliamentary government since 1932.

Unlike many of his predecessors, Prem became prime minister in March 1980 not by a coup, the traditional route to power, but by consensus among key politicians. At that time he was the commander in chief of the Royal Thai Army, a post that was long considered to be the most powerful in the country. With little dissent from any quarter, he succeeded Kriangsak Chomanand, who had resigned as prime minister amid mounting economic and political tensions. A group of disgruntled officers, popularly known as "the Young Turks," attempted coups against Prem in 1981 and 1985. These attempts, however, had no disruptive effect on political stability.

Despite these failed coups, in 1987 the military as a whole continued to play a major role in Thai politics. Increasingly, this role was tempered as so-called "enlightened" officers realized that a coup was no longer acceptable to the public and that the military could bring its influence to bear politically by working within the constitutional system. The military continued to believe, nonetheless, that politics and government were too important to be left entirely in the hands of civilian politicians, whom they tended to disdain as corrupt, divisive, and inefficient.

Barring early dissolution or resignation of his cabinet, Prem's mandate was scheduled to lapse in July 1990. Who would succeed him and, more important, how it would happen were the key questions because of their far-reaching implications for parliamentary democracy in Thailand. A related question concerned the future role of the monarchy and whether or not it would continue to command the reverence and loyalty of all segments of society and maintain its powerful symbolism as the sole conferrer of political legitimacy.

In the 1980s, a growing number of Thai favored a constitutional amendment requiring that only an elected member commanding a parliamentary majority could become prime minister. Citing Prem as an example, others argued that, even in the absence of a constitutional amendment, orderly succession was possible if a nationally reputable figure were acceptable to a majority of the country's political leaders. In any case, many observers agreed that, rather than imitating a foreign political model, Thailand should develop the political system best suited to the kingdom's particular needs and circumstances. The quest for a so-called "Thai-style democracy" was still under way in 1987, although the form and process of such a democracy remained largely undefined.

During the 1980s, Thailand pursued three major foreign policy objectives: safeguarding national security, diversifying and expanding markets for Thai exports, and establishing cordial relations with all nations. On the whole, Thailand conducted what it called "omnidirectional foreign policy," and it did so in a highly pragmatic and flexible manner. Relations with such major powers as the United States, China, and Japan were increasingly cordial, and relations with the Soviet Union were correct. The Thai were suspicious of Soviet intentions because Moscow was perceived to be aiding and abetting Vietnam, Laos, and Cambodia. Beginning in the mid-1970s, Indochina had come to be viewed as the major threat to Thailand's security. The normalization of relations with these Indochinese neighbors remained the principal unresolved issue for Bangkok, which continued to address the problem directly as well as indirectly through a regional forum called the Association of Southeast Asian Nations (ASEAN).

The Constitutional Framework

The Constitution, promulgated on December 22, 1978, is the country's twelfth such document since 1932, when Thailand, then called Siam, first became a constitutional monarchy (see 1932 Coup, ch. 1). Thailand's numerous constitutions resulted, in part, from various coup leaders revoking an old constitution and announcing an interim one in order to legitimize their takeover until a permanent constitution could be promulgated. Political maneuvers aimed at amending constitutional provisions have often shed light on the interplay of Thai political forces and the personalities and issues involved (see Political Developments, 1980–87, this ch.).

The Constitution provides for a parliamentary form of government with the king as titular head of state. In theory, the monarch exercises popularly derived power through the National Assembly, the Council of Ministers, and the courts. In reality, power is wielded by the prime minister—the head of government—who chairs the Council of Ministers, or cabinet.

The Constitution includes a long chapter on the rights and liberties of the people, in which are guaranteed due process of law; sanctity of the family; rights of property and inheritance; freedom from forced labor, except by law in times of national emergencies or armed hostilities; and the inviolability of the person and private communications. Censorship is banned except by law for the purpose of "public order or good morals, public safety, or for maintaining the security of the state." Also guaranteed are freedom of the press, freedom of speech, freedom of religious worship, and the right of peaceful assembly; freedom of residence and movement within the kingdom; the right to organize voluntary associations; the right to establish a political party and engage in political activities within a democratic framework; and the right to petition against public institutions. These rights and liberties, however, are not to be used against the interest of "the Nation, religion, the King, and the Constitution."

Affairs of state must conform to a set of principles, which, among other things, obligate the state to maintain the monarchy, provide compulsory and free education, and promote public understanding of and belief in a democratic form of government with the king as its head. The state is also directed to ensure that the people enjoy the right of self-government as prescribed by law. Other directive principles urge the state to encourage private economic initiatives, raise the economic and social status of the citizenry to the level of "comfortable livelihood," and secure either landownership or land use rights for all farmers by means of land reform or other appropriate measures. The state is also called upon to promote culture, environmental protection, planned parenthood, and public health.

The power of the state, exercised through a centralized form of government, is divided into legislative, executive, and judicial categories. The state revolves around the king, the bicameral legislature, the cabinet, the judiciary, the local government, and the Constitutional Tribunal.

The Constitution may be amended by motions introduced either by the cabinet or by one-third of the members of the lower house of the National Assembly; in the latter case, a motion must be in accordance with a resolution adopted by the political party to which the proponents of the amendment belong. This provision is designed to encourage responsible party politics by prohibiting motions by members acting in defiance of party discipline. An amendment bill is deliberated in three readings and must be approved by more than one-half of the total members of both houses.

The interpretation of the Constitution is under the jurisdiction of both the National Assembly and the Constitutional Tribunal. Except for matters reserved for the Constitutional Tribunal, questions relating to the power and duty of the legislature are resolved by the assembly sitting in joint session. The tribunal is responsible for deciding the legality of a bill passed by the National Assembly. If at least one-fifth of the National Assembly members object to a given bill before it is given royal assent, they may request the president of either chamber to refer the disputed bill to the tribunal for adjudication. The prime minister also may raise an objection to the tribunal directly. Decisions by the Constitutional Tribunal are final and cannot be appealed.

The Central Government

In the 1980s, the governmental system remained unitary, with all important decisions emanating from the traditionally powerful bureaucratic elite in Bangkok. Composed of senior members of the civil and military wings of the bureaucracy, this elite dominated the governmental process from the national level down to the district level. In this process, the Ministry of Interior continued to play a key role as the administrative framework of the state, resisting reforms and changes (see fig. 12).

The King

The Constitution stipulates that the king is "enthroned in a position of revered worship" and is not to be exposed "to any sort of accusation or action." As ceremonial head of state, the monarch is endowed with a formal power of assent and appointment, is above partisan affairs, and does not involve himself in the decision-making process of the government. In the 1980s, King Bhumibol Adulyadej remained the nation's most respected figure because he was popularly perceived to be the embodiment of religion, culture, and history. He ensured political stability and unity by lending legitimacy to important government actions and, in potentially destabilizing situations, as during the abortive coups in 1981 and 1985, by discreetly signaling his support of the incumbent government.

In discharging his formal duties, the king was assisted by the Privy Council, whose president and not more than fourteen members were royal appointees. These members could not hold other public offices, belong to political parties, or show loyalty to any partisan organization. Also assisting the king were the Office of His Majesty's Principal Private Secretary and the Bureau of the Royal Household, agencies responsible for organizing ceremonial functions and administering the finances and logistics of the royal palace.

The mode of succession was set forth in the Palace Law on Succession. In the absence of a crown prince, or if the crown prince declined succession, a princess could succeed, subject to parliamentary approval. When the throne became vacant, an heir was to be appointed by the Privy Council. Until the heir formally ascended the throne, the president of the Privy Council would act as regent. Prince Vajiralongkorn, the only son of King Bhumibol and Queen Sirikit, was designated as heir on December 28, 1972, at the age of twenty.

National Assembly

In the 1980s, the bicameral parliament, unable to successfully challenge the tradition of bureaucratic dominance over state affairs, was overshadowed by the executive branch. The National Assembly continued to be an instrument of cabinet rule, with its legislative agenda issuing for the most part from the executive branch.

Under the Constitution, the National Assembly was structured to accommodate both the military and civilian bureaucratic elite and the electorate. The influence of the traditionally powerful bureaucracy was channeled through the Senate, whose members were nominated by the prime minister for pro forma appointment by the king. Up to 85 percent of the Senate membership in the late 1980s was drawn from the armed forces and the police. The intent of this arrangement was to encourage the military to play its traditional political role through the upper house rather than through a coup or countercoup.

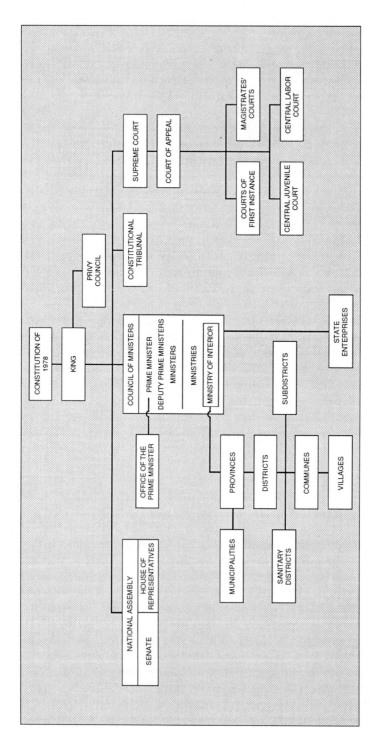

Figure 12. The Governmental System of Thailand, 1987

Senators served a term of six years, and one-third of them were retired every two years. Retirees could be reappointed for an unlimited number of terms. A senator was required to be at least thirty-five years of age, a Thai citizen by birth, and not a member of any political party. Other membership qualifications were broadly phrased, including the requirement that appointees have "knowledge and experience in various branches of learning or affairs which will be useful to the administration of the state."

House of Representatives members represented the populace. They were elected for a four-year term by direct suffrage and secret ballot at the ratio of a member to each 150,000 inhabitants. Each province (*changwat*), regardless of population, was entitled to at least one seat. A constituency with a population in excess of 75,000 also qualified for a seat. A candidate had to be at least twenty-five years of age, a Thai citizen by birth, and a member of a political party. As a rule, an election had to be held within sixty days from the expiration of the four-year term of the lower house. When the House was dissolved by royal decree (on the recommendation of the prime minister), a new election was required within ninety days.

The two chambers conducted their business separately under their respective presidents (speakers) and vice presidents, who were chosen from among the membership. Under the Constitution, the president of the Senate was automatically the speaker of the National Assembly and in that capacity was empowered to play a strategic role in the selection of the prime minister.

In the 1980s, lower house members demanded that their president, rather than the president of the upper house, have a decisive role in the process of selecting the prime minister. This policy was necessary, they said, because the House of Representatives, not the military-dominated Senate, collectively represented the will of the electorate. A bill to amend the Constitution to make the lower house speaker the president of the National Assembly was introduced in 1986 but failed to pass.

In 1987 the customary role of the Senate as a major vehicle for the power of the bureaucracy and a counterweight to the elective lower house remained little changed, even though its stature seemed to have diminished somewhat after April 1983. At that time, certain senatorial powers granted under temporary clauses of the Constitution expired despite the army's efforts to have these clauses extended (see Political Developments 1980–87, this ch.). Under these clauses, the Senate had had the power to deliberate jointly with the lower chamber on annual appropriation bills, on "an important bill relating to the security of the Kingdom, the Throne, or the national economy," and the power to vote on no-confidence motions. The army and its political allies in parliament failed to have the clauses extended because of factious squabbles. If they had succeeded, the military's political power would have been enhanced greatly.

The lapse of the transitory provisions, however, did not affect the Senate's power to address such matters as the appointment of a regent, the royal succession, reconsideration of a bill vetoed by the prime minister, constitutional interpretation, a declaration of war, the ratification of treaties, the appointment of members of the Constitutional Tribunal, and constitutional amendments. In joint sessions senators also could render their opinion on any aspect of affairs of state to the prime minister when requested to do so by the latter. Such opinion was advisory and nonbinding.

Bills could be introduced only by the Council of Ministers or the members of the House of Representatives. Major legislation originated mostly in the cabinet, but only the lower house, with the prior endorsement of the prime minister, could initiate an appropriations bill. An ordinary bill had to be sponsored by a political party and endorsed by at least twenty party members. Bills were passed by a majority, the quorum being not less than one-half of the total members of either house in which the bills originated.

A bill passed by the House was sent to the Senate. The Senate was required to act on an ordinary bill within ninety days and on an appropriations bill within sixty days. If the Senate failed to act in either case, the bill was considered to have been consented to by the Senate, unless the lower chamber had extended the time. Disagreements between the two houses were resolved by a joint committee. When the dispute pertained to an appropriations bill and the lower house voted to reaffirm the bill it had originally passed, the prime minister was required to present the bill to the king for his assent and promulgation. At that point, the prime minister could exercise his important legislative role. He might advise the king to approve or veto the bill; in the latter event, the National Assembly needed two-thirds of its total membership to override the royal objections (actually the prime minister's objections).

Members of the assembly, who had parliamentary immunity, could question formally a cabinet minister or the prime minister on any appropriate issue except one in which executive privilege was involved. A motion of no-confidence against either an individual minister or the cabinet en masse could be initiated only by members of the lower house. Such a motion required an affirmative vote of at least one-half of the lower house membership. Senators could not take part in no-confidence debates.

Council of Ministers

The cabinet, the center of Thai political power, consisted of forty-four members, including the prime minister, deputy prime ministers, ministers, and deputy ministers. Individually and collectively the members were accountable to the House of Representatives and had to retain its confidence. The cabinet was required to resign en masse if a no-confidence motion against it was passed by the House. The four-party coalition cabinet formed in August 1986 had no civil servants or active-duty military officers. Under the Constitution, cabinet members were not allowed to hold political posts as part of an effort to strengthen the political party system.

Under the customary rules of parliamentary government, Thailand could have a prime minister whose party or electoral alliance had earned the mandate of this office outright by winning a majority of seats in the House of Representatives. Whether or not anyone would command a majority in the next election was uncertain, given the highly fragmented political party system. In any case, a public opinion survey conducted in March 1987 by the Social Research Institute of Chulalongkorn University showed that 91 percent of those interviewed in Bangkok favored an elected prime minister. For a requirement that the prime minister be elected, however, the Constitution would have to be amended. In 1987 the Royal Command appointing the prime minister had to be countersigned by the president of the National Assembly, the leader of the military-dominated Senate, who had the power to block the installation of anyone unacceptable to the military establishment. Until the basic law is revised, the selection of the prime minister will continue to be determined by behind-the-scenes power brokers, including the military (especially the army), the monarchy, and leaders of various political parties representing business groups.

The prime minister held the real powers of appointment and removal, which he exercised in the name of the king. He countersigned royal decrees and wielded a wide range of executive powers, including the power to declare a national emergency to ensure "national or public safety or national economic security or to avert public calamity." The legality of an emergency decree had to be validated by the next session of the National Assembly. The prime minister could also proclaim or lift martial law, declare war with the advice and consent of parliament, and conclude peace treaties, armistices, and other treaties—all in the king's name.

As of mid-1987, the executive branch had thirteen ministerial portfolios: agriculture and cooperatives; commerce; communications; defense; education; finance; foreign affairs; industry; interior; justice;

public health; science, technology, and energy; and university affairs. The heads of these ministries (except for justice; science, technology, and energy; and university affairs) were aided by one or more cabinet-rank deputy ministers. Each ministry was divided into departments, divisions, and sections. Traditionally, the ministries of defense, interior, and finance were regarded as the most desirable by aspiring politicians and generals. In the 1980s, the ministries of agriculture and cooperatives, industry, and communications grew in stature as the economic value of resources steadily increased.

In 1987 the Office of the Prime Minister continued to be the nerve center of the government. With the assistance of several cabinet-rank ministers attached to the office and of the Secretariat of the Prime Minister, this office monitored, coordinated, and supervised the activities of all government agencies and state enterprises. The secretariat was headed by a cabinet-rank secretary general, who supervised the work of sixteen agencies attached to the prime minister's office. Among these agencies were the Bureau of the Budget, the National Security Council, the Department of Central Intelligence, the Civil Service Commission, and the National Economic and Social Development Board. In August 1986, the secretary general was also placed in charge of a new unit called the National Operations Center established in the Office of the Prime Minister to provide essential data for efficient decision making. Specifically, the task of the National Operations Center was to handle crisis management, cope with threats to internal and external security, and keep the prime minister informed of public sentiment throughout the country.

Outside the regular administrative structure, but subject to its control and supervision, approximately sixty-eight state enterprises were engaged as of 1987 in commercial and economic activities of major importance. In these enterprises, the government was either the sole owner or the dominant partner. Managed by senior civil servants, retired military officers, or politicians, the state enterprises permitted a major government role in virtually every facet of the economic life of the country. In fiscal year (FY—see Glossary) 1986, their total budget was 9 percent more than the total budget of the government and accounted for 65 percent of external public debt. The inefficiency of these enterprises continued to affect the government's fiscal stability. Privatization of the enterprises was listed as one of the ten major programs of the country's Sixth Economic Development Plan, for 1987–91 (see Public Finance, ch. 3).

Coronation of King Bhumibol Adulyadej in 1950
Courtesy Royal Thai Embassy

Judiciary

The legal system remained an amalgam of the traditional and the modern. In several southern provinces, for example, Islamic law and custom were applicable to matrimonial and inheritance matters among the Muslims. A large part of the modern legal system was made up of criminal, civil, and commercial codes adopted from the British and other European legal systems with some modifications borrowed from India, Japan, China, and the United States. Also, an extensive body of administrative law consisted of royal decrees, executive orders, and ministerial regulations.

The judiciary provided for three levels of courts: the courts of first instance, the Court of Appeal, and the Supreme Court. The courts came under two separate jurisdictions. The Ministry of Justice appointed and supervised the administrative personnel of the courts and instituted reform in judicial procedures; the Judicial Service Commission, which was responsible for the independence of the courts, appointed, promoted, and removed judges. As a rule, judges retired at age sixty, but their service could be extended to age sixty-five.

The country was divided into nine judicial regions, which were coextensive with the nine administrative regions (*phag*), in contrast

193

to the four geographic regions (North, Northeast, Center, and South). At the base of the judiciary system were the courts of first instance, most of which were formally known as provincial courts with unlimited civil and criminal jurisdiction. Petty civil and criminal offenses were handled by magistrates' courts, which were designed to relieve the increasing burden on provincial courts. Offenses committed by Thai citizens on the high seas and outside the country were tried before the Criminal Court in Bangkok. Labor disputes were adjudicated by the Central Labor Court established in Bangkok in 1980. Offenses by persons under eighteen years of age were referred to the Central Juvenile Court and its counterparts in several regional centers.

The Court of Appeal in Bangkok heard cases from all lower courts (except the Central Labor Court) relating to civil, juvenile, criminal, and bankruptcy matters. At least two judges were required to sit at each hearing. Cases of exceptional importance had to be heard by plenary sessions of the court. The appellate court could reverse, revise, or remand lower court decisions on questions of both law and fact.

The Supreme Court, which was the highest court of appeal, also had original jurisdiction over election disputes. Although decisions of the court were final, in criminal cases the king could grant clemency. A dispute over court jurisdiction was settled by the Constitutional Tribunal.

Local Government

Local government comprised both regular territorial administrative units and self-governing bodies. Local autonomy was limited, however, by the high degree of centralization of power. The Ministry of Interior controlled the policy, personnel, and finances of the local units at the provincial and district levels. Field officials from the ministry as well as other central ministries constituted the majority of administrators at local levels.

In 1987 there were seventy-three provinces (*changwat*), including the metropolitan area of Bangkok, which had provincial status (see fig. 8). The provinces were grouped into nine regions for administrative purposes. As of 1984 (the latest year for which information was available in 1987), the provinces were divided into 642 districts (*amphoe*), 78 subdistricts (*king amphoe*), 7,236 communes (*tambon*), 55,746 villages (*muban*), 123 municipalities (*tesaban*), and 729 sanitation districts (*sukhaphiban*).

The province was under a governor (*phuwarachakan*), who was assisted by one or more deputy governors, an assistant governor, and officials from various central ministries, which, except for the

Ministry of Foreign Affairs, maintained field staffs in the provinces and districts. The governor supervised the overall administration of the province, maintained law and order, and coordinated the work of ministerial field staffs. These field officials carried out the policies and programs of their respective ministries as line administrators and also served as technical advisers to the governor. Although these officials were responsible to the governor in theory, in practice they reported to their own ministries in Bangkok and maintained communication with other province-level and district-level field staffs.

The governor also was responsible for district and municipal administration, presiding over a provincial council composed of senior officials from the central ministries. The council, which served in an advisory capacity, met once a month to transmit central government directives to the district administrators. Apart from the council, an elected provincial assembly exercised limited legislative oversight over provincial affairs.

District administration was under the charge of a district officer (*nai amphor*), who was appointed by the minister of interior and reported to the provincial governor. Larger districts could be divided into two or more subdistricts, each under an assistant district officer. The district or the subdistrict was usually the only point of contact between the central authority and the populace; the central government had no appointed civil service officials below this level.

The district officer's duties as overseer of the laws and policies of the central government were extensive. He supervised the collection of taxes, kept basic registers and vital statistics, registered schoolchildren and aliens, administered local elections at the commune and village levels, and coordinated the activities of field officials from Bangkok. Additionally, the district officer convened monthly meetings of the headmen of the communes and villages to inform them of government policies and instruct them on the implementation of these policies. As the chief magistrate of the district, he also was responsible for arbitration in land disputes; many villagers referred these disputes to the district officer rather than to a regular court.

The commune was the next level below the district. An average of nine contiguous, natural villages were grouped into one commune, whose residents elected a headman (*kamnan*) from among the village headmen (*phuyaibun*) within the commune. The commune chief was not a regular government official, but because of his semiofficial status, he was confirmed in office by the provincial governor. He also was entitled to wear an official uniform and receive a monthly stipend. Assisted by a small locally recruited staff,

195

the *kamnan* recorded vital statistics, helped the district officer collect taxes, supervised the work of village headmen, and submitted periodic reports to the district officer.

Below the commune level was the village government. Each village elected a headman, who generally served as the middleman between villagers and the district administration. The headman's other duties included attending meetings at the district headquarters, keeping village records, arbitrating minor civil disputes, and serving as village peace officer. Generally the headman served five years or longer and received a monthly stipend. In the 1980s, the importance of a village headman seemed to be declining as the authority of the central government expanded steadily through the provincial and local administrations.

Municipalities in Thailand included Bangkok, seventy-two cities serving as provincial capitals, and some large district towns. According to the 1980 census, municipalities had a combined population of 7.6 million, or about 17 percent of the national total. The municipalities consisted of communes, towns, and cities, depending on population. Municipal residents elected mayors and twelve to twenty-four municipal assemblymen; the assemblymen chose two to four councillors from among their number, who together with the mayors made up executive councils.

In theory, the municipal authorities were self-governing, but in practice municipal government was an administrative arm of the central and provincial authorities. The Ministry of Interior had effective control over municipal affairs through the provincial administration, which had the authority to dissolve municipal assemblies and executive councils. Moreover, such key officials as the municipal clerk and section chiefs were recruited, assigned, and retired by the ministry, which also had the power to control and supervise the fiscal affairs of the perennially deficit-ridden municipalities.

Until 1985 Bangkok's governor and assemblymen were appointed by the central government. In November of that year, however, for the first time an election was held as part of the constitutionally mandated effort to nurture local self-government. Chamlong Srimuang, a former major general running as an independent, won the governorship by a landslide.

At the next lower level of local government, every district had at least one sanitation district committee, usually in the district capital. This committee's purpose was to provide services such as refuse collection, water and sewage facilities, recreation, and road maintenance. The committee was run by ex-officio members headed by the district officer. Like municipalities, the sanitation districts were financially and administratively dependent on the government, notably the district administration.

Civil Service

A civil service career continued in 1987 to be widely regarded as a desirable route to financial security, social status, and power. As a result, despite the universal complaint about the inadequacy of government salaries, and despite many well-paid jobs becoming available in the commercial and industrial sectors, the civil service continued to attract many of the most promising young men and women.

Personnel administration was in theory centralized under the Civil Service Commission, which reported to the prime minister. In actuality the commission's functions were limited to standardization, general guidance, coordination, and record keeping. Recruitment, assignment, promotion, and discipline were handled by each ministry and other public entities. After 1975 government service was divided into eleven position classifications. The top five grades (seven through eleven) were "special grade officers"—the elite of the civilian wing of the bureaucracy. Entry level for college graduates was grade two, and, for those with master's degrees, grade three. Ordinarily, the district officer was either grade five or six, and the district section head was grade three. The provincial governor, deputy governors, and assistant governors were special grade officials, as were mid- to top-level managerial officers of the central ministries. Provincial section chiefs were grade four.

An informative study by Thai political scientist Likhit Dhiravegin revealed that as of 1977 the Ministry of Interior had the largest bloc of special and first grade officials (29 percent and 26 percent, respectively) because of its role as the backbone of the country's far-flung administrative system. This study indicated that the administrative service continued to be elitist, dominated by families of government officials and businessmen. In 1977, although these families accounted for only 10 percent (1 percent and 9 percent, respectively) of the national population, they claimed 41 percent and 33 percent, respectively, of the special grade category and 31 percent and 27 percent, respectively, of the first grade category. This meant that these families produced a combined total of 74 percent of the special grade officers and 58 percent of the first grade functionaries.

Geographically, a strong bias favored the Center (including Bangkok), which had 32 percent of the total population but had 68 percent and 63 percent, respectively, of the special and first grade officers assigned there; Bangkok alone had 39 percent and 33 percent of these two categories. In terms of male-female ratio, of the special grade and first grade officers, only 11 percent and 23 percent, respectively, were women. Many of the female officers were in the ministries of university affairs, education, and public health. Likhit pointed out that, insignificant as it might seem, the number of women in managerial positions was impressively high when compared with other Asian countries.

In terms of education, about 93 percent and 77 percent of the civil servants in the special and first grade categories, respectively, had college educations, which compared favorably with other Asian countries such as Japan, the Republic of Korea (South Korea), Singapore, and Burma. The Likhit study also showed that 33 percent and 20 percent of the elite categories had foreign training, the United States accounting for 71 percent and 78 percent and Britain for 11 percent and 9 percent. The British-United States connection was attributable to Thailand's close relationship with Britain before World War II and with the United States since that time.

According to the Likhit study, foreign influence was least evident in the ministries of interior, justice, and public health—ministries that had the largest number of locally trained civil service officials at the elite level. Most of the locally trained senior judges, public prosecutors, lawyers, district officers, and provincial governors were graduates of Thammasat University. In the 1980s, several other Thai universities were expected to have an increased share of graduates applying for government service.

Civil service promotion was based on merit, but many observers believed that favoritism was an important factor in career advancement. A civil servant normally retired at age sixty. In 1980, however, the law was changed to permit extension of tenure up to age sixty-five in cases of extreme necessity for the benefit of the country.

The Media

In the mid-1980s, the media played an important role as the principal source of domestic and foreign news and, to a lesser degree, as a source of public entertainment. All major daily newspapers were privately owned, but radio and television stations were controlled by the government and operated as commercial enterprises. Newspapers were generally regarded as more credible than the government-controlled broadcast media.

Mass media were under the broad supervision of the Public Relations Department in the Office of the Prime Minister. This department served as the principal source of news and information about the government and its policies. It issued daily news

Throne Hall (Anantasamakom),
the assembly hall for the Thai government
Courtesy National Archives

bulletins on domestic and foreign affairs for use by the print and electronic media. News bulletins were also issued by other government agencies, including the Thai News Agency, established in 1976 under the Mass Communications Organization of Thailand, a state enterprise under the Office of the Prime Minister. The Thai News Agency concentrated mostly on domestic affairs; foreign news was gathered from international wire services, which maintained offices or representatives in Bangkok.

The Constitution guarantees freedom of the press, which may not be curbed except by law ''for the purpose of maintaining the security of state or safeguarding the liberties, dignity or reputation of other persons or maintaining public order or good morals or preventing deterioration of the mind or health of the public.'' Most observers agreed that the Thai press enjoyed considerable freedom. Nevertheless, in the 1980s editorial writers and reporters continued to exercise self-censorship, mindful that there were unwritten but real government constraints, especially on coverage relating to the monarchy, government affairs, internal security matters, and Thailand's international image. The existing statutes gave broad powers to the director general of the Thailand National Police Department, including the authority to revoke or suspend the license of an offending publication. The severity of penalties varied, depending on the political climate and the sensitivity of an issue. In 1987 a new press bill was pending before the National Assembly, the intent of which was to give the press as much autonomy as possible except in time of war or in a state of emergency, in which case the press officer would be allowed to exercise censorship.

Daily newspapers were concentrated heavily in Bangkok, where at least 65 percent of the adults read a daily paper, compared with about 10 percent in rural areas. Newspapers were generally independent, and many were financially solvent, deriving their income from sales and advertising. The government was forbidden by law to subsidize private newspapers. Foreign ownership of newspapers was also banned as a safeguard against undue foreign or subversive influence.

In the 1980s, Thai journalistic standards improved steadily, as reflected in the print media's growing emphasis on political and economic issues, as well as on major foreign news events. This could be attributed to the emergence of a more discriminating readership. On the negative side, sensationalist coverage and insufficient professional training continued to mar the reputation of the Thai press.

There were about 150 newspapers, including 30 dailies in Bangkok and 120 provincial papers in 1985. Some Bangkok dailies were considered to be national newspapers because of their countrywide distribution. Most provincial papers appeared every two, five, seven, or ten days. In Bangkok twenty-one dailies appeared in Thai, six in Chinese, and three in English. Of an estimated daily circulation of 1.6 million for all Bangkok dailies in 1985, *Thai Rath* (800,000 circulation) and the *Daily News* (400,000 circulation) together claimed about 75 percent of the total circulation. These two newspapers reportedly were popular among white-collar groups. The most successful among the remaining newspapers were *Ban Muang, Matichon, Siam Rath,* and *Naew Na.* The English-language dailies were the *Bangkok Post, The Nation,* and the *Bangkok World,* which were popular among the well-educated and influential members of Thai society and were regarded by many as more reliable than the Thai dailies. Some of the editorial positions on the *Bangkok Post* and the *Bangkok World* were held by foreigners, mostly British; *The Nation,* on the other hand, was almost entirely staffed by Thai and tended to view the world from a Thai perspective.

Unlike the English-language dailies, whose circulation was increasing in the early 1980s, Chinese-language dailies were declining in readership. Their total circulation was probably around 70,000. Two leading Chinese-language dailies were *Sing Sian Yit Pao* and *Tong Hua Yit Pao.* These dailies were noted for responsible coverage of domestic and international affairs, but they refrained from taking strong stands on local political questions.

All aspects of radio and television broadcasting, such as operating hours, content, programs, advertising, and technical requirements, were set by the Broadcasting Directing Board, which was under the Office of the Prime Minister and headed by a deputy prime minister. In 1987 the country had 275 national and local radio stations. The Public Relations Department, under the Office of the Prime Minister, was responsible for Radio Thailand and the National Broadcasting Services of Thailand (NBT). NBT was the official government broadcasting station, which transmitted local and international news mandatorily broadcast on all stations. News was also broadcast daily in nine foreign languages over Radio Thailand's World Service. Radio stations were run also as commercial enterprises by such government agencies as the Mass Communications Organization of Thailand; units of the army, the navy, and the air force; the police; the ministries of communications and education; and several state universities. In 1985 there were 7.7 million radio sets in use.

As a major official channel of communication, all television stations avoided controversial viewpoints and independent political comment in their programming. The Army Signal Corps and the Mass Communications Organization of Thailand directly operated television channels 5 and 9. Two other channels were operated under license by private groups, the Bangkok Entertainment Company, which ran Channel 3, and the Bangkok Television Company, in charge of Channel 7. Channel 11 was operated by the government primarily as an educational station.

By 1980 television had become the dominant news medium among urban Thai. Household television set ownership (about 3.3 million sets in 1984) was as widespread as radio in all urban areas of the country. As of 1984, television exceeded radio ownership in the Center and South and was about even with radio ownership in the North and the Northeast. Nine out of ten Bangkok households had at least one television set. Ownership of color television was also widespread among urban Thai in the South (58 percent), Bangkok (54 percent), the Northeast (49 percent), the central plain (47 percent), and the North (43 percent).

Political Developments, 1980–87

In 1987 Thailand was stable under Prime Minister Prem's eighth consecutive year of administration, even though his leadership was criticized for alleged indecisiveness and weakness. The country had not experienced a successful military coup since October 1977, and in 1987 few politically or economically destabilizing issues existed. As in past decades, the military continued to be influential in the political process. Significantly, however, "one of the most surprising aspects of recent Thai politics," as American political scientist Ansil Ramsay noted, "is that political change has occurred within a parliamentary framework instead of through military coups."

In January 1980, while dismissing as obsolete the flurry of seasonal rumors of an imminent coup, then-Prime Minister Kriangsak declared that "our military officers who are pursuing a democratic course" would never allow it to happen. He did not, however, rule out a coup if there were good reason, but only as a last resort. He also made the point that he would step down if there was a majority political party run by trustworthy and efficient political party executives.

At the end of February, Kriangsak stepped down, not, however, because there was a party he could trust. Rather, the factious military was unable to give the former army commander in chief the unified support he needed at the time to weather a political storm brought on by economic troubles. Predictably, he was succeeded by Prem, the army commander in chief at the time, making Kriangsak the first ex-military prime minister ever to give up power voluntarily (see table 14, Appendix). Prem survived two attempted coups and provided years of stability, which the country needed for the institutionalization of a political process based on the party system. The development of party politics was still under way in 1987, albeit with occasional setbacks.

Although Prem initially ruled through a coalition cabinet of three parties—the Democrat (Prachathipat) Party, the Social Action (Kit Sangkhom) Party, and the Chart Thai (Thai Nation) Party—his real political base was the armed forces, the traditional source and guarantor of political power (see Political Parties, this ch.). In 1980, as from the early 1970s, the military was divided into several cliques. One of the more influential cliques called itself "the Young Military Officers Group," popularly nicknamed "the Young Turks." The influential members of this group belonged to Class Seven (1960 graduates) of the elite Chulachomkhlao Royal Military Academy. Their aim was to enhance military professionalism as well as to ensure a decisive role for the military in the Thai political process. In 1980 their support was key to Prem's ascension to the prime ministership. In April 1981, however, they turned against Prem, who at that time was still army commander in chief. Apparently the Young Turks believed that Prem had betrayed their trust by consorting with political opportunists and party politicians in his coalition government and, worse yet, by taking sides with rival

military cliques opposed to the Young Turks. For two days, the Young Turks controlled the capital city, but they failed to win the monarch's tacit consent, which had been crucial to the traditional legitimization of a coup. Thirty-eight coup plotters—including their leaders, Colonel Manoon Rupekahorn and Colonel Prachak Sawangchit—were dismissed from the army. After the abortive coup, General Arthit Kamlangek, who was credited with a key role in thwarting the attempt, was promoted to commander of the First Army Region; traditionally, this post was regarded as the most strategic one in the making of coups and countercoups (see Military Structure, ch. 5). It was also noticeable that Class Five (1958 graduates) of the military academy, the Young Turks' chief rival faction, were promoted to some key army posts.

In August 1981, Prem relinquished his post as army commander in chief but continued to head his second coalition cabinet. This coalition was formed in March 1981, after a cabinet crisis brought on by the withdrawal of the Social Action Party from the ruling coalition. The second coalition comprised the Chart Thai Party, the Democrat Party, and the United Democracy (Saha Prachathipatai) Party, the latter a loose alliance of minor parties. In December 1981, this cabinet was reorganized to make room for the Social Action Party, which decided to return to Prem's third cabinet.

Another notable development of the year was Kriangsak's entry into partisan politics when he won a parliamentary by-election in

August. For this purpose, he founded the National Democracy (Chart Prachathipatai) Party in June. Thus, he became the first former army commander in chief and prime minister to enter party politics through the so-called front door—the parliamentary route. Because of his background and experience, Kriangsak was often mentioned as an alternative to Prem.

Another frequently mentioned alternative was General Arthit, a palace favorite, whose rapid rise to the post of commander in chief of the army in October 1982 was unprecedented. To some Thai observers, outspoken Arthit was "the strongman of the future," destined to become the next prime minister.

It was not unusual for a Thai general to air his views publicly on socioeconomic or political issues, and such utterances were often considered important. As political scientist John L.S. Girling noted, "The power and authority of the military-bureaucratic regime, which had been so long in existence, depended not so much on the physical means of coercion that it possessed . . . as in the acceptance by extrabureaucratic elements of the inevitability of that power and their inability to challenge it."

In the 1980s, the military dominance in politics, however, seemed to be undergoing some change, partly because the officer corps was not as cohesive as it had been previously and hence was less able to impose its will. For example, the lack of unity among the officers and their allies in the Senate and the political parties was largely to blame for the failure to amend the Constitution in 1983 (see National Assembly, this ch.). Factionalism continued unabated, particularly between members of Class Seven and of Class Five of the Chulachomkhlao Royal Military Academy. The relative influence of these factions was reflected in the annual reshuffle of the military high command—the traditional barometer of real political power—announced each year in September. By 1983 the Class Five faction, sometimes known as the "democratic soldiers" group, seemed to be particularly influential.

Another factor bearing on the military's changing political role was the generals' own growing perception that a coup was undemocratic, if not uncivilized. As a result, an increasing number of generals and colonels in retirement chose to involve themselves in party politics. In the election held on April 18, 1983, for example, the Chart Thai Party captured 73 of 324 seats in the House of Representatives—nearly twice its 1979 total (see table 15, Appendix). Led by Major General (retired) Pramarn Adireksan, this party had a large number of retired military officers. After the election, the Chart Thai Party emerged as the top party in parliament with 108 seats by absorbing independents and other minor party members. Nonetheless, it was not included in Prem's fourth coalition cabinet. This exclusion reportedly was because of the party's aggressive postelection maneuvers for what it claimed as the moral right to form a new government. Such aggressiveness antagonized other parties, which wanted Prem for another term as their consensus prime minister. Prem's fourth coalition consisted of four parties: Social Action Party, Democrat Party, Prachakorn Thai (Thai People) Party, and National Democracy Party (see Political Parties, this ch.).

The political situation was volatile during 1984, with rumors of a coup, a cabinet reorganization, and a rift between Prem and Arthit—two of the most frequently mentioned political actors. Arthit continued to project a forceful image with his confrontational approach, a sharp contrast to Prem's low-keyed, conciliatory approach. Also serving as the supreme commander of the armed forces beginning in September 1983, Arthit at times challenged the propriety of important government policies. In November, for example, he made a televised condemnation of the government's policy of devaluation. Also in 1984, apparently with Arthit's blessing, some active-duty and retired army officers pressed for constitutional amendments aimed at enhancing their political influence through the Senate and the cabinet. A showdown between Arthit's camp and Prem's ruling coalition seemed imminent. Arthit backed off, however, urging the army officers to abandon, at least for the time, the drive for amendments. It appeared that the monarchy played a key role in defusing the tension. In this context, Thai political scientist Juree Vichit-Vadakan commented that the monarchy was "likely to be the single most important force capable of holding the country together during times of chaos and crisis and of assuring the viability of a democratic process in Thailand. With a clear commitment of the monarchy to a constitutional government, democracy Thai style ultimately may have a chance to take root."

In 1985 Thailand survived another military challenge to its constitutional government in the form of an abortive coup, again led by Manoon, the Young Turks colonel who had engineered the unsuccessful coup in 1981. On September 9, a small band of army and air force officers with several hundred men and twenty-two tanks made a vain predawn bid for power. The coup collapsed after ten hours, but not before seven persons were killed and scores wounded. Manoon was allowed to go into exile as part of a deal to avert further bloodshed. Among those detained for complicity were Kriangsak, Prem's predecessor and leader of the National Democracy Party; the former army commander in chief and supreme commander of the armed forces, General Sern Na Nakorn; the former deputy army commander in chief, General Yos Thephasdin na Ayutthaya; the former deputy supreme commander of the armed forces, Air Chief Marshal Krasae Intharathat; and the still-serving deputy supreme commander of the armed forces Air Chief Marshal Arun Prompthep.

The facts surrounding the affair were still unclear as of mid-1987, but observers generally suggested two reasons for the failure of the coup. One was factiousness in the military. The other was the perceived obsolescence of a coup, a view shared by a widening circle of military officers, senior civil servants, businessmen, financiers, industrialists, white-collar executives, intellectuals, and, significantly, by the king as well. According to this perception, popular demand for participation and representation, whetted by the advent of industrialization in Thailand, could be better accommodated by a parliamentary government than by an authoritarian and narrowly based military regime. Despite the absence of a successful coup since 1977, however, few informed Thai seemed to believe that the country was on a steady course toward fuller democratic rule. Thai political scientist Likhit Dhiravegin observed in December 1986, ''[If] one probes deeper, one would get a feeling that despite the existence of the elected assembly and a Cabinet consisting of civilians, the final say on who should be the prime minister still rests mainly with the military.''

In partisan politics, the Democrat Party, the oldest and the best organized party, fared well. Of the seven seats at stake in five by-elections held in 1985, the Democrats won five, four of them in Bangkok, where they also captured thirty-eight seats in the election for the fifty-four-member city council. One of the winning Democrats was General Harn Linanond, a former commander of the Fourth Army Region who quit the army in 1984 in a dispute with General Arthit. In 1985 Harn, who was deputy leader of the Democrat Party, and his party colleagues opposed a one-year extension of service for Arthit, who was due for retirement in September 1985. The army had reportedly ordered its personnel in Bangkok to vote for former Lieutenant General Vitoon Yasawas, Harn's rival, running on the Social Action Party ticket.

Tensions between the army and the Democrat Party also surfaced in Thailand's first gubernatorial election for Bangkok in November 1985. This contest was won handily by former Major General Chamlong Srimuang, a devout Buddhist, former chief aide to Prem and former leader of the Class Seven military academy graduates. Chamlong ran as an independent but was strongly supported by Arthit, who publicly urged his subordinates and their

The Royal Family in the early 1980s
Courtesy Royal Family Thai Embassy

families to vote against any party that had an antimilitary orientation. His urging was directed particularly against the Democrat Party. Arthit's support would have made little difference in the outcome of the contest because of Chamlong's immense personal appeal to nearly every segment of the Bangkok electorate.

The eventful year of 1986 augured well for the future of party politics. Prem's coalition overcame a minor cabinet crisis, reined in outspoken Arthit, held the third parliamentary election since 1979, and improved the climate for professionalization of the military. At the root of the cabinet crisis was endemic factional strife within the Social Action Party, the senior partner in Prem's four-party coalition. This problem necessitated a cabinet reorganization in January and, worse still, caused the coalition government an embarrassing parliamentary defeat on a routine legislative bill. Facing the certainty of a major parliamentary fight over a motion of no-confidence against his government, Prem consulted King Bhumibol and dissolved the House of Representatives, with an election slated for July 27—eleven months ahead of schedule. The political arena was explosive at that juncture, as a result of mounting tension between the two competing poles of power—Prem and Arthit. Relations between them had become steadily strained since Arthit's public assault on the government's fiscal and monetary policies in November 1984.

Another complicating factor was Arthit's decision to set up the army's "election-monitoring center" in connection with the forthcoming election, an action some Thai criticized as an unwarranted foray into politics. Still another complication was active lobbying by Arthit's loyalists to have the army commander in chief's term extended another year to September 1987. If these loyalists had had their way, the extension would have enabled them to influence political realignment to their advantage in 1987—after Prem's four-year mandate expired in April. A new election, to be held within sixty days from mid-April, would have been held while the army was still under Arthit's direction.

On March 24, 1986, the government announced that Arthit would be retired as scheduled on September 1. Then on May 27, the government stunned the nation by dismissing the army commander in chief and replacing him with General Chaovalit Yongchaiyut, a Prem loyalist. Prior to that, no army commander in chief had been fired before the expiration of his term. This unprecedented action came amid the flurry of rumors that Arthit was involved in behind-the-scenes maneuvers to undermine Prem's chances for another premiership after the July election. Arthit, whose largely ceremonial post as supreme commander of the armed forces until September 1986 was not affected by the dismissal order, denied any role in such maneuvers.

Chaovalit quickly set the tone of his army leadership by promising to keep the military out of politics, by dissolving the army's election watchdog center, and by pledging military neutrality in the election. Later in August, the army announced that twenty-eight of the thirty-eight Young Turks officers cashiered in the wake of the abortive coup in 1981 had been reinstated to active service; Colonel Manoon officially remained a fugitive from prosecution. The reinstatement, though mostly to nonsensitive noncommand positions, was widely welcomed as an important step toward restoring unity in the army and improving the prospect for military professionalism. In the annual September reshuffle of senior military officials, Chaovalit strengthened his power base by appointing Class Five graduates of the military academy to key senior commands.

The July 1986 election involved the participation of 3,810 candidates representing 16 parties. Candidates of the outgoing coalition parties campaigned, generally avoiding any association with Prem. The contest literally was wide open; no single party was expected to win an electoral mandate outright in the newly enlarged 347-seat House of Representatives. As in 1983, Prem declined to run in this election, citing the "need to maintain my neutrality and to let the election be held . . . free from any factor that may sway the people.'' Nevertheless, because he might again be picked as the compromise choice of major parties to lead the postelection government, the issue of an elected or nonelected prime minister became a focus of campaign debate. Regardless of partisanship, however, nearly all agreed that the austerity measures that had been initiated by the outgoing government should be scuttled as a major step toward accelerating economic recovery and boosting rural incomes. Evidently Bangkok's powerful banking and business families, who had suffered as a result of such measures since late 1984, effectively brought their influence to bear on many candidates. The army did not intervene, but Chaovalit warned that the military would not stand idly by if the postelection government failed the people's trust.

Predictably, no party emerged with a majority, although the Democrat Party captured the largest bloc of seats with 100, which was 44 more than it had in 1983. Most observers agreed that a coalition led by the Democrat Party would stand little chance of survival; the party had nowhere near a majority and, moreover, was traditionally the most outspoken critic of military involvement in politics. Thus, despite the lack of any ground swell for a non-elected prime minister, Prem again emerged as the compromise leader most acceptable to the army, the palace, and the major political parties.

The new coalition cabinet Prem unveiled in August consisted of four parties, with a combined strength of 232 seats distributed among the Democrat Party (100), the Chart Thai Party (63), the Social Action Party (51), and the Rassadorn (People) Party (18). These four were among the seven parties that initially agreed to support Prem; the remaining three not in the coalition were the Prachakorn Thai Party (24), the Ruam Thai (Thai Unity) Party (19), and the Community Action (Kit Prachakhorn) Party (15). The three parties later formed an opposition bloc with several other minor parties. The United Democracy Party, which commanded thirty-eight seats, agreed to support the opposition bloc in voting against the government on an issue-by-issue basis.

In September 1986, the fifty-four-year-old army commander in chief, Chaovalit, pledged his support for ''the parliamentary government,'' adding that there would be ''no more coups'' as long as he was in charge of the army. Earlier, he had expressed an intention to retire in 1988 (reaffirmed in July 1987); if he did not, he could remain in his post until official retirement in 1992, or 1993 with a one-year extension of service.

On April 22, 1987, the Prem administration faced a no-confidence debate in parliament, the second one since October 1986. Eighty-four opposition members sponsored the no-confidence motion against the entire cabinet. However, amid allegations of bribery and rumors of a coup or a parliamentary dissolution, the censure bid failed. Fifteen of the sponsors, under heavy outside pressure, withdrew their names on the day the debate was scheduled to take place, leaving the motion one vote shy of the minimum seventy votes. Opposition leaders vowed to resubmit another no-confidence motion later.

Political Parties

In the late 1980s, the Thai political party system continued to evolve, albeit spasmodically. It was at a delicate stage of transition from its past status as an adjunct to the bureaucratic establishment to a more substantial role as a channel for popular representation and a provider of top political executives.

The concept of party politics dated back to the early 1930s, but its impact was generally insignificant, having been overshadowed by the military-bureaucratic elite. The struggle for power was nearly always settled by coup, and the pluralistic demands of the society were accommodated through either bureaucratic channels or patron-client connections. For decades political parties had an uncertain status. When they existed, they did so at the sufferance of generals, who abolished or revived them at will. Parties were unable to maintain continuity, nor could they develop a mass base. Part of the problem was the bad image of partisan politics, which the politicians brought on themselves through their unscrupulous pursuit of self-interest.

Party politics received a major impetus from the student uprising of October 1973 (see Thailand in Transition, ch. 1). Forty-two parties participated in the 1975 parliamentary election, and thirty-nine participated the following year. The freewheeling partisan politics during the so-called democratic period of 1973–76 ended in the coup of October 1976. Kriangsak, the army commander in chief, appointed a civilian-led government, but the Thanin Kraivichien regime turned out to be overly repressive and was overthrown in 1977. Assuming the office of prime minister himself, Kriangsak permitted the resumption of party politics banned by Thanin. Of the 39 parties that took part in the April 1979 election, 7 parties captured about 70 percent of the 301 contested seats.

As a result of the confusion stemming from the proliferation of minor parties, a new political parties act was passed in July 1981.

The act, which became effective in 1983, specified that to participate in an election, a party must have a minimum of 5,000 members spread throughout the country's four geographical regions.
In each region, at least five provinces must have members, the minimum per province being fifty. The membership requirement was
designed to foster the development of mass-based parties catering
to broad national interests rather than narrow, sectional interests.
Another provision of the act stipulated that a party must put up
candidates for at least half the total lower house seats, or 174 seats.
As a result, in the 1983 and 1986 elections, the number of participating parties was reduced to fourteen and sixteen, respectively.
In order to satisfy the legal requirements, some parties fielded candidates recruited from among recent college graduates.

In the 1980s, the country's multiparty system continued to suffer
from traditional long-standing problems. These included organizational frailty and lack of discipline, endemic factionalism, the
emphasis on personalities over issues, and the politicians' penchant
for vote-buying and influence-peddling. Parties were formed, as
before, by well-known or wealthy individuals to promote their own
personal, familial, parochial, or regional interests. Observers
expressed concern that failure to improve the party system could
result in a return to authoritarian military rule.

The perception that political parties and politicians were unwor-
thy of trust was widespread in 1987. However, a coup was ruled
out by Chaovalit, the new army commander in chief, even though
he publicly castigated politicians as venal and hypocritical. In February he asserted that political parties, the Constitution, and elections alone would not make for a genuine democracy in Thailand,
where, he argued, the party system and elections were controlled
by a wealthy few who used the trappings of democracy for their
own benefit. Appearing before a parliamentary committee in April
1987, Chaovalit maintained that to build a real Thai-style democracy with the king as head of state, the ever-widening income disparity must be narrowed first and that at the same time political
parties and all government entities including the military "must
join hands and walk ahead together."

The major Thai parties, which Chaovalit had criticized, were
mostly right-of-center. Their numerical representation in the House
of Representatives varied considerably from one election to another.
Of the four ruling coalition parties in 1987, the Democrat Party
was considered to be somewhat liberal, despite its beginning in 1946
as a conservative, monarchist party. Seni Pramoj, prime minister
in 1946 and again in 1976, led the party from its inception until
1979. In 1974 the party suffered major fragmentation and lost some

key figures, including Kukrit, Seni's brother, who formed the Social Action Party that year. In the 1979 election, the Democrats suffered a major setback but rebounded in 1983. Over the years, this party consistently opposed military involvement in politics and actively sought to broaden its base of support across all social segments and geographical regions. In recent years, particularly after July 1986, the Democrats were racked by internal strife. Their leader Bhichai Rattakul, deputy prime minister in Prem's coalition, was reconfirmed in a factional showdown in January 1987. Afterward, retired Lieutenant Colonel Sanan Khachornprasart was named secretary general, in place of Veera Musikapong, whose faction had been backed by wealthy Bangkok businessman Chalermphan Srivikorn.

The Chart Thai Party, sometimes called the "generals' party," was founded in 1974 by a group of retired generals and was led until July 1986 by Pramarn Adireksan, retired major general and former president of the Association of Thai Industries and the Thai Textile Association. Aggressively anticommunist, Chart Thai was backed by a number of prominent industrialists. After the July 1986 election, it was led by retired General Chatichai Choonhaven, whose relationship with Prem was friendly.

The Social Action Party, a 1974 offshoot of the Democrat Party, was led by Thai statesman Kukrit Pramoj until he stepped down in December 1985. The party was led thereafter by the former deputy party leader and minister of foreign affairs, Siddhi Savetsila, a retired air chief marshal. More than any other party, the Social Action Party was identified with a free enterprise economy. In the 1986 election, the party suffered a severe loss, brought on in no small part by its own internal strife. In May 1986, a splinter faction led by seventy-four-year-old Boontheng Thongsawasdi formed the United Democracy Party with financial support from big business—amid a spate of rumors that General Arthit was also among the party's behind-the scenes backers. In the July 1986 election and afterward, the United Democracy Party was outspokenly critical of the Prem administration.

The Rassadorn Party, the fourth member of the ruling coalition, was formed only a few months before the July 1986 election; until May 1986 it was known as the National Union (Sahachat) Party. Its leader was Thienchai Sirisamphan, retired deputy army commander in chief. Rassadorn came to be known as a *pak taharn* (military party) because its key party posts were held by retired generals. Its entry into partisan politics was welcomed by many for providing a constructive channel for military involvement in parliamentary government.

Former Prime Minister
Kukrit Pramoj
Courtesy
Royal Thai Embassy

The exclusion of the United Democracy Party from the fifth coalition government was predictable in light of its anti-Prem stance. However, it probably came as a surprise to Samak Sundaravej, leader of the Prachakorn Thai Party formed in 1978, that his right-wing and monarchist group was not invited to join the coalition. Before the election, master orator Samak stated that the new postelection government should continue its strong military ties and should once again be led by outgoing Prem. In so doing, he rejected the suggestion that Kukrit Pramoj, who had retired from party politics altogether in May 1986, should head the new postelection regime.

The Ruam Thai Party and the Community Action Party, both formed in 1986, were also among the seven parties supporting Prem for continued premiership; but they, too, were left out of the coalition. The leader of the Ruam Thai Party, Narong Wongwan, was a former member of the Social Action Party and outgoing minister of agriculture and cooperatives. The Community Action Party was led by its founder Boonchu Rojanasathien, one-time deputy prime minister in charge of economic affairs, ex-deputy leader of the Social Action Party, and former president of the Bangkok Bank.

The remaining seven parties with one or more elected House of Representatives members formed the "Group of Nineteen," so named because of their combined total of nineteen members. These

213

parties agreed in August 1986 to join with other noncoalition parties to form a united front in an attempt to ensure efficient and systematic monitoring of the government. In a crucial showdown over a no-confidence motion against the Prem government in April 1987, however, the opposition bloc suffered a major political embarrassment because of the last-minute defection from the censure debate by fifteen of its members. Boonchu, chief strategist of the five-member opposition leadership team, expelled five members from his Community Action Party for their action.

Foreign Affairs

Diplomacy has served Thailand well, enabling the kingdom to manage its foreign affairs flexibly and relatively unencumbered by intrusions of major foreign powers. Remarkably adaptive to shifts in international currents, Thailand has almost always aligned itself with the dominant power in the region in its effort to ensure security, increase trade, and preserve national independence. In the 1980s, its primary concern was to normalize relations with Cambodia and Laos—relations that were complicated by the Vietnamese military presence in these countries.

Background

Since World War II, no single factor has shaped the style and substance of Thai foreign relations more than the establishment of a communist-run government in China in 1949. The communist triumph aroused a Thai fear of southward Chinese expansion, in which the economically powerful and ethnocentrist Chinese minority in Bangkok might serve as a potential fifth column. Chinese intervention in Korea in 1950 and growing evidence of clandestine communist Chinese roles in local insurgencies in Southeast Asia reinforced Thai resolve to act in concert with other anticommunist nations. The formal installation of a communist administration in Hanoi after the decisive defeat of the French at Dien Bien Phu in May 1954 set the stage for Thailand's signing of the Manila Pact, a collective security agreement, in September 1954. The resulting Southeast Asia Treaty Organization (SEATO), as the regional body was formally called, had as its members Australia, Britain, France, New Zealand, Pakistan, the Philippines, Thailand, and the United States. SEATO headquarters was in Bangkok.

Nevertheless, Thailand viewed the effectiveness of collective security with some degree of skepticism. On March 6, 1962, in an attempt to allay Thai apprehensions, the United States and Thailand reached a new understanding under what came to be known as the Rusk-Thanat agreement (named after then-Secretary of State Dean Rusk and then-Minister of Foreign Affairs Thanat Khoman). Under the agreement, the United States pledged that, in the event of aggression it would help Thailand unilaterally without prior agreement of all other parties to the Manila Pact.

During the 1960s, Thailand maintained close economic and security ties with the United States, while at the same time striving to foster regional cooperation with its noncommunist neighbors. Its assumption was that regional solidarity and national security were mutually reinforcing and would provide an effective deterrence to communism. In 1961 Thailand joined Malaya (since 1963, Malaysia) and the Philippines in launching the Association of Southeast Asia as a nonmilitary, nonpolitical vehicle for consultation and mutual assistance in economic, cultural, scientific, and administrative matters.

In 1967 the Association of Southeast Asia was replaced by a broader regional group, the Association of Southeast Asian Nations (ASEAN), comprising Indonesia, Malaysia, the Philippines, Singapore, and Thailand. The members agreed to cooperate in food production, industry and commerce, civil aviation, shipping, tourism, communications, meteorology, science and technology, and Southeast Asian studies. Consultation and cooperation were to take place through an annual ministerial conference held in each of the five ASEAN countries in alphabetical rotation. As a result of the formation of the regional organization, consultation between Thailand and the other ASEAN countries on external problems increased greatly in the 1970s.

The Thai response to the external uncertainties of the 1970s was a graphic demonstration of the flexibility of its foreign policy. The external catalyst was an apparent shift in American strategic thinking with regard to China and the Vietnam conflict. The shift was sensed in Bangkok in the late 1960s—in March 1968, when President Lyndon B. Johnson expressed his intention to seek a negotiated peace in Vietnam and again in July 1969, when President Richard M. Nixon told Thai leaders in Bangkok of his intention to lower the future American military profile in Asia without undertaking any new security obligations. At that time, Nixon reaffirmed the United States resolve to "honor its present commitments in Southeast Asia" and to continue its support of Thai efforts in the areas of security and economic development. Not surprisingly, in 1968, before the "Nixon Doctrine" was proclaimed in 1969, Thailand hinted at its desire to open channels of communication with China, the Democratic People's Republic of Korea (North Korea), and the Democratic Republic of Vietnam (North Vietnam).

These channels were considered necessary by the Thai in order to solve difficulties and achieve peaceful coexistence. In late 1970, a government committee was set up to explore the possibility of normalizing relations with China.

After 1971, as the United States and China moved toward reconciliation and détente, Thai soul-searching began in earnest. In 1972 Thailand sent sports teams to China, and in 1973 Thailand made overtures to Hanoi for a dialogue shortly after the United States and North Vietnam signed a cease-fire agreement. In 1974 a Thai delegation conferred with Chinese premier Zhou Enlai in Beijing on measures to improve bilateral relations. At that time Zhou was reported to have assured the Thai delegation that China would stop aiding communist insurgents in Thailand, while underlining his concern over increasing Soviet influence in Southeast Asia. In December 1974, the Thai government lifted a fifteen-year ban on trade with China. In March 1975, a month before Saigon fell, Thailand announced its decision to recognize and normalize diplomatic relations with China.

In the wake of communist takeovers in Phnom Penh and Saigon in April 1975, Thailand moved expeditiously to realign its foreign policy. Thailand's security ties with the United States—the pillar of Bangkok's foreign relations for nearly three decades—were downplayed as part of accentuating a policy of friendship with all nations. In July 1975, the Thai revoked a military accord with the United States under which American troops had been allowed on Thai soil. Thailand also agreed with the Philippines in principle that SEATO, having outlived its usefulness, should be phased out as early as possible. The crowning moment of the policy of readjustment came in July 1975, when Thailand and China signed a formal agreement on establishing diplomatic relations. Noteworthy was the absence of a Chinese demand for the prior removal of American troops from Thailand, in striking contrast to Hanoi's insistence that Thailand should first renounce its policy of "collusion" with the United States before any reconciliation could take place.

The normalization of relations with its Indochinese neighbors became pressing as refugees from Laos, Cambodia, and Vietnam streamed across the Thai frontier, straining Thai resources and raising tensions in the border regions. Relations with Laos, bound to Thailand by a shared history, religion, ethnicity, culture, and language, were tense. Much of the problem centered on Laotian Meo tribespeople who had taken refuge in Thailand after the communist-led Pathet Lao forces gained control of Vientiane in May 1975. For years the Meo and some Thai irregular troops had

*The Thai delegation to the Southeast Asia Treaty Organization
(SEATO) conference in Bangkok in 1955
Courtesy National Archives*

waged clandestine operations against the Pathet Lao forces, reportedly with the knowledge and cooperation of the government of
Thailand. After intermittent clashes on the Mekong River, Thailand
in November 1975 closed the frontier with Laos, causing hardship
in Vientiane; this action prevented oil, food, and other essential
goods from reaching Laos through Thai territory, the historical
transit route to the landlocked country. Tension eased somewhat
after January 1976, when the border was reopened following Thai
recognition of the new Laotian regime. In August 1976, the two
countries signed an agreement on the transport of Laotian goods
through Thailand in exchange for Thai air routes over Laos to Vietnam and Hong Kong. Nonetheless, recurring border incidents led
to a temporary Thai economic blockade of Laos in late 1977. By
the end of the year, Laotian refugees accounted for 73,000 of about
95,000 Indochinese refugees encamped in Thailand.

In April 1975, Thailand was the first country in Southeast Asia
to recognize the new regime of the communist Khmer Rouge (see
Glossary) in Phnom Penh. In October the two countries agreed
in principle to resume diplomatic and economic relations; the agreement was formalized in June 1976, when they also agreed to erect
border markers in poorly defined border areas.

217

Meanwhile, the withdrawal of all American troops from Thailand by July 1976 paved the way for the Thai-Vietnamese agreement in August on normalizing relations. In January 1978, Bangkok and Hanoi signed an accord on trade and economic and technical cooperation, agreeing also to exchange ambassadors, reopen aviation links, resolve all problems through negotiations, and consult on the question of delimiting sea boundaries. Progress toward improved relations with the Indochinese states came to an abrupt halt, however, after Vietnam invaded Cambodia in December 1978, and in January 1979 installed in Phnom Penh a new communist regime friendly to Hanoi.

This invasion not only provoked a Chinese attack on Vietnam in February 1979 but also posed a threat to Thailand's security. Bangkok could no longer rely on Cambodia as a buffer against Vietnamese power. Bangkok was forced to assume the role of a frontline state against a resurgent communist Vietnam, which had 300,000 troops in Cambodia and Laos. The Thai government began increasing its defense capabilities. While visiting Washington in February 1979, Prime Minister Kriangsak asked for and received reassurances of military support from the United States. His government also launched a major diplomatic offensive to press for the withdrawal of all Vietnamese forces from Cambodia and for continued international recognition of Democratic Kampuchea under Pol Pot's Khmer Rouge regime. As part of that offensive, Kriangsak also journeyed to Moscow in March 1979—the first visit ever by a Thai prime minister—to explain the Thai position on the Cambodian question and to reassure the Soviets that Thailand's anti-Vietnamese position was neither anti-Soviet nor pro-Chinese. Such reassurances were believed to be necessary in view of Vietnamese accusations that Thailand collaborated with China and the United States in aiding and abetting the Khmer Rouge forces against the Heng Samrin regime.

The Thai offensive, backed by Bangkok's ASEAN partners, was rewarded in a United Nations (UN) General Assembly resolution adopted in November 1979. The resolution called for immediate withdrawal of all foreign forces from Cambodia, asked all nations to refrain from interfering in, or staging acts of aggression against, Cambodia, and called on the UN secretary general to explore the possibility of an international conference on Cambodia.

Foreign Relations since 1980

In the 1980s, the Cambodian-Vietnamese question was a principal concern of Thai foreign policy makers, who found common cause with countries that also opposed the Vietnamese occupation of Cambodia. Security once again became an important consideration in the determination of Bangkok's foreign policy.

In 1979 the ASEAN members were apparently divided over the Cambodian-Vietnamese situation. Indonesia and Malaysia were reportedly more conciliatory toward Hanoi than Thailand and Singapore, viewing China rather than Vietnam as the principal threat to regional stability. Indonesia and Malaysia wanted a strong and stable Vietnam as a potential ally, or at least as a buffer, against Chinese expansionism. They were inclined to tolerate to a degree the Vietnamese presence in Cambodia and to recognize the Heng Samrin regime, provided that some Vietnamese troops were withdrawn from Cambodia and the political base of the regime was reconstituted more broadly.

The ASEAN differences were turned aside in June 1980, when Vietnamese troops crossed the border into Thailand. The incursion, which coincided with an annual ASEAN ministerial conference in Kuala Lumpur, was contrary to earlier Vietnamese assurances that they would not encroach on Thai territory. The ASEAN foreign ministers strongly condemned the incursion as "an act of aggression" and reaffirmed their undivided support for the UN resolution of November 1979. They also reaffirmed their recognition of the deposed government of Democratic Kampuchea—their rationale being that to recognize the Heng Samrin regime would be tantamount to rewarding Vietnamese aggression in Cambodia. At the first UN-sponsored international conference on Cambodia held in New York in July 1981, Thailand and its ASEAN allies played a key role in seeking a political settlement of the Cambodian question. The conference was attended by delegates from seventy-nine countries and observers from fifteen others, but it was boycotted by Vietnam, Laos, the Soviet Union and its allies, and some nonaligned nations. The conference adopted a resolution that, among other things, called for a cease-fire by all armed Cambodian factions, the withdrawal of all foreign troops under the supervision of a UN observer group, the restoration of Cambodian independence, the establishment of a nonaligned and neutral Cambodia, and the establishment of an ad hoc committee comprising Japan, Malaysia, Nigeria, Senegal, Sri Lanka, Sudan, and Thailand to advise the UN secretary general on ways to implement the resolution.

Relations between Thailand and China improved steadily in the 1980s, with Beijing sharing Bangkok's opposition to Vietnamese military occupation of Cambodia and affirming its support for the Thai and ASEAN stance on the Cambodian question. China sought to reassure Bangkok of its withdrawal of support for the Communist

Party of Thailand and offered military assistance to Thailand in the event the latter was attacked by Vietnam. In the mid-1980s, Chinese arms and supplies for the Khmer Rouge resistance forces reportedly were being shipped through Thai territory. In 1985 a telephone hotline was established between Thailand and China in an effort to coordinate their activities in the event of a major Vietnamese incursion into Thailand. Cordiality in Thai-Chinese relations was evident in a military assistance agreement signed in Beijing in May 1987. This agreement allowed Thailand to purchase, on concessional terms, Chinese tanks, antiaircraft guns, missiles, ammunition, and armored personnel carriers.

Despite some friction over trade issues, Thai relations with the United States were very close, especially from 1979 onward. The United States reassured its commitment to Thai security under the Rusk-Thanat agreement of 1962 as well as the Manila Pact of 1954. In addition to backing the ASEAN position on Cambodia, Washington steadily increased its security assistance to Thailand and also took part in a series of annual bilateral military exercises. Spurred by Vietnamese incursions in 1985 and the arrival in Vietnam of Soviet-piloted MiG-23s, Thailand decided to buy twelve F-16 fighter-bombers from General Dynamics in the United States. Moreover, under an accord reached in October 1985, the two countries began to set up a war reserve weapons stockpile on Thai soil, making Thailand the first country without a United States military base to have such a stockpile. The stockpile, subject to approval by the United States Congress, was to be used only in a "nation-threatening emergency" or to repulse possible armed invasion by Soviet-supported Vietnamese and other forces from Cambodia.

Trade was an irritant in Thai-American relations, but many observers agreed that the trade problems would not likely affect the long-standing friendship and cooperation between the two countries. The United States was a major trading partner and by 1985 had become the largest and most important export market for Thai goods. Thailand enjoyed a trade surplus with the United States, which grew from a modest US$100 million in 1983 to about US$1 billion in 1986 (see International Trade, ch. 3). Meanwhile, there was growing Thai criticism that the United States had become protectionist in trade relations with Thailand. By 1987, however, many informed Thai had come to believe that problems in Thai-American trade relations would be temporary.

In 1987 Thailand continued to express its desire for mutually beneficial relations with the Soviet Union and to affirm its neutrality in the Sino-Soviet rivalry. Relations with Moscow, however, were merely correct, if not cool, as a result of Thai apprehension over Soviet intentions toward Southeast Asia in general and Vietnam in particular. Thai concern was prompted by Moscow's military aid to Vietnam and its continued support of Hanoi's involvement in Cambodia. During his visit to Moscow in May 1987, Minister of Foreign Affairs Siddhi Savetsila of Thailand told his Soviet counterpart that Cambodia was "the test case" of Soviet intentions toward Asia and the Pacific region. He urged the Soviet Union to use its "immense influence and prestige" to bring about a quick and durable settlement of the Cambodian question. Such settlement, according to Siddhi, entailed an early withdrawal of some 140,000 Vietnamese troops from Cambodia, Cambodian exercise of the right of self-determination, and the formation of a neutral and nonaligned Cambodia posing no threat to its neighbors. At the end of the May visit, a protocol was signed establishing a Thai-Soviet trade commission.

As Thailand and Japan celebrated the centennial of their relationship in 1987, Japan continued to be Thailand's principal trading partner and largest foreign investor (see International Trade and Finance, ch. 3). The generally cordial relations between the two countries—dating back to 1887, when Japan was the first country to set up a foreign embassy in Bangkok—were marred in the 1970s and 1980s by a continuous imbalance of trade. In 1984 Thailand's trade deficit with Japan accounted for 62 percent of its total trade deficit for the year, up from 46 percent in the previous year. Japan's economic dominance was much criticized as exploitive and, in late 1984, was the target of a campaign against Japanese goods launched by university students. The Thai government stated that such a campaign offered little or no solution to the deficit problem. Thailand's preferred solution was for Japan to open its market to Thai products, increase its aid and loans to Thailand, set up export-oriented industries in Thailand, and enhance economic cooperation through more active transfers of technology. In 1986 Thailand's trade deficit with Japan decreased 32 percent from the 1984 figure.

In 1987 a major foreign policy goal for Thailand was the restoration of its traditionally cordial ties with Laos, strained since 1975, when Bangkok came to perceive Laos as a client state of Vietnam. In 1979 Thailand and Laos agreed to improve their relations by promoting bilateral trade and allowing free access to the Mekong River by border residents. Nonetheless, relations between Bangkok and Vientiane continued to be tense, marred by frequent shooting incidents on the Mekong. In 1981 Thailand banned 273 "strategic" commodities from export or transshipment to Laos. In mid-1984 armed clashes occurred over the status of three remote border villages. Laos raised this issue in the UN Security

Council, rejecting Thailand's proposal to determine the territoriality of the villages through a joint or neutral survey team. Meanwhile, one important economic link continued to be unaffected by political or security matters: Laos sold electricity to Thailand, earning as much as 75 percent of its annual foreign exchange from this transaction.

On the initiative of Laos, the two sides met in November 1986 to reaffirm their commitment to the 1979 accord on neighborly relations. At about the same time, Thailand began to relax its trade embargo, thereby decreasing the number of banned items to sixty-one. Apparently, this action was taken under pressure from Thai businessmen, whose exports to Laos had dropped sharply from 81 percent of the total imports of Laos in 1980 to 26 percent in 1984. Thai exports to Laos increased in 1985 and 1986, but the future of economic links between the two countries was uncertain. With Soviet assistance, the Laotians planned to complete by 1988 a major highway from Savannakhet across Laos to the Vietnamese port of Danang, thus lessening the traditional dependence of Laos on Thailand for access to the sea for foreign trade.

In March 1987, the two sides met again to discuss matters of mutual concern but made no progress. Although 40,000 to 60,000 Vietnamese troops were still present on Laotian soil, Laos continued to accuse Thailand of harboring its historic ambition to dominate the region. Moreover, Vientiane accused Bangkok of being in collusion with the United States in engaging in unfriendly acts to destabilize the Laotian government. The alleged acts, along with Thai occupation of the three "Lao villages," were stated by Vientiane to be the main barriers to improvement of Laotian-Thai relations. For its part, Thailand charged that Laos was aiding the Pak Mai (New Party), a small, pro-Vietnamese, Thai communist insurgent group that had split from the Chinese-backed Communist Party of Thailand in 1979. Furthermore, Thailand accused Laos of turning a blind eye to heroin production inside Laos and of refusing to cooperate in the suppression of narcotics trafficking between Laos and Thailand. In March 1987, the *Bangkok Post* lamented in an editorial, "It is strange but true that the country with which Thailand has just about everything to share except ideology should happen to be one of the hardest to deal with."

Nevertheless, Thailand was committed to solving its problems with the neighboring states of Indochina—Cambodia, Laos, and Vietnam. The Thai flexibility in foreign policy that had enabled the country to avoid conquest or colonization by foreign powers included a dedication to maintaining good relations with all nations, great and small. Given this commitment and adaptability, it was likely that Thailand, perhaps in concert with its ASEAN partners, would soon reach a mutually agreeable accommodation with its Indochinese neighbors.

*   *   *

Thailand: Buddhist Kingdom as Modern Nation-State by Charles F. Keyes is a good general introduction to the socioeconomic and political setting of Thailand. Equally informative are *Thailand: Society and Politics* by John L.S. Girling, which provides an excellent perspective on Thai politics from 1963 to 1977, based on the author's professional, as well as scholarly, experience in Thailand; Thak Chaloemtiarana's *Thailand: The Politics of Despotic Paternalism*, which has an informative discussion on the dynamics of military rule from 1947 to 1970; and *Modern Thai Politics: From Village to Nation*, edited by Clark D. Neher, a collection of useful articles dealing with Thai political culture and process at all levels. Political dynamics, particularly "the actual events, people, and institutions active during the period of open politics" (1973–76), are given excellent treatment in *Political Conflict in Thailand* by David Morell and Chai-anan Samudavanija.

The Thai Young Turks by Chai-anan Samudavanija is highly useful for understanding the role of the military in Thai politics, with particular attention to the Class Seven (1960) graduates of the Chulachomkhlao Royal Military Academy. David F. Haas's *Interaction in the Thai Bureaucracy* offers a useful discussion on the way district-level civil servants behave in response to the structural and cultural parameters of Thailand's bureaucratic polity. *The Bureaucratic Elite of Thailand* by Likhit Dhiravegin is an insightful study of senior-level Thai civil servants.

In addition, for an understanding of political events, issues, personalities, and institutions active in the political evolutions of the 1980s, specific articles on Thailand in the following publications are recommended: *Southeast Asian Affairs, Asian Survey,* and the annual *Far Eastern Economic Review Asia Yearbook.* (For further information and complete citations, see Bibliography.)

Chapter 5. National Security

Scene depicting the sixteenth-century "War of the Seven White Elephants" in which Queen Suriyothai of Ayutthaya, disguised as a warrior, was killed by a Burmese spear while defending her husband, King Chakraphat

OVER THE LAST CENTURY, Thailand has been highly successful in maintaining its independence and national security in a part of the world where dissension, struggles for power, territorial takeovers, armed insurgency, and war have been common. The Thai managed to avoid the direct colonial rule that led many other Southeast Asian countries into years of struggle, and they remain proud of their legacy of independence and wary of international developments they perceive as threatening. As of the late 1980s, the Thai had not fought a major war on their own soil since the eighteenth century, having avoided foreign military encroachment largely through adroit diplomatic maneuvering.

The pragmatism inherent in Thai national security policy brought the country safely through World War II and into the postwar period. Rather than capitulating to the Japanese, the Thai entered into an alliance with them. At the same time, they maintained an active resistance movement that enjoyed the tolerance of the wartime Thai government. This lack of support for their wartime "ally," combined with Thai diplomatic skill, achieved a postwar accommodation with the victorious Allies. In the face of communist advances in parts of Asia after World War II, Thai leaders sought protection against a possible threat from China by joining other countries for collective security through the 1954 Manila Pact, which laid the groundwork for the Southeast Asia Treaty Organization (SEATO). SEATO's lack of military forces in the tradition of the stronger North Atlantic Treaty Organization, however, left Thai authorities apprehensive about depending on the organization.

In 1962 the country received the added security assurance it sought in the form of the Rusk-Thanat agreement, which stated that the security obligations under the Manila Pact were bilateral as well as collective. The agreement confirmed a long-term protective alliance with the United States, which supplied vast quantities of economic, internal security, and military aid. The close association between the two countries later facilitated United States use of Thai military bases and other facilities during the Second Indochina War (1954–75).

In the mid-1970s, however, Thai leadership began to question the wisdom of depending solely on a protective alliance with the United States. The communists had been successful in Indochina, and the United States role in the region had declined, while the Soviet Union was increasing its support for Thailand's traditional regional rival, Vietnam. Accordingly, Thailand established diplomatic relations with China in 1975, a step that harmonized with the new policy of accommodation between the United States and China. For Thailand this pragmatic course seemed wise in view of the growing threat posed by Vietnam. Once again, Thai flexibility in national security matters reflected the traditional analogy of bamboo bending with the wind.

Although Thai flexibility improved relations with Vietnam, the Thai viewed the Treaty of Friendship and Cooperation in 1978 between Hanoi and Moscow, combined with Vietnam's continued domination of Laos and the Vietnamese invasion of Cambodia, as a serious threat to Thailand's national security.

State of National Security

Persistent armed insurgency had been viewed by a succession of Thai governments as the nation's greatest long-term security problem. In the early 1980s, although insurgent activity had been virtually eliminated, the Thai government continued to fear a recurrence of the problem. Bounded on the west by Burma and on the south by Malaysia, where domestic insurgencies also plagued governing powers, Thailand continued to guard against the spread of such activity across its borders. With the threat of its own communist-supported insurgency lessened by the early 1980s, the Thai government strengthened its defenses against attack by external armed forces as large contingents of Vietnamese army troops continued to occupy neighboring Cambodia.

Insurgency

By the late 1980s, armed insurgency—a national problem that had plagued a series of Thai governments and dominated police and army activities for more than twenty years—had been virtually eliminated. From a peak strength of about 12,000 armed insurgents in the late 1970s, the number of armed guerrillas and separatists had declined to fewer than 2,000. Careful and coordinated government efforts combining military and police actions with social and economic policies had succeeded in reducing the level of insurgency. In addition, in the 1950s the United States had provided extensive military aid and technical assistance to the counterinsurgency program.

A number of insurgent elements had enjoyed fair success in the 1970s. They included the armed Communist Party of Thailand (CPT), Malaysian Communist Party (MCP) guerrillas, disaffected hill tribes people, and Muslim separatists. Their ranks had been increased by an influx of youthful, idealistic supporters who turned to the insurgents as a result of the 1976 military coup and the conservative policies of the Thanin Kraivichien government that followed it. By the mid-1980s, however, the government's coordinated counterinsurgency program had succeeded in eliminating all but a few small pockets of rebels.

Foreign observers disagree on the importance of communist ideology to the insurgency (see Ethnic and Regional Relations, ch. 2). Neglect by past governments, whose primary interests and attention were centered on the capital city of Bangkok, had alienated many rural inhabitants and particularly many ethnic minorities in peripheral areas of the country. Communist militants were able to exploit the discontent that grew steadily during the 1960s and 1970s in those remote regions.

The Thai communist movement had begun in the late 1920s. Dominated by ethnic Chinese, the movement also appealed to other neglected minorities, including the various hill tribes, the Malay, and the Vietnamese (see Ethnicity, Regionalism, and Language, ch. 2). Despite their long residence in the country, these groups had not been accepted by the Thai, who regarded them with suspicion and distrust. In December 1942, a number of small ethnic communist groups merged to form the CPT under predominantly Chinese leadership.

Outlawed by the Anti-Communist Act of 1933, the party began a clandestine existence, surfacing briefly when the act was rescinded in late 1946 but going underground again in 1952, when legislation prohibiting communist political action was adopted. The 1952 law also banned the communist-controlled Central Labor Union, the majority of whose 50,000 members were of mixed Chinese-Thai ancestry. When Sarit Thanarat took control of the government in October 1958, he abolished the Constitution, declared martial law, and intensified the government's anticommunist drives. Nonetheless, the CPT continued its clandestine activities in schools and associations that had large Chinese-Thai memberships and among villagers in border regions. In 1959 the party began to recruit and train limited numbers of Hmong hill people in the North geographical region for use as cadres in antigovernment activities.

The CPT also sought support in the Northeast, appealing to both Thai-Lao and non-Tai minorities, and among the Malay in southern Thailand. Promising a better future to rural peasants in the historically neglected Northeast, the CPT tried to exploit antigovernment sentiments in the area, which for decades had been the center of political dissidence. As a result, the Thai media accused the international communist world of conspiring to break off fifteen northeastern Thai provinces and integrate them into a Greater Laos.

In the peninsular provinces adjoining the Malaysian border in the South the CPT sought to capitalize on Malay minority sentiments for a separate state or a union with Malaysia. This effort was enhanced by popular perceptions of Bangkok's long history of neglect of the socioeconomic development of the Muslim minority.

Despite these countrywide efforts, the CPT failed to gain widespread popular support and sympathy. For one thing, the country's long history of national independence made it difficult for the CPT to present itself as an anticolonial, nationalist movement—a tactic that had been successful in other Asian countries. The large influx in the 1980s of refugees from Cambodia and Vietnam, with their stories of hardship and repression under communist rule, cooled potential popular support for communism (see The Indochinese Refugee Question, ch. 2). For many Thai citizens a sense of shared language, customs, and traditions, together with an ingrained attachment to the king and the Buddhist religion, also presented a psychological barrier to adopting communist goals.

Consequently, the principal energy for the CPT came from external Asian sources. As early as 1959, and particularly after the early 1960s, China and the Democratic Republic of Vietnam (North Vietnam) began providing Thai cadres with training, money, and matériel for insurgency, subversion, and terrorism. Training camps were set up in Vietnam, in the Pathet Lao-controlled areas of neighboring Laos, and in Yunnan Province in China. In early 1962, a clandestine radio station—the Voice of the People of Thailand (VOPT)—began broadcasting from Kunming in Yunnan, transmitting Thai-language propaganda opposing the Bangkok government, as did Radio Hanoi and Radio Beijing.

In the 1960s, because of growing evidence that the CPT was building support structures among villagers in the Northeast, the government began to institute limited countermeasures designed to improve both the defense and the living conditions in villages in threatened areas. Information teams sought to identify villagers' problems and needs and to establish better communication with local authorities. Mobile development units dispatched to vulnerable areas attempted to establish the government's presence and improve its image among isolated villagers. The units were designed to stimulate village self-help and to meet immediate local health, educational, and economic needs by furnishing guidance, materials, and tools. Failure to complete many of the projects, however, limited the effectiveness of the program.

In 1964 Thai authorities further increased their countermeasures. As a follow-up to the mobile development unit scheme, they initiated an accelerated rural development program in security-sensitive areas, constructing roads, wells, marketplaces, health clinics, and schools. Despite these initial government steps, insurgent activity increased steadily after 1965.

Insurgency also became much more active in the South, where dissidents staged ambushes and held propaganda meetings in isolated villages along the Thai-Malaysian border. Many of these rebels were remnants of the MCP that had been driven north across the border into the jungles of southern Thailand by British counterinsurgency action against the MCP in the late 1950s. Roving groups of bandits compounded the security problems in the area. The leading Muslim separatist movement in the South after the early 1970s was the Pattani United Liberation Organization (PULO), whose objective was the formation of an independent Muslim state. PULO enjoyed support from radical Muslims in both southern Thailand and northern Malaysia. The MCP, CPT, and several Muslim separatist organizations, as well as opportunistic bandit groups, all conducted operations against Thai security forces and area residents.

By the mid-1970s, the multifaceted insurgency had become a part of life in the kingdom. The Thai government and the United States had spent vast amounts of money to combat the various insurgencies, but success was limited at best. When the United States withdrew from the counterinsurgency effort in the mid-1970s, a stalemate set in. The infusion of substantial funds by the United States (estimates for the 1951–76 period range from a low of US$100 million to a high of US$1 billion) had failed to gain "victory." There had been too great a diffusion of responsibility among the myriad Thai and American agencies planning and carrying out counterinsurgency operations. In addition, the 1976 coup had sent as many as 5,000 students into the jungles to join the CPT. Total CPT strength was estimated at 12,000 armed fighters in the peak year of 1979.

Beginning in the mid-1970s, the Thai government tried to increase the effectiveness of its counterinsurgency operations. In 1974, in order to eliminate the customary competition for power among government agencies, a new coordinating and command agency, the Internal Security Operational Command (ISOC), was established directly under the military's Supreme Command. In 1987 Prime Minister Prem Tinsulanonda took over as director of a reorganized ISOC, signaling an increased emphasis on political rather than military counterinsurgency programs.

In the early 1980s, the operational policy of Thai counterinsurgency forces had also changed. Rather than concentrating on military actions designed to kill insurgents, the counterinsurgency focused on neutralizing CPT tactics by reclaiming remote areas and their people from control by the communists. The approach demanded increased and better use of coordinated civic action, police, and military operations.

In 1980 the government also began a new policy addressing the complex political and social aspects of the insurgency problem. A directive from the prime minister laid out the broad political strategy, which featured an offer of amnesty to all insurgents and a promise to accord them respect and security. The document also outlined measures to improve the social and political conditions that had contributed to CPT strength. A companion directive issued in 1982 called for a coordinated offensive against insurgent centers in the remote mountainous areas. King Bhumibol Adulyadej (Rama IX, 1946–) had played a role in formulating this strategy, and his enthusiastic support for it quickly spread throughout the military and civilian agencies implementing it.

The government's new approach—referred to as communist suppression rather than counterinsurgency—resulted in the surrender of more than 2,000 insurgents during the first ten months. Many who rallied to the government side during this period were students who had fled to the remote jungles and joined the CPT forces after the repressive action of the Thai police at Bangkok's Thammasat University in early October 1976 (see Thailand in Transition, ch. 1). Some had grown disillusioned with CPT goals and tactics. Others were simply tired of the hardships endured in years of fighting under spartan conditions in the remote countryside. Former student leader Thirayuth Bunmee's surrender after 5 years with the CPT gained wide publicity for the amnesty program, as did the mass defection of 250 armed insurgents and hundreds of unarmed family members and supporters at Mukdahan in December 1982.

At the same time, the Thai armed forces conducted selective but increasingly aggressive and effective operations against longtime guerrilla bases in the Northeast and North. The capture and destruction in 1981 of the Khao Khor base astride the border between Phetchabun and Phitsanulok provinces in the North was a serious blow to the insurgency. In the South, more aggressive Thai military operations, political and social strategy, and a series of combined operations with Malaysian armed forces exacted a similar toll on the MCP, CPT, and Muslim separatists. By 1981 MCP strength had declined by one-third, to about 2,000. The steady pounding by the military and the political defections also rapidly depleted CPT strength. By the end of 1982, the number of armed CPT forces had decreased from 12,000 in 1979 to fewer than 4,000 countrywide. The coordinated military, political, economic, and social strategy had proved successful.

The phaseout of matériel support from China also weakened the insurgency. The rift in Sino-Vietnamese relations in Asia benefited Thailand. Beginning by closing the clandestine guerrilla radio station (VOPT), which had broadcast for years from Yunnan Province, China eventually halted virtually all support for the CPT and minority separatists. At the same time the CPT, plagued for many years by factionalism and ideological differences, was paralyzed by a break between Maoists and Leninists. Faced with the loss of border sanctuaries in Laos and China and deprived of Cambodian sanctuaries by the Vietnamese invasion, CPT cadres faced ever-increasing hardship, and only the most dedicated revolutionaries remained in the field. Thai authorities expressed concern over the emergence of a small, Vietnam-oriented faction of the CPT, but that faction posed little threat to stability in the country.

In mid-1987 the government estimated that there were about 600 armed, active communist insurgents operating in Thailand. Of this number, approximately 65 to 70 were thought to be in the North, 85 to 115 in the Northeast, 260 to 350 in the South, and 55 to 60 in the Center (see fig. 13). The MCP, which had been reduced to fewer than 1,500, operated in two factions along the Thai-Malaysian border. Muslim separatists—PULO and the smaller Barisan Revolusi Nasional (National Revolutionary Front)—numbered between 350 and 400 altogether.

Although, by the late 1980s most of the insurgencies had been defeated, dedicated revolutionaries remained, both within Thailand and abroad. The government was particularly concerned about a new CPT strategy that stressed urban operations. Moreover, there had long been a suspicion that not all the heralded defectors had indeed renounced their communist beliefs. Nonetheless, the Thai government had achieved significant success in defeating an array of insurgents during the 1980s.

Potential External Threats

Having controlled the insurgencies within Thailand, in the early 1980s the government turned to protecting the country from outside aggression. Although Vietnamese forces in Cambodia were viewed as the primary external threat, border tensions, caused partly by ill-defined boundaries, between Thailand and Laos and between Thailand and Burma also created concern (see Boundaries, ch. 2). For the most part, diplomacy enabled the government to resist external pressures and to keep the use of armed force to a minimum, but the Vietnamese invasion and occupation of Cambodia

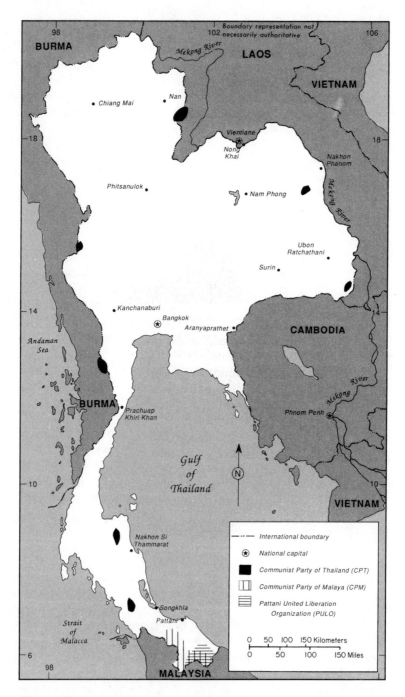

Figure 13. Areas of Insurgent and Separatist Activity, 1987

in December 1978 caused severe tension along the Thai-Cambodian border. The Vietnamese stationed 140,000 troops along that frontier, along with 30,000 Cambodian troops, whom they trained, organized, and directed. The immediate presence of heavily armed and capable Vietnamese divisions on its border reinforced Thailand's decision to improve its relations with China. In January 1979, Prime Minister Kriangsak Chomanand of Thailand and senior Chinese policy makers met secretly at Thailand's Utapao Air Base to forge a Thai-Chinese cooperation policy. That meeting resulted in China's halting moral and matériel support for the CPT and establishing Thailand as a conduit for Chinese support to the Khmer Rouge (see Glossary) faction of the Khmer resistance movement.

Thailand deployed elements of several divisions along the Cambodian border to deal with all aspects of the Vietnamese threat. There had been a history of strife along this border resulting from ethnic prejudices, poor demarcation of the boundary, and profitable cross-border smuggling, but the Vietnamese invasion of Cambodia seriously aggravated the situation. Vietnamese efforts to eliminate Cambodian resistance forces drove thousands of refugees into areas along the Thai border (see The Indochinese Refugee Question, ch. 2). Admitting large numbers of the refugees into Thailand posed severe problems for Thai authorities, not only because providing for the refugees strained the local economy but also because Khmer troops and some Vietnamese soldiers disguised as civilian refugees infiltrated Thailand. Thai security forces attempted to disarm all military infiltrators and return them to Cambodia.

Thailand supported Khmer resistance efforts as soon as the magnitude of the Vietnamese invasion became apparent in 1979. This resistance consisted of three major factions, the largest and most effective of which were remnants of the ousted communist Khmer Rouge. The noncommunist resistance groups—the forces loyal to Prince Norodom Sihanouk and the Khmer Peoples National Liberation Front (KPNLF)—also maintained their own armed combatants separate from the Khmer Rouge. All three groups, loosely aligned in the Coalition Government of Democratic Kampuchea, had their headquarters and primary bases just inside Thai territory. This situation allowed Thailand to exercise considerable control over the forces and their operations inside Cambodia, but it also provided targets for Vietnamese attack. Thailand viewed assistance to the resistance movements as essential to Thai security and, along with fellow Association of Southeast Asian Nations (ASEAN) members, waged a highly visible campaign for international assistance to Cambodian refugees and resistance forces (see Foreign Affairs, ch. 4). Assistance from China, ASEAN, the United States, and others was essential for continued viability of the Khmer resistance movement.

Vietnamese operations against the resistance along the Thai border provoked numerous clashes with Thai security forces, resulting in some casualties among Thai civilians living near the border, as well as among Thai forces. Vietnamese troops concentrated on trying to eliminate the Khmer resistance forces and to close resistance infiltration routes. They also conducted artillery attacks and made limited incursions, occupying small portions of Thai territory, notably in the border area where Thailand, Laos, and Cambodia meet.

The pattern of conflict along the Thai-Cambodian border showed little change between 1979 and 1984. Vietnamese forces conducted offensives against the Cambodian resistance forces during the dry season each year and then withdrew to consolidated positions and internal security operations well within the interior of Cambodia during the rainy season. This pattern changed with the major dry season campaign in 1984–85. In its largest and most successful series of operations, Vietnamese forces eliminated most major resistance bases along the Thai border and inflicted casualties on both refugees and armed resistance fighters. Following that offensive, Vietnamese forces remained deployed along the border during the rainy season and attempted to seal the border against the resistance forces. These efforts did not seriously hamper resistance infiltration, although they made movement into the interior of Cambodia more difficult. In the late 1980s, sizable Vietnamese forces with the limited support of units from the Khmer People's Revolutionary Armed Forces (KPRAF) continued to be deployed along the border.

Vietnam repeatedly assured Thailand and other ASEAN countries that it had no intention of invading Thailand, and contacts among these parties continued sporadically for several years as they explored the possibility of a political solution to the Cambodian conflict. Vietnam stated that it intended to withdraw the bulk of its forces by 1990, when it would have armed and trained the KPRAF into a credible national army. However, in mid-1987 observers doubted that the Vietnamese-supported Cambodian government would be able to assume the burden of its own defense by 1990. Even if Vietnam met its self-imposed 1990 deadline, observers expected that, as in Laos, a number of Vietnamese troops would remain in Cambodia to "advise" the KPRAF and secure Vietnamese interests in the country.

In mid-1987 the 800-kilometer Thai-Cambodian border was fully garrisoned by Vietnamese and Cambodian forces. An estimated three Vietnamese divisions and two Cambodian regiments were deployed along the northern Cambodian border adjacent to Ubon Ratchathani, Surin, Buriram, and Sisaket provinces. In the tightly contested region between Poipet in Cambodia and Aranyaprathet in Thailand's Prachin Buri Province, there were parts of two Vietnamese divisions and three Cambodian regiments. In the former Khmer Rouge stronghold of the Phnom Milai Mountains south of Poipet, two Vietnamese divisions and one Cambodian regiment were deployed. From this region southward to the Gulf of Thailand, there were two Vietnamese divisions and three independent Vietnamese regiments. (A Vietnamese infantry division usually consists of about 10,500 officers and men; an independent regiment has a strength of about 3,000.)

Although the situation along the Cambodian border posed the greatest external threat to Thai security, other areas presented problems as well (see fig. 14). Thailand faced security challenges of varying intensity in each sector of its 2,800-kilometer border with Burma, Laos, and Malaysia. Sporadic clashes with Laos received publicity but did not pose major security threats. Armed clashes in the mountains of Nan and Uttaradit provinces were more serious but were contained by Thai security forces. This mountainous area suffered from a poorly demarcated border and was host to migrations of nomadic hill tribes and pockets of CPT resistance.

Thai security concerns along the lengthy border with Burma were complex and vexing. The numerous Burmese separatist movements posed a touchy diplomatic problem for Thailand. Annual Burmese government military operations against Mon, Karen, and Kayah separatist groups resulted in wholesale border crossings by fleeing insurgents and refugees. Thailand, however, was able to disarm and control these annual migrations. More serious were the activities of narcotics traffickers and the private armies that provided security for the narcotics trade. These elements operated along the northwestern Thai border and until the early 1980s encountered only weak response from Thai security forces. Thereafter, pressure from the United States, world opinion in general, and a new spirit of cooperation between the Thai and Burmese governments on the narcotics issue began to change the situation (see Criminal Activity and the Narcotics Trade, this ch.).

Faced with various threats along its borders, the Thai government attempted to apply the principles of its highly successful counterinsurgency program to the country's external security problems. Encouraged by the success that road building had had in destroying

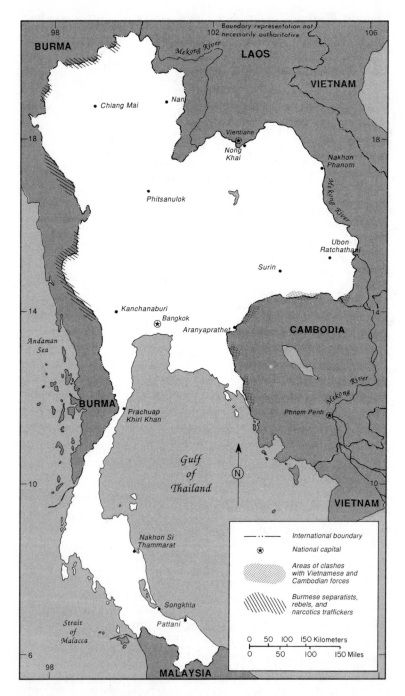

Figure 14. Areas of External Threat and Instability, 1987

the Khao Khor insurgent base, Thailand developed an extensive network of new roads along the Laotian border in Nan and Uttaradit provinces and along much of the length of the Burmese border. These roads provided easier access for security forces to remote border regions and served as a base for developing the local political, social, and economic infrastructure. Volunteer local security organizations established throughout the country in the 1980s played an important role both in containing insurgency and in enhancing security in border regions. Village security units were organized and trained by the army. Civilian agencies taught development techniques, safety measures, and village administration and provided improved health, agricultural, and educational facilities. The Rangers were locally recruited contract paramilitary forces trained in counterinsurgency and border security operations. They often joined with the army and the Border Patrol Police (BPP) to form units of forty to fifty called Santi Nimitr (Dream of Peace) teams, which carried out community development projects in remote villages where CPT front activities were reported or external threats detected. In 1987 there were more than 200 such teams operating throughout the country.

During the mid-1980s, the government continued to consolidate its political and military gains against insurgencies while turning its attention to the external threat. The government directed major efforts toward securing its borders, improving access to remote mountain regions, and strengthening domestic perceptions of the Vietnamese threat. The combination of army and BPP operations, road building and associated economic development, and resettlement resulted in a closer integration of formerly isolated areas with the rest of the country.

The Armed Forces

The Thai military establishment historically has played an important role in the country's national life. Composed of heterogeneous elements of regular cadres and conscripts, the armed forces in mid-1987 had a total strength of approximately 273,000 officers and enlisted personnel on active duty. Component services included the Royal Thai Army of 190,000, the Royal Thai Navy of 40,000, and the Royal Thai Air Force of 43,000. The navy's personnel strength included 20,000 marines.

The military's reputation as the center of political power manifested itself in nearly a score of coups and countercoups between 1932 and 1987. Over the years, its role as a political instrument had detracted from its abilities as a professional military force. Doubts about the state of combat readiness had been expressed by some members of the Thai officer corps as well as by foreign military observers. By the 1980s, the military had acted to increase the professionalism of its personnel—particularly the officer corps—and to modernize its units and weaponry.

General Development

From early times, the country's kings were, with few exceptions, military leaders, and the history of their reigns is replete with accounts of armed conflict. The Thai peasants followed their kings and nobles into war and then between wars returned to the land. The few professional retainers and mercenaries who made up the permanent military establishment neither enjoyed special privileges or prestige nor exercised any particular influence over national life. Military leaders were usually members or favorites of the royal family with an aptitude for military organization and command. Their authority and tenure, however, were subject to the king's pleasure.

During the fifteenth and sixteenth centuries the Thai learned much from their campaigns against the Khmer and the Burmese. Following the Khmer example, King Trailok (1448–88) established administrative divisions and increased the proficiency of his army. A successor, Ramathibodi II (1491–1529), wrote a treatise on warfare and further improved Thai military capability by reorganizing his army and instituting compulsory service. In the early sixteenth century, the Portuguese introduced firearms into the kingdom and taught the Thai the arts of casting bronze cannon and constructing stone fortifications. Portuguese mercenaries also served the king as bodyguards, armorers, and instructors in musketry.

The Thai-Burmese struggle continued into the seventeenth century, and the exploits of King Naresuan (1590–1605) contributed greatly to emerging Thai military traditions. In a battle in 1593 that secured his kingdom against an invading Burmese army, Naresuan killed the enemy crown prince in a famous duel in which the contenders were mounted on elephants. His exploits were recounted in later school texts as part of the country's heritage of courage and valor.

King Mongkut (Rama IV, 1851–68) took the first steps toward the development of modern fighting forces. Under his rule and that of his son, King Chulalongkorn (Rama V, 1868–1910), the Thai were particularly receptive to Western ideas and methods. They established military and naval cadet schools, brought in limited numbers of foreign advisers, and began reorganizing the army along European lines. In 1894 the Ministry of Defense was formed, giving the military for the first time a recognized position in the governmental hierarchy.

These developments laid the groundwork for the creation of a professional military officer class and for the establishment of a permanent and relatively modern military organization. Although the king maintained complete control, princes and other high-ranking members of the royal family continued to hold key positions within the military. In 1905 a law was passed designating the crown prince as commander in chief of the army. In 1912 King Vajiravudh (Rama VI, 1910–25) established the National Defense Council, composed of military and civilian officials, with himself at the head. During this same period antimonarchist sentiment found its first clandestine expression in a small group of army and navy officers who resented the king's favoring units that served as the palace guard. Powerful princes of the time also indicated their displeasure at the king's practice of appointing commoners to high government positions, including senior military posts.

In succeeding years, Thai kings gave increasing attention to building a modern military establishment, which they began to use to further the country's international interests. In World War I Thailand joined the Allied Powers and sent a small contingent of soldiers to France. The kingdom's demonstrated ability to develop its own military force with only limited foreign assistance became an effective argument in obtaining favorable revision of treaties with France and Britain in the early 1920s. During this period the first full-fledged Thai army, a force consisting of roughly 30,000 officers and men, was organized and trained according to European military concepts and practices.

The acceptance of Western influence by the Thai ruling elite at the beginning of the twentieth century significantly affected the role of the military. By the 1930s, many officers had attended European military schools, where they learned not only modern fighting tactics but also new social concepts and political patterns. Similarly, many civilians who had studied abroad had become interested in liberalizing the governmental system. These civilian leaders enlisted support among the military, and the resulting coup d'état in June 1932 brought about the transformation of the absolute monarchy into a constitutional government (see Beginning of the Constitutional Era, ch. 1). It also established the military as a dominant force in national political life.

During World War II the Thai armed forces grew in strength to about 60,000. In the period of political instability following the war, however, the size of the military establishment fluctuated markedly. When the military elite was in power as a result of a coup d'état, the armed forces expanded. When countercoups brought civilian-led administrations, military force reductions followed.

In 1950 the Thai entered into various aid agreements with the United States and received grants through the latter's Military Assistance Program (MAP). Under this arrangement, the Thai initiated a comprehensive modernization program based on American advice, equipment, and training (see Foreign Security Assistance, this ch.). Two decades later these measures had transformed the Thai military into a modern armed force with greatly improved capabilities for national defense and internal security. By 1970 the armed forces had increased to approximately 155,000. Their growth maintained a moderate pace thereafter (see table 16, Appendix).

Place in National Life

The country's military establishment was developed essentially to protect and defend an ethos that is still widely upheld: adherence to the monarchy, practice of Buddhism, and devotion to one's country. Over the years, the armed forces have generally ensured a sufficient level of peace, order, and domestic security to maintain political stability. In this respect the Thai military's place in national life has been like that of many other nations. However, military officers—particularly in the army—were much more deeply involved in the country's governmental and business operations than were their counterparts in most Western nations (see National and Urban Structures: Class and Status, ch. 2; Political Developments, 1980–87, ch. 4).

Seizing power in 1951, ostensibly to protect the country and its traditional institutions from the threat of communist influences, military leaders firmly reinforced the traditional Thai values of peace, order, and security within the political fabric of society. Although military control of the country gave way in succeeding years to democratic periods of varying lengths, the population still regarded the armed forces as an institution that could be relied on when political stability was needed. One result of this attitude was the persistent involvement of senior military leaders in affairs in which the military in Western countries usually are not allowed to engage. It became commonplace for high-ranking officers to pursue military careers while taking an active role in lucrative business activities that in turn added to their influence in national affairs. The military service also became for many a career that provided as much opportunity for political achievement as did the civil service.

Royal Thai Army troops inspecting shipment
of United States military equipment in 1954
Courtesy National Archives

Liberal-minded observers deplored the inordinate influence the armed forces had on the country's sociopolitical existence. Such criticism focused on allegations of repressive power tactics, greed, and corrupt practices. Defenders of the military, however, countered that in developing countries these abuses were minor in relation to the armed forces' success in thwarting communist takeovers and ensuring stability. In the late 1980s, the military establishment remained an integral part of Thai society.

The Military Roles

From the early days of their development, the Thai armed forces have been primarily responsible for defending the country's territorial integrity against foreign aggressors. In addition, they have traditionally served as a backup for the police in maintaining internal security and protecting citizens and their property. For several decades, elements of all three services have been included to varying degrees in military actions to contain, dispel, or crush insurgency.

The army's main purpose was to defend the country against invasion by any foreign ground force. To be prepared for wartime tasks, the army was charged with training and equipping itself in peacetime in order to achieve and maintain a satisfactory state of combat readiness.

Although the national police frequently demonstrated their ability to handle isolated domestic disorders, problems generated by insurgents at times required the assistance of the stronger and better equipped military forces, particularly the army. Throughout the 1960s and early 1970s, a large part of the army was committed to counterinsurgency efforts and played a crucial role in the coordinated operations that virtually eliminated the communist insurgency. At times the armed forces found themselves in competition with the police for control of the national counterinsurgency effort. To eliminate this contention, the police defined their responsibility as maintaining law and order and combating low levels of insurgent activity, while the army was to locate and destroy guerrilla bases and fight in major encounters.

After 1975, however, the military leadership grew increasingly concerned over incursions by Vietnamese forces from Cambodia and by Laotian forces along the lengthy northern and northeastern border. With the defeat of most of the insurgency, the army concentrated on establishing defensive positions and developing the forces needed to counter the Vietnamese and Laotian threats.

The navy's basic mission continued to be protecting the sea approaches to the country and assisting the internal security forces in suppressing insurgent activity. The navy was also responsible for conducting river patrols and antipiracy efforts in the Gulf of Thailand. The air force was charged with providing tactical air support to ground and naval forces. It also had a limited capability for aerial strikes against invading ground forces and air-to-air combat. Its counterinsurgency aircraft and trained air crews were deployed on numerous occasions to assist the army and the BPP against guerrilla bands.

In addition to their basic military roles, the armed forces participated in a variety of civic action programs designed to support the country's development efforts. Public service by the armed forces included such major projects as road building and repair in remote regions, disaster relief, construction of dams and reservoirs, assistance in building irrigation works, and participation in agricultural reform efforts among the hill tribes. Aimed at preventing villagers and peasant farmers in the border regions from falling under the influence of insurgents, military civic action appeared highly successful.

Manpower: Sources and Quality

Thai law required that all male citizens serve in the military. The 1978 Constitution, in a section entitled "Duties of the Thai People," states, "every person shall have a duty to defend the country [and] . . . to serve in the armed forces as provided by law.'' Similar requirements appear in the 1978 document's numerous predecessors. The Military Service Act, administered by the army, implemented these requirements. The act—a national conscription law—required two years of active military duty.

All Thai males were required to register when they became eighteen years of age but were not liable for compulsory service until they reached twenty-one. At that time they were notified to report for a physical examination, on the basis of which they were assigned to one of four categories: those who were fully qualified to serve in combat units; those who were partially disabled and only eligible for duty in support units; those with minor physical disqualifications that could be corrected before the next call-up; and those who were physically disqualified and exempt.

In addition to those exempted for physical reasons, Buddhist monks, career teachers, cadets attending the military academies, students in certain technical courses, naturalized citizens, and persons convicted of a crime subject to a penalty of ten years' imprisonment were not drafted. Waivers were granted in cases of personal hardship, for example, when an individual was the sole support of parents or minor children. Students in the later stages of their education also found it easy to obtain deferment. The exemption granted to naturalized citizens was designed to exclude the country's Chinese from the armed forces, but selective application of the law to other ethnic minorities as well resulted in a military establishment composed largely of members of the Thai Buddhist majority.

Thailand has always had an ample source of manpower for its military needs. In 1987 population estimates indicated that the country had nearly 13.6 million males aged 15 to 49, of whom an estimated 8.4 million were considered physically fit for military service. Roughly 520,000 young men reached the age of 18 each year, but the total annual induction averaged only about 30,000 men. Because the supply exceeded the demand, only those in the best physical condition were selected for service. Many inductees came from rural areas and were reliable, hardy, physically fit, adaptable, and accustomed to working outdoors in tropical heat, humid climate, and monsoon rains; many possessed a keen interest in learning and developing new skills. The average conscript accepted his military obligation as a necessary duty.

Inductees were usually sent to the nearest army, navy, or air force installation where the need was greatest. There the conscripts were assigned to units for training and then to appropriate service elements for duty. After a two-year commitment, conscripts who did not choose to reenlist (or were not permitted to do so) were released and placed on unassigned reserve status for an additional twenty-three years. During this period of reserve service they were subject to recall whenever a need arose. The priority of recall was based on age, the youngest reserves being reinducted first. In mid-1987 observers estimated that the system had produced more than 500,000 reserves whose military training and physical fitness made them reasonably available for emergency use in the army.

Noncommissioned officers (NCOs) were, in most cases, former conscripts who had reenlisted to make a career of the military service. On the basis of past performance, they were selected to attend an NCO school and upon graduation returned to their units in their new status. A limited number of NCOs were procured by placing on active duty graduates of reserve training programs conducted by the Ministry of Defense.

The officer corps of the armed forces was composed mainly of graduates of the service academies and officer candidate schools. It also included a small number of reserve officers who had completed training courses while in college and subsequently assumed military careers. A few officers with special qualifications were commissioned directly from civilian life. In the past the practice of appointing civilians to military positions was fairly widespread and had important political effects. Under the Civil Service Act of 1928 (amended in 1954), a number of high-ranking officials once prominent in the political bureaucracy became generals and acceded to prominent positions within the military hierarchy without undergoing military training or rising through the ranks. Although most of these senior officers worked as administrators on headquarters staffs, they had political clout and were important members of the contending military cliques that figured prominently in the coups and countercoups after 1932. Thailand's laws governing mandatory military retirement eventually eliminated these old guard generals and admirals, but the established pattern of rival cliques within the armed forces—particularly the army—persisted in the late 1980s.

Within the army, in particular, military academy classmate groupings were important. Officers identified with their classmates, and detailed records were kept of each academy class. Most Thai officers knew with which class any other officer had graduated. In the mid-1980s, officers from Class Five, led by Lieutenant General Suchinda Kraprayoon, the army deputy chief of staff, commanded seven of the army's thirteen divisions and formed a crucial base of political support for Prime Minister Prem.

Royal Thai Army
commander in chief,
General
Chaovalit Yongchaiyut
Courtesy
Voice of America

Little information was publicly available on promotion criteria and the rate of upward mobility within the officer corps. It was known, however, that the pay—even for senior officers—was low by Western standards. This fact of military life encouraged officers of every rank to engage in outside commercial activities—a practice that not only supplemented their service income but also enhanced their influence within the society. Many in important military positions served simultaneously on corporate directorates, family real estate companies, and other business ventures. For the most part, the Thai citizenry had come to accept their leaders' threefold roles as soldiers, businessmen, and politicians.

Following the coups of the 1950s and 1960s, officers in the losing factions were either purged or relegated to positions of little importance or potential threat. Falls from grace, however, were less permanent or violent in the Thai system than in some other countries. At the same time, officers who backed the winning group were usually promoted and given assignments supporting the new leaders. Other officers played important roles in expanding the power of governing regimes by transferring from the army to the police and from the military to the bureaucracy.

After the coup of October 1977, which brought Kriangsak, the supreme commander of the armed forces, into national power as prime minister, much publicity was given to the role played by a faction within the officer corps commonly referred to as the Young

Turks. Composed largely of Class Seven academy graduates, many of whom were key battalion commanders, the group was depicted as symbolic of the growing disparity between the conservative old guard of the politico-military establishment and the foreign-trained younger officers who were seeking to modernize society. The reformist Young Turks were critical of the extravagant life-style of the military leadership, especially when contrasted with the living conditions of ordinary soldiers fighting the insurgents. The young reformist officers aided Kriangsak's takeover and helped nullify the power of the old guard officers' faction.

However, the coup attempt of April 1981, in which many Young Turk officers had major roles, tarnished the reputation of the group, and those involved were expelled from military service. When a few Young Turks led a second unsuccessful coup attempt in September 1985, their credibility declined further. Nonetheless, in a spirit of reconciliation typical of the Thai system, most Young Turk officers were permitted by the army chief of staff, General Chaovalit Yongchaiyut, to return to active duty in 1986. Although they were assigned to less important staff positions, the move to heal rifts and establish unity enhanced the political credentials of General Chaovalit.

By the late 1980s, the Thai army had a large group of well-trained, forward-looking officers, many of whom occupied influential command and staff posts. This group of younger officers was described as increasingly outraged at the inefficient, expensive Thai-style democracy. Their growing influence was reflected in the increased attention given to their views by the government.

Defense Spending

Beginning in the 1950s, when the country undertook to build up and modernize its armed forces to withstand perceived threats from communist expansion in Southeast Asia, there was a relatively steady increase in government expenditures for defense. During that time, social and economic developments had to compete with an expanding military establishment for limited financial resources. The high cost of maintaining a credible defense posture was compounded by a desire to stay abreast of weaponry advances in a rapidly changing technological age as well as by rising inflation rates and economic retrenchment.

During the three decades of Thai military modernization, the amounts of money budgeted and expended for defense varied somewhat according to whether or not a military regime controlled the government. Predictably, defense expenditures tended to rise moderately when military governments were in power, but even then the percentages of total government outlays for the armed forces were not inordinate when compared with defense expenditures in some other countries, nor were they high when compared with amounts spent on social needs, such as education and health.

In the mid-1980s, defense spending averaged about 30 percent of the government's annual current expenditures and about 4.2 percent of the gross national product (GNP). Additional costs of internal security, which were attributed in government statistics to the Ministry of Interior rather than to the Ministry of Defense, further increased the country's total current security burden by an average of about 6 percent annually. But even with internal security costs added, government statistics still did not reflect the total defense bill. Reports of funds budgeted and expended reflected only amounts covering current accounts and did not include the cost of new equipment acquired to update the armed forces' fighting capabilities.

Although the country's armed forces did not constitute a large military establishment when compared with those of some other Asian nations, the costs of maintaining combat readiness began, by the late 1980s, to pose problems for the government treasury. The country was experiencing many of the economic problems common to developing countries undergoing rapid economic change. Among these were a worrisome trade deficit inherited from previous regimes and the continuing impact of rising oil prices (see International Trade and Finance, ch. 3). At the same time, moreover, the government was still coping with a persistent possibility of insurgency and with the threat from Vietnam.

During the era of American involvement in the war in Vietnam, the United States met most of Thailand's military equipment needs with a steady flow of hardware, mainly in the form of grant aid (see Foreign Security Assistance, this ch.). In the mid-1970s, the United States Congress dramatically reduced the role of grant military assistance, relying instead on foreign military sales and direct commercial sales. To make up for the loss of United States grants and to cover the costs of equipment needed in the country's efforts to modernize its armed forces, the government in 1976 authorized its Ministry of Finance to obtain US$1 billion in loans from private banks in the United States and Western Europe over the next 6 to 8 years. Approximately one-half of this amount was devoted to hardware requirements of the army; air force and navy needs were to be met by equal portions of the remaining one-half. This approximate distribution of funds was the pattern for defense expenditures followed by succeeding governments.

Although it was not a common practice for private banks to lend money to foreign governments for military purposes, banks in the United States, Britain, Canada, and the Federal Republic of Germany (West Germany) had loaned Thailand more than US$335 million by the late 1980s. Thailand's unconventional approach to its defense needs was aided by its generally high credit rating among the world's private banks and the judgment of most bankers that the money would be used for the country's own defense rather than for purposes of aggression.

Domestic Defense Industry

Before the 1970s, domestic defense production was extremely limited. Local industrial plants made items such as uniforms, storage batteries, glassware, preserved foods, some electronic devices, and certain pharmaceutical and chemical products. The production of armaments, began on a modest scale in 1969 and received increasing government assistance. In August 1976, the Ministry of Defense announced that it had invested more than US$200 million since 1969 in developing domestic production of ordnance items. This investment resulted in the local production of 5.56mm, 7.62mm, and .30 calibre ammunition. In addition, the government operated facilities for limited rebuilding and modernization of military vehicles, aircraft engines, and helicopters. A modern dockyard provided similar improvements as well as maintenance on naval vessels and their armaments. Most of these capabilities were achieved with American technical assistance.

In December 1977, Prime Minister Kriangsak announced plans to establish a number of new factories to increase the strength of the country's arms industry. In particular, he hoped to meet internal security requirements for ammunition and light weapons. The industrial expansion called for private as well as government-owned facilities. The primary vehicle for this was a privately owned company called Thai Interarms, which received substantial government aid. Divided into four subunits, the company manufactured small arms, ammunition, gunpowder, and other explosives. In addition, a factory established in Ta Khli, a joint venture between the Thai government and the Winchester Company of the United States, had a projected production capability of 1 million tons of ammunition annually, including rockets.

To strengthen the navy's combat readiness, the government expanded its naval repair facilities with aid from the United States, Italy, and Japan. As a result, Thailand produced a variety of naval vessels, including six fast coastal patrol boats, and had an LST (landing ship, tank) under construction in 1987. Despite the

Former Prime Minister Kriangsak Chomanand
Courtesy Royal Thai Embassy

ambitious scope of plans for a domestic defense industry, however, production failed to reach the levels desired.

Foreign Security Assistance

Although other Western nations—notably Britain, West Germany, and Italy—have provided Thailand with moderate amounts of military aid, the chief source of armament and training assistance since 1950 has been the United States. From 1950 through early 1976, the substantial majority of United States aid was in the form of grants under the Military Assistance Program (MAP). Additional aid was offered in the form of Foreign Military Sales (FMS) credits, part of which carried United States guarantees of payment to American commercial suppliers if necessary.

The goal of United States assistance was to strengthen Thailand's military capability through buildup and modernization of its equipment, improvement of its operational tactics, and increased training for its personnel. As the communist-supported insurgency became a potential threat to the kingdom's political stability in the 1960s, increased military aid was channeled to support the Thai internal security forces in their counterinsurgency actions. To assist the Thai in meeting requirements for military aid and to supervise the United States program in the field, increasing numbers

251

of American military specialists were assigned to the Joint United States Military Assistance Group (JUSMAG) in Bangkok.

During the Second Indochina War (1954–75), the United States and Thailand negotiated an unsigned agreement to permit American naval and air units to use Thai territory. Although units of the United States Navy operated from modern facilities established at Sattahip on the Gulf of Thailand, the vast majority of American-occupied bases in the country were used by combat squadrons and supporting units of the United States Air Force. In addition to a number of intelligence outposts scattered about the North and Northeast, there were seven air bases from which United States aircraft flew combat missions against targets throughout Indochina.

These bases were at Udon Thani, Nakhon Phanom, Nam Phong, Nakhon Ratchasima, Ubon Ratchathani, Ta Khli, and Ban U Taphao. Constructed at a cost to the United States of several hundred million dollars, most of the facilities were former Thai installations that were modernized to accommodate the American squadrons. After completion of the renovation and expansion work by Thai civilian contractors, the bases had permanent buildings, sophisticated ground support equipment, and runways capable of accommodating modern combat aircraft. During the height of the war the bases were used by more than 500 American airplanes, including several squadrons of B–52 heavy bombers of the Strategic Air Command. At some of the bases, facilities were shared with training units of the Royal Thai Air Force.

Thai reaction to the United States military presence was mixed. Senior Thai officers tended to believe that the presence of the United States combat squadrons provided assurance against potentially aggressive designs of communist countries in the region. Some in the government, however, were concerned that the installations would invite hostile political or military action against Thailand. The presence of roughly 45,000 United States servicemen also had a pronounced socioeconomic effect—one that was increased by the large number of American personnel who came to Bangkok on rest and recreation leaves from the Vietnam combat zone.

A phased withdrawal of the American presence began in 1969, when United States participation in the war in Indochina decreased, and it proceeded through the early 1970s as internal political tensions rose in the Thai kingdom (see Thailand in Transition, ch. 1). By late July 1976, at the request of the Thai government, the last of the United States air and naval units had departed. The facilities at Sattahip and the seven air bases were turned over to the Thai government, with much of the sophisticated ground support equipment removed. Considerable controversy ensued between

Thai military and government officials over the future of the abandoned network of airfields. Ultimately the military retained control over the bases, even though most were in excess of their needs and of the government's ability to pay for upkeep. Nakhon Ratchasima alone had cost the United States approximately US$2.5 million a year to maintain. Consolidating the equipment left by departing United States units in accordance with government-to-government agreements, the Thai air force assumed use of some of the installations.

After 1976 MAP aid to Thailand declined, and FMS credits increased. By 1979 Thailand had been dropped from the United States shrinking list of grant aid recipients. But later that year, after Vietnam invaded Cambodia, President Jimmy Carter expedited delivery of approximately US$400 million in arms and military supplies that the Thai government had under contract from American companies. This action set a precedent for expedited equipment deliveries on a periodic basis to demonstrate American support for Thailand in the face of the Vietnamese threat in Cambodia. In the mid-1980s, as the country was increasingly caught between economic retrenchment and the need to upgrade its defense capabilities, the United States Congress approved resumption of a limited military grant aid program for Thailand.

Beginning in the early 1980s, the country hosted a series of joint Thai-United States military exercises. A major annual combined exercise called Cobra Gold, as well as many smaller exercises, served to enhance relations between the two countries' armed forces. All four United States services sent troops to take part in the exercises, which were designed as training vehicles for both countries.

In 1986 the United States and Thailand agreed to establish a war reserve weapons pool in Thailand. This concept was first raised by a former Thai supreme commander of the armed forces, General Saiyud Kerdphon in 1982, and the proposal received bilateral support during a meeting between Prime Minister Prem and Secretary of Defense Caspar W. Weinberger in April 1986. As the plan was formulated, these war reserve stocks were designed to improve Thailand's ability to withstand aggression and were to be used only in the event of a "nation-threatening emergency."

According to United States government statistics, between 1950 and 1987 the United States provided Thailand with more than US$2 billion in military assistance. Approximately US$1.2 billion was in the form of grant aid and covered arms purchases, training of military personnel, and transfer of excess items from the United States military equipment inventory. The remainder—almost US$1 billion—was made available in the form of FMS credits to be applied against commercial sales of military items from American manufacturers. The FMS credit program was expected to continue into the 1990s.

Military Structure

Largely because of the advice and military aid received from the United States in the decades since World War II, Thailand's military establishment reflected to some degree the influence of American defense practices. This was particularly apparent in the organizational structure of its high command (see fig. 15).

Although the 1978 Constitution—like its predecessors—declares that the king is the head of the armed forces, his role is chiefly ceremonial. Until 1957 functional control was generally exercised by the prime minister through the minister of defense. Both positions were important in the national power structure, but they were usually held by political appointees who had little actual authority over the troops.

As the military establishment grew in size and proficiency, control over its operations became vested in the supreme commander of the armed forces. Over the years the influence inherent in the job marked it as a logical springboard to the prime minister's office. Even in periods dominated by military regimes, the various heads of government watched the activities of the supreme commander warily, realizing that their own positions of authority were subject in large measure to his concurrence. This pattern is exemplified by the military coup d'état of September 1957 in which Sarit Thanarat took over the government. Assuming control of the military establishment as prime minister, Sarit further ensured his position of authority in April 1960 by securing a royal decree that designated him supreme commander as well. This title was similarly assumed by Field Marshal Thanom Kittikachorn, who succeeded Sarit as prime minister in 1963.

Despite past successes in using this seemingly traditional basis of influence, the supreme commander with political ambitions was still subject to the military retirement system. According to the Military Service Act of 1954, retirement at age sixty was mandatory for all military personnel. A year after General Kriangsak became prime minister in 1977 he had to relinquish his additional position as supreme commander of the armed forces because of the military retirement age.

Throughout the history of military governments in Thailand, the effective authority wielded by the prime minister depended, in large measure, on support from the real center of military power—the army commander in chief, who controlled the field forces—and on the adroitness of the prime minister in garnering such support for himself. Prime Minister Kriangsak was successful in this regard in 1978 when he appointed the commander of the Second Army, General Prem Tinsulanonda—a respected professional soldier—commander in chief of the army. In June 1979 Prem was given the additional position of minister of defense within the Council of Ministers. Prem went on from these posts to succeed Kriangsak as prime minister in 1980. General Arthit Kamlangek served as both army commander in chief and supreme commander of the armed forces until 1986, when he lost the former title as a result of his outspoken opposition to Prime Minister Prem. Arthit retired from active duty in 1986.

On national security matters that required coordinated cabinet action or presented a serious threat to the country's sovereignty, the prime minister was advised by the National Security Council. This body consisted of the prime minister as chairman; his deputies; the council's secretary general; the ministers of defense, foreign affairs, interior, communications, and finance; and the supreme commander of the armed forces. Traditionally the prime minister dominated the workings of the council.

The Ministry of Defense supervised the operations and administration of the military establishment and coordinated military policies with those of other governmental agencies concerned with national security. The defense minister received advice on military matters—particularly those pertaining to draft laws, budget allocations, mobilization, training, and deployment of the armed forces in response to national need—from the ministry's Defense Council. This body comprised the minister of defense as chairman; his two deputy ministers; the undersecretary of defense; the supreme commander of the armed forces; the chief of staff of the Supreme Command; the commanders in chief of the three services, their deputies, and chiefs of staff; and not more than three additional general officers selected for their outstanding ability.

Each of the three armed services was headed by a commander in chief who was directly responsible to the supreme commander of the armed forces for the combat readiness and operation of his units (see fig. 16). Although the three components were equal under the law, the army was in fact the dominant service. Key positions in both the armed forces high command structure and the cabinets of military regimes traditionally were held by senior army officers. In order to ensure support from the other services, however, senior officers from the navy, air force, and police occasionally were appointed to a few key ministries. In general the structural form of service units and the method of their employment were similar

255

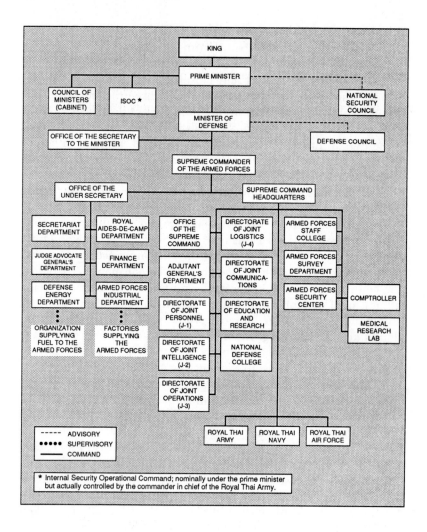

Figure 15. High Command of the Royal Thai Armed Forces, 1987

to those of comparable United States military components, although they differed in size and in the technological sophistication of their equipment.

Royal Thai Army

The oldest and largest of the military services, the Royal Thai Army traditionally served as the mainstay of the kingdom's defense system. The commander in chief and his large staff of military specialists, headquartered in Bangkok, directed the army in carrying out its mission. For tactical and administrative purposes, the army operated through four regional army commands. The First Army, headquartered in Bangkok, was responsible for the country's western and central provinces and the capital city (see fig. 17). The northeastern quadrant was the territorial home of the Second Army, and its regional headquarters were in Nakhon Ratchasima. The region of the Third Army, with headquarters in Phitsanulok, consisted of the northern and northwestern parts of the kingdom. The Fourth Army's region was southern Thailand; its headquarters were in Nakhon Si Thammarat.

Tactically, the army was organized into seven infantry divisions (including five tank battalions), one armored division, one cavalry division (with an armor capability), eight independent infantry battalions, two special forces divisions trained and geared for small unit special and airborne operations, one field artillery division, and one air defense artillery division. Three airmobile companies provided the ground force units with battlefield support.

Although the army's primary mission was to defend the country against aggression by foreign ground forces, for many years invasion was considered an unlikely possibility by Thai civilian and military leaders, in part because of the defense umbrella provided by the United States. Moreover, many Thai leaders believed that such a threat probably could be circumvented politically without need for a military response. Furthermore, some assurance was derived from the fact that Cambodia and Laos, which were not regarded as serious potential threats, were between Thailand and Vietnam, the region's most belligerent power. Consequently, from the 1960s through the mid-1970s field action by army units concentrated mostly on dispelling insurgency. Devoting its training programs, equipment inventory, and operational capabilities to counterinsurgency, the army thus shelved its primary mission and for more than a decade concentrated on providing internal security.

Because there was such a mélange of security forces combating the insurgency, the army's units were dispersed throughout the country—often in a manner that negated their value as frontline defenders in the event of invasion. For many years the single armored division was committed to counterinsurgency action in the North and operated as infantry; most other tank battalions were on permanent duty in Bangkok, partly for internal political reasons. These scattered units could not have regrouped rapidly and effectively enough to support an infantry struggling to repel invaders. Similarly, artillery units were dispersed in small detachments designed to engage in limited action. The bulk of the infantry divisions were garrisoned in the interior at regional army command headquarters.

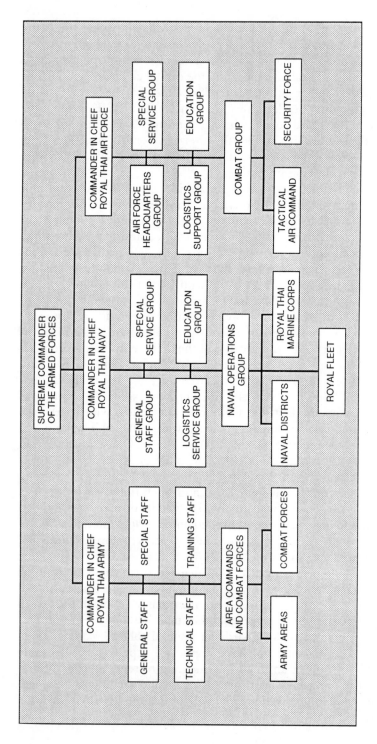

Figure 16. Field Command of the Royal Thai Armed Forces, 1987

Concentrating large numbers of troops in the interior rather than deploying them to border defense positions helped reduce financial costs because government regulations required that combat troops in field operations receive per diem payments of the equivalent of about US$1.00 in addition to regular salaries. (The police and civil servants also received this compensation when they were on government field operations or travel status.) The shortage of per diem money plagued defense and internal security operations, even during the years of United States military aid.

The army's top-heavy organizational structure and its role in political affairs also diluted its effectiveness as a conventional combat force. Because the country could not afford to maintain a large trained military, the army was organized to depend for the majority of its troops below the NCO ranks on conscripts serving their two-year service obligations. Most of these conscripts did not reenlist after their required commitments, and therefore a large percentage of their active service was spent in training. There were able officers at all levels of command, but the staffs at higher headquarters were inflated with high-ranking officers using their positions as opportunities for promotion and political advancement, particularly if they were assigned in Bangkok.

Key units of the First Army, stationed permanently in the capital, frequently provided the military backup for the coup d'état attempts of senior army officers. At other times they were used by military leaders in power to forestall the coup aspirations of rival factions. The First Army also furnished detachments that served as the king's bodyguard and other units that took part in ceremonial activities in Bangkok.

Vietnam's invasion of Cambodia in December 1978 eliminated this complacent approach to national defense. Thailand scrambled to redeploy its combat forces and to provide its frontline units with the equipment and munitions needed to combat the Vietnamese threat along the Cambodian border. The Thai army's lack of readiness to provide border defense soon became apparent. Prime Minister Kriangsak flew to Washington in February 1979 to seek assistance in updating the army's military equipment inventory, which was ill-suited to modern defensive operations, particularly against the better equipped and more experienced Vietnamese. Despite the sympathetic response of the United States, the task of revamping the Royal Thai Army to meet potential threat was formidable, as the service's weapons inventory revealed.

To upgrade its state of combat readiness the army sought to increase its holdings of tanks and armored personnel carriers, improve its antitank capabilities, add heavier and longer range guns

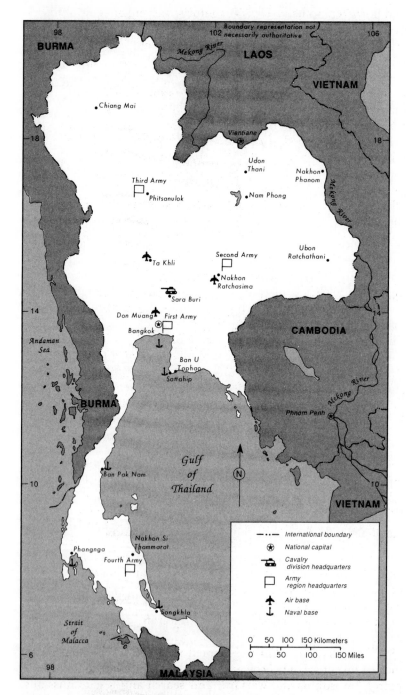

Figure 17. Major Thai Military Installations, 1987

and howitzers to its artillery inventory, and enhance its ability to provide adequate battlefield defense against attacking enemy aircraft. These modernization efforts were hampered by economic retrenchment throughout the 1980s (see table 17, Appendix).

Other changes contemplated for the early 1990s included plans to upgrade the four infantry divisions stationed along the Cambodian border to mechanized or light infantry configurations. New training guidelines were designed to pare training time and establish a pool of trained reservists to draw upon as needed. General Chaovalit Yongchaiyut, in 1987 army commander in chief, called for reducing the number of ''idle'' generals by decreasing the number of general officers on active duty from more than 200 to about 80. Army troop strength was held at about 190,000 by lowering the conscription rate as the force moved toward becoming a totally volunteer army. Thai military planners proposed to upgrade the training and size of the army reserve force, studying systems used in Singapore and Israel.

Royal Thai Navy

Although Thailand had small naval components throughout much of its long history, the development of a modern navy capable of carrying out combat missions dated from the post-World War II period. Thereafter, the size and efficiency of the Royal Thai Navy increased steadily. Of the three service branches, the navy was the least involved in national politics and therefore was able to concentrate more of its time and efforts on its security mission.

Naval affairs were directed by the country's most senior admiral from his Bangkok headquarters. The naval commander in chief was supported by staff groups that planned and administered such activities as logistics, education and training, and various special services. The headquarters general staff functioned like those of corresponding staffs in the army and air force command structures.

The navy's combat forces included the Royal Fleet and the Royal Thai Marine Corps. The latter was organized into two regiments composed of one artillery battalion, six infantry battalions, and one amphibious assault battalion; a light tank battalion was also proposed. The 130 vessels of the Royal Fleet included frigates equipped with surface-to-air missiles, fast attack craft armed with surface-to-surface missiles, large coastal patrol craft, coastal minelayers, coastal minesweepers, landing craft, and training ships (see table 18, Appendix). In addition, a small naval air component flew a modest inventory of helicopters and light aircraft in reconnaissance, patrol, antisubmarine warfare, and search-and-rescue missions. Major operational bases for the fleet, the marines, and the air units were the naval stations in Bangkok and Songkhla and the major naval bases at Sattahip and Ban Pak Nam.

In 1977 the government began construction of a new naval base in Ban Thap Mo District of Phangnga Province facing the Andaman Sea and approaches to the southern region. The new Phangnga naval base, completed by 1983, had a large steel-reinforced concrete wharf, dockyard, arsenal, living quarters for naval personnel, and other military facilities. The new base gave the Thai navy a modest but much-needed operations and support facility on the west coast of the Isthmus of Kra.

Royal Thai Air Force

The Royal Thai Air Force was the most recently formed of the three services. The air force had a command structure consisting of five groups: headquarters, logistics support, education, special services, and combat forces. The headquarters group in Bangkok performed the usual general staff functions, including planning and directing operations of the combat elements. The logistics support group provided engineering, communications, ordnance, transportation, quartermaster, and medical services support. The education group coordinated and supervised all air force training programs. The special service group was responsible for the welfare of air force personnel and coordinated the activities of Thai civil aviation with those of the air force.

The operational units of the air force were organized into two functional elements: a tactical air command structured and equipped for conventional warfare and an aerial security force trained and geared for counterinsurgency and other internal security missions. In 1987 the tactical air command had a combat force of one squadron committed to forward ground attack, two squadrons of fighter-interceptors also used for armed reconnaissance, a separate reconnaissance squadron that also served in a training role, three transport squadrons, one utility squadron, two helicopter squadrons, and one training squadron. The security force consisted of seven counterinsurgency squadrons, equipped with helicopter gunships, and other light aircraft suitable for counterinsurgency operations. Airfield security was provided by four battalions of troops trained in perimeter defense tactics.

The air force maintained a number of modern bases from which it conducted its administrative, transport, and training operations. The bases, which were constructed between 1954 and 1968, had permanent buildings, sophisticated ground support equipment, and some of the best runways in Asia. All but one were part of the network of airfields built and used by United States forces until their withdrawal from Thailand in 1976. Consolidating the equipment left by the departing units in accordance with government-to-government agreements, the Thai air force assumed use of the installations at Ta Khli and Nakhon Ratchasima. In the late 1980s, these bases and Don Muang Air Base outside Bangkok, which the air force shared with civil aviation, remained the primary operational holdings. Maintenance of the facilities at other bases abandoned by the United States proved too costly and exceeded Thai needs. Nonetheless, all runways were still available for training and emergency use.

The American withdrawal had quickly revealed to the Thai Supreme Command the inadequacy of its air force in the event of a conventional war in Southeast Asia. Accordingly, in the 1980s the government allotted large amounts of money for the purchase of modern aircraft and spare parts. Thirty-eight F-5E and F-5F fighter-bombers purchased from the Northrop Corporation formed the nucleus of the air force's defense and tactical firepower. The F5Es were accompanied by training teams of American civilian and military technicians, who worked with members of the Thai air force. In addition to the F-5E and F-5F fighter-bombers, OV-10C aircraft, transports, and helicopters were added to the air force equipment inventory (see table 19, Appendix). In 1985 the United States Congress authorized the sale of the F-16 fighter to Thailand. A total of twelve of these aircraft were scheduled for delivery in 1988.

Training

With increased funding for instructional purposes and with guidance from JUSMAG personnel stationed in the country, the Thai armed forces continued to improve their ability to handle sophisticated weapons and to employ the tactics of modern warfare. Over the years, Thailand expanded its training facilities, sent a large number of Thai officers to the United States for military instruction, and augmented conventional training with counterinsurgency instruction.

New army conscripts customarily underwent a sixteen-week program of instruction, half devoted to basic training and half to more specialized requirements. This initial program was followed by a three-phase unit training cycle that lasted the rest of the first year. Roughly two months were allotted to instruction and testing in squad and platoon tactics. Next came a second phase consisting of exercises at company and battalion levels. The third phase usually included some form of battalion maneuver.

Naval basic training lasted from eight to eleven weeks, depending on the ultimate assignment of the conscript. The course covered the elementary aspects of seamanship, navigation, ordnance, gunnery, and damage-control procedures. Marine recruits received the same basic training, but those selected for advanced training received additional instruction in counterinsurgency amphibious warfare. Unit training was generally conducted at the naval squadron level. Shipboard drills, including team gunnery and other underway operations, took place throughout the entire instruction cycle.

The training program of the Royal Thai Air Force was patterned on that of its American counterpart. Upon completion of basic training, recruits and conscripts were selected for more advanced programs. Flight training for pilots and other aircrew members was conducted at Khorat Air Base (near Nakhon Ratchasima). Most air technical instruction took place at the school complex assigned to Don Muang Air Base near Bangkok. More advanced training was provided by the specialized schools of each branch of the armed forces and the entire system of military education coordinated by the Directorate of Education and Research at Supreme Command Headquarters. This directorate also supervised the operation of the combined and special service schools, such as the National Defense College and the Armed Forces Staff College. The National Defense College in Bangkok was the highest level military school in the country. Its major objective was to foster cooperation between senior military and civilian authorities in planning and directing national security activities. Its course of instruction, conducted for a limited number of high-ranking military, police, and civilian officials each year, covered military, political, and economic subjects. The Armed Forces Staff College in Bangkok, the second highest military school, was intended to produce senior general staff officers who were qualified to serve on joint or combined staffs. Annual enrollment was confined to a small number of officers selected from the three armed services. Attendance at either the Armed Forces Staff College or a service staff college was considered mandatory for advancement beyond the rank of major or lieutenant commander.

In addition to its staff college, each of the armed forces operated its own service academy. The army's Chulachomkhlao Royal Military Academy was the largest and oldest of these. In 1986 it was moved from its central Bangkok location to a new campus in Nakhon Nayok Province. The Royal Thai Naval College was at Ban Pak Nam and the Royal Thai Air Force Academy at Don

Muang Air Base. The five-year academies served as the principal sources of junior officers for all three services.

Each service also had intermediate military schools similar to those operated by the United States military establishment. In addition, a sizable number of officers from all branches received training in American institutions as well as in advanced technical training schools in the United States. The armed forces also maintained a variety of schools to provide technical training for NCOs. These were oriented primarily toward career enlisted men and offered courses that varied in length, depending on the particular vocational specialty involved.

Uniforms, Ranks, and Insignia

To build institutional solidarity and esprit de corps, each Thai service component developed its own distinctive uniforms, ranking system, and insignia. Many Thai military uniforms reflected historical foreign influences. For example, most of the distinctive service uniforms were patterned on those of the United States, but lower ranking enlisted navy personnel wore uniforms resembling those of their French counterparts. The early influence of British advisers to the Thai royal court and the historical role of the military in royal pomp and ceremony contributed to the splendor of formal dress uniforms worn by high-ranking officers and guards of honor for ceremonial occasions.

The rank structures of the three armed services were similar to those of the respective branches of the United States Armed Forces, although the Thai system had fewer NCO and warrant officer designations (see fig. 18; fig. 19). The king, as head of state and constitutional head of the armed forces, personally granted all commissions for members of the officer corps. Appointments to NCO ranks were authorized by the minister of defense. In theory, the authority and responsibilities of officers of various ranks corresponded to those of their American counterparts. However, because of a perennial surplus of senior officers—in 1987 there were some 600 generals and admirals in a total force of about 273,000—Thai staff positions were often held by officers of higher rank than would have been the case in the United States or other Western military establishments.

Thai military personnel were highly conscious of rank distinctions and of the duties, obligations, and benefits they entailed. Relationships among officers of different grades and among officers, NCOs, and the enlisted ranks were governed by military tradition in a society where observance of differences in status was highly formalized. The social distance between officers and NCOs was

THAILAND RANK ARMY	ROI TRI	ROI THO	ROI EG	PHAN TRI	PHAN THO	PHAN EG	PHAN EG PHISET	PHON TRI	PHON THO	PHON EG	CHOM PHON
U.S. RANK TITLES	2D LIEUTENANT	1ST LIEUTENANT	CAPTAIN	MAJOR	LIEUTENANT COLONEL	COLONEL	BRIGADIER GENERAL	MAJOR GENERAL	LIEUTENANT GENERAL	GENERAL	GENERAL OF THE ARMY
THAILAND RANK NAVY	RUA TRI	RUA THO	RUA EG	NAWA TRI	NAWA THO	NAWA EG	NAWA EG PHISET	PHON RUA TRI	PHON RUA THO	PHON RUA EG	CHOM PHON RUA
U.S. RANK TITLES	ENSIGN	LIEUTENANT JUNIOR GRADE	LIEUTENANT	LIEUTENANT COMMANDER	COMMANDER	CAPTAIN	COMMODORE ADMIRAL	REAR ADMIRAL	VICE ADMIRAL	ADMIRAL	FLEET ADMIRAL
THAILAND RANK AIR FORCE	RUA AAKAAD TRI	RUA AAKAAD THO	RUA AAKAAD EG	NAWA AAKAAD TRI	NAWA AAKAAD THO	NAWA AAKAAD EG	NAWA AAKAAD EG PHISET	PHON AAKAAD TRI	PHON AAKAAD THO	PHON AAKAAD EG	CHOM PHON AAKAAD
U.S. RANK TITLES	2D LIEUTENANT	1ST LIEUTENANT	CAPTAIN	MAJOR	LIEUTENANT COLONEL	COLONEL	BRIGADIER GENERAL	MAJOR GENERAL	LIEUTENANT GENERAL	GENERAL	GENERAL OF THE AIR FORCE

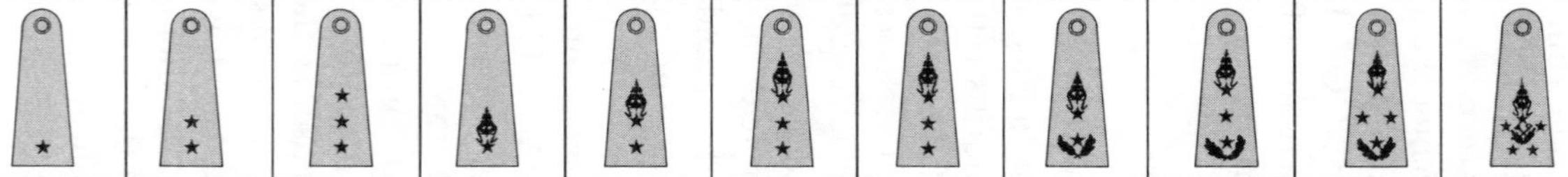

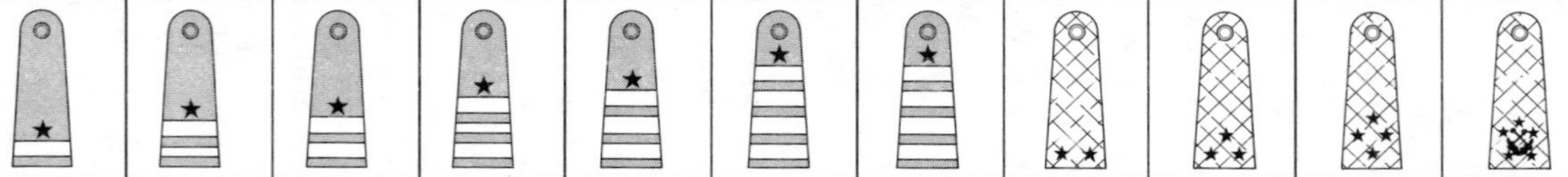

NOTE- Phan Eg Phiset and Nawa Aakaad Eg Phiset grades wear shoulder insignia of Phan Eg and Nawa Aakaad Eg, respectively, and collar insignia of general officers; Nawa Eg Phiset grade wears shoulder insignia of Nawa Eg and collar insignia of flag officers.

Figure 18. Officer Rank Insignia, 1987

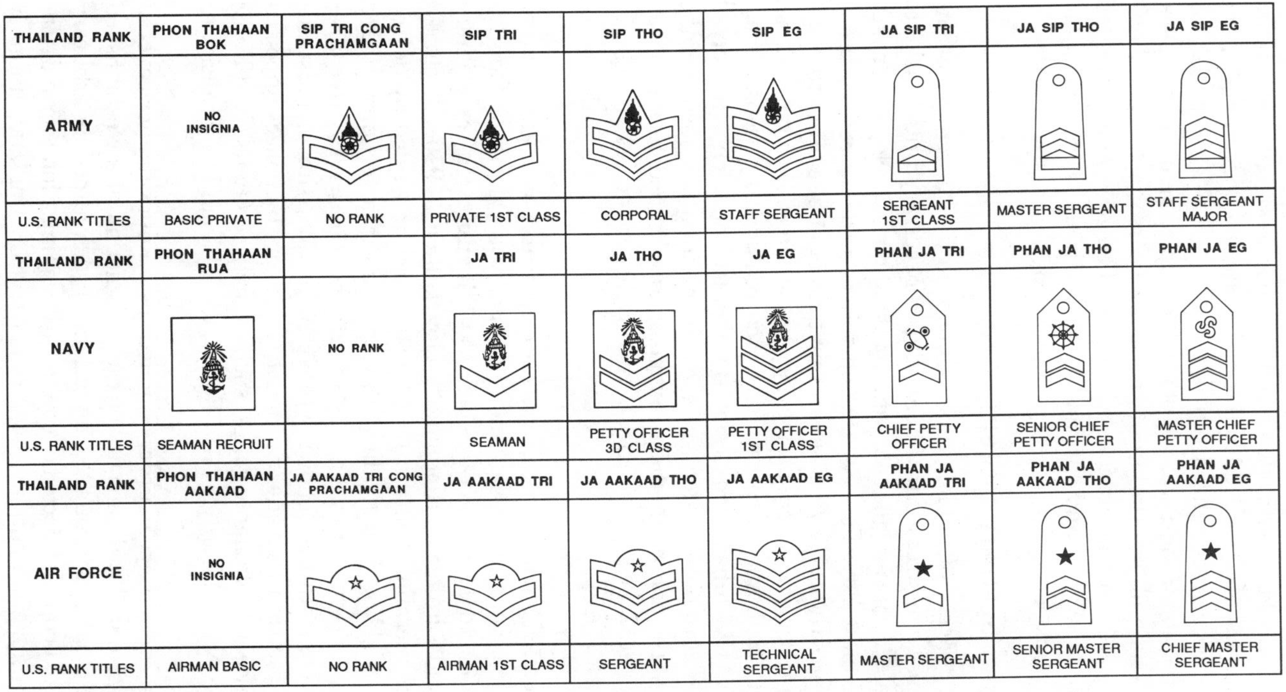

	PHON THAHAAN BOK	SIP TRI CONG PRACHAMGAAN	SIP TRI	SIP THO	SIP EG	JA SIP TRI	JA SIP THO	JA SIP EG
ARMY (THAILAND RANK)	NO INSIGNIA							
U.S. RANK TITLES	BASIC PRIVATE	NO RANK	PRIVATE 1ST CLASS	CORPORAL	STAFF SERGEANT	SERGEANT 1ST CLASS	MASTER SERGEANT	STAFF SERGEANT MAJOR
NAVY (THAILAND RANK)	PHON THAHAAN RUA		JA TRI	JA THO	JA EG	PHAN JA TRI	PHAN JA THO	PHAN JA EG
	NO RANK							
U.S. RANK TITLES	SEAMAN RECRUIT	NO RANK	SEAMAN	PETTY OFFICER 3D CLASS	PETTY OFFICER 1ST CLASS	CHIEF PETTY OFFICER	SENIOR CHIEF PETTY OFFICER	MASTER CHIEF PETTY OFFICER
AIR FORCE (THAILAND RANK)	PHON THAHAAN AAKAAD	JA AAKAAD TRI CONG PRACHAMGAAN	JA AAKAAD TRI	JA AAKAAD THO	JA AAKAAD EG	PHAN JA AAKAAD TRI	PHAN JA AAKAAD THO	PHAN JA AAKAAD EG
	NO INSIGNIA							
U.S. RANK TITLES	AIRMAN BASIC	NO RANK	AIRMAN 1ST CLASS	SERGEANT	TECHNICAL SERGEANT	MASTER SERGEANT	SENIOR MASTER SERGEANT	CHIEF MASTER SERGEANT

Figure 19. Enlisted Rank Insignia, 1987

widened by the fact that officers usually were college or military academy graduates, while most NCOs had not gone beyond secondary school. There was often a wider gap between officers and conscripts, most of whom had had even less formal education, service experience, or specialized training.

Formal honors and symbols of merit occupied an important place in the Thai military tradition, and service personnel received and wore awards and decorations with pride. The government granted numerous awards, and outstanding acts of heroism, courage, and meritorious service received prompt recognition.

Internal Security System

The concept of public order founded on the supremacy of law has long been stressed in Thailand as a necessary prerequisite to internal security and the achievement of national development goals. For the most part, Thai governments, in accordance with constitutional provisions, have dealt with matters of public order through a comprehensive system of statutory law enforced by a professional police force. Some exceptions have occurred during periods of martial law, which has been declared to control dissidence perceived as a threat to public safety. In such times, summary justice at the hands of the police and the army has stressed expediency in a way that has drawn criticism from human rights advocates throughout the world.

One of these periods of martial law occurred after the bloody October 1976 coup d'état, which brought to power the military junta known as the National Administrative Reform Council (NARC) and Thanin Kraivichien as prime minister (see Military Rule and Limited Parliamentary Government, 1976–83, ch. 4). The regime abolished the 1974 constitution and ruled by decree and martial law. During the following year the government issued a series of decrees known as NARC orders. These restrictive measures were instituted following the brutal suppression of leftist student demonstrations at Thammasat University by police-supported and ultra-right vigilante gangs, such as the Red Gaurs (Red Bulls) and the Nawa Phon, or New Force (see Thailand in Transition, ch. 1).

Most of the NARC orders applied to activities neither covered by the criminal code nor under the jurisdiction of the established system of criminal courts. The orders were enforced by arbitrary arrests of people suspected of communist leanings; long-term detention or imprisonment, often without charge or trial; and summary execution of major offenders. Military courts had authority to try those defendants who were allowed a hearing, but the right of appeal was denied. The government also imposed press censorship, revoking the publication licenses of newspapers that criticized government activities.

One of the most repressive of the decrees—NARC Order 22—defined nine categories of offenses, six involving criminal violations and three identifying political activities that "endanger society." The political offenses were defined as "instigating confusion," advocating political systems other than those headed by the king, and undertaking labor strikes. The decree stated that political detainees could be held for thirty days and could subsequently be required to attend democracy-training schools for periods as long as three months. These schools, operated under the government's reeducation program, provided lectures on democracy and Thai national institutions. Some NARC orders were retained by the Kriangsak regime immediately after it gained power in 1977 by ousting Thanin, but they were gradually phased out during conciliation efforts that led to adoption of the new Constitution in December 1978.

In early February 1979, the National Assembly unanimously adopted the new Anti-Communist Activities Act, which had universal application throughout the country. Later in the month martial law was temporarily lifted as the government prepared for the national elections to be held in April. In August NARC Order 22 was abolished, and the government revealed that nearly 12,000 people had been detained or imprisoned indefinitely under the decree's provisions since its imposition in October 1976. All who were still incarcerated solely on "danger to society" charges were granted amnesty and released. Although these actions drew favorable responses from some human rights critics, others saw continuing problems in the criminal justice system under the Anti-Communist Activities Act of 1979.

The Anti-Communist Activities Act gave Thai security forces authority to search suspected individuals and establishments at any time without a court warrant and to detain suspects for a maximum of 480 days. Moreover, the act gave provincial governors and regional military commanders broad powers to control the activities of local populations by imposing curfews, banning demonstrations and meetings, confiscating mail, monitoring telephone conversations, and reviewing business employers' personnel files. Human rights organizations, such as Amnesty International and the Union of Democratic Thai, regarded the new act as tantamount to a state of martial law. Most provisions of the Anti-Communist Activities Act were not enforced in the late 1980s because insurgent activities had been virtually eliminated. Most of the other aspects of arbitrary justice gave way to safeguards assured by the Constitution. Although laws mandating harsh sentences for certain major crimes remained, they were infrequently implemented.

Police and Paramilitary Forces

Primary responsibility for the maintenance of public order through enforcement of the kingdom's laws was exercised by the Thailand National Police Department (TNPD), a subdivision of the Ministry of Interior. Charged with performing police functions throughout the entire country, the TNPD was a unitary agency whose power and influence in Thai national life had at times rivaled that of the army.

The formal functions of the TNPD included more than the enforcement of laws and apprehension of offenders. The department also played an important role in the government's efforts to suppress the remnants of the insurgency. In the event of an invasion by external forces, much of the police force would come under the control of the Ministry of Defense to serve with, but not be incorporated into, the military forces.

Originally modeled on the pre-World War II national police force of Japan, the TNPD was reorganized several times to meet changing public order and internal security needs. American advice, training, and equipment, which were provided from 1951 through the early 1970s, did much to introduce new law enforcement concepts and practices and to aid in the modernization of the TNPD. During this era the strength and effectiveness of the police grew steadily.

All components of the police system were administered by the TNPD headquarters in Bangkok, which also provided technical support for law enforcement activities throughout the kingdom (see fig. 20). The major operational units of the force were the Provincial Police, the Border Patrol Police (BPP), the Metropolitan Police, and smaller specialized units supervised by the Central Investigation Bureau.

In mid-1987 the total strength of the TNPD, including administrative and support personnel, was estimated at roughly 110,000. Of this number, over one-half were assigned to the Provincial Police and some 40,000 to the BPP. More than 10,000 served in the Metropolitan Police. Quasi-military in character, the TNPD was headed by a director general, who held the rank of police general. He was assisted by three deputy directors general and five assistant directors general, all of whom held the rank of police lieutenant general. Throughout the TNPD system, all ranks except the lowest (constable) corresponded to those of the army. The proliferation of high ranks in the TNPD organizational structure, as in the military, indicated the political impact of the police on national life.

Provincial Police

The Provincial Police formed the largest of the TNPD operational components in both manpower and geographic responsibility. It was headed by a commander, who reported to the director general of the TNPD, and administered through four police regions—geographic areas of responsibility similar to those of the army regional commands. This force provided police services to every town and village throughout the kingdom except metropolitan Bangkok and border areas. The Provincial Police thus handled law enforcement activities and in many cases was the principal representative of the central government's authority in much of the country.

During the 1960s and early 1970s, as the police assumed an increasing role in counterinsurgency operations, a lack of coordination among security forces operating in the rural areas became apparent. Observers noted that the overall police effort suffered because of conflicting organizational patterns and the highly centralized control system that required decisions on most matters to emanate from the various police bureaus of TNPD headquarters in Bangkok.

A reorganization of the TNPD in 1978 and 1979 gave more command authority to the four police lieutenant generals who served as regional commissioners of the Provincial Police. Thereafter, the senior officers of each region not only controlled all provincial police assigned to their respective geographic areas but also directed the railroad, highway, marine, and forestry police units operating there, without going through the chain of command to the Central Investigation Bureau in Bangkok. Although this change increased the workload of the four regional headquarters, it resulted in greater efficiency and improved law enforcement.

Border Patrol Police

Developed in the 1950s with assistance from the United States Central Intelligence Agency, the paramilitary Border Patrol Police (BPP) has remained the country's most effective internal security force. Although technically part of the TNPD, the BPP has always enjoyed a great deal of basic autonomy within the national headquarters as well as in its multifaceted field operations. Because the royal family was a principal patron of the organization, the BPP developed the esprit de corps of an elite unit. This traditional relationship benefited both the palace and its paramilitary protectors.

271

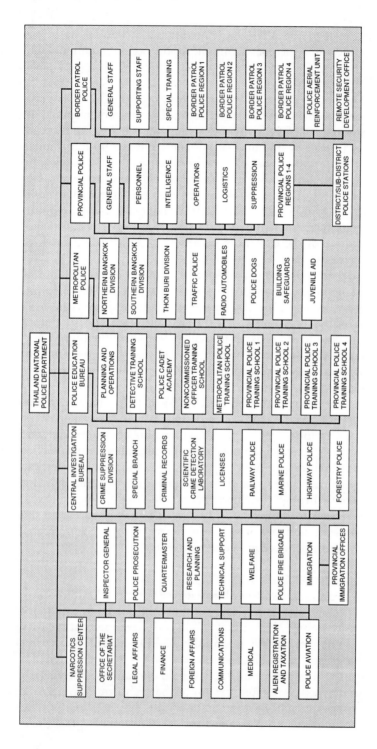

Figure 20. Organization of the Thailand National Police Department, 1987

At the same time, the BPP retained direct links with the larger Royal Thai Army—a relationship that afforded it an additional degree of political strength. Most BPP commanders were former army officers whose military ties were of considerable value in BPP operations.

Charged with border security along some 4,800 kilometers of land frontiers, the BPP's mission included collecting information on the activities of smugglers, bandits, illegal immigrants, refugees, infiltrators, and communist insurgents. To fulfill its mission, it employed an extensive intelligence network and maintained surveillance over villages and farming districts that had a history of cross-border activities. When armed force was required, the BPP was able to respond effectively. Despite its modest size in comparison with the army, the BPP became a primary counterinsurgency force because of its training, motivation, and unique skills.

Thirty-two-man platoons functioning as security teams formed the basic operating units of the BPP. Each platoon was supported by one or more heavy weapons platoons stationed at the regional and area police headquarters. A special police aerial reinforcement unit airlifted BPP platoons to troubled areas when an emergency arose. Relatively well armed with modern light infantry equipment, the BPP also benefited from training by United States Army Special Forces advisers, who helped establish an instruction program during the 1960s.

The BPP served as an important adjunct to the Thai military and often operated under army (and sometimes marine corps) control during counterinsurgency operations. BPP units stationed along the Cambodian and Laotian borders following the Vietnamese invasion of Cambodia in 1979 often served as the first line of defense and bore the brunt of Vietnamese attacks.

In order to carry out its primary intelligence mission, the BPP worked to establish rapport with remote area villagers and hill tribes. They engaged in civic action projects to gain the confidence and loyalty of rural peoples, building and operating more than 200 schools in remote areas and helping the army to construct offices for civilian administration. In addition, they established rural medical aid stations, gave farmers agricultural assistance, and built small airstrips for communication and transportation purposes.

Responding to village complaints of banditry and harassment by elements the central government considered subversive, the BPP supported the development of a local law enforcement adjunct known as the Volunteer Defense Corps (VDC). Established in 1954, the corps was intended to provide law and order, much like a civilian militia responsible to local authorities, in the event of defense emergencies or natural disasters. The paramilitary VDC had the main responsibility for protecting local inhabitants from threats and intimidation by guerrillas who infiltrated the border provinces from neighboring Laos, Cambodia, and Malaysia. One of its chief tactics was to deny the insurgents access to the food and other supplies that made villages and farms favorite targets. VDC members received training from the BPP, and their effectiveness in both law enforcement and civic action was of considerable value to government goals.

In the late 1980s, VDC strength was estimated at roughly 33,000, down from a peak of about 52,000 in 1980. Part of the reduction was absorbed by the formation of a new organization called the Thahan Phran. With a strength of about 14,000, the Thahan Phran was a volunteer irregular force deployed in active trouble spots along the Cambodian and Burmese borders. The organization followed a military structure and had 32 regiments and 196 companies. The Thahan Phran gained considerable publicity and incurred significant casualties during Vietnamese bombardments and local assaults along the Cambodian border.

Metropolitan Police

Responsible for providing all law enforcement services for the capital city of Bangkok and its suburbs, the Metropolitan Police was probably the most visible and publicly recognizable of all TNPD components. This largely uniformed urban force operated under the command of a commissioner, who held the rank of police major general and was assisted by six deputy commissioners. Organizationally, the force consisted of three divisions, each responsible for police services in one of the three urban areas: northern Bangkok, southern Bangkok, and Thon Buri. Together they accounted for about forty police precincts, which were patrolled around the clock.

In addition to covering the city with foot patrols, the Metropolitan Police maintained motorized units, a canine corps, building guards, traffic-control specialists, and law enforcement personnel trained to deal with juvenile problems. The Traffic Police Division also provided mounted escorts and guards of honor for the king and visiting dignitaries and served as a riot-control force to prevent unlawful demonstrations and to disperse unruly crowds within the capital city.

Central Investigation Bureau

Having jurisdiction over the entire country, the Central Investigation Bureau was organized to assist both provincial and metropolitan components of the TNPD in preventing and suppressing criminal activity and in minimizing threats to national security. The specialized units of the bureau, including the railway, marine, highway, and forestry police, employed up-to-date technical equipment, law enforcement techniques, and training. In addition to the specialized units, five other divisions and offices employed modern procedures to assist in investigating and preventing crime. The Crime Suppression Division—one of the bureau's largest components—was responsible for conducting most of the technical investigations of criminal offenses throughout the kingdom. Its emergency unit coped with riots and other public disorders, sabotage, counterfeiting, fraud, illegal gambling operations, narcotics trafficking, and the activities of secret societies and organized criminal associations. The Special Branch—sometimes referred to by critics as the "political police"—was responsible for controlling subversive activities and served as the TNPD's chief intelligence organization. The Criminal Records Office collected and maintained records required in the conduct of police work, including dossiers and fingerprints of known criminals and persons suspected of wrongdoing. At the well-equipped Scientific Crime Detection Laboratory, technicians performed the requisite chemical and physical analyses. The Licenses Division registered and licensed firearms, vehicles, gambling establishments, and various other items and enterprises as required by law.

Education Bureau

The Police Education Bureau of the TNPD was responsible for training police personnel in the latest methods of law enforcement and the use of modern weapons. It operated the Police Officers Academy at Sam Phran, the detective training school at Bang Kaen, the Metropolitan Police Training School at Bang Kaen, and the Provincial Police training centers at Nakhon Pathom, Lampang, Nakhon Ratchasima, and Yala.

The bureau also supervised a number of sites established and staffed by the BPP to train its field platoons in counterinsurgency operations. These sites included a large national facility at Hua Hin and smaller facilities in Udon Thani, Ubon Ratchathani, Chiang Mai, and Songkhla.

Criminal Justice

Until the nineteenth century the source of criminal law in the kingdom was ancient Thai law based on the Indian *Dharmashastra* (a Hindu legal code attributed to Manu), which was introduced into the country during the Ayutthaya era (see The Ayutthaya Era, 1350–1767, ch. 1). Over the centuries this code was augmented by numerous and sometimes conflicting royal laws and decrees, and there was little uniformity in the interpretations and applications made by different judges. The resulting tangle of legal concepts and arbitrary judicial decisions was strongly criticized by Western countries whose nationals were brought in as advisers or engaged in commerce in the kingdom during the nineteenth century. Objecting to the complexities, cruel punishments, delays, and injustices of the legal system, each Western government insisted that its nationals and others under its protection in the kingdom be subject only to the jurisdiction of its own extraterritorial courts. By the middle of the nineteenth century, the system of extraterritoriality was firmly established and had further complicated an already confusing legal structure.

Concerned by the limitations on the country's sovereignty and encouraged by treaty promises that extraterritoriality would be ended when the laws and judiciary were modernized, the Thai rulers set about making legal reforms. Whereas earlier kings had attempted to codify existing law and eliminate many of the harsher punishments, King Mongkut upon his accession to the throne in 1851 went further. Proclaiming the equality of all people before the law, he tried to improve standards of judicial honesty and competence and to abolish the delays and conflicting rules that had become so much a part of the judicial administration.

During the reign of King Chulalongkorn, who succeeded Mongkut in 1868, legal reform took a new direction. Whereas previous kings had tried to revise and adapt ancient law to meet modern needs, Chulalongkorn believed that the problem would be solved not by revising the old system but by replacing it. He created the Ministry of Justice in 1892, extending its powers to all courts of the kingdom. The ministry's first task was to develop a modern uniform court structure, a process that continued until 1920, ten years after Chulalongkorn's death.

During this period existing statutory and customary laws were collected and codified, and an enormous volume of new legislation was added. In 1897 a commission composed almost entirely of French and Belgian lawyers was appointed to draw up a penal code, which was promulgated in 1908. The constitutional monarchy established after the coup of 1932 brought about further legal reforms, promulgated in 1935 in the Criminal and Civil Procedures Code. This new legislation was based on Thai and Western legal practices that provided substantial safeguards in the administration of justice. In response to these legal reforms and the incorporation into Thai law of some Western concepts of jurisprudence, the system of extraterritoriality was completely eliminated by 1938.

Touring Laotian border front in late 1970s,
Crown Prince Vajiralongkorn,
Prime Minister Thanom Kittikachorn,
and King Bhumibol Adulyadej (left to right)
Courtesy Royal Thai Embassy

Further legal refinements resulted in the Criminal Code of 1956, which in the late 1980s remained the core of Thai criminal law.

Criminal Code

The Criminal Code listed twelve kinds of offenses categorized as felonies. The first consisted of crimes against the security of the kingdom, including those against the royal family, treason, espionage, and acts that damaged friendly relations with foreign countries. Crimes relating to public administration, such as malfeasance in office and offenses against public officials, constituted a second major category. Crimes relating to justice, such as perjury or offenses against the police or the judiciary, formed a third major group. Other felonies included crimes against Buddhism; acts against public order and safety; offenses relating to the counterfeiting of money, seals, stamps, and documents; crimes against trade, including the use of false weights and measures and misrepresentation of goods; sexual offenses; crimes against the person; crimes against liberty and reputation, such as false imprisonment, kidnapping, and libel; crimes against property; and offenses such as misappropriation and receipt of stolen property. The code also

277

listed a wide assortment of petty offenses that were classed as misdemeanors, defined officially as violations punishable by imprisonment for not more than one month, a modest fine, or both.

Five penalties for violating the code's various provisions were stipulated: death, imprisonment, detention (restricted residence), fines, and forfeiture of property to the state. The death sentence was mandatory for murder or attempted murder of any member of the royal family or for any offense likely to endanger the life of a king; murder of a public official or anyone assisting a public official in the performance of his or her duty; murder committed in perpetrating another offense or in an attempt to escape punishment; matricide or patricide; premeditated murder; or murder accompanied by torture. Other homicides could be punished by death but usually brought only imprisonment. Execution was carried out by a firing squad. A sentence of life imprisonment usually meant incarceration for twenty years, the maximum prison term.

Children under eight years of age were not subject to criminal penalties. Juveniles between the ages of seven and fifteen were not fined or imprisoned but could be restricted to their homes, placed on probation, or sent to a vocational training school. Juvenile delinquents were, however, admonished by the court, and their parents were required to show that they had taken measures to ensure against repeated violations. Offenses committed by minors between the ages of fifteen and seventeen resulted in fines or periods of confinement amounting to one-half the penalties prescribed for adults committing the same crimes.

Procedures in Criminal Law

Responsibility for the administration of criminal law was shared by the Ministry of Interior and the Ministry of Justice. Appropriate branches of the TNPD were charged with detecting and investigating crimes, collecting evidence, and bringing the accused before the court. The Public Prosecution Department of the Ministry of Interior represented the state in criminal proceedings and conducted the prosecution. The Ministry of Justice supervised the operation of the courts.

The first step in a criminal case was a preliminary investigation carried out by a police officer; the investigation might include searches of suspects, their homes, and others thought to be implicated. The required warrants for these searches stated the reason for the search, the identity of the person or place to be searched, the name and official position of the officer making the search, and the nature of the offense charged. The police generally adhered to this requirement except in instances covered by the Anti-Communist Activities Act of 1979.

Similar procedures applied for arrest warrants, but a senior police officer was permitted to make an arrest without a warrant when the offense was of a serious nature, or when someone was apprehended in the commission of a crime or in possession of a weapon or instrument commonly used for criminal purposes. Private citizens were permitted to arrest without warrant anyone caught in the act of committing a serious crime. Arrested suspects were required to be taken promptly to a police station, where the arrest warrant was read and explained to them. They were then held or released on bail. The provisions for bail and security were defined by law.

After an arrest, a further and more detailed investigation of the case was made, but not until the complainant—the state or a private individual—had submitted and signed a full bill of particulars. At the beginning of this phase, accused persons were warned that any statement they made might be used against them in court. The investigator was not permitted to use threats, promises, or coercion to induce the accused to make self-incriminating statements.

When the investigation was completed, a report was filed with the public prosecutor, who then prepared an indictment and gave a copy to the accused or his counsel, who entered a plea of guilty or not guilty. Based on the plea and the evidence that had been gathered, the judge either accepted a case for trial or dismissed all charges. Trials were normally held in open court, and the accused was presumed to be innocent until proven guilty. If the defendant had no counsel and wished to be represented, the court appointed a defense attorney. During trials, accused persons or their counsels could cross-examine prosecution witnesses and reexamine defense witnesses. They could also refuse to answer questions or to give evidence that might be self-incriminating. At the conclusion of the argument the court usually recessed while the judge reached a decision; the court was required, however, to reconvene within three days and the judgment be read to the accused in open court. The presiding judge, after pronouncing sentence, frequently canceled half of the term of the sentence if the accused confessed to his crime. A convicted person wishing to appeal was required to do so within fifteen days. The case then was transferred to the Court of Appeal, which could reverse or reduce, but not increase, the sentence imposed by the original trial court.

Although periodic revisions of the Criminal Code improved the quality of criminal justice, the system still suffered from disparity in sentences. In many cases the court experienced difficulty in determining appropriate sentences because the minimum punishment specified by the Criminal Code was often quite severe. In order that sentences for the same offense be consistent without hampering the court's discretion, judges had a list of standard sentences derived from past practices and consideration of other relevant factors. These guidelines, however, were not compulsory. To permit judges to exercise informed discretion, the Ministry of Justice stressed the importance of accurate information about the causes of the crime, the nature of the accused, and other circumstances pertinent to judicial decisions. Even so, the criminal courts showed some difficulty in overcoming the historical tendency to regard punishment solely as retribution for past misdeeds and deterrence of future antisocial behavior.

Penal System

The penal system was administered by the Department of Corrections within the Ministry of Interior. The government's stated policy in operating the system was to use its facilities to reduce crime by correcting and rehabilitating offenders rather than only punishing them. Rehabilitation of convicted offenders was a relatively recent penal concept in Thailand, however, and proper facilities, programs, and specially trained penal staff were limited.

In the late 1980s, the system consisted of forty-six regular penal institutions, including seven central prisons, five regional prisons, twenty-three prison camps, seven correctional institutions, three reformatories, and one detention home. In addition, all metropolitan, provincial, and district police stations had jails of varying adequacy for offenders whose sentences did not exceed one year.

The seven central and five regional prisons housed the majority of prisoners with long-term sentences. Khlong Prem Central Prison in Bangkok, with a capacity of 6,000 inmates, was one of the oldest and largest. A maximum security institution for habitual criminals was operated at Nakhon Pathom. Twenty-three prison camps were located on Ko Tarutao, an island in the Strait of Malacca. The camps accommodated an average of fifty good-conduct prisoners, who worked principally in agriculture, preparing themselves for employment after their release.

Two correctional institutions, one at Ayutthaya and one in Bangkok, held primarily offenders eighteen to twenty-five years old serving terms of up to five years. The Women's Correctional Institution was also located in Bangkok, and the specialized Medical Correctional Institution for drug addicts and other prisoners who required medical attention was located in Pathum Thani Province north of the capital. Minimum security correctional centers were located at Rayong and Phitsanulok.

Of the three reformatories, the Ban Lat Yao facility, just north of Bangkok, with a capacity of about 2,000, received the majority of the more recalcitrant juvenile delinquents. Limited rehabilitation activities were undertaken there; those who failed to respond were sent to a second reformatory near Rayong, which was operated on the prison farm principle. A third reformatory at Prachuap Khiri Khan, about 200 kilometers southwest of Bangkok, was used only to accommodate the overflow from the other two institutions.

Additional special facilities for juvenile offenders, called observation and protection centers, were administered by the Central Juvenile Court and the Central Observation and Protection Center of the Ministry of Justice. Attached to each juvenile court, the centers assisted in caring for and supervising delinquent children charged with criminal offenses, both before and after trial. Probation officers, social workers, and teachers assigned to the centers aided the court by collecting information on the background and home environment of offenders, by taking them into custody pending trial, by accompanying the defendants into court, and by reporting to the court on their mental and physical conditions.

Health conditions in all types of penal institutions improved during the 1970s and 1980s, but more hospital facilities were needed. Prison education facilities conducted literacy classes for 20,000 prisoners each year. Vocational training workshops also were established in some prisons. Products from prison labor were sold, and 35 percent of the net profit was returned to the prisoners. Some of this income could be spent during incarceration, but most of it went into a savings fund to assist the prisoner in making a new start after release.

Criminal Activity and the Narcotics Trade

The crime rate appeared to have risen throughout the 1970s and early 1980s—perhaps an inevitable by-product of a society changing under the pressures of population increases and economic and social modernization. The TNPD reports revealed increases in murder, assault, theft, armed robbery, smuggling, and petty violations. The major share of these criminal activities occurred in Bangkok and some of the larger towns in outlying areas. The high incidence of theft by youthful gangs also caused the police considerable concern.

In general, organized crime appeared to be rare, except for the illicit trade in opium, heroin, and cannabis, which persisted in spite of ever-increasing government efforts during the 1970s and 1980s to cope with a problem that had not only serious domestic implications but also escalating international repercussions. The drug trade had originated with the growing of poppies as a traditional primary cash crop by hill tribes in the Thai section of the notorious Golden Triangle—a mountainous border region including parts of Burma and Laos. For many years peasant cultivators in this region produced a major share of the world's opium.

According to estimates by the Thai government and international drug-control agencies, the average crop year yielded from 500 to 1,000 tons of opium, which, when processed in clandestine laboratories, produced from 50 to 100 tons of heroin. An estimated one-half of each annual crop found its way into the world market, destined primarily for addicts in Western Europe and the United States. The other half supplied users in Thailand, Malaysia, and other Asian countries. In the late 1980s, it was believed that Thailand alone had roughly 500,000 addicts who depended on illicit supplies of opium and heroin. For years the Thai government maintained that there were relatively few opium users among the cultivators. But a medical survey, conducted in 1976–77 by health researchers from Chulalongkorn University, indicated that the rate of addiction in 6 sample villages varied from 6.6 to 16.8 percent of all inhabitants over the age of 10. This survey and subsequent studies convinced the Thai leadership that trafficking in illegal narcotics had become a domestic problem requiring action, rather than a low-priority international problem.

The opium-heroin trade of the 1980s stemmed from a history of international political machinations in the countries of and around the Golden Triangle—a maze compounded in more recent times by increasing profitability. The hill tribes grew the opium. Insurgents and separatists in Burma transported it. Yunnan Chinese living in northern Thailand taxed it, and Chaozhou Chinese (overseas Chinese living in Bangkok and Hong Kong) bought and exported it. Any clear understanding of the complicated system requires careful study of the region's ethnic and political hierarchy.

The Chinese appeared to have been heavily involved in the opium trade, but that was mainly before the advent of Mao Zedong. The Yunnan Chinese who traded in opium were a hodgepodge of private armies, including representatives of the Guomindang (Kuomintang—KMT) forces that fled China at the time of the communist takeover in the late 1940s. The rebel Chinese bands in the Golden Triangle were the remnants of the KMT who were unable to escape to Taiwan but instead sought refuge in Burma. Over the intervening years their fanatical anticommunist attitude kept them active in southern China as well as in Burma, Laos, and northern Thailand. For many years their fierce independence and swashbuckling military courage was regarded by many Western

King Bhumibol Adulyadej meeting with hill tribespeople
participating in crop substitution program
Courtesy Royal Thai Embassy

governments as helpful in stemming communism in Southeast Asia. That attitude, however, predated the international heroin problem and the rapprochement between the West and China.

The Chaozhou Chinese (originally from Chaozhou District, Guangdong Province) traced their roots in drug trafficking back to the days of organized crime in Shanghai after China's defeat in the Opium War (1839–42). Operating their maze of syndicates from Hong Kong, the Chaozhou Chinese had a virtual monopoly on the illicit opium and heroin trade, and the technology they used in converting opium to more easily transportable heroin was handed on to Chinese living in Thailand. The syndicates' intricate system of international couriers operated within Thailand to transport drugs both to local dealers and to the vast array of worldwide customers.

Faced with increasing use of illicit drugs among young people in the United States in the 1960s and a rising incidence of addiction among its servicemen in Vietnam, the United States government focused on the flow of heroin from Thailand. On September 28, 1971, the two governments signed a memorandum of understanding, reaffirming their intention to cooperate with each other in combating the illicit international traffic in dangerous drugs. Under the terms of the accord, the Thai government agreed to step up its efforts to eliminate poppy production and to control narcotics

283

traffic within the country. The United States agreed to provide support, such as training, equipment, advisory assistance, and funds, to improve the effectiveness of the Thai programs. For several years the cooperative efforts of the two governments produced limited results, partly because certain corrupt senior Thai officials in the bureaucracy, the army, and the police had personal interests in the drug trade.

By the 1980s, successive Thai governments had played an increasingly effective role in the suppression and control of illicit drugs originating in Southeast Asia. The agents of the Narcotics Suppression Center, established under the TNPD, were highly regarded by foreign narcotics representatives for their efficiency and incorruptibility. Personnel of the Provincial Police and the BPP received training in narcotics work, and new equipment—including helicopters—had been procured to aid in aerial surveillance. Coordination between the TNPD specialists and Interpol provided the Thai with valuable information and suggestions from the police representatives of countries such as Canada, France, Britain, Sweden, the Netherlands, and the United States as well as the metropolitan police of Hong Kong. Many foreign governments, including the United States, assigned professional narcotics specialists to their embassies in Bangkok to work with the Thai government on the illicit drug problem.

Thai citizens, threatened by the problems stemming from drug abuse in their country, strongly supported such measures as preventive education, treatment, and rehabilitation. In addition, tough amendments were added to the Criminal Code to deter those trafficking in narcotics. Legislation passed in March 1979 mandated the death penalty or life imprisonment for persons convicted of possessing, manufacturing, or transporting more than 100 grams of heroin. Despite limited success in the legal and enforcement areas of antinarcotics programs, the Thai government and its foreign advisers believed that the most logical long-term solution lay in persuading the opium-growing hill people to abandon their traditional crop and switch instead to other cash crops, such as coffee, beans, tea, and tobacco. This effort received aid from the United Nations, which started a pilot project along these lines in 1973. The United States provided funds to assist in the development of a highland marketing system for the hill tribes' produce and for a system of roads to provide growers with easier access to lowland consumers.

During the 1980s, as the number of narcotics addicts in Thailand continued to grow, the Thai government renewed its attention to narcotics eradication and interdiction programs. These efforts received strong support from the United States and other countries. Thailand and Burma, always suspicious neighbors, increased cooperation in the effort to eliminate narcotics traffic along their border. The two governments arranged for limited intelligence exchange on narcotics refineries and trade routes along the border and also cooperated in combined tactical missions against the narcotics traffic. Progress in the battle against illicit narcotics was slow, partly because of the vested interests of certain influential figures within Thailand. It was also difficult to combat the problem because of the remote and rugged terrain and the international border. Observers predicted drug traffic would continue for many years to come and might never be completely eradicated.

*   *   *

Although an abundance of material exists concerning various aspects of national security in Thailand, there are no definitive studies in English that provide the entire picture. Readers interested in further details on the country's insurgency problem may consult former United States Agency for International Development officer Robert F. Zimmerman's succinct 1976 article, "Insurgency in Thailand," and former United States special assistant for counterinsurgency George K. Tanham's informative book *Trial in Thailand*. Hans U. Luther's extensive article, "Peasants and State in Contemporary Thailand," provides an informative explanation of the insurgency's socioeconomic basis. Thomas Lobe's well-researched and provocative monograph, *United States National Security Policy and Aid to the Thailand Police,* offers interesting exploration of the myriad problems encountered in counterinsurgency efforts through the mid-1970s. Moreover, a clear picture of the roles and activities of the kingdom's prime internal security force is offered in Thomas Lobe and David Morell's chapter, "Thailand's Border Patrol Police: Paramilitary Political Power," in *Supplementary Military Forces,* edited by Louis A. Zurcher and Gwyn Harries-Jenkins. An understanding of national security policy is greatly assisted by the chapter on Thailand in *Strategies of Survival* by Charles E. Morrison and Astri Suhrke. But no analysis of the national security situation, using publicly available sources, would be possible without the extensive coverage provided by the periodical *Far Eastern Economic Review.* (For further information and complete citations, see Bibliography.)

Appendix

Table 1. Metric Conversion Coefficients and Factors

When you know	Multiply by	To find
Millimeters	0.04	inches
Centimeters	0.39	inches
Meters	3.3	feet
Kilometers	0.62	miles
Hectares (10,000 m²)	2.47	acres
Square kilometers	0.39	square miles
Cubic meters	35.3	cubic feet
Liters	0.26	gallons
Kilograms	2.2	pounds
Metric tons	0.98	long tons
....	1.1	short tons
....	2,204	pounds
Degrees Celsius	9	degrees Fahrenheit
(Centigrade)	divide by 5 and add 32	

Table 2. Chakkri Dynasty, 1782–1987

Regnal Title	Reign	Conventional Form Used in the West	Systematic Romanization [1]
Rama I [2]	1782–1809	Yot Fa	Phutthayotfa Chulalok
Rama II [2]	1809–1824	Loet La	Phutthaloetla Naphalai
Rama III	1824–1851	Nang Klao	Nangklao
Rama IV	1851–1868	Mongkut	Chomklao
Rama V	1868–1910	Chulalongkorn	Chunlachomklao
Rama VI	1910–1925	Vajiravudh	Mongkutklao
Rama VII	1925–1935 [3]	Prajadhipok	Pokklao
Rama VIII	1935–1946 [4]	Ananda Mahidol	Anantha Mahidon
Rama IX	1946 [5]–	Bhumibol Adulyadej	Phumiphon Adunlayadet

[1] As adopted by the Library of Congress, except for the omission of diacritical markings.
[2] Conferred posthumously.
[3] Abdicated; died 1941.
[4] Regency until 1945; died 1946.
[5] Regency until 1951.

289

Table 3. *Population Growth, 1911-85*

Census Year	Total Population	Rate of Increase (in percentage) [1]
1911	8,266,408	
		.... 1.4
1919	9,207,355	
		.... 2.2
1929	11,506,207	
		.... 3.0
1937	14,464,105	
		.... 1.9
1947	17,442,689	
		.... 3.2
1960	26,257,916	
		.... 3.4
1970	34,397,374	
		.... 2.6
1980	44,824,540	
		.... 2.5
1985	51,571,000 [2]	

[1] Average annual increase during the period between censuses.
[2] Estimated.

Table 4. *School Enrollment, 1980-84*

Level of Education	1980	1981	1982	1983	1984
Preprimary	349,827	379,400	408,687	471,597	532,097
Primary	7,370,846	7,449,219	7,413,571	7,272,153	7,229,064
Secondary					
Lower secondary ...	1,343,937	1,104,339	1,188,911	1,222,037	1,302,131
Upper secondary ...	266,349	468,248	516,199	532,888	557,095
Total secondary ..	1,610,286	1,572,587	1,705,110	1,754,925	1,859,226
Teacher training	70,837	71,978	85,016	76,957	70,877
Vocational	356,700	492,597	539,865	588,470	577,147
University*					
Undergraduate	71,096	88,796	96,662	102,696	106,562
Graduate	11,092	11,305	12,178	13,418	14,257
Total university ..	82,188	100,101	108,840	116,114	120,819
TOTAL	9,840,684	10,065,882	10,261,089	10,280,216	10,389,230

* Excludes Ramkhamhaeng University and Sukhothai Thammathirat Open University, in 1980 excluded Srinakharinwirot University.

Source: Based on information from Thailand, Office of the Prime Minister, National Statistical Office, *Statistical Handbook of Thailand, 1985,* Bangkok, 40-41.

Table 5. Gross Domestic Product, by Sector, 1983–86

	1983 Value [1]	1983 Percentage of GDP [2]	1984 Value [1]	1984 Percentage of GDP [2]	1985 Value [1]	1985 Percentage of GDP [2]	1986 Value [1]	1986 Percentage of GDP [2]
Agriculture								
Crops	149,973	16.2	139,547	14.1	127,051	12.2	124,905	11.4
Livestock	28,840	3.1	26,328	2.7	24,371	2.3	26,669	2.4
Fisheries	14,466	1.6	13,129	1.3	14,807	1.4	17,564	1.6
Forestry	11,164	1.2	12,274	1.2	12,304	1.2	13,899	1.3
Total agriculture	204,443	22.1	191,278	19.3	178,533	17.1	183,037	16.7
Nonagriculture								
Mining and quarrying ...	16,480	1.8	21,291	2.2	29,240	2.8	23,347	2.1
Manufacturing	176,200	19.0	196,257	19.8	209,014	20.1	226,571	20.6
Construction	47,129	5.1	52,772	5.3	54,373	5.2	55,682	5.1
Electricity and water supply	16,319	1.8	18,884	1.9	24,070	2.3	28,182	2.6
Transportation and communications .	73,708	8.0	83,588	8.5	95,160	9.2	101,827	9.3
Wholesale and retail trade	165,812	17.9	181,993	18.4	189,736	18.2	204,095	18.6
Banking, insurance, and real estate ..	72,381	7.8	80,577	8.2	84,922	8.2	87,248	7.9
Ownership of dwellings	11,210	1.2	12,337	1.2	13,608	1.3	14,909	1.3
Public administration and defense ..	42,551	4.6	43,182	4.4	47,136	4.5	49,139	4.5
Services	98,680	10.7	106,704	10.8	115,562	11.1	124,325	11.3
Total nonagriculture ..	720,470	77.9	797,585	80.7	862,821	82.9	915,325	83.3
TOTAL	924,913	100.0	988,863	100.0	1,041,354	100.0	1,098,362	100.0

[1] In millions of baht (for value of the baht—see Glossary).
[2] Gross domestic product.

Source: Based on information from Bank of Thailand, *Quarterly Bulletin*, Bangkok, June 1987, 88.

Table 6. *Government Expenditures, Selected Years, 1978-86*
(in millions of baht) *

	1978	1980	1982	1984	1986
Economic classification					
Current	58,518	94,370	125,904	154,481	173,557
Capital	18,991	26,603	31,113	27,747	30,722
Major functional classification					
Economic services	17,012	22,804	27,902	28,573	29,928
Social services	23,831	35,474	47,940	55,419	60,156
Defense	15,310	24,398	31,350	36,034	41,125
General administration .	9,526	17,705	18,134	24,304	25,761
Unallocable items	11,830	20,592	31,691	37,898	47,309
TOTAL	77,509	120,973	157,017	182,228	204,279

* For value of the baht—see Glossary.

Source: Based on information from Bank of Thailand, *Quarterly Bulletin*, Bangkok, June
1987, 36.

Table 7. *Balance of Payments, 1982–86*
(in millions of baht) *

	1982	1983	1984	1985	1986
Exports	157,203.4	145,076.1	173,520.0	191,703.0	231,481.4
Imports	-193,319.6	-234,278.5	-242,283.6	-253,333.7	-245,690.3
Nonmonetary gold	-20.5	-34.7	-32.2	-40.8	-159.8
Balance of trade	-36,136.7	-89,237.1	-68,795.8	-61,671.5	-14,368.7
Net goods and services	-27,341.7	-72,662.3	-53,596.4	-46,418.9	584.1
Unrequited transfers	4,203.5	6,376.6	4,128.1	4,494.1	5,913.6
Balance on current account	-23,138.2	-66,285.7	-49,468.3	-41,924.8	6,497.7
Capital movements	15,207.0	-31,604.9	8,896.4	9,508.1	17,851.3
Net errors and omissions	-11,892.7	13,526.9	1,691.5	2,955.8	15,726.8
Overall balance	3,314.3	-18,078.0	10,587.9	12,463.9	33,578.1

* For value of the baht—see Glossary.

Source: Based on information from Bank of Thailand, *Quarterly Bulletin,* Bangkok, June 1987, 68–69.

293

Table 8. *Principal Exports, Selected Years, 1981–86*
(in millions of baht) [1]

Item	1981	1983	1985	1986
Rice	26,366	20,157	22,524	20,315
Rubber products	10,841	11,787	13,567	15,116
Maize	8,349	8,486	7,700	9,261
Cassava products	16,446	15,387	14,969	19,086
Tin	9,091	5,265	5,647	3,096
Sugar	9,572	6,338	6,247	7,271
Integrated circuits	6,163	5,829	8,248	12,818
Textile products	12,570	14,351	23,578	31,268
Marine products [2]	7,859	10,682	15,934	23,013
Precious stones	4,486	6,214	6,350	8,150
Tobacco leaves	1,739	1,791	1,580	1,487
Mung beans	1,693	1,552	2,284	1,463
Frozen fowl	1,187	946	1,467	3,121
Sorghum	904	790	1,048	657
Fresh fruit	426	525	684	736
Orchids	402	354	490	387
Raw cotton	267	268	210	96
Kapok fiber	285	250	230	205
Tungsten	379	132	150	64
Coffee	231	452	883	1,722
Fluorite	332	289	363	230
Canned pineapple	2,039	1,871	3,292	3,183
Molasses	696	609	758	1,018
Iron or steel pipes	580	429	1,649	1,502
Leather gloves	242	223	347	420
Artificial flowers	383	481	913	1,146
Wall and floor tiles	227	302	315	519
Wood products	1,367	1,336	1,901	2,235
Jute products	1,245	1,100	1,561	1,265
Footwear	956	1,743	2,368	3,185
Furniture	707	981	1,317	1,866
Plastic products	689	938	1,262	1,414
Jewelry	526	1,028	2,168	5,014
Other	23,756	23,586	41,362	51,054
TOTAL	153,001	146,472	193,366	233,383

[1] For value of the baht—see Glossary.
[2] Includes fresh and canned fish, crustaceans, and mollusks.

Source: Based on information from Bank of Thailand, *Quarterly Bulletin*, Bangkok, June 1987, 54–57.

Table 9. Exports by Sector, Selected Years, 1981–86
(in millions of baht) *

Sector	1981	1983	1985	1986
Agriculture	72,998	66,484	73,398	79,397
Fishing	6,632	8,225	10,590	14,853
Forestry	143	109	365	620
Mining	11,814	6,806	10,126	6,283
Manufacturing	54,743	61,358	95,615	129,170
Samples and other unclassified goods .	2,632	1,340	1,518	1,772
Reexports	4,039	2,150	1,754	1,288
TOTAL	153,001	146,472	193,366	233,383

* For value of the baht—see Glossary.

Source: Based on information from Bank of Thailand, *Quarterly Bulletin,* Bangkok, June 1987, 52–53.

Table 10. Foreign Trade, 1981–86
(in millions of baht) *

Country	Trade	1981	1982	1983	1984	1985	1986
Brunei	Exports	240	187	221	237	388	388
	Imports	3,338	2,278	2,760	5,165	8,971	4,716
China	Exports	4,064	7,053	2,468	4,295	7,367	7,252
	Imports	6,983	5,374	6,099	7,449	6,073	6,917
Hong Kong	Exports	7,350	7,934	7,281	6,646	7,807	9,306
	Imports	1,942	2,059	2,704	3,050	2,931	3,659
Indonesia	Exports	2,958	4,251	2,754	1,101	1,176	1,516
	Imports	524	532	777	1,868	1,657	1,641
Iran	Exports	4,602	2,287	2,373	2,937	1,769	1,061
	Imports	263	127	1	1	999	282
Japan	Exports	21,704	21,947	22,087	22,787	25,828	33,134
	Imports	52,521	46,086	64,757	66,059	66,587	63,656
South Korea	Exports	3,214	1,888	2,097	2,887	3,575	6,420
	Imports	3,017	3,589	5,602	6,822	5,069	5,731
Malaysia	Exports	6,968	8,342	6,561	8,278	9,646	10,025
	Imports	5,891	10,214	12,738	11,921	14,825	10,118
Philippines	Exports	445	806	1,554	542	1,451	760
	Imports	435	444	356	470	1,616	1,841
Qatar	Exports	32	45	52	82	109	187
	Imports	7,075	4,219	2,907	273	153	1,534
Saudi Arabia	Exports	3,118	4,261	4,245	4,599	4,382	5,398
	Imports	29,395	29,819	24,431	20,865	7,121	2,522

Table 10.—Continued

Country	Trade	1981	1982	1983	1984	1985	1986
Singapore	Exports	11,991	11,654	11,913	14,722	15,350	20,689
	Imports	14,949	12,455	14,623	19,373	18,746	15,845
Taiwan	Exports	2,014	1,916	1,472	2,431	3,130	3,691
	Imports	4,589	5,501	6,762	6,797	7,793	8,730
Belgium	Exports	1,595	1,730	1,432	1,676	2,323	2,342
	Imports	1,944	1,449	2,759	2,238	2,043	2,791
Britain	Exports	2,464	3,042	2,990	3,918	4,703	7,443
	Imports	5,851	5,023	5,390	5,739	6,335	7,767
France	Exports	2,833	3,030	2,813	3,015	3,595	5,301
	Imports	3,918	2,917	3,593	4,116	6,783	3,947
West Germany	Exports	4,934	5,355	5,105	5,799	7,220	10,827
	Imports	9,336	7,624	11,065	10,304	13,586	13,924
Italy	Exports	2,147	2,577	2,072	3,082	3,248	3,847
	Imports	2,488	2,107	3,195	2,848	2,929	2,584
Netherlands	Exports	18,674	21,013	15,883	17,472	13,772	16,996
	Imports	2,786	2,275	2,672	2,721	2,482	2,429
Soviet Union	Exports	6,752	4,212	1,505	1,720	1,703	1,893
	Imports	328	300	388	380	480	560
Switzerland	Exports	2,044	1,745	1,662	1,923	1,941	2,526
	Imports	1,971	1,837	2,534	2,560	3,577	4,033
Canada	Exports	681	657	1,226	2,110	2,368	3,200
	Imports	2,903	2,769	3,403	2,965	3,102	2,984
United States	Exports	19,794	20,257	21,895	30,102	38,016	42,219
	Imports	28,087	26,220	29,708	32,679	28,434	34,518

Table 10.—Continued

Country	Trade	1981	1982	1983	1984	1985	1986
Algeria	Exports	2,008	1,561	2,907	1,133	1,990	394
	Imports	—	—	3	1	—	—
Australia	Exports	1,749	1,715	2,148	2,866	3,370	4,180
	Imports	4,223	4,339	4,279	4,621	4,155	4,241
Other	Exports	18,626	20,263	19,756	28,877	27,139	32,388
	Imports	21,989	17,059	23,103	23,870	34,722	34,388
TOTAL	Exports	153,001	159,728	146,472	175,237	193,366	233,383
	Imports	216,746	196,616	236,609	245,155	251,169	241,358

— means negligible.
* For value of the Baht—see Glossary.

Source: Based on information from Bank of Thailand, *Quarterly Bulletin*, Bangkok, June 1987, 42–43.

Table 11. Imports by Sector, 1981–86
(in millions of baht) *

Category	1981	1982	1983	1984	1985	1986
Consumer goods						
Nondurable						
Food and beverages						
Dairy products	2,451	1,937	2,447	2,418	2,589	2,528
Cereals and derivatives .	1,101	730	947	782	880	843
Fruits and vegetables ..	716	715	896	991	794	523
Coffee, tea, and spices .	166	191	237	190	261	263
Other	1,532	1,417	1,530	1,670	1,840	1,946
Total food and beverages	5,966	4,990	6,057	6,051	6,364	6,103
Tobacco products	71	100	85	105	111	113
Toiletries and cleaning products	991	957	1,165	1,230	1,442	1,519
Clothing and footwear ...	1,054	1,756	2,158	2,065	1,816	2,111
Medicinal and pharmaceutical products	2,377	2,496	2,786	2,733	3,072	3,136
Total nondurable ...	10,459	10,299	12,251	12,184	12,805	12,982
Durable						
Household goods	2,573	2,471	2,885	3,044	3,524	3,646
Electrical appliances	3,519	3,625	5,263	5,549	5,682	5,777
Wood and cork products .	126	122	121	103	115	98
Leather and leather products	38	30	47	75	269	402
Furniture	70	81	105	131	128	102
Bicycles, motorcycles, and parts	1,225	1,024	1,310	1,284	947	842
Small arms	253	253	326	322	496	617
Total durable	7,804	7,606	10,057	10,508	11,161	11,484
Total consumer goods	18,263	17,905	22,308	22,692	23,966	24,466
Intermediate products and raw materials						
Chiefly for consumer goods						
Fish and fish products ...	481	648	984	2,020	3,754	7,462
Animal and vegetable crude materials	3,149	2,782	2,987	4,010	2,494	3,129
Tobacco, unprocessed ...	865	1,639	603	974	1,409	1,252
Lumber and wood products	3,642	2,992	3,783	3,489	3,677	3,501
Textile fibers	3,915	3,247	4,516	5,388	5,673	5,638
Natural	3,443	2,451	3,882	4,507	4,919	4,825
Synthetic	472	796	634	881	754	813
Textile yarn and thread ..	1,278	1,094	1,399	1,514	1,445	2,359
Fabrics	2,676	2,044	2,810	3,459	3,397	4,225
Jewelry, including silver bars	1,352	1,772	3,141	2,591	2,541	4,149
Paper and paperboard ...	2,856	2,535	3,109	2,914	3,656	3,370
Chemicals	18,011	16,138	20,790	20,730	23,061	26,106
Total chiefly for consumer goods	38,225	34,891	44,122	47,089	51,107	61,191

Table 11. — Continued

Category	1981	1982	1983	1984	1985	1986
Chiefly for capital goods						
Crude minerals	1,055	1,035	1,105	1,150	1,318	966
Base metals	18,804	17,134	21,247	21,374	23,347	22,176
Iron and steel	12,039	11,323	13,860	14,035	15,942	15,737
Other	6,765	5,811	7,387	7,339	7,405	6,439
Total chiefly for capital goods	19,859	18,169	22,352	22,524	24,665	23,142
Total intermediate products and raw materials	58,084	53,060	66,474	69,613	75,772	84,333
Capital goods						
Fertilizers and pesticides .	5,180	4,723	6,232	6,162	6,748	6,660
Cement	175	8	27	19	17	29
Construction materials ...	412	242	292	298	317	227
Tubes and pipes	650	458	824	834	1,066	619
Glass and other mineral manufactures	1,443	1,183	1,527	1,256	1,455	1,483
Rubber manufactures	504	511	620	630	697	675
Metal manufactures	5,147	2,986	4,046	3,952	4,977	4,221
Nonelectrical machinery and parts	25,842	21,172	33,061	34,992	34,720	32,299
Electrical machinery and parts	11,080	11,422	16,372	18,085	15,848	25,561
Scientific and optical instruments	2,991	3,256	4,598	4,088	4,356	4,779
Aircraft and ships	3,222	2,171	1,427	3,176	3,493	1,642
Locomotives and rolling stock	339	60	788	115	1,710	121
Total capital goods ..	56,985	48,192	69,814	73,607	75,404	78,316
Other imports						
Vehicles and parts	9,568	7,687	11,416	11,834	9,292	8,939
Petroleum Products	65,100	60,765	57,065	57,353	56,719	32,354
Gold bullion	n.a.	20	35	32	41	160
Miscellaneous	8,746	8,987	9,497	10,024	9,975	12,790
Total other imports ..	83,414	77,459	78,013	79,243	76,027	54,243
TOTAL	216,746	196,616	236,609	245,155	251,169	241,358

n.a.—not available.
* For value of the baht—see Glossary.

Source: Based on information from Bank of Thailand, *Quarterly Bulletin,* Bangkok, June 1987, 44–47.

Table 12. Production of Major Crops, Selected Years, 1960–86
(in thousands of tons)

Crop	1960	1970	1975	1981	1985	1986
Rice	6,770.0	13,410.0	13,386.0	17,800.0	20,599.0	19,026.0
Rubber	171.8	287.2	348.7	502.0	722.0	790.0
Maize	543.9	1,938.2	2,863.2	4,000.0	5,030.0	4,092.0
Cassava	1,222.0	3,431.0	8,100.0	17,744.0	19,263.0	15,255.0
Sugarcane	5,382.0	6,585.9	19,910.0	30,260.0	24,000.0	24,410.0
Mung beans	60.3	150.5	120.6	283.7	323.4	325.0
Ground nuts	152.0	124.9	99.9	146.5	171.0	171.0
Soybeans	25.6	50.4	113.9	131.5	307.8	350.0
Sesame	18.6	20.2	17.4	28.5	25.4	32.6
Coconuts	1,040.0	714.0	677.0	709.6	980.8	890.0
Castor beans	43.0	42.7	38.5	36.0	32.9	28.5
Cotton	45.5	26.8	28.7	175.7	101.5	57.0
Jute and kenaf	187.5	384.9	307.6	208.0	266.0	240.0
Kapok and bambax fiber	n.a.	103.0	106.4	39.2	43.5	41.6
Tobacco leaves (Virginia)	n.a.	20.2	36.9	51.6	35.2	31.3

n.a.—not available.

Source: Based on information from Bank of Thailand, *Quarterly Bulletin,* Bangkok, June
1987, 75.

Table 13. Forest and Fisheries Production, 1979–85

Production	1979	1980	1981	1982	1983	1984	1985
Forest production (in thousands of cubic meters)							
Teak	179.6	97.3	73.2	58.1	58.2	48.2	39.2
Yang wood *	627.4	551.1	289.4	n.a.	n.a.	n.a.	n.a.
Other woods	2,293.7	1,895.8	1,435.9	1,646.9	1,761.5	1,983.6	1,786.1
Firewood	825.2	635.7	643.0	857.2	772.5	816.5	690.6
Charcoal	418.0	234.2	256.9	340.7	291.9	441.2	363.9
Commercial fish catch (in thousands of tons)							
Marine fish	1,813.2	1,648.0	1,824.4	1,986.6	2,100.0	1,973.0	2,057.8
Freshwater fish	133.2	145.0	164.6	133.6	150.0	161.8	167.5

n.a.—not available.
* Yang wood recorded with other woods beginning in 1982.

Source: Based on information from Bank of Thailand, *Quarterly Bulletin*, Bangkok, June 1987, 75.

Table 14. Prime Ministers, 1932–87

Prime Minister	Term of Office
Phraya Manopakonnitithada (Phraya Manopakorn; Kot Hutasing)	August 28, 1932–June 20, 1933
Phraya Phahonphonphayuhasena (Phot Phahonyothin)	June 21, 1933–December 16, 1938
Luang Phibunsongkhram (Plaek Phibunsongkhram; Phibun)	December 16, 1938–July 24, 1944
Khuang Aphaiwong	August 1, 1944–August 17, 1945
Thawi Bunyaket	August 31, 1945–September 17, 1945
M.R.W. Seni Pramoj	September 17, 1945–January 31, 1946
Khuang Aphaiwong	January 31, 1946–March 18, 1946
Pridi Phanomyong	March 24, 1946–August 21, 1946
Luang Thamrongnawasawat (Thawan Thamrongnawasawat)	August 23, 1946–November 8, 1947
Khuang Aphaiwong	November 10, 1947–April 8, 1948
Luang Phibunsongkhram	April 8, 1948–September 16, 1957
Pote Sarasin	September 21, 1957–December 26, 1957
Thanom Kittikachorn	January 1, 1958–October 20, 1958
Sarit Thanarat	February 9, 1959–December 8, 1963
Thanom Kittikachorn	December 9, 1963–October 14, 1973
Sanya Dharmasakti (Sanya Thammasak) ..	October 14, 1973–February 15, 1975
M.R.W. Seni Pramoj	February 15, 1975–March 6, 1975
M.R.W. Kukrit Pramoj	March 14, 1975–January 12, 1976
M.R.W. Seni Pramoj	April 20, 1976–October 6, 1976
Thanin Kraivichien	October 8, 1976–October 20, 1977
Kriangsak Chomanand .....'..........	November 11, 1977–February 28, 1980
Prem Tinsulanonda	March 3, 1980–

Table 15. Parliamentary Elections, 1979–86

Participants	1979	1983	1986
Political party			
Democrat (Prachathipat)	32	56	100
Chart Thai (Thai Nation) [1]	38	73[1]	63
Social Action (Kit Sangkhom)	83	92	51
United Democracy (Saha Prachathipatai)	—	—	38
Prachakorn Thai (Thai People)	32	36	24
Ruam Thai (Thai Unity)	—	—	19
Rassadorn (People)	—	—	18
Community Action (Kit Prachakhorn)	—	—	15
Progressive (Koa Nar)	—	3	9
Muan Chon (Mass)	—	—	3
National Democracy (Chart Prachathipatai)	—	15	3
Liberal (Seriniyom)	—	—	1
Democratic Labor (Raeng Ngam Prachathipatai) ..	—	0	1
New Force (Phalang Mai)	8	0	1
Puangchon Chao Thai (Thai Mass)	—	0	1
Rak Thai (Love Thai)	—	—	0
Freedom and Justice (Seritham)	21	—	—
Siam Democracy (Siam Prachathipatai)	—	18	—
Other parties	24	7	—
Independents [2]	63	24	—
Total	301	324	347
Number of participating political parties	38	14	16
Number of candidates	1,630	1,862	3,810
Voter turnout (in percentage)	44	51	61

— means did not participate.

[1] After the 1983 election, this party increased its strength to 108 by absorbing most independents and members of minor parties.

[2] Independents were required by a 1983 law to join existing parties.

Table 16. Defense Expenditures and Manpower Levels, Fiscal Years 1980-86

Fiscal Year [1]	Defense Expenditures [2] (in billions of baht) [3]	Defense as Percentage of Total Expenditures	Defense as Percentage of GNP [4]	Military Manpower	Paramilitary Forces [5]
1980	22.4	20.1	4.0	230,000	67,000
1981	27.7	19.5	3.8	233,000	67,000
1982	33.1	30.4	4.2	235,000	71,000
1983	35.5	30.3	4.2	256,000	71,000
1984	39.4	30.6	4.2	256,000	73,000
1985	41.4	30.8	4.2	265,000	75,000
1986	41.2	30.8	4.3	273,000	80,000

[1] Fiscal year extends from October 1 through the following September 30, e.g., fiscal year 1980 began October 1, 1979.
[2] Accounts do not include expenditures for internal security or major military equipment purchases.
[3] For value of the baht—see Glossary.
[4] Gross national product.
[5] Includes Thahan Phran, Rangers, Village Defense Corps, Border Patrol Police, Marine Police, Police Aviation, and Special Action Forces.

Table 17. *Major Army Equipment, 1987*

Type and Description	Country of Origin	In Inventory
Tanks		
M-48A5 Patton (medium with 90mm gun)	United States	65
M-41 Walker Bulldog (light) with 76mm gun	-do-	200
Scorpion (light) with 76mm gun	Britain	154
Type 59	China	n.a.
Armored personnel carriers		
M-113A1 (amphibious)	United States	300
LVTP-7 amphibious assault vehicle	-do-	40
V-150 Commando	-do-	114
Shortland Mk3 reconnaissance vehicle	Britain	32
Saracen	-do-	20
Howitzers and guns		
M-101A1 105mm, towed	United States	300
M114 155mm, towed	-do-	56
M-198 155mm, towed	-do-	62
155mm, towed	Israel	24
85mm antitank gun	China	n.a.
105mm Kittikhachorn multiple rocket launcher	Thailand	n.a.
Mortars		
81mm	United States	550
60mm	-do-	900
Recoilless rifles		
57mm	-do-	360
75mm	-do-	200
106mm	-do-	150
Antiaircraft guns		
40mm	-do-	40
20mm Vulcan	-do-	48
Missiles		
BGM-71A TOW antitank missile	-do-	215
FGM-77A Dragon antitank missile	-do-	500
M-72 self-contained, disposable, antitank missile launcher	-do-	n.a.
Redeye	-do-	40
Blowpipe surface-to-air missile	Britain	n.a.

Appendix

Table 17.—Continued

Type and Description	Country of Origin	In Inventory
Aircraft		
Cessna O-1 utility/liaison	-do-	90
Bell UH-1B/D helicopter	-do-	90
Boeing-Vertol CH-47 Chinook helicopter ...	United States	4
Bell OH-13 Sioux helicopter	-do-	24
Fairchild FH-1100 helicopter	-do-	16
Bell 206 helicopter	-do-	3
Bell 212 helicopter	-do-	2
Bell 214B helicopter	-do-	2
Fairchild OH-23F helicopter	-do-	6
Beech BE-99 light transport	-do-	1
Kawasaki KH-4 helicopter	-do-	28
Short 330-UTT transport	Britain	n.a.

n.a.—not available.

Source: Based on information from International Institute for Strategic Studies, *The Military Balance, 1986-1987,* London, 1986; and *Far Eastern Economic Review Asia Yearbook,* Hong Kong, 1987.

Table 18. Major Navy Equipment, 1987

Type and Description	Country of Origin	In Inventory
Frigates		
Yarrow class; 1,650 tons displacement; armed with two 4.5-inch deck guns, two 40mm Bofors antiaircraft guns, Sea Cat surface-to-surface missiles, one antisubmarine Lombo mortar, and two depth charge projectors; serves as flagship of Royal Fleet	Britain	1
PF–103 class, 900 tons displacement; armed with two 3-inch deck guns, two 40mm antiaircraft guns, Hedgehog antisubmarine launchers, and six torpedo tubes	United States	2
Cannon class; 1,240 tons displacement; armed with three 3-inch deck guns, six 40mm antiaircraft guns, six torpedo tubes, and eight depth-charge projectors; ex-USS *Hemminger*	-do-	1
Tacoma class; 1,430 tons displacement; armed with three 3-inch deck guns, two 40mm and nine 20mm antiaircraft guns, eight depth-charge projectors, and six torpedo tubes; ex-USS *Glendale* and ex-USS *Gallup*	-do-	2
Tacoma MK–16 class; 1,430 tons displacement; armed with 76mm main guns, 40mm antiaircraft gun, Stingray torpedoes, Harpoon and Albatross surface-to-air missiles	United States	1
Fast attack craft (missile)		
Breda BMB 30 design; 235 tons displacement; armed with four Exocet surface-to-surface missiles, one 76mm deck gun, and one 40mm Bofors antiaircraft gun	Italy	3
Sea Hawk class; 224 tons displacement; armed with five Gabriel missile launchers, one 57mm Bofors and one 40mm Bofors antiaircraft guns	Singapore	3
Large patrol craft		
Trad class; 318 tons displacement; armed with two 3-inch deck guns, one 40mm and two 20mm antiaircraft guns, and four torpedo tubes	Italy	4
Liulom class (former United States PC class); 280 tons displacement; armed with one 3-inch deck gun and two torpedo tubes	United States	7
Klongyai class; 110 tons displacement; armed with one 3-inch deck gun, one 20mm antiaircraft gun, and two torpedo tubes	Thailand	1
PGM 71 class; 130 tons displacement; armed with one 40mm and four 20mm antiaircraft guns and two .50 caliber machine guns; former United States vessels	United States	10

Table 18.—Continued

Type and Description	Country of Origin	In Inventory
Cape class (former United States Coast Guard cutters); 95 tons displacement; armed with one 20mm antiaircraft gun, depth charges, and two Hedgehog anti-submarine launchers	-do-	4
Coastal patrol craft		
Small craft; 87.5 tons displacement; armed with one 40mm and one 20mm antiaircraft gun	Thailand	6
Swift class; 20 tons displacement; armed with two 81mm mortars and two .50 caliber machine guns; transferred from United States Navy to Royal Thai Navy	United States	12
River patrol craft		
PBR type; 10.4 tons displacement; armed with two .50 caliber and two .30 caliber machine guns; former United States vessels	-do-	6
Fiberglass trimaran	Thailand	1
Mine warfare vessels		
Bangrachan-class coastal minelayer; 368 tons displacement; armed with two 3-inch deck guns, two 20mm antiaircraft guns, and 142 mines	Italy	2
Bluebird-class coastal minesweeper; 330 tons displacement; armed with two 20mm anti-aircraft guns	United States	4
Riverine minesweeper; armed with 20mm deck guns, one 12.7mm machine gun, and two 40mm grenade launchers	Thailand	10
Mine-warfare support ship	Japan	1
Amphibious vessels		
Landing ship, tank (LST)	United States	5
Landing ship, medium (LSM)	-do-	3
Landing craft, medium/mechanized (LCM) ..	-do-	26
Landing craft, utility (LCU)	-do-	6
Landing craft, vehicle and personnel	-do-	8
Landing craft, assault (LCA)	Thailand	n.a.
Aircraft		
Grumman S–2F Tracker for antisubmarine search and attack	United States	10
Grumman HU–16B Albatross	-do-	2
Bell UH–N for antisubmarine search and attack	-do-	8
Canadair CK–215 multipurpose amphibian for search and rescue	Canada	2
F–27 Maritime	Netherlands	3
Nomad	Australia	3

Table 18.—Continued

Type and Description	Country of Origin	In Inventory
Missiles		
Short Seacat surface-to-air missile	Britain	12
IAI Gabriel-2 surface-to-surface missile	Israel	15
Aerospatiale MM–38 Exocet surface-to-surface missile	France	12

n.a.—not available.

Source: Based on information from International Institute for Strategic Studies, *The Military Balance, 1986–1987,* New York, 1986; and Far Eastern Economic Review, *Asia Yearbook 1987,* Hong Kong, 1987.

Table 19. Major Air Force Equipment, 1987

Type and Description	Country of Origin	In Inventory
Fighter-bombers		
Northrop F-5A/B Freedom Fighter	United States	13
Northrop F-5E Tiger II	-do-	34
Northrop F-5F Tiger II two-seat fighter-trainer	-do-	4
F-16A fighter	-do-	8
F-16B two-seat fighter-trainer	-do-	4
Counterinsurgency aircraft		
North American-Rockwell T-28D	-do-	20
North American-Rockwell OV-10C Bronco ..	-do-	24
Cessna A-37B	-do-	14
Fairchild AU-23A Peacemaker	-do-	25
Armed reconnaissance aircraft		
Northrop RF-5A Freedom Fighter	-do-	4
Lockheed T-33A	-do-	4
Lockheed RT-33A	-do-	3
Transports and utility aircraft		
McDonnell Douglas C-47 Dakota	-do-	15
Fairchild C-123B/K Provider	-do-	30
McDonnell Douglas AC-47 Dakota	-do-	10
Cessna O-1	-do-	35
Swearingen Merlin IVA turboprop	-do-	3
Lockheed C-130H Hercules	-do-	4
Hawker-Siddeley HS-748	Britain	2
Britten-Norman Islander	-do-	1
Fairchild/Pilatus Turbo-Porter	Britain and Switzerland	10
Lipnur/CASA C-212 Aviocar	Indonesia and Spain	4
McDonnell Douglas DC-8	United States	3
Boeing 737	-do-	1
Helicopters		
Bell UH-1H Iroquois	-do-	30
CH-34	-do-	16
Trainers		
de Havilland DHC-1 Chipmunk	Britain	4
Cessna T-37B primary jet trainer	United States	20
Cessna T-41D Mescalero light utility	-do-	11
SIAI-Marchetti SF-260MT single piston engine	Italy	15
AESL CT-4	New Zealand	15
Missiles		
NWC AIM-9J Sidewinder air-to-air missile ..	United States	96

Source: Based on information from International Institute for Strategic Studies, *The Military Balance 1986-1987,* London, 1986; and Far Eastern Economic Review, *Asia Yearbook,* 1987, Hong Kong, 1987.

Bibliography

Chapter 1

Akin, Rabibhadana. *The Organization of Thai Society in the Early Bangkok Period, 1782-1873.* (Southeast Asia Program, Data Paper, No. 74.) Ithaca: Department of Asian Studies, Cornell University, 1969.

Allen, Richard. *A Short Introduction to the History and Politics of Southeast Asia.* New York: Oxford University Press, 1970.

Alsop, Joseph. "Rewriting Human History," *Washington Post,* September 8, 1975, A26.

Asian Development Bank. *Southeast Asia's Economy in the 1970s.* New York: Praeger, 1971.

Bastin, John, and Harry J. Benda. *A History of Modern Southeast Asia: Colonialism, Nationalism, and Decolonization.* Englewood Cliffs, New Jersey: Prentice-Hall, 1968.

Batson, Benjamin A. (ed.). *Siam's Political Future: Documents from the End of the Absolute Monarchy.* (Southeast Asia Program, Data Paper, No. 96.) Ithaca: Department of Asian Studies, Cornell University, 1974.

Benda, Harry J., and John Larkin, with Sidney L. Mayer. *The World of Southeast Asia: Selected Historical Readings.* New York: Harper and Row, 1967.

Benedict, Ruth F. *Thai Culture and Behavior.* (Southeast Asia Program, Data Paper, No. 4.) Ithaca: Department of Asian Studies, Cornell University, 1952.

Berrigan, Darrell. "Thailand: New Cast, Same Play," *Reporter,* No. 17, November 28, 1957, 12-14.

_____. "Thailand: Phibun Tries Prachathipatai," *Reporter,* No. 14, June 14, 1956, 30-34.

Bowie, Theodore (ed.). *The Arts of Thailand.* Bloomington: Indiana University Press, 1960.

Bowring, John. *The Kingdom and the People of Siam.* (2 Vols.) London: John W. Parker, 1857.

Briggs, Lawrence P. "The Appearance and Historical Usage of the Terms Tai, Thai, Siamese, and Lao," *Journal of the American Oriental Society,* 69, April-June 1949, 60-73.

Bruce, Helen. *Nine Temples of Bangkok.* Bangkok: Progress Books, 1960.

Buchanan, Keith. *The Southeast Asian World: An Introductory Essay.* Garden City, New York: Anchor Books, Doubleday, 1968.

Bunnag, Tej. *The Provincial Administration of Siam, 1892–1915: The Ministry of Interior under Prince Ranajubhab.* Kuala Lumpur: Oxford University Press, 1977.

Cadet, J.M. *The Ramakien: The Thai Epic.* Tokyo: Kodansha International, 1970.

Cady, John F. *Southeast Asia: Its Historical Development.* New York: McGraw-Hill, 1964.

Chandran Mohandas Jeshurun. *The Contest for Siam 1889–1902: A Study in Diplomatic Rivalry.* Kuala Lumpur: Penerbit University Kebangsaan Malaysia, 1977.

Charnvit Kasetsiri. *The Rise of Ayudhya: A History of Siam in the Fourteenth and Fifteenth Centuries.* Kuala Lumpur: Oxford University Press, 1976.

Chatthip Nartsupha, and Suthy Prasartset (eds.). *Socio-Economic Institutions and Cultural Change in Siam, 1851–1910: A Documentary Survey.* (Southeast Asian Perspectives Series, No. 4.) Singapore: Institute of Southeast Asian Studies, 1977.

Chula Chakrabongse. *Lords of Life: The Paternal Monarchy of Bangkok, 1782–1932.* New York: Taplinger, 1960.

Coedès, Georges. *The Indianized States of Southeast Asia.* Honolulu: East-West Center Press, 1968.

———. *The Making of South East Asia.* Berkeley and Los Angeles: University of California Press, 1969.

Conze, Edward. *The Buddhist Wisdom Books.* London: Allen and Unwin, 1958.

Crozier, Brian. *South-East Asia in Turmoil.* Harmondsworth, Middlesex, United Kingdom: Penguin, 1968.

Darling, Frank C. "Marshal Sarit and Absolutist Rule in Thailand," *Pacific Affairs* [Vancouver], 33, December 1960, 347–60.

———. "Modern Politics in Thailand," *Review of Politics,* 24, April 1962, 163–82.

———. *Thailand and the United States.* Washington: Public Affairs Press, 1965.

———. "Thailand in 1977: The Search for Stability and Progress," *Asian Survey,* 18, No. 2, February 1978, 153–63.

Dhani Nivat. "The Old Siamese Conception of the Monarchy," *Journal of the Siam Society* [Bangkok], 36, 1947, 91–106.

Direk, Jayanama. *Siam and World War II.* Bangkok: Social Science Association of Thailand Press, n.d.

Donner, Wolf. *The Five Faces of Thailand: An Economic Geography.* (Institute of Asian Affairs, Hamburg.) New York: St. Martin's Press, 1978.

Engel, David M. *Law and Kingship in Thailand During the Reign of King Chulalongkorn.* Ann Arbor: University of Michigan Center for South and Southeast Asian Studies, 1975.

Fifield, Russell H. *The Diplomacy of Southeast Asia: 1945–1958.* New York: Harper and Row, 1958.

Frederic, Louis. *The Art of Southeast Asia: Temples and Sculpture.* New York: Abrams, 1965.

Girling, John L.S. *Thailand: Society and Politics.* Ithaca: Cornell University Press, 1981.

Graham, Walter A. *Siam.* (2 Vols, 2d ed.) London: Alexander Moring, 1924.

Hall, D.G.E. *A History of South-East Asia.* (2d ed.) London: Macmillan, 1964.

Hanks, Lucien M. "Merit and Power in the Thai Social Order," *American Anthropologist,* 64, No. 6, December 1962, 1247–61.

Hearn, Robert (ed.). *A Guide to Research Materials on Thailand and Laos.* Auburn, New York: Asia Library Services, 1977.

Heine-Geldern, Robert G. *Conceptions of State and Kingship in Southeast Asia.* (Southeast Asia Program, Data Paper, No. 18.) Ithaca: Department of Asian Studies, Cornell University, 1956.

Higham, Charles, and Amphan Kijngam. "Ban-Chiang and Northeast Thailand—Palaeoenvironment and Economy," *Journal of Archaelogical Science,* 6, No. 3, September 1979, 211–34.

Ho Kwon Ping. "Thailand's Broken Ricebowl," *Far Eastern Economic Review* [Hong Kong], 102, No. 48, December 1, 1978, 40–46.

Ingram, James C. *Economic Change in Thailand, 1850–1970.* Stanford: Stanford University Press, 1971.

Insor, D. *Thailand: A Political, Social, and Economic Analysis.* New York: Praeger, 1963.

Ishii, Yoneo (ed.). *Thailand: A Rice-Growing Society.* (Monographs of the Center for Southeast Asian Studies, Kyoto University.) Honolulu: University Press of Hawaii, 1978.

Jones, Robert R. *Thai Titles and Ranks: Including a Translation of Traditions of Royal Lineage in Siam by King Chulalongkorn.* (Southeast Asia Program, Data Paper, No. 81.) Ithaca: Department of Asian Studies, Cornell University, 1971.

Keyes, Charles F. *Thailand: Buddhist Kingdom as Modern Nation-State.* Boulder, Colorado: Westview Press, 1987.

Kirk, Donald. *Wider War: The Struggle for Cambodia, Thailand, and Laos.* New York: Praeger, 1971.

Kunstadter, Peter (ed.). *Southeast Asian Tribes, Minorities, and Nations.* (2 Vols.) Princeton: Princeton University Press, 1967.

Lebar, Frank M., et al. *Ethnic Groups of Mainland Southeast Asia.* New Haven, Connecticut: Human Relations Area Files Press, 1964.

Lent, John A. (ed.). *The Asian Newspapers' Reluctant Revolution.* Ames: Iowa State University Press, 1971.

Lester, Robert C. *Theravada Buddhism in Southeast Asia.* Ann Arbor: University of Michigan Press, 1973.

McAlister, John T. (ed.). *Southeast Asia: The Politics of National Integration.* New York: Random House, 1973.

Malalasekera, G.P. "Theravada Buddhism." Pages 161–94 in Ismail R. al Faruqi (ed.), *Historical Atlas of the Religions of the World.* New York: Macmillan, 1974.

Martin, James V., Jr. "Thai-American Relations in World War II," *Journal of Asian Studies,* 22, No. 4, August 1963, 451–67.

Mills, Lennox A. *Southeast Asia: Illusion and Reality in Politics and Economics.* Minneapolis: University of Minnesota Press, 1964.

Moffat, Abbot Low. *Mongkut: The King of Siam.* Ithaca: Cornell University Press, 1961.

Morrison, Charles E., and Astri Suhrke. *Strategies of Survival: The Foreign Policy Dilemmas of Smaller Asian States.* New York: St. Martin's Press, 1979.

Moseley, George V.H. *The Consolidation of the South China Frontier.* (Center for Chinese Studies, University of California.) Berkeley and Los Angeles: University of California Press, 1973.

Murti, T.R.V. *The Central Philosophy of Buddhism.* London: Allen and Unwin, 1955.

Niksch, Larry A. "Thailand in 1981: the Prem Government Feels the Heat," *Asian Survey,* 22, No. 2, February 1982, 191–99.

Panikkar, K.M. *Asia and Western Dominance.* New York: Collier Books, 1969.

Peterson, Alec. "Britain and Siam: The Latest Phase," *Pacific Affairs* [Vancouver], 19, December 1946, 364–72.

Punyaratabandhu-Bhakdi, Suchitra. "Thailand in 1982: General Arthit Takes Center Stage." *Asian Survey,* 23, No. 2, February 1983, 172–77.

_____. "Thailand in 1983: Democracy, Thai Style." *Asian Survey,* 24, No. 2, February 1984, 187–94.

Ramsay, Ansil. "Thailand 1978: Kriangsak—the Thai Who Binds." *Asian Survey,* 19, No. 2, February 1979, 104–14.

Rawson, Phillip. *The Art of Southeast Asia.* London: Thames and Hudson, 1967.

Riggs, Fred W. *Thailand: The Modernization of a Bureaucratic Polity.* Honolulu: East-West Center Press, 1966.

Robinson, Warren C. "Economic Policy and Population Change in Thailand," *World Development* [Oxford], 6, Nos. 11–12, 1978, 1261–69.

Salmony, Alfred. *Sculpture in Siam.* New York: Harker Art Books, 1972.

Sarasin, Viraphol. *Sino-Siamese Trade, 1652–1853.* Cambridge: Harvard University Press, 1977.

Seidenfaden, Eric. *The Thai Peoples, I: The Origins and Habitats of the Thai Peoples with a Sketch of Their Material and Spiritual Culture.* Bangkok: Siam Society, 1958.

Shaplen, Robert. *Time Out of Hand: Revolution and Reaction in Southeast Asia.* New York: Harper and Row, 1969.

Sharp, Lauriston, and Lucien M. Hanks. *Bang Chan: Social History of a Rural Community in Thailand.* Ithaca: Cornell University Press, 1978.

Siffin, William J. *The Thai Bureaucracy: Institutional Change and Development.* Honolulu: East-West Center Press, 1966.

Silpa, Bhirasri. *Thai Architecture and Painting.* (4th ed.). Bangkok: National Culture Institute, 1956.

Skinner, George William. *Chinese Society in Thailand: An Analytical History.* Ithaca: Cornell University Press, 1957.

Skinner, George William, and A. Thomas Kirsch (eds.). *Change and Persistence in Thai Society: Essays in Honor of Lauriston Sharp.* Ithaca: Cornell University Press, 1975.

Smith, Bardwell L. (ed.). *Religion and Legitimation of Power in Thailand, Laos, and Burma.* (South and Southeast Asia Studies.) Chambersburg, Pennsylvania: Anima Books, 1978.

Smith, Harold E. *Historical and Cultural Dictionary of Thailand.* (Historical and Cultural Dictionaries of Asia, No. 6.) Metuchen, New Jersey: Scarecrow Press, 1976.

Solheim, Wilhelm G. "New Light on a Forgotten Past," *National Geographic Magazine,* 139, No. 3, March 1971, 330–39.

Steinberg, David Joel (ed.). *In Search of Southeast Asia: A Modern History.* New York: Praeger, 1971.

Tarling, Nicholas. *A Concise History of Southeast Asia.* New York: Praeger, 1966.

Textor, Robert B. "Cultural Futures for Thailand: An Ethnographic Enquiry," *Futures,* 10, October 1978, 347–60.

Thak Chaloemtiarana. "Reflections on the Sarit Regime and the Process of Political Change in Thailand: Some Conceptual and Theoretical Reassessments," *Southeast Asian Studies,* 16, No. 3, December 1978, 400–10.

Thamsook Numnonda. *Thailand and the Japanese Presence, 1941–45.* (Research Notes and Discussions Series, No. 6.) Singapore: Institute of Southeast Asian Studies, October 1977.

Thompson, Virginia. "Government Instability in Siam," *Far Eastern Survey*, 27, 1948, 185–89.

Trumbull, Robert. *The Scrutable East: A Correspondent's Report on Southeast Asia*. New York: David McKay, 1964.

Van Roy, Edward. *Economic Systems of Northern Thailand: Structure and Change*. Ithaca: Cornell University Press, 1971.

Vella, Walter F. *Chaiyo: King Vajiravudh and the Development of Thai Nationalism*. Honolulu: University Press of Hawaii, 1978.

_____. *The Impact of the West on Government in Thailand*. (University of California Publications in Political Science, 4, No. 3.) Berkeley and Los Angeles: University of California Press, 1955.

_____. *Siam under Rama III, 1824–1851*. (Monographs of the Association for Asian Studies, No. 4.) Locust Valley, New York: Augustin, 1957.

Von Der Mehden, Fred R. *South-East Asia 1930–1970: The Legacy of Colonialism and Nationalism*. New York: Norton, 1974.

Wales, Horace Geoffrey Quaritch. *Ancient Siamese Government and Administration*. London: Bernard Quaritch, 1934.

_____. *Siamese State Ceremonies*. London: Bernard Quaritch, 1931.

Warren, William. "Out of Thai Soil an Archeological Upheaval," *ASIA*, 4, No. 3, September–October 1981, 26–28, 52–54.

Wenk, Klaus. *The Restoration of Thailand under Rama I, 1782–1809.* (Association for Asian Studies Monographs and Papers, No. 24.) Tucson: University of Arizona Press, 1968.

Werner, Jayne, et al. "October 1976: The Coup in Thailand," *Bulletin of Concerned Asian Scholars*, 9, No. 3, July–September 1977, 2–51.

Wilson, David A. "The Military in Thai Politics." Pages 326–39 in Robert O. Tilman (ed.), *Man, State, and Society in Contemporary Southeast Asia*. New York: Praeger, 1969.

_____. *Politics in Thailand*. Ithaca: Cornell University Press, 1962.

_____. "Thailand." Pages 3–72 in George McTurnan Kahin (ed.), *Governments and Politics in Southeast Asia*. (2d ed., Southeast Asia Program, Cornell University.) Ithaca: Cornell University Press, 1964.

Wyatt, David K. *The Politics of Reform in Thailand: Education in the Reign of King Chulalongkorn*. (Yale Southeast Asia Studies, Cultural Report Series, No. 4.) New Haven: Yale Univesity Press, 1969.

_____. *Thailand: A Short History*. New Haven: Yale University Press, 1984.

Young, Gordon. *The Hill Tribes of Northern Thailand*. New York: AMS Press, 1982.

(Various issues of the following periodicals were also used in the preparation of this chapter: *Asian Survey, Asiaweek* [Hong Kong]; *Bangkok Post* [Bangkok]; and *Far Eastern Economic Review Asia Year Book.*)

Chapter 2

Amnesty International. "Health Concern, Thailand: Damri Reaungsutham, Aged 62." (ASA 39/04/85.) London: December 1985, 1-2.

_____. "Lao People's Democratic Republic: Arrests Following Forcible Repatriation." (ASA 26/01/87.) London: April 10, 1987, 1-2.

Anderson, Ben. "Withdrawal Symptoms: Social and Cultural Aspects of the October 6 Coup," *Bulletin of Concerned Asian Scholars,* 9, No. 3, July–September 1977, 13-30.

"Another Victory," *Asiaweek* [Hong Kong], 13, No. 15, April 27, 1987, 25.

Aran Suwanbubpa, and Amnoyvit Schoovong. "An Investigation into the Etiology of Heroin Addiction Among Narcotic Prisoners." *Journal of the National Research Council* [Bangkok], 11, No. 1, January–June 1979, 39-45.

Arnold, Fred, Robert D. Retherford, and Anuri Wanglee. "The Demographic Situation in Thailand." (Papers of the East-West Population Institute, Vol. 45.) Honolulu: East-West Center, July 1977.

Arong Suthasana. "The Impact of Modern Development in Southeast Asia: A Thai Case." Pages 54-61 in *International Seminar on Islam in Southeast Asia.* Jakarta: Lembaga Penelitian Iain Syarif Hidayatullah, 1986.

Ayal, Eliezer B. (ed.). *The Study of Thailand: Analyses of Knowledge, Approaches, and Prospects in Anthropology, Art History, Economics, History, and Political Science.* (Southeast Asia Program, Southeast Asia Series, No. 54.) Athens: Ohio University Center for International Studies, 1978.

Boonsanong Panyodyana. "Chinese-Thai Differential Assimilation in Bangkok: An Exploratory Study," (Southeast Asia Program, Data Paper, No. 79.) Ithaca: Department of Asian Studies, Cornell University, 1971.

Botan. *Chotmai Chak Muang Thai* (Letters from Thailand.) Bangkok: D.K. Book House, 1977.

Brummelhuis, Han ten, and Jeremy H. Kemp (eds.). *Strategies and Structures in Thai Society.* Amsterdam: Universiteit van Amsterdam, Antropologisch-Sociolgisch Centrum, 1984.

Bunnag, Jane. *Buddhist Monk, Buddhist Layman: A Study of Urban, Monastic Organization in Central Thailand.* Cambridge: Cambridge University Press, 1973.

Buri Rangsan. *Patiwat Prachathipatai* (Revolutionary Democracy). Nonthaburi, Thailand: Samnakphim Santhitham, 1985.

Burrows, Rob. "Thailand: Closing Khao-I-Dang," *Refugees* [Geneva], No. 40, April 1987, 9–11.

Chase, Susan. "AID in Thailand," *Front Lines,* 26, No. 11, November 1986, 7–10.

Cheang, Wee Soo. "How Thailand's Deaf Made Themselves Heard," *Nation* [Bangkok], December 16, 1984, 19.

Chetana Nagavajara. *Thang Bisu Watthanatham Haeng Kanwichan* (Towards Literary Criticism). Bangkok: Borisat Samnakphim Duang Komon Chamkat, 1981.

_____. "Thai Literary Historiography: From Self-Assertion Through Self-Criticism Towards Self-Knowledge." (Unpublished paper for the Southeast Asian Summer Institute Conference held at the University of Michigan at Ann Arbor, n.d.)

Chote Suvatti. "Chao Thai Lae Chon Tangpao Nai Mu'ang Thai" (Thai and Its Relatives in Thailand). *Journal of the National Research Council* [Bangkok], 8, No. 2, July–December 1976, 1–100.

Cochrane, Susan H. "The Population of Thailand: Its Growth and Welfare." (World Bank Staff Working Paper, No. 337.) Washington: World Bank, Development Economic Department, Development Policy Staff, June 1979.

Crossette, Barbara. "Thais Pressing Ouster of Laotians," *New York Times,* March 19, 1987, A14.

Darunee Tantiwiramanond, and Shashi Pandey. "The Status and Role of Thai Women in the Pre-Modern Period: A Historical and Cultural Perspective," *Sojourn* [Singapore], 2, No. 1, February 1987, 125–49.

Deyo, Frederic C. "Ethnicity and Work Culture in Thailand: A Comparison of Thai and Thai-Chinese White-Collar Workers," *Journal of Asian Studies,* 34, No. 4, August 1975, 995–1015.

Donner, Wolf. *The Five Faces of Thailand: An Economic Geography.* (The Institute of Asian Affairs, Hamburg), New York: St. Martin's Press, 1978.

Embree, John F. "Thailand—A Loosely Structured Social System," *American Anthropologist,* 52, 1950, 181–93.

Evers, Hans-Dieter, and T.H. Silcock. "Elites and Selection." Pages 84–104 in T.H. Silcock (ed.), *Thailand: Social and Economic Studies in Development.* Durham, North Carolina: Duke University Press, 1967.

Evers, Hans-Dieter (ed.). *Loosely Structured Social Systems: Thailand in Comparative Perspective.* (Southeast Asia Studies. Cultural Report Series, No. 17.) New Haven: Yale University Press, 1969.

Flood, E. Thadeus. "The Vietnamese Refugees in Thailand: Minority Manipulation in Counterinsurgency," *Bulletin of Concerned Asian Scholars,* 9, No. 3, July–September 1971, 31–47.

Foster, Brian L. *Commerce and Ethnic Differences: The Case of the Mon in Thailand.* (Southeast Asia Program, Papers in International Studies Series, No. 59.) Athens, Ohio: Center for International Studies, 1982.

_____. "Friendship in Rural Thailand," *Ethnology.* 15, No. 3. July 1976, 251–67.

_____. *Social Organization of Four Mon and Thai Villages.* New Haven, Connecticut: Human Relations Area Files Press, 1977.

Geddes, William Robert. *Migrants of the Mountains: The Cultural Ecology of the Blue Miao (Hmong Njua) of Thailand.* New York: Oxford University Press, 1976.

Girling, John L.S. *Thailand: Society and Politics.* Ithaca: Cornell University Press, 1981.

Grace, Brewster. *A Note on Thailand: The Student Rebellion and Political Change.* (American Universities Field Staff. Fieldstaff Reports. Southeast Asia Series, 22, No. 4.) Hanover, New Hampshire: AUFS, 1974.

_____. *The Politics of Income Distribution in Thailand.* (American Universities Field Staff. Fieldstaff Reports. Southeast Asia Series, 25, No. 7.) Hanover, New Hampshire: AUFS, 1977.

_____. *Population Growth in Thailand Part I: Population and Social Structure.* (American Universities Field Staff. Fieldstaff Reports. Southeast Asia Series, 22, No. 1.) Hanover, New Hampshire: AUFS, 1974.

_____. *Population Growth in Thailand Part II: Population and Employment.* (American Universities Field Staff. Fieldstaff Reports. Southeast Asia Series, 22, No. 2.) Hanover, New Hampshire: AUFS, 1974.

_____. *Recent Developments in Thai Rice Production.* (American Universities Field Staff. Fieldstaff Reports. Southeast Asia Series, 23, No. 3.) Hanover, New Hampshire: AUFS, 1975.

Griswold, A.B., and Prasert na Nagara. "The Inscription of King Rama Gamhen of Sukodaya (1292 A.D.)" *Journal of the Siam Society* [Bangkok], 59, No. 2, July 1971, 179–228.

Gua, Bo. "Opium, Bombs and Trees: The Future of the H'mong Tribesmen in Northern Thailand," *Journal of Contemporary Asia* [London], 5, No. 1, 1975, 70–81.

Hanks, Lucien M. *Rice and Man: Agricultural Ecology in Southeast Asia.* Chicago: Aldine Atherton, 1972.

Hearn, Robert M. *Thai Government Programs in Refugee Relocation and Resettlement in Northern Thailand.* Auburn, New York: Thailand Books, 1974.

Heine-Geldern, Robert G. *Conceptions of State and Kingship in Southeast Asia.* (Southeast Asia Program, Data Paper, No. 18.) Ithaca: Cornell University, 1956.

Hiebert, Murray. "Laos: Flexible Policies Spark Tenuous Recovery," *Indochina Issues,* No. 37, May 1983, 1–7.

"Hok Sinlapin Thai Nai Amerika" (Six Thai Artists in America). *Sayamrat Sapda Wichan* [Bangkok], 33, No. 4, July 1986, 34–7.

Hussain, Zakir. *The Silent Minority: Indians in Thailand.* Bangkok: Social Research Institute, Chulalongkorn University, 1982.

Ibrahim Syukri. *History of the Malay Kingdom of Patani.* (Southeast Asian Series, No. 68.) Athens: Ohio University, Center for International Studies, 1985.

Ingersoll, Jasper. "The Priest Role in Central Village Thailand." Pages 51–76 in Manning Nash, et al., *Anthropological Studies in Theravada Buddhism.* New Haven: Southeast Asia Studies, Yale University, 1966.

Ishii, Yoneo. *Sangha, State, and Society: Thai Buddhism in History.* Monographs of the Center for Southeast Asian Studies, Kyoto University. Honolulu: University of Hawaii Press, 1986.

Karuna Kusalasaya. *Buddhism in Thailand: Its Past and Its Present.* The Wheel Publication No. 85–86. Kandy, Ceylon: Buddhist Publication Society, 1965.

Keye, Peter. "Tide is Turning Against Pirates," *San Diego Union,* June 15, 1987, A1.

Keyes, Charles F. *Thailand: Buddhist Kingdom as Modern Nation-State.* Boulder, Colorado: Westview Press, 1987.

_____. "Local Leadership in Rural Thailand." Pages 219–50 in Fred R. von der Mehden and David A. Wilson (eds.), *Local Authority and Administration in Thailand.* Los Angeles: University of California Academic Advisory Council for Thailand, 1970.

_____. "Political Crisis and Militant Buddhism in Contemporary Thailand." Pages 147–64 in Bardwell L. Smith (ed.), *Religion and Legitimation of Power in Thailand, Laos, and Burma.* Chambersburg, Pennsylvania: Anima Books, 1978.

Keyes, Charles F. (ed.). *Ethnic Adaptation and Identity: The Karen on the Thai Frontier with Burma.* Philadelphia: Institute for the Study of Human Issues, 1979.

Khrongkan Phak Prachachon Haeng Chat (A Plan for the People's Party). Bangkok: Rongphim Ruan Kaeo Kanphim, 1986.

Kunstadter, Peter (ed.). *Southeast Asian Tribes, Minorities, and Nations.* (2 Vols.) Princeton: Princeton University Press, 1967.

"Laos Rides a New Line." *Asiaweek* [Hong Kong], 13, No. 14, April 15, 1987, 28–45.

Le Xuan Khoa. "Shift to Immigration," *Bridge,* 3, No. 4, December, 1986, 1, 20.

Lebar, Frank M., Gerald C. Hickey, and John K. Musgrave. *Ethnic Groups of Mainland Southeast Asia.* New Haven, Connecticut: Human Relations Area Files Press, 1964.

Lewis, Paul, and Elaine Lewis. *Peoples of the Golden Triangle: Six Tribes in Thailand.* London: Thames and Hudson, 1984.

Lissak, Moshe. *Military Roles in Modernization: Civil-Military Relations in Thailand and Burma.* Beverly Hills, California: Sage Publications, 1976.

Luong Thu Thuy, and Walter E.J. Tips. "Women and Development in Ho Chi Minh City, Vietnam: A Comparison with Thailand, Malaysia, and the Philippines." (Working Paper, No. 118.) East Lansing: Michigan State University, 1986.

Luther, Hans U. "Peasants and State in Contemporary Thailand," *International Journal of Politics* [Hamburg], 8, No. 4, Winter 1978–79, 1.

Lutpi Ibrahim (ed.). *Islamika: Esei-esei Sempena Abad Ke-15 Hijrah* (Islam: Blessed Essays for the Fifteenth Century After the Hijah). Kuala Lumpur, Malaysia: Sarjana Enterprise, 1981.

Malalasekera, G.P. "Theravada Buddhism." Pages 161–94 in Ismail R. al Faruqi (ed.), *Historical Atlas of the Religions of the World.* New York: Macmillan, 1974.

Martin, Linda G. (ed.). *The ASEAN Success Story: Social, Economic, and Political Dimensions.* (Based on proceedings of the East-West Center Conference on ASEAN and the Pacific Basin, 1985.) Honolulu: University of Hawaii Press, 1987.

Mattani Mojdara Rutin. "The Development of Theatre Studies at the University Level," *Journal of the National Research Council* [Bangkok], 14, No. 2, July–December 1982, 1–19.

McKinnon, John, and Wanat Bhruksasri (eds.). *Highlanders of Thailand.* Kuala Lumpur, Malaysia: Oxford University Press, 1983.

Mizuno, Koishi. *Social System of Don Daeng Village: A Community Study in Northeast Thailand.* (Discussion Papers 12–22.) Kyoto: Kyoto University, Center for Southeast Asian Studies, 1971.

Moerman, Michael. *Agricultural Change and Peasant Choice in a Thai Village.* Berkeley and Los Angeles: University of California Press, 1968.

_____. "Ban Ping's Temple: The Center of a 'Loosely-Structured' Society." Pages 137-74 in Manning Nash, et al., *Anthropological Studies in Theravada Buddhism* (Southeast Asia Studies, Cultural Report Series, No. 13.) New Haven: Yale University Press, 1966.

_____. "Ethnic Identification in a Complex Civilization: Who are the Lue?" *American Anthropologist,* 67, No. 5, October 1965, 1215-30.

_____. "Kinship and Commerce in a Thai-Lue Village," *Ethnology,* 5, No. 4, October 1966, 360-64.

_____. "A Thai Village Headman as a Synaptic Leader," *Journal of Asian Studies,* 28, No. 3, May 1969, 535-49.

Mole, Robert L. *Thai Values and Behavior Patterns.* Rutland, Vermont: C.E. Tuttle, 1973.

Mudannayake, Ivan (ed.). *Thailand Year Book 1975-76.* Bangkok: Temple Publicity Services, 1975.

Murray, Charles A. *A Behavioral Study of Rural Modernization: Social and Economic Change in Thai Villages.* New York: Praeger, 1977.

Muscat, Robert J. *Development Strategy in Thailand. A Study of Economic Growth.* New York: Praeger, 1966.

National Minorities Questions Editorial Panel. *Questions and Answers About China's Minority Nationalities.* Beijing: New World Press, 1985.

"Panha Dek Lae Yaowachon Phlae Ruarang Khong Sangkhom" (Social Problems of Children and Youth in Bangkok). *Sayamrat Sapda Wichan* [Bangkok], 33, No. 22, November 16-22, 1986, 23-27.

Pasuk Phongpaichit. *From Peasant Girls to Bangkok Masseuses.* (Women, Work, and Development Series, No. 2.) Geneva: International Labour Office, 1982.

Phillips, Herbert P. *Modern Thai Literature: With an Ethnographic Interpretation.* Honolulu: University of Hawaii, 1987.

_____. *Thai Peasant Personality: The Patterning of Interpersonal Behavior in the Village of Bang Chan.* Berkeley and Los Angeles: University of California Press, 1966.

Piker, Steven. "Sources of Stability and Instability in Rural Thai Society," *Journal of Asian Studies,* 27, No. 4, August 1968, 777-90.

Poole, Peter A. "The Vietnamese in Thailand: Their Continuing Role in Thai-Vietnamese Relationships," *South-East Asian Spectrum,* 4, No. 2, January-March 1976, 40-43.

Potter, Jack M. *Thai Peasant Social Structure.* Chicago: University of Chicago Press, 1976.

Potter, Sulamith Heins. *Family Life in a Northern Thai Village.* Berkeley and Los Angeles: University of California Press, 1977.

Proschan, Frank. "Tradition and Survival: Khmu Highlanders in America." Pages 87–90 in Thomas Vennam, Jr., *1986 Festival of American Folklife.* Washington: Smithsonian Institution Press, 1986.

Pryor, R.J. *Migration and Development in South-East Asia.* New York: Oxford University Press, 1979.

Puey Ungphakorn. *Sinlatham Lae Sasana Nai Kanphatthana Chat* (Role of Ethnics and Religion in National Development). Chiang Mai, Thailand: Sapha Kritsatchak nai Prathet Thai, 1969.

"Rangoon Attacks," *Asiaweek* [Hong Kong], 13, No. 2, January 11, 1987, 18.

"Refugee Problem in Thailand," *Thailand Foreign Affairs Newsletter* [Bangkok], No. 3, March 1986, 11–14.

"The Rites of Homage to the Teachers," *Thai Life* [Bangkok], 1, No. 2, June 1982, 4–5.

Ryan, N.J. *The Making of Modern Malaysia and Singapore: a History From Earliest Times to 1966.* (4th ed.), Kuala Lumpur: Oxford University Press, 1969.

Sangharakshita, Bhikshu. *The Three Jewels: An Introduction to Buddhism.* London: Rider, 1967.

Shaplen, Robert. "Letter from Bangkok," *New Yorker,* July 24, 1978, 43–57.

Sharp, Lauriston, et al. *Siamese Rice Village: A Preliminary Study of Bang Chan, 1948–1949.* Bangkok: Cornell Research Center, 1953.

Skinner, George William. *Chinese Society in Thailand: An Analytical History.* Ithaca: Cornell University Press, 1957.

_____. *Leadership and Power in the Chinese Community of Thailand.* Ithaca: Cornell University Press, 1958.

Skinner, George William, and A. Thomas Kirsch (eds.). *Change and Persistence in Thai Society: Essays in Honor of Lauriston Sharp.* Ithaca: Cornell University Press, 1975.

"Slaking a Thirst for Success," *Asiaweek* [Hong Kong], 11, No. 16, April 19, 1985, 52–53.

Smith, Bardwell L. (ed.). *Religion and Legitimation of Power in Thailand, Laos, and Burma.* (South and Southeast Asia Studies.) Chambersburg, Pennsylvania: Anima Books, 1978.

Smith, Harold E. *Historical and Cultural Dictionary of Thailand.* (Historical and Cultural Dictionaries of Asia, No. 6.) Metuchen, New Jersey: Scarecrow Press, 1976.

Somboon Suksamran. *Political Buddhism in Southeast Asia: The Role of the Sangha in the Modernization of Thailand.* New York: St. Martin's Press, 1976.

Somkiat Onvimol. Unpublished speech on current Thai foreign policy at The Fletcher School for Law and Diplomacy, Tufts University. Conference on Thailand, Fall 1982.

325

"Somkiat Tops TV News Survey Poll," *Nation* [Bangkok], November 30, 1986, 2.

"Southeast Asian Refugee Arrivals in the U.S. and Third Countries: (April 1975 through September 1986)," *Bridge,* 3, No. 4, December 1986, 10.

Sriprinya Ramakomud. "Theravada Buddhist Value and Economic Development." Unpublished paper given at Northern Illinois University in November 1982 for a conference "Two Hundred Years of the Chakkri Dynasty," 1-7.

Sternstein, Larry. *Thailand: The Environment of Modernization.* Sydney: McGraw-Hill, 1976.

Stifel, Lawrence. "Technocrats and Modernization in Thailand," *Asian Survey,* 16, No. 12, December 1976, 1184-96.

Subhadradis Diskul, M.C. *Art in Thailand: A Brief History.* Bangkok: Amarin Press, 1981.

Suhrke, Astri. "Loyalists and Separatists: The Muslims in Southern Thailand," *Asian Survey,* 57, No. 3, March 1977, 237-50.

Surin Pitsuwan. *Islam and Malay Nationalism.* Bangkok: Thai Khadi Research Institute, Thammasat University, 1985.

Suryadinata, Leo. *China and the ASEAN States: The Ethnic Chinese Dimension.* Singapore: Singapore University Press, 1985.

Sutthiphon Chiraphan. *Landlessness in Central Thailand.* Bangkok: Division of Research and Planning, Agricultural Land Reform Office, Ministry of Agriculture and Cooperatives, 1981.

Svantesson, Jan-Olaf. *Khmu Phonology & Morphology.* Malmo, Sweden: CWK Gleerup, 1983.

Swanson, Herbert R. *Khrischak Muang Nua: A Study in Northern Thai Church History.* Bangkok: Chuan Printing Press, 1984.

Tambiah, S.J. "The Persistence and Transformation of Tradition in Southeast Asia, with Special Reference to Thailand," *Daedalus,* 102, No. 1, Winter 1979, 55-84.

_____. *Buddhism and the Spirit Cults in Northeast Thailand.* Cambridge: Cambridge University Press, 1970.

Tapp, N. "Buddhism and Ethnic Minorities: Wat Tam Krabok," *Seeds of Peace* [Bangkok], 1, No. 2, October 1985, 19-23.

Textor, Robert B. "Cultural Future for Thailand: An Ethnographic Inquiry", *Futures,* 10, October 1978, 347-60.

Thailand. Bank of. *Thailand: Economic Conditions in 1986 and Outlook for 1987: Special Supplement.* Bangkok: 1987.

_____. Embassy in Washington. Press release on the closing down of the Khao-I-Dang Holding Center, December 31, 1986.

_____. Ministry of Education. *Educational Development in Thailand (1979-1980): Report to the 38th Session of the International Conference on Education, Geneva, November 1981.* Bangkok: 1981.

Bibliography

_____. Ministry of Interior. Department of Public Welfare. *Raingan Pracham Pi 1983* (Annual Report 1983). Bangkok: 1984.

_____. Office of the Prime Minister. Government Public Relations Department. Foreign News Division. *Facets of Thai Cultural Life.* Bangkok: 1984.

_____. Office of the Prime Minister. National Statistical Office. *Statistical Handbook of Thailand 1985.* Bangkok: n.d.

_____. Office of the Prime Minister. National Statistical Office. Statistical Reports Division. *Warasan Sathiti Raidaimat* (Quarterly Bulletin of Statistics) [Bangkok], 32, No. 3, September 1984.

_____. Office of the Prime Minister. National Identity Office. *Thailand in the 80s.* Bangkok, 1984.

_____. Office of the Prime Minister. Office of the National Economic and Social Development Board. *Development Plan For Women for the Period of Five Years, 1982–1986.* Bangkok: 1981.

_____. Office of the Prime Minister. *Thailand 1982: Plans, Problems, and Prospects.* Bangkok: 1982.

Thailand's Policy Toward the Vietnam-Kampuchea Conflict. Bangkok: Chulalongkorn University, Institute of Asian Studies, 1985.

Turton, Andrew. "National Minority Peoples in Indochina," *Journal of Contemporary Asia* [London], 4, No. 3, 1974, 332–46.

_____. "Northern Thai Peasant Society: Twentieth Century Transformation in Political and Social Structures," *Journal of Peasant Studies,* 3, No. 3, April 1976, 267–98.

United Nations. Department of International Economic and Social Affairs and Fund for Population Activities. *Population Policy Compendium. Thailand.* n. pl: January 1979.

United Nations. Economic and Social Commission for Asia and the Pacific. *The Population of Thailand.* (Country Monograph Series, No. 3.) Bangkok: 1976.

_____. Economic and Social Commission for Asia and the Pacific. "Thailand." Pages 572–92 in *Statistical Yearbook for Asia and the Pacific, 1983,* Bangkok, 1984.

United States. Congress. 96th, lst Session. Senate. Committee on the Judiciary. *Refugee Crisis in Southeast Asia. Results of the Geneva Conference.* Washington: GPO, July 26, 1979.

_____. Department of Commerce. Bureau of the Census. *Country Demographic Profiles: Thailand.* (ISP DP 15.) Washington: GPO, April 1978.

_____. Department of State. "Refugees," *Department of State Bulletin: The Official Monthly Record of United States Foreign Policy,* 79, No. 2031, October 1979, 1–8.

Vajiranana Varoros. *Autobiography: the Life of Prince-Patriarch Vajiranana of Siam, 1860–1921.* Athens: Ohio University Press, 1979.

327

Valaiporn Bhavabhutanonda. "Botbat Khong Phrasong Thai Thi Ben Mo Phra Nai Dan Kanbambat Raksa Rok Kae Chumnum-chon" (The Medical Role of the 'Doctor Bhikku' in Bangkok and Rural Communities), *Journal of the National Research Council* [Bangkok], 12, No. 2, July–December 1980, 11–60.

Wain, Barry. *The Refused: The Agony of the Indochina Refugees.* New York: Simon and Schuster, 1981.

Wenk, Klaus. *Restoration of Thailand Under Rama I, 1782–1809.* (Association for Asian Studies Monographs and Papers, No. 24.) Tucson: University of Arizona Press, 1968.

Wibha Senanan. *The Genesis of the Novel in Thailand.* Bangkok: Thai Watana Panich, 1975.

World Bank. *World Development Report, 1979.* Washington: 1979.

Wyatt, David K. *The Politics of Reform in Thailand: Education in the Reign of King Chulalongkorn.* (Southeast Asia Studies, Cultural Report Series, No. 4.) New Haven: Yale University Press, 1969.

―――. *Thailand: A Short History.* New Haven: Yale University Press, 1984.

Chapter 3

"The Baht Devaluation: The Final Panacea to Thailand's Economic Ills?" *Business Review* [Bangkok], No. 13, November 1984, 32–34.

Baldwin, W. Lee, and W. David Maxwell (eds.). *The Role of Foreign Financial Assistance to Thailand in the 1980s.* Lexington, Massachusetts: Lexington Books, D.C. Heath, 1975.

Berkoff, D.J.W. "Land and Development in South Thailand," *South-East Asian Spectrum* [Bangkok], 4, No. 2, January–March 1976, 44–55.

Blanchard, Wendell, et al. *Thailand: Its People, Its Society, Its Culture,* New Haven, Connecticut: Human Relations Area Files Press, 1957.

Brannon, Russell H. *The Agricultural Sector in Thailand: A Brief Assessment* (Staff Paper, No. 66.) Lexington: Department of Agricultural Economics, University of Kentucky College of Agriculture, April 1978.

Caldwell, J. Alexander. *American Economic Aid to Thailand.* Lexington, Massachusetts: Lexington Books, D.C. Heath, 1974.

Chamlong Attanatho, and Suthiporn Chirapanda. "Current Land Reform in Thailand, 1977." Pages 183–92 in Vichitvong Na Pombhejara (ed.), *Readings in Thailand's Political Economy.* Bangkok: Bangkok Printing Enterprise, May 1978.

Connell, John. "Thailand's Southern Land Settlement Schemes,"
Asian Profile [Hong Kong], 6, No. 6, December 1978, 577–55.
Cooper, Robert. *Resource Scarcity and the Hmong Response: Patterns
of Settlement and Economy in Transition.* Singapore: Singapore
University Press, National University of Singapore, 1984.
"A Critique of the New Government's Economic Policy," *Bangkok
Bank Monthly Review,* No. 24, June 1983, 253–62.
Cumming-Bruce, Nicholas. "Austerity Comes to Thailand," *Euro-
money,* May 1985, 211.
Donner, Wolf. *The Five Faces of Thailand: An Economic Geography.*
(The Institute of Asian Affairs, Hamburg.) New York: St.
Martin's Press, 1978.
Dowling, J.M. "The Supply Response of Rubber in Thailand,"
Southern Economic Journal, 45, January 1979, 795–805.
"The Export Economy: 20 Years of Growth and Diversification;
Where Do We Go From Here?" *Bangkok Bank Monthly Review,*
No. 25, February 1984, 47–55.
Fredericks, L.J., and R.J.G. Wells. "Some Aspects of Tenancy
Reform Measures in Southeast Asia," *Asian Survey,* 18, No. 6,
June 1978, 644–58.
"Government Budget 1984," *Bangkok Bank Monthly Review,* No. 24,
October 1983, 407–09.
Grace, Brewster. *The Politics of Income Distribution in Thailand.*
(American Universities Field Staff. Fieldstaff Reports. Southeast
Asia Series, 25, No. 7.) Hanover, New Hampshire: AUFS, 1977.
_____. *Population Growth in Thailand. Part II: Population and Employ-
ment* (American Universities Field Staff. Fieldstaff Reports.
Southeast Asia Series, 22, No. 2.) Hanover, New Hampshire:
AUFS, 1974.
"Grass Roots Aids for Thai Farmers," *Business Review* [Bangkok],
No. 11, June 1983, 43–45.
"Growth of Industrial Sector in 1983 and Prospect for 1984," *Busi-
ness Review* [Bangkok], No. 12, June 1984, 21–22.
Hanson, James A., and Craig R. Neal. *Interest Rate Policies in Selected
Developing Countries, 1970–82.* Washington: World Bank, 1984.
Ho, Robert, and E.C. Chapman (eds.). *Studies of Contemporary
Thailand.* Canberra: Australian National University, Research
School of Pacific Studies, 1973.
Holtsberg, Christer Per. "Effects of a New Feeder Road on Unem-
ployment and Income Distribution: A Case Study in Thailand,"
International Labour Review [Geneva], 118, No. 2, March–April
1979, 237–49.
Ingram, James C. *Economic Change in Thailand, 1850–1970.* Stan-
ford: Stanford University Press, 1971.

Ishii, Yoneo (ed.). *Thailand: A Rice-Growing Society.* (Monographs of the Center for Southeast Asian Studies, Kyoto University.) Honolulu: University of Hawaii Press, 1978.

"Japan's Overseas Investments (2): Thailand," *Oriental Economist* [Tokyo], 47, No. 819, January 1979, 49–59.

Kunstadter, Peter, E.C. Chapman, and Sanga Sabhasri (eds.). *Farmers in the Forest: Economic Development and Marginal Agriculture in Northern Thailand,* Honolulu: East-West Center, 1978.

"Labour and Unemployment: Objectives of the Sixth Five-Year Plan," *Bangkok Bank Monthly Review,* No. 24, November 1983, 441–45.

Laramee, Peter A. "Problems of Small Farmers Under Contract Marketing, with Special Reference to a Case in Chiengmai Province, Thailand," *Economic Bulletin for Asia and the Pacific,* 26, Nos. 2–3, September–December 1975, 43–57.

Lin, Sein, and Bruce Esposito. "Agrarian Reform in Thailand," *Pacific Affairs* [Vancouver], 49, No. 3, Fall 1976, 425–42.

Luther, Hans U. "Peasants and State in Comtemporary Thailand," *International Journal of Politics* [Hamburg], 8, No. 4, Winter 1978–79, 1–120.

Mabry, Bevars D. "The Thai Labor Movement," *Asian Survey,* 17, No. 10, October 1977, 931–51.

Meesook, Oey Astra. "Income, Consumption, and Poverty in Thailand, 1962–63 to 1975–76." (World Bank Staff Working Paper, No. 364.) Washington: World Bank, 1979.

Mudannayake, Ivan (ed.). *Thailand Year Book, 1975–76.* Bangkok: Temple Publicity Services, 1975.

Murray, Charles A. *A Behavioral Study of Rural Modernization: Social and Economic Change in Thai Villages.* New York: Praeger, 1977.

"New Forces in Thailand," *Asian Finance,* No. 11, April 1985, 117–23.

Ng, R.C.Y. "Development and Change in Rural Thailand," *Asian Affairs* [London], 10 (new series.) February 1979, 62–68.

Nicol, Kenneth J., Somnuk Sriplung, and Earl O. Heady (eds.). *Agricultural Development Planning in Thailand.* Ames: Iowa State University Press, 1982.

Nikom Chandravithun. "Labour Relations: Thailand's Experience." Pages 281–85 in Vichitvong Na Pombhejara (ed.), *Readings in Thailand's Political Economy.* Bangkok: Bangkok Printing Enterprise, 1978.

Prizzia, Ross. "The Labor Movement in Thailand: A Brief Overview," *Asia Quarterly* [Brussels], No. 2, 1978, 93–108.

Race, Jeffrey. "The Future of Thailand," *Pacific Community* [Tokyo], 8, No. 2, January 1977, 303–26.

Randolph, R. Sean. "The Limits of Influence: American Aid to Thailand 1965–1970," *Asian Affairs: An American Review,* 6, No. 4, March–April 1979, 243–266.

Ravenholt, Albert. *Milling Rice Makes the Difference.* (American Universities Field Staff. Fieldstaff Reports. Southeast Asia Series, 24, No. 1.) Hanover, New Hampshire: AUFS, 1976.

"Repercussions of the Oil Price Decrease," *Bangkok Bank Monthly Review,* 24, April 1983, 159–74.

Robinson, Warren C. "Economic Policy and Population Change in Thailand," *World Development* [Oxford], 6, Nos. 11–12, 1978, 1261–69. "The Role of the Bank of Thailand in Providing Financial Assistance to Priority Economic Sectors," *Bank of Thailand Quarterly Bulletin,* No. 23, June 1983, 27–39.

Rubin, Herbert J. *The Dynamics of Development in Rural Thailand.* (Special Report No. 8.) De Kalb: Center for Southeast Asian Studies, Northern Illinois University, 1974.

Sabatini, Omero. *The Agricultural Economy of Thailand.* Washington: United States Department of Agriculture, Economic Research Service, January 1972.

Saeng Sanguanroang. *Development Planning in Thailand: The Role of the University.* Singapore: Regional Institute of Higher Education and Development, September 1973.

Silcock, T.H. *The Economic Development of Thai Agriculture.* Canberra: Australian National University Press, 1970.

Srisilpavongse, Kanitha. "Privatisation: Dream or Reality?" *Bangkok Bank Monthly Review,* No. 26, April 1985, 79–182.

Sternstein, Larry. *Thailand: The Environment of Modernization.* Sydney: McGraw-Hill, 1976.

Sura Sanittanont. "The Role of Japanese Investment in Thailand." Pages 254–67 in Vichitvong Na Pombhejara (ed.), *Readings in Thailand's Political Economy.* Bangkok: Bangkok Printing Enterprise, 1978.

"The Thai Economy in 1983," *Bangkok Bank Monthly Review,* No. 25, March 1984, 87–102.

"Thai-Japanese Relations," *Business Review* [Bangkok], No. 12, June 1984, 83–100.

"The Thai-Korean Nexus," *Business Review* [Bangkok], No. 11, August 1983, 73–75.

Thailand. Bank of. *Annual Economic Report, 1986.* Bangkok: 1986.

_____. Bank of. Department of Economic Research. *Thailand: Economic Conditions in 1987 and Outlook for 1988.* Bangkok: 1987.

_____. Bank of. *Quarterly Bulletin.* Bankgok: June 1983.

_____. National Economic and Social Development Board. *External Assistance Requirements for the Fourth National Economic and Social Development Plan (1977–1981).* Bangkok: March 1977.

Thailand. Office of the Prime Minister. National Economic and Social Development Board. *Summary of the Fourth Five-Year Plan, 1977-1981,* Bangkok: n.d.

──────. *The Third National Economic and Social Development Plan (1972-1976).* Bangkok: 1973.

"Thailand: The Middle Way," *Euromoney,* October 1983, 345.

"Thailand: Trade Unions Are Facing Formidable Problems," *Financial Times* [London], December 18, 1979, 32.

Turton, Andrew. "The Current Situation in the Thai Countryside," *Journal of Contemporary Asia* [London], 8, No. 1, 1978, 104-41.

Unakul, Snoh. "Thailand's 'Growth Plus Four' Analogy," *United Malaysian Banking Corporation Economic Review* [Kuala Lumpur, Malaysia], 2, No. 19, 1983, 12-16.

United States. Department of Labor. Bureau of International Labor Affairs. *Country Labor Profile: Thailand.* Washington: GPO, 1979.

──────. Department of State. *Foreign Economic Trends and Their Implications for the United States: Thailand.* (International Marketing Information, No. 79-037.) Washington: GPO, March 1979.

Vichitvong Na Pombhejara (ed.). *Readings in Thailand's Political Economy.* Bangkok: Bangkok Printing Enterprise, May 1978.

Vijetbhakdi, Norani. "Eastern Seaboard Development Plan," *Bangkok Bank Monthly Review,* No. 25, April 1984, 140-87.

Wang, K.P. *Far East and South Asia* (Mineral Perspectives, MP-1.) Washington: United States. Department of the Interior, Bureau of Mines, 1977.

Wibulswasdi, Chaiyawat. "Strategies and Measures to Maintain Thailand's Economic Stability in the 1980s," *Bank of Thailand Quarterly Bulletin,* No. 23, March 1983, 27-47.

Williams, Llewelyn. *Thailand, Current and Potential Crops: An Evaluation of Germplasm Requirements.* Washington: United States Department of State, Agency for International Development, January 1974.

Wong, John. *ASEAN Economies in Perspective: A Comparative Study of Indonesia, Malaysia, the Philippines, Singapore, and Thailand.* Philadelphia: Institute for the Study of Human Issues, 1979.

World Bank. *Bangchak Oil Refinery Restructuring Project.* Washington: April 22, 1985.

──────. *Coal Development Potential and Prospects in the Developing Countries.* Washington: October 1979.

──────. *Thailand: Coping with Structural Change in a Dynamic Economy.* Washington: December 23, 1980.

──────. *Thailand: Growth with Stability—A Challenge for the Sixth Plan Period—A Country Economic Report.* Washington: June 5, 1986.

_____. *Thailand: Land Reform Areas Project.* Washington: August 23, 1982.

_____. *Thailand: Perspectives for Financial Reform.* Washington: July 31, 1983.

_____. *Thailand: Rural Growth and Employment.* (A World Bank Country Study.) Washington: 1983.

_____. *Thailand: Second Accelerated Rural Electrification Project.* Washington: May 23, 1980.

_____. *Thailand: Second Agricultural Credit Project.* (Staff Appraisal Report.) Washington: May 10, 1983.

_____. *The World Bank Atlas, 1985.* Washington: 1985.

_____. *World Development Report 1986.* Washington: 1986.

(Various issues of the following periodicals were also used in the preparation of this chapter: *Asia Research Bulletin* [Singapore]; *Bangkok Post* [Bangkok]; Bank of Thailand, *Monthly Bulletin* [Bangkok], Joint Publications Research Service (JPRS) *Southeast Asia Report; Quarterly Bulletin* [Bangkok], and *Statistical Bulletin* [Bangkok]; *Far Eastern Economic Review* [Hong Kong]; *Standard Chartered Review* [London].)

Chapter 4

Alpern, Stephen I. "Insurgency in Northeast Thailand: A New Cause for Alarm," *Asian Survey,* 15, No. 8, August 1975, 684–92.

Ampa, Santimatanedol. "Brainwave Idea for Way out of Politics Impasse?" *Bangkok Post,* May 8, 1987, 4.

"Army Chief under Sharper Scrutiny," *Bangkok Post,* April 11, 1987, 4.

"Arthit Obeys His Orders," *Asiaweek* [Hong Kong], 12, No. 14, April 6, 1986, 18–19.

Bowring, Philip. "Shifts in Foreign Policy," *Financial Times* [London], December 18, 1979, 30.

Burgess, John. "Despite Democratic Facade, Thai Military Retains Power," *Washington Post,* February 20, 1980, A22.

Buszynski, Leszek. "Thailand and the Manila Pact," *World Today* [London], 36, No. 2, February 1980, 45–51.

Caldwell, Malcolm. "Thailand: Towards the Revolution," *Race and Class,* 18, Autumn 1976, 129–53.

Chadin, Tephaval. "Parliament is Stuttering Along," *Bangkok Post,* January 1, 1987, 27.

Chai-anan, Samudavanija. *The Military in Thai Politics: The Young Turks and the Democrat Soldiers.* Bangkok: Krungthep Bannakij, 1983.

Thailand: A Country Study

------. *The Thai Young Turks.* Singapore: Institute of Southeast Asian Studies, 1982.

Chakrit, Noranitipadungkarn. *Elites, Power Structure, and Politics in Thai Communities.* Bangkok: National Institute of Development Administration, 1970.

"Chavalit: Prem Still the Peoples' Choice: Premier 'as strong as ever'," *Bangkok Post,* May 21, 1987, 1.

China in Thai Perspective: Research Report. (Asian Studies Monographs, No. 27.) Bangkok: Institute of Asian Studies, Chulalongkorn University, April 1980.

"Civil Servants Viewed with Fearful Respect," *Far Eastern Economic Review* [Hong Kong], 132, No. 25, June 19, 1986, 44–48.

"Coalition Mum on Chavalit's Charge," *Bangkok Post,* February 16, 1987, 1.

Darling, Frank C., "Political Functions of the United States Embassy in Thailand," *Asian Survey,* 18, No. 11, November 1978, 1191–1207.

------. "Thailand in 1976: Another Defeat for Constitutional Democracy," *Asian Survey,* 16. No. 2, February 1977, 116–32.

------. "Thailand in 1977: The Search for Stability and Progress," *Asian Survey,* 18, No. 2, February 1978, 153–63.

------. "Thailand: Return to Military Rule," *Current History,* 71, December 1976, 197–200.

Davies, Derek. "A right royal example: King Bhumibol Acts As a Catalyst for Progress," *Far Eastern Economic Review* [Hong Kong], 131, No. 4, January 23, 1986, 22–25.

"Despite Strain, Thai-US Ties Still Strong," *Bangkok Post,* November 7, 1986, 7.

"Dr. Khien Offers a Thai Perspective on Indochina," *Bangkok Post,* November 13, 1986, 2.

Evans, Grant. "Thai-Lao Relations: Three Villages Not Trade Is the Key," *Nation* [Bangkok], February 22, 1987, 11.

"The Firing of Arthit," *Asiaweek* [Hong Kong], 12, No. 23, June 8, 1986, 17–18.

Forbes, Andrew D.W. "Thailand's Muslim Minorities: Assimilation, Secession, or Coexistence?" *Asian Survey,* 22, No. 11, November 1982, 1056–73.

Ghosh, Suchita. "Role of the Military in Thailand," *Institute for Defence Studies and Analysis Journal* [New Delhi], 10, No. 2, October–December 1977, 140–56.

Girling, John L.S. "Is Small-holder Cultivation Viable? A Question of Political Economy with Reference to Thailand," *Pacific Affairs* [Vancouver], 59, No. 2, Summer 1986.

------. *Thailand: Society and Politics.* Ithaca: Cornell University Press, 1981.

334

Grace, Brewster. *A Note on Thailand: The Student Rebellion and Political Change.* (American Universities Field Staff, Fieldstaff Reports. Southeast Asia Series, 22, No. 4.) Hanover, New Hampshire: AUFS, 1974.

Gurevich, Robert. "Teachers, Rural Development, and the Civil Service in Thailand," *Asian Survey*, 15, No. 10, October 1975, 870–81.

Haas, David F. *Interaction in the Thai Bureaucracy: Structure, Culture, and Social Exchange.* Boulder, Colorado: Westview Press, 1979.

Hong, Lysa. *Thailand in 1984: Towards a Political Modus Vivendi.* Page 319 in Lim Joo-Jack (ed.), *Southeast Asian Affairs, 1985*, Singapore: Institute of Southeast Asian Studies, 1985.

Jackson, Kare D., and M. Hadi Soesastro (eds.). *ASEAN Security and Economic Development.* (Research Papers and Policy Studies.) Berkeley: Institute of East Asian Studies, University of California, 1984.

Jha, Ganganath. *Foreign Policy of Thailand.* New Delhi: Radiant Publishers, 1979.

Juree Vichit-Vadakan. "Thailand in 1984: Year of Administering Rumors," *Asian Survey*, 25, No. 2, February 1985, 232–40.

——. "Thailand in 1985: Year of Facing up to Facts," *Asian Survey*, 26, No. 2, February 1986, 174–85.

Kasem, Udyanin, and Rufus D. Smith. *The Public Service in Thailand: Organization, Recruitment, and Training.* Brussels: International Institute of Administrative Sciences, 1954.

Kershaw, Roger. "Thailand's Return to Limited Democracy," *Asian Affairs* [London], 10, Part 3, October 1979, 304–13.

Keyes, Charles F. *Thailand: Buddhist Kingdom as Modern Nation-State.* Boulder, Colorado: Westview Press, 1987.

Khien, Theeravit. "Thai-Kampuchean Relations: Problems and Prospects," *Asian Survey*, 22, No. 6, June 1982, 561–76.

Konthi, Suphamongkon. "Thailand's Democracy: The Sticky Experiment," *Bangkok Post*, July 7, 1987, 4.

Kramol, Tongdhamachart. *Toward a Political Party: Theory in Thai Perspective.* (Occasional Paper, No. 68.) Singapore: Institute of Southeast Asian Studies, 1982.

Krannich, Ronald L. *Mayors and Managers in Thailand: The Struggle for Political Life in Administrative Settings.* (Southeast Asia Series, No. 51.) Athens: Ohio University Center for International Studies, 1978.

——. "The Politics of Intergovernmental Relations in Thailand," *Asian Survey*, 19, No. 5, May 1979, 506–22.

"Kukrit: Plan for 'Revolution' Won't Succeed," *Bangkok Post*, April 2, 1987, 1.

"Kukrit Says Professional Premier Is Needed," *Bangkok Post,* December 11, 1986, 3.

Lent, John A. "The Burnt-Out Candle: Thailand's Brief Press Freedom," *Index on Censorship* [London], 6, No. 4, July–August 1977, 45–50.

Likhit Dhiravegin. *The Bureaucratic Elite of Thailand: A Study of Their Sociological Attributes, Educational Backgrounds, and Career Advancement Pattern.* Bangkok: Thai Khadi Research Institute, Thammasat University, 1978.

_____. *Political Attitudes of the Bureaucratic Elite and Modernization in Thailand.* Bangkok: Thai Watana Panich, 1973.

_____. "Three Cardinal Principles for Thai-Japan Relations," *Bangkok Post,* December 17, 1986, 4.

"Looking to Prem," *Asiaweek* [Hong Kong], 12, No. 32, August 10, 1986, 44–45.

Luther, Hans U. "Peasants and State in Contemporary Thailand," *International Journal of Politics* [Hamburg], 8, No. 4, Winter 1978–79, 2–119.

Mabry, Bevars D. "The Thai Labor Movement," *Asian Survey,* 17, No. 10, October 1977, 931–51.

McBeth, John. "Arms for Peace: The US and Thailand Near an Accord on a Munitions Stockpile," *Far Eastern Economic Review* [Hong Kong], 131, No. 12, March, 20, 1986, 50–51.

_____. "New Political Waters: Thai Voters Elect a Bizarre Mix of Powerful Men to Parliament," *Far Eastern Economic Review* [Hong Kong], 133, No. 35, August 28, 1986, 14–15.

_____. "Political Crossroads," *Far Eastern Economic Review* [Hong Kong], 132, No. 25, June 19, 1986, 40–44.

_____. "Pre-emptive Strike: Prem Fires Arthit to Stop Army Meddling in Election," *Far Eastern Economic Review* [Hong Kong], 132, No. 23, June 5, 1986, 13–15.

_____. "Prem-ature Election," *Far Eastern Economic Review* [Hong Kong], 132, No. 20, May 15, 1986, 12–13.

McBeth, John and Paisal Sricharatchanya. "Awaiting a Call-up," *Far Eastern Economic Review* [Hong Kong], 133, No. 32, August 7, 1986, 10–11.

_____. "Prem's Portfolio Power," *Far Eastern Economic Review* [Hong Kong], 133, No. 34, August 21, 1986, 12–13.

Morell, David, and Chai-anan Samudavanija. *Political Conflict in Thailand: Reform, Reaction, Revolution.* Cambridge, Massachusetts: Oelgeschlager, Gunn and Hain, 1981.

_____. "Thailand's Revolutionary Insurgency: Changes in Leadership Potential," *Asian Survey,* 19, No. 4, April 1979, 315–32.

Morrison, Charles E., and Astri Suhrke. *Strategies of Survival: The Foreign Policy Dilemmas of Smaller Asian States.* New York: St. Martin's Press, 1979.

Neher, Clark D. *The Dynamics of Politics and Administration in Rural Thailand.* Athens: Ohio University, 1974.

_____. "Move to Censure Prem 'May Spark a Coup'," *Bangkok Post,* March 20, 1987, 3.

_____. "Political Forces in Thailand," *Current History,* 83, No. 497, December 1984, 418-21.

_____. *Politics and Culture in Thailand.* (Politics and Culture Series.) Ann Arbor: Center for Political Studies, Institute for Social Research, University of Michigan, 1987.

_____. "Thailand in 1986: Prem, Parliament, and Political Pragmatism," *Asian Survey,* 27, No. 2, February 1987, 219-30.

Neher, Clark D. (ed.). *Modern Thai Politics: From Village to Nation.* Cambridge, Massachusetts: Schenkman Publishing Company, 1976.

Niksch, Larry A. "Thailand in 1980: Confrontation with Vietnam and the Fall of Kriangsak," *Asian Survey,* 21, No. 2, February 1981, 223-31.

_____. "Thailand in 1981: The Prem Government Feels the Heat," *Asian Survey,* 22, No. 2, February 1982, 191-99.

"No Star, But a Stirring Campaign Start," *Asiaweek* [Hong Kong], 12, No. 25, June 22, 1986, 22-23.

"No United Front As Censure Date Nears," *Bangkok Post,* April 11, 1987, 5.

"Once Again, It's Premier Prem," *Asiaweek* [Hong Kong], 12, No. 33, August 17, 1986, 19.

"Opposition to Resubmit No-Confidence Motion," *Bangkok Post,* April 23, 1987, 1.

Paisal, Sricharatchanya. "City on the Mend: Governor Chamlong Srimuang Brings Some Order to the Capital," *Far Eastern Economic Review* [Hong Kong] 134, No. 52, September 4, 1986, 18-19.

_____. "Promise of the Good Life: A Plethora of Parties Offers Quick Fixes for a Sagging Economy," *Far Eastern Economic Review* [Hong Kong], 133, No. 29, July 17, 1986, 36-37.

_____. "Queen Sirikit Helps Peasants Generate Extra Income," *Far Eastern Economic Review* [Hong Kong], 131, No. 4, January 23, 1986, 26-28.

_____. "Renewing Old Ties: Thai Visit to Lao Helps Improve Relations," *Far Eastern Economic Review* [Hong Kong], 134, No. 51, December 18, 1986, 29-30.

Pauker, Guy J. "The ASEAN Energy Scene in Global Perspective," *Asian Survey,* 19, No. 6, June 1979, 627–38.

Phuangkasem, Corrine. *Thailand's Foreign Relations 1964–80.* (Occasional Paper, No. 74.) Singapore: Institute of Southeast Asian Studies, 1984.

Pichai Chuensuksawadi, Banyat Tasaneeyavej, and Nattaya Chetchotiros. "Democracy, Army-Style?" *Bangkok Post,* March 13, 1987, 4.

Pike, Douglas. "Communist vs Communist in Southeast Asia," *International Security,* Summer, 1979, 20–39.

Prachyadavi, Tavedikul. "Breakthrough in Indochina?" *Bangkok Post,* December 5, 1986, 4.

_____. "Soul Searching in Thai Foreign Policy," *Bangkok Post,* January 1, 1987, 28.

"Prem Set to Face Challenge in House: Supporters Bid to Block Debate," *Bangkok Post,* April 21, 1987, 1.

Punyaratabandhu-Bhakdi, Suchitra. "Thailand in 1982: General Arthit Takes Center Stage," *Asian Survey,* 23, No. 2, February 1983, 172–77.

_____. "Thailand in 1983: Democracy, Thai Style," *Asian Survey,* 24, No. 2, February 1984, 187–94.

Race, Jeffrey. "The January 1975 Thai Elections: Preliminary Data and Inferences," *Asian Survey,* 15, No. 4, April 1975, 375–81.

_____. "Thailand in 1974: A New Constitution," *Asian Survey,* 15, No. 2, February 1975, 157–65.

Ramsay, Ansil. "Tenancy and Landlessness in Thailand: How Severe a Problem?" *Asian Survey,* 22, No. 11, November 1982, 1074–92.

_____. "Thailand 1978: Kriangsak—The Thai Who Binds," *Asian Survey,* 19, No. 2, February 1979, 104–14.

_____. "Thailand 1979: A Government in Trouble," *Asian Survey,* 20, No. 2, February 1980, 112–22.

_____. "Thailand: Surviving the 1980s," *Current History,* 86, No. 519, April 1987, 164–67.

Randolph, R. Sean "The Limits of Influence: American Aid to Thailand, 1965-1970," *Asian Affairs: An American Review,* 6, No. 4, March–April 1979, 243–66.

"Rangers Lay Siege to Kukrit's House," *Bangkok Post,* April 6, 1987, 1.

Richburg, Keith B. "Thailand's Army Chief Touches Off Debate: Call for Peaceful Revolution Draws Fire," *Washington Post,* April 16, 1987, A36.

_____. "Thai Scandals Raise Army's Concerns," *Washington Post,* November 9, 1986, A28.

The Royal Thai Government—A Directory 1982. Bangkok: Business Information and Research Company, 1982.

"Rural Voters Support Individual, Not Parties," *Far Eastern Economic Review* [Hong Kong], 132, No. 25, June 19, 1986, 44–45.

"Secret Fund: Army Prevails," *Bangkok Post,* December 13, 1986, 4.

Seah, Chee-Meow. "Student Activism and the Political Process of ASEAN Countries," *Pacific Community* [Tokyo], 7, No. 4, July 1976, 551–66.

Sermsuk, Kasitipradit. "Democrat Party Showdown," *Bangkok Post,* January 10, 1987, 4.

_____. "Military in Move to Foil Censure Bid," *Bangkok Post,* April 14, 1987, 6.

Siffin, William J. *The Thai Bureaucracy: Institutional Change and Development.* Honolulu: East-West Center Press, 1966.

Simon, Sheldon W. "The ASEAN States: Obstacles to Security Cooperation," *ORBIS,* 22, No. 2, Summer 1978, 415–34.

Somboom, Suksamran. *Political Buddhism in Southeast Asia: The Role of the Sangha in the Modernization of Thailand.* New York: St. Martin's Press, 1976.

Somsakdi, Xuto, et al. *Thailand in the 1980s: Significant Issues, Problems, and Prospects.* Bangkok: Tura Institute, 1981.

Somvichian, Kamol. "The Oyster and the Shell: Thai Bureaucrats in Politics," *Asian Survey,* 18, No. 8, August 1978, 829–37.

Stifel, Laurence D. "Technocrats and Modernization in Thailand," *Asian Survey,* 16, No. 12, December 1976, 1184–96.

Stuart-Fox, Martin. "Factors Influencing Relations Between the Communist Parties of Thailand and Laos," *Asian Survey,* 19, No. 4, April 1979, 333–52.

Suhrke, Astri. "Loyalists and Separatists: The Muslims in Southern Thailand," *Asian Survey,* 17, No. 3, March 1977, 237–50.

_____. "Thailand: Politics as Usual," *Current History,* 77, No. 452, December 1979, 210–13.

Surachai Sirikrai. "General Prem Survives on a Conservative Line," *Asian Survey,* 22, No. 11, November 1982, 1093–1104.

Surin, Pitsuwan. "The Political Will, Military Might . . . and Democracy," *Bangkok Post,* October 20, 1986, 4.

Thailand. *Constitution of the Kingdom of Thailand.* (Certified correct English translation by Juridical Council. Document originally published in the Government Gazette, Vol. 95, Part 146, Special Issue, 1978). Bangkok: December 22, 1978.

_____. Office of the Prime Minister. Public Relations Department. *Thai Government Organizational Directory, 1986,* Bangkok: 1986.

_____. *Thailand in Brief.* Bangkok: August 1985.

Thak Chaloemtiarana. "Reflections on the Sarit Regime and the Process of Political Change in Thailand: Some Conceptual and Theoretical Reassessments," *Southeast Asian Studies,* 16, No. 3, December 1978, 400–10.

_____. *Thailand: The Politics of Despotic Paternalism.* Bangkok: Thammasat University Printing Press, 1979.

Thawatt Mokarapong. *History of the Thai Revolution: A Study in Political Behaviour.* Bangkok: Chaalermnit, 1972.

Theh, Chongkhadikij. "An Important Year for General Prem," *Bangkok Post,* January 1987, 27.

_____. "Prasong Calls for Changes in Constitution," *Bangkok Post,* July 9, 1987, 1.

_____. "Prem Reveals Formula for National Success," *Bangkok Post,* March 4, 1987, 1.

_____. "Siddhi Reveals Shift in Policy on Kampuchean Issue," *Bangkok Post,* August 14, 1986, 1.

"Total Viet Withdrawal Unrealistic—Scientist," *Bangkok Post,* December 22, 1986, 3.

Turton, Andrew, Jonathan Fast, and Malcolm Caldwell, *Thailand: Roots of Conflict.* Nottingham, United Kingdom: Bertrand Russell Home, 1978.

United States. United States Information Agency. "Mass Media Usage in Bangkok 1984." (Research Memorandum.), Washington: January 16, 1985.

_____. "Thai Use of Local Media for Foreign News" (Research Memorandum), Washington: April 2, 1985.

Wilson, David A. *The United States and the Future of Thailand.* New York: Praeger, 1970.

Wong, John. *ASEAN Economies in Perspective: A Comparative Study of Indonesia, Malaysia, the Philippines, Singapore, and Thailand.* Philadelphia: Institute for the Study of Human Issues, 1979.

Wyatt, David K. *Thailand: A Short History.* New Haven: Yale University Press, 1984.

Yah, Lim Chong. "ASEAN's Internal Advances and External Unity," *Asia Pacific Community* [Tokyo], No. 6, Fall 1979, 31–43.

Zimmerman, Robert F. "Insurgency in Thailand," *Problems of Communism,* 25, May–June 1976, 18–39.

_____. "Thailand 1975: Transition to Constitutional Democracy Continues," *Asian Survey,* 16, No. 2, February 1976, 159–72.

(Various issues of the following periodicals were also used in the preparation of this chapter: *Asian Recorder* [New Delhi]; *Asian Survey; Bangkok Post; Christian Science Monitor; Deadline Data on World Affairs; Far Eastern Economic Review* [Hong Kong]; *Far Eastern Economic*

Review Asia Yearbook [Hong Kong]; *Financial Times* [London]; *Foreign Broadcast Information Service Daily Reports: Asia and Pacific;* Joint Publications Research Service (JPRS) *Southeast Asia Report; Keesings Contemporary Archives* [Edinburgh]; *New York Times; Southeast Asian Affairs* [Singapore]; *Washington Post; Washington Star.*)

Chapter 5

Alpern, Stephen I. "Insurgency in Northeast Thailand: A New Cause for Alarm," *Asian Survey,* 15, No. 8, August 1975, 684-92.
_____. "Insurgency in Thailand: An Analysis of the Government Response," *Military Review,* 55, No. 7, July 1975, 10-17.
Ball, George W. "Thailand Next?" *Washington Post,* November 2, 1979, A17.
Barang, Marcel. "The Struggle for Hearts and Minds," *Far Eastern Economic Review* [Hong Kong], 96, No. 16, April 22, 1977, 13.
Bowring, Philip. "Shifts in Foreign Policy," *Financial Times* [London], December 18, 1979, 30.
_____. "Thailand: Further Aid for Rural Areas," *Financial Times* [London], December 18, 1979, 29.
Bowring, Philip, and Paisal Sricharatchanya. "Shaking the Pillars," *Far Eastern Economic Review* [Hong Kong], 112, No. 26, June 19, 1981, 38-43.
Burgess, John. "Thais Turn to Bank Loans for Defense," *Washington Post,* September 6, 1978, D3.
Chai-anan Samudavanija. *The Thai Young Turks.* Singapore: Institute of Southeast Asian Studies, 1982.
Chanda, Nayan. "Battles Along the Border," *Far Eastern Economic Review* [Hong Kong], 97, No. 32, August 12, 1977, 16.
_____. *Brother Enemy: The War After the War, A History of Indochina Since the Fall of Saigon.* New York: Harcourt Brace Jovanovich, 1986.
Clifford, W. "Science, Culture, and Criminal Justice in Asia," *International Journal of Comparative and Applied Criminal Justice,* 2, No. 2, Winter 1978, 191-205.
Copeley, Gregory R. (ed.). *Defense and Foreign Affairs Handbook 1977-78.* New York: Franklin Watts, 1978.
Crozier, Brian (ed.). *Thailand: The Dual Threat to Stability.* (Conflict Studies, No. 44.) London: Institute for the Study of Conflict, 1974.
Darling, Frank R. "Thailand." Pages 290-93 in Richard F. Staar (ed.), *Yearbook on International Communist Affairs, 1979.* Stanford, California: Hoover Institution Press, 1979.

Das, K. "Strife Among the Rebels," *Far Eastern Economic Review* [Hong Kong], 112, No. 19, May 1, 1981, 13–14.

_____. "Thailand: Transitional Military Rule?" *Current History*, 73, No. 434, December 1978, 208–11.

_____. "Operation People's War," *Far Eastern Economic Review* [Hong Kong], 96, No. 16, April 22, 1977, 10–12.

Day, Booner. "U.S. in the Pacific: Overcommitted and Undermanned," *Air Force Magazine*, No. 11, November 1979, 92–97.

De Beer, Patrice. "History and Policy of the Communist Party of Thailand." Pages 143–57 in Andrew Turton, Jonathon Fast, and Malcolm Caldwell (eds.), *Thailand: Roots of Conflict*. Nottingham, United Kingdom: Spokesman, 1978.

Dorey, Marcia A. and George J. Swidler, *World Police Systems: A Factual Text*. Boston: Northeastern University, 1975.

Depuy, Trevor N., Grace P. Hayes, and John A.C. Andrews. *The Almanac of World Military Power*. New York: Bowker, 1974.

Foreign Military Markets: South America/Australasia. (Market Intelligence Reports.) Greenwich, Connecticut: Defense Marketing Service, 1979.

Ghosh, Suchita. "Role of the Military in Thailand," *Institute for Defence Studies and Analysis Journal* [New Delhi], 10, No. 2, October–December 1977, 142–56.

Goldstein, Carl. "Letter from Mae Salong," *Far Eastern Economic Review* [Hong Kong], 105, No. 33, August 17, 1979, 70.

Gooi, Kim. "Letter from Aranyaprathet," *Far Eastern Economic Review* [Hong Kong], 105, No. 39, September 28, 1979, 86.

_____. "The Lure of Pol Pot's Gold," *Far Eastern Economic Review* [Hong Kong], 105, No. 31, August 3, 1979, 32–33.

Gua, Bo. "Opium, Bombs, and Trees: The Future of the H'mong Tribesman in Northern Thailand," *Journal of Contemporary Asia* [London], 5, No. 1, January 1975, 70–81.

Gwertzman, Bernard. "A Vietnamese Drive Along Thai Border is Reported by U.S.," *New York Times*, January 31, 1980, A1.

Haseman, John B. *The Thai Resistance Movement During the Second World War*. De Kalb: Northern Illinois University, 1978.

Hatcher, Dave. "Rapprochement Under Fire," *Far Eastern Economic Review* [Hong Kong], 99, No. 1, January 6, 1978, 810.

Ho Kwon Ping. "Thailand's Broken Ricebowl," *Far Eastern Economic Review* [Hong Kong], 102, No. 48, December 1, 1978, 40–45.

International Institute for Strategic Studies. *The Military Balance*, London: 1986, 170.

Jane's Weapon Systems, 1985–86. London: Jane's Publishing, 1986.

Kamm, Henry. "Thailand Steps Up Its Arms Purchases From U.S.," *New York Times,* January 6, 1980, 6.

Keyes, Charles F. *Buddhist Kingdom as Modern Nation-State.* Boulder, Colorado: Westview Press, 1987.

Levine, Charles (ed.). *Thailand.* Singapore: APA Publications, 1977.

Lissak, Moshe. *Military Roles in Modernization: Civil-Military Relations in Thailand and Burma.* Beverly Hills, California: Sage Publications, 1976.

Liu, Melinda. "The Triangle's Pecking Order," *Far Eastern Economic Review* [Hong Kong], 105, No. 37, September 14, 1979, 38–40.

Lobe, Thomas. *United States National Security Policy and Aid to the Thailand Police.* (Monograph Series in World Affairs, Graduate School of International Studies, 14, No. 2.). Denver: University of Denver, 1977.

Lobe, Thomas, and David Morell. "Thailand's Border Patrol Police: Paramilitary Political Power." Pages 153–78 in Louis A. Zurcher and Gwyn Harries-Jenkins (eds.), *Supplementary Military Forces: Reserves, Militias, Auxiliaries.* Beverly Hills, California: Sage Publications, 1978.

Luther, Hans U. "Peasants and State in Contemporary Thailand," *International Journal of Politics* [Hamburg], 8, No. 4, Winter 1978–79, 1–120.

Marks, Thomas A. "The Military and Politics in Thailand: An Analysis of the Two October Coups (1976–1977)," *Issues and Studies* [Taipei], 14, January 1978, 58–90.

McBeth, John. "Decline and Defection," *Far Eastern Economic Review* [Hong Kong], 118, No. 50, December 10, 1982, 15–16.

_____. "The Disappearing Army," *Far Eastern Economic Review* [Hong Kong], 131, No. 2, January 9, 1986, 30.

_____. "Hanoi's Troops Shift Inland," *Far Eastern Economic Review* [Hong Kong], 131, No. 20, March 15, 1986, 28.

_____. "A Long, Tough March Towards Total Security," *Far Eastern Economic Review* [Hong Kong], 132, No. 16, April 17, 1986, 30–33.

_____. "Open-Arms Cache," *Far Eastern Economic Review* [Hong Kong], 132, No. 17, April 24, 1986, 44–46.

_____. "A Profile of the Young Turks' Camp," *Far Eastern Economic Review* [Hong Kong], 112, No. 26, June 19, 1981, 44–53.

McBeth, John and Paisal Sricharatchanya, "The Coup Mentality," *Far Eastern Economic Review* [Hong Kong], 130, No. 47, November 28, 1985, 4–37.

Morell, David, and Chai-anan Samudavanija. "Thailand's Revolutionary Insurgency: Changes in Leadership Potential," *Asian Survey*, 19, No. 4, April 1979, 315–32.

Moritz, Frederic A. "Pol Pot Troops Slip In and Out of Thai Sanctuaries," *Christian Science Monitor*, November 28, 1979, 13.

————. "Tough Thai Armor Forces Ready if Viets Attack This Month," *Christian Science Monitor*, December 3, 1979, 3.

Morrison, Charles E., and Astri Suhrke, *Strategies of Survival: The Foreign Policy Dilemmas of Smaller Asian States*. New York: St. Martin's Press, 1979.

Morrow, Michael. "Bases: Costly Legacy for Thais," *Far Eastern Economic Review* [Hong Kong], 92, No. 14, April 2, 1976, 40–43.

Mudannayake, Ivan (ed.). *Thailand Year Book 1975–76*. Bangkok: Temple Publicity Services, 1975.

Nations, Richard. "Thailand's Tactical Retreat," *Far Eastern Economic Review* [Hong Kong], 105, No. 27, July 6, 1979, 52–53.

Noranit Setabutr, *The Role of the Military in Thailand: 1958–1970*, Bangkok: Praepittaya, 1971.

"October 1976: The Coup in Thailand," (Special Supplement.) *Bulletin of Concerned Asian Scholars*, 9, No. 3, July–September 1977, 2–51.

Olsen, Edward A. and Stephen Jurika, Jr. (eds.). *The Armed Forces in Contemporary Asian Societies*. Boulder, Colorado: Westview Press, 1986.

Paisal Sricharatchanya. "The Army Fights To Win the Cities of the Mind," *Far Eastern Economic Review* [Hong Kong] 119, No. 7, February 17, 1983, 18.

————. "The Army's New Role," *Far Eastern Economic Review* [Hong Kong], 135, No. 8, February 19, 1987, 24–25.

————. "How the Communists Crumbled in Two Years of Border War," *Far Eastern Economic Review* [Hong Kong], 114, No. 42, October 9, 1981, 23–24.

————. "A 'Lean, Mean Machine'," *Far Eastern Economic Review* [Hong Kong], 135, No. 8, February 19, 1987, 26–27.

————. "Malaysian Reds Under Fire," *Far Eastern Economic Review* [Hong Kong], 128, No. 20, May 23, 1985, 50–51.

————. "The Muslims Move In," *Far Eastern Economic Review* [Hong Kong], 114, No. 42, October 9, 1981, 23.

————. "Winning Hearts and Minds," *Far Eastern Economic Review* [Hong Kong], 135, No. 10, March 5, 1987, 38–40.

Race, Jeffrey. "Thailand in 1974: A New Constitution," *Asian Survey*, 15, No. 2, February 1975, 157–65.

Randolph, R. Sean. "The Limits of Influence: American Aid to Thailand, 1965–1970," *Asian Affairs: An American Review*, 6, No. 4, March–April 1979, 243–66.

Richardson, Michael. "Keeping up the Momentum," *Far Eastern Economic Review* [Hong Kong], 99, No. 10, March 10, 1978, 16.

Schneider, Robert J., Phon Sangsingkeo, and Serin Punnahita-nond. "A Survey of Thai Student Use of Illicit Drugs," *The International Journal of the Addictions,* 12, February–March 1977, 227–39.

Somvichian, Kamol. "The Oyster and the Shell: Thai Bureaucrats in Politics," *Asian Survey,* 18, No. 8, August 1978, 829–37.

Sorenson, Torkil, and John McBeth. "The Fast-ebbing Tide," *Far Eastern Economic Review* [Hong Kong], 125, No. 29, July 19, 1984, 28.

Suhrke, Astri. "Loyalists and Separatists: The Muslims in Southern Thailand," *Asian Survey,* 17, No. 3, March 1977, 237–50.

_____. "Thailand: Politics as Usual," *Current History,* 74, No. 446, December 1979.

Suwanwela, Charas, et al. "The Hill Tribes of Thailand: Their Opium Use and Addiction," *Bulletin on Narcotics,* 30, No. 2, April–June 1978, 1–19.

Tanham, George K. *Trial in Thailand.* New York: Crane, Russak, 1974.

Thailand. *Constitution of the Kingdom of Thailand* (Certified correct English translation by Juridical Council. Document originally published in Government Gazette, Vol. 95, Part 146, Special Issue, 1978), Bangkok: December 22, 1978.

Thak Chaloemtiarana. *Thailand: The Politics of Despotic Paternalism.* Bangkok: Thammasat University, 1979.

Thomas, M. Ladd. "The Malayan Communist Insurgents and Thai Malaysian Relations," *Asian Affairs: An American Review,* 4, No. 6, July–August 1977, 371–84.

United States. Congress. 92d, 2d Session. Senate. Committee on Foreign Relations. Subcommittee on U.S. Security Agreements and Commitments Abroad. *Thailand, Laos, and Cambodia: January 1972.* (Staff Report.) Washington: GPO, May 8, 1972.

_____. Congress. 96th, 1st Session. House of Representatives. Committee on Foreign Affairs. Subcommittee on Asian and Pacific Affairs. *Security and Stability in Asia: 1979.* Washington: GPO, May 1979.

_____. Department of State. *Cooperation in Combating Illicit International Traffic in Narcotics and Other Dangerous Drugs: Memorandum of Understanding Between the United States of America and Thailand* (Signed at Washington September 28, 1971. Treaties and Other International Acts, Series 7185.) Washington: GPO, 1971.

_____. General Accounting Office. *Withdrawal of U.S. Forces from Thailand: Ways to Improve Future Withdrawal Operations.* (Report to the Congress by the Comptroller General of the United States.) Washington: GPO, November 1, 1977.

――――. "Thailand." Pages 424–31 in *Report on Human Rights Practices in Countries Receiving U.S. Aid.* (Report submitted to the Committee on Foreign Relations, United States. Senate, and Committee on Foreign Affairs, United States House of Representatives, February 8, 1979.) Washington: GPO, 1980.

Van der Kroef, Justus M. "Thailand: A New Phase in the Insurgency?" *Pacific Community* [Tokyo], 8, No. 4, July 1977, 600–24.

Weintraub, Peter, and David Lawton. "Thailand's Drug Trade Tangle," *Far Eastern Economic Review* [Hong Kong], 100, No. 17, April 28, 1978, 23–27.

Wilson, David A. "The Military in Thai Politics," Pages 253–431 in Johnson, John J. (ed.), *The Role of the Military in Underdeveloped Countries.* Princeton: Princeton University Press, 1962.

Wyatt, David K. *Thailand: A Short History.* New Haven, Connecticut: Yale University Press, 1984.

Zimmerman, Robert F. "Insurgency in Thailand," *Problems of Communism,* 25, May–June 1976, 18–39.

(Various issues of the following periodicals were also used in the preparation of this section: *Bangkok Post; Deadline Data; Far Eastern Economic Review* [Hong Kong]; *Far Eastern Economic Review Asia Year Book* [Hong Kong]; *Foreign Broadcast Information Service Daily Reports: Asia and Pacific;* Joint Publications Research Service (JPRS) *Southeast Asia Report; Keesing's Contemporary Archives* [Edinburgh]; *The Military Balance* [London]; *New York Times;* and *Washington Post.*)

Glossary

baht (B)—Basic currency unit, divided into 100 satang. In 1984 the value of the baht was tied to a basket of foreign currencies, including the United States dollar, that were significant to the Thai economy. The exchange rate per US$1 was B25.74 in September 1987.

chaophraya—Traditional title given to the highest ranking official in the civil government.

fiscal year (FY)—October 1 to September 30.

General Agreement on Tariffs and Trade (GATT)—A multilateral trade agreement signed at the Geneva Conference in 1947, which both sets out rules of conduct for international trade relations and provides a forum for multilateral negotiations on trade problems and the gradual elimination of tariffs and other trade barriers.

gross domestic product (GDP)—The total value of goods and services produced within a country's borders during a fixed period, usually one year. Obtained by adding the value contributed by each sector of the economy in the form of compensation of employees, profits, and depreciation (consumption of capital). Subsistence production is included and consists of the imputed value of production by the farm family for its own use and the imputed rental value of owner-occupied dwellings.

gross national product (GNP)—Gross domestic product (*q.v.*) plus the income from overseas investments and wages, minus the earnings of foreign investors and workers in the home economy.

Khmer Rouge—The name given to Khmer communists by Prince Sihanouk in the 1960s. Later (although a misnomer) it was applied to the Cambodian insurgents of varying ideological backgrounds who opposed the Khmer Republic of Lon Nol. Between 1975 and 1978 it also became an informal designation for the regime of Democratic Kampuchea, whose leaders were the radical Pol Pot faction of the Kampuchean (or Khmer) Communist Party. After the Vietnamese invasion of Cambodia in December 1978, the Khmer Rouge became one of the three components of the Coalition Government of Democratic Kampuchea that contested the Vietnamese presence and the Hanoi-installed regime of the People's Republic of Kampuchea.

khwan—Body-spirit or life-soul, generally thought to reside in the head; illness and death follow loss of the *khwan*.

luang—Title of distinction designating that its bearer is in royal service.

nai—Literally, master. Lowest rank in the traditional nobility, the term is also used as a mark of respect for employers or any person of superior status. Under the *sakdi na (q.v.)* system, it identified its bearer as a landholder to whom labor service was due. Variant form is *naaj.*

phi—General term for a variety of spirits believed to have power over human beings. Specific kinds of spirits may have particular names.

phra—Traditional princely title prefix designating that its bearer is a relative of the king; functional title given to holders of ranks in the civil administration below that of *phraya (q.v.)*; honorific for monks or persons and objects having religious associations.

phrai—Generic term for commoners, variously translated as servant, serf, or, incorrectly, as slave. The *phrai* was bound to the land in the service of a *nai (q.v.)* under the *sakdi na (q.v.)* system.

phraya—Traditional princely title conferred on holder of second highest rank in the civil government and on viceroys of tributary states. Sometimes seen as *phrajaa* or *phya.*

sakdi na—Literally, *sak* (power in the sense of resources); *na* (paddy land). A system of social ranking originally based on the king's allocation of specific quantities of rice land to persons according to their rank, each such rank being defined in terms of so-called quality points (or dignity marks). The size of the allotment was closely associated with the number of persons owing labor service to an individual of a given rank; by the beginning of the Chakkri Dynasty in 1782, an individual's rank in the system was thought of primarily in relation to the number of persons owing him service, regardless of the amount of land he controlled.

shifting cultivation—A traditional method of agriculture characterized by the rotation of fields rather than crops, the use of short cropping periods and long fallow periods, and the maintenance of fertility by allowing natural vegetation to regenerate on fallow land. Clearing of new or previously cropped land is often accomplished by cutting and burning vegetation. Also known as slash-and-burn or swidden agriculture. Thai term is *tam rai.*

Siam—Official name of the Thai kingdom from 1855 to 1939 and again from 1946 to 1949. Used conventionally in European sources from the late sixteenth century for the kingdom of Ayutthaya and later the kingdom of Bangkok, hence the term Siamese *(q.v.)* to describe their inhabitants.

Siamese—Inhabitants of Siam (*q.v.*). Historically used by Mon and Khmer to distinguish Tai (*q.v.*)-speaking settlers in the Chao Phraya Valley from those in other regions. The term was extended in conventional usage to inhabitants of Siam. Between 1939 and 1946 and since 1949, Thai (*q.v.*) and not Siamese has been employed to describe the dominant ethnic group of Thailand and Central Thai to denote the Thai of the Chao Phraya Valley.

Sino-Thai—Term used by observers of Thailand for persons of Chinese and Thai ancestry. It does not apply to a clearly delineated, cohesive group; some such persons have been essentially assimilated into Thai society; others (usually with a recent Chinese forebear) have not.

Tai—A family of languages spoken in Southeast Asia and southern China including Thai (*q.v.*); by extension the peoples speaking languages of that family.

Thai—A national of Thailand; one or more persons of the (regionally varied) ethnic group dominant in Thailand; the (dialectically varied) language of the Thai people, one of several grouped in Tai (*q.v.*) family of languages; also used adjectivally.

World Bank—Informal name used to designate a group of three affiliated international institutions: the International Bank for Reconstruction and Development (IBRD), the International Development Association (IDA), and the International Finance Corporation (IFC). The IBRD, established in 1945, has the primary purpose of providing loans to developing countries for productive projects. The IDA, a legally separate loan fund but administered by the staff of the IBRD, was set up in 1960 to furnish credits to the poorest developing countries on much easier terms than those of conventional IBRD loans. The IFC, founded in 1956, supplements the activities of the IBRD through loans and assistance specifically designed to encourage the growth of productive private enterprises in the less developed countries. The president and certain senior officers of the IBRD hold the same positions in the IFC. The three institutions are owned by the governments of the countries that subscribe their capital.

Index

administrative law, 193
administrative regions, 193, 194
Agricultural Land Reform Act of 1975, 152
agricultural land reform program, 164
Agricultural Land Rent Control Act of 1974, 152
agricultural sector, xv, xxv, 123; credit availability to, 129–30; effect of commercialization of, 87; employment in, xv, 132; expansion of, 144; increase in land requirements, 162, 164, 165; manufactured products of, xv, 139; in North region, 62; production of, xv, 46, 155; tenancy in, 149–50
AIDS, 115
air bases, 252–53, 262–63
airport, 174
Airport Authority of Thailand (AAT), 174
air power: supplements to, 263
Akha (Kaw) people, 75
American troops. See military assistance; military bases; United States
ammunition manufacture, 250
Amnesty International, 116, 269
Ananda Mahidol (Rama VIII), 27–28, 32
Angkor, 7
Anglo-Burmese War, 19
animal husbandry, 160
anticommunist policy (see also counterinsurgency operations; infrastructure development; military assistance; national security), 32, 38, 214; Anti-Communist Activities Act (1979), 269; Anti-Communist Act of 1933, 229; legislation, 46, 269; in remote villages, 230–31
antimonarchist factions, 241
armed forces (see also Royal Thai Air Force; Royal Thai Army; Royal Thai Marines; Royal Thai Navy), xviii; civic program participation of, 244; officer corps in, 246–47; rank structure of, 265, 268; reliance for political stability on, 242; role in counterinsurgent actions, 243–44; strength of, 239; structure of, 254–56; training

programs and facilities of, 263–65; uniforms of, 265
armies, private, 237
army reserves, 246, 261
Army Signal Corps, 201
art, 113
Arthit Kamlangek, 203–8, 255
ASA. See Association of Southeast Asia (ASA)
ASEAN. See Association of Southeast Asian Nations (ASEAN)
assimilation: of Chinese people, xxvi, 80, 91; of Mon people, 78–79; policy of, 70, 80; of South Asian people, 81
Association of Southeast Asia (ASA), 39, 215
Association of Southeast Asian Nations (ASEAN), 184, 215; support for Cambodian resistance groups, 235–36; Thailand as member, 45, 215
automobile industry, domestic, 172
Ayutthaya kingdom, xxi, 10–11, 13, 60; economic importance of, 15, 17; foreign trade of, 17
Ayutthaya Thai. See Central Thai

Bangkok: First Army headquarters in, 257, 259; government of, 196; headquarters of Royal Thai Air Force, 262; location of, 65; as major air traffic center, 174; as major port, 168, 173; population of, 67, 69
Bangkok Entertainment Company, 201
Bangkok Stock Exchange. See Security Exchange of Thailand
Bangkok Television Company, 201
Bangkok-Thon Buri metropolitan area, 46
Bang Pakong, 179
Bank for Agriculture and Agricultural Cooperatives (state-owned), 128, 130
Bank of Thailand (central bank), 128, 142
banks: commercial, 128, 130–31; foreign, 125, 249–50
Ban Pak Nam naval base, 262
Ban Pho hydroelectric facility, 176
Ban U Taphao, 252

351

Foreign Military Sales (FMS) credits, 251, 254; increase after 1976, 253
foreign policy, 45; effect of sending troops in World War I, 241; flexibility of, xxviii, 215, 222-23; objectives of, xviii, 184, 235; toward Laos, 221, 221-22; toward United States, 124, 135, 220; toward Vietnam, 184, 218
foreign trade: composititon of, xvi, 140; importance of, 123-24; with newly industrializing countries (NICs), 135; in reign of Mongkut, 20-21; trading partners in, xvi, 134-35
Forest Industry Organization, 164
forests (*see also* reforestation; teak industry), 62; destruction by farmers of, 162, 164, 165; reduction of, xv, 162; state ownership of, 162
fowl production, 161
France: effect of imperialism, 22; support by Thailand for Indochina campaign, 34; treaty revision with, 241
freedom of the press, 199-200
Free Thai Movement, 30, 31
fruit, 134, 155
Funan state, 5, 7
furniture, 134

GATT. *See* General Agreement on Tariffs and Trade (GATT)
gem industry, 167
General Agreement on Tariffs and Trade (GATT): effect of Tokyo Round of, 135
geography, xiii; diversity of regions, 62
Girling, John L. S., 204
Golden Triangle, 75, 282
government, xvii; agencies for industrial policy, 142; interdependence with *sangha* of, 104-5; interim, 1947, 33
government bond repurchase market, 129
Government Housing Bank (state-owned), 128
Government Savings Bank (state-owned), 128
Great Britain (*see also* Bowring Treaty; Burney Treaty), 17-18, 20; effect of imperialism, 22; treaty revision with, 241
gross domestic product, 124; ratio of agriculture to total, 144
Group of Nineteen, 213-14
guerrilla activity, 41

guerrilla radio station. *See* Voice of the People of Thailand (VOPT)

Harn Linanond, 206
health (*see also* public health), xv,113-15
heterogeneity: of lower urban social stratum, 92-93; of urban middle class, 92
highway system, national, 172
hill people: Akha (Kaw), 75; Hmong (Meo, Miao), 75, 77, 115-16, 147; insurgent elements of, 228; Karen, 70, 74, 75, 146; Lahu (Mussur) people, 75; languages of, 76; Lisu (Lisaw), 75, 147; Mien (Yao), 75, 77
Hindu religion: coexistence with Buddhism, 7; influence on Mon people, 7; rites for birth, death, and marriage, 102
Hindus, 81, 109
Hmong (Meo, Miao) people, 75, 77, 147; migration to Thailand of, 115-16
homogeneity of society, xxi, xxv, 69
Hong Kong, 135
household network, rural, 86-87
House of Representatives: role in National Assembly of, 189-90
housing, 114, 123
human capital as national asset, xxi, xxv
human rights organizations, 116, 269
hydroelectric power facilities, 154, 175-76

IFCT. *See* Industrial Finance Corporation of Thailand (IFCT)
imperialism, 22
imports, 124
independence, 3-4, 23
Indonesia, 135
industrial development plans, 141-42
Industrial Finance Corporation of Thailand (IFCT), 128, 130, 142
industrial policy, 142-44
Industrial Restructuring Committee, 142
industrial sector: contribution to economic growth, xv, 139
infiltration, military, 235; actions of Border Patrol Police (BPP) in, 273-74
inflation, 49, 132
infrastructure development, xv, 239
insurgent activity (*see also* revolutionaries), decrease by mid-1987, 233; increase after 1965, 231; as threat to national security, 228

water supply (*see also* irrigation), 114; control system, 153–54; pollution of parts of, 162

waterways (*see also* canals), xvi, 168, 171

weapons pool. *See* war reserve weapons pool

Weinberger, Caspar, 253

Western influence, xxii, 21–22, 28, 33; effect on military establishment of, 241–42; on legal system, 275–76

Winchester Arms Company, 250

wood as fuel, 175

World Bank: assistance for highway development from, 172; financial assistance for railway system, 171; financial assistance from, 154; loans for natural gas exploitation, 179

World War I, 25, 241

World War II, xxiii, 29–30

yams, 155

Yot Fa (Rama I): contributions of, 19

Young Turks, 202–3, 205, 247–48

zinc mining and production, 168

Published Country Studies

(Area Handbook Series)

550-65	Afghanistan	550-153	Ghana
550-98	Albania	550-87	Greece
550-44	Algeria	550-78	Guatemala
550-59	Angola	550-174	Guinea
550-73	Argentina	550-82	Guyana
550-169	Australia	550-151	Honduras
550-176	Austria	550-165	Hungary
550-175	Bangladesh	550-21	India
550-170	Belgium	550-154	Indian Ocean
550-66	Bolivia	550-39	Indonesia
550-20	Brazil	550-68	Iran
550-168	Bulgaria	550-31	Iraq
550-61	Burma	550-25	Israel
550-37	Burundi/Rwanda	550-182	Italy
550-50	Cambodia	550-30	Japan
550-166	Cameroon	550-34	Jordan
550-159	Chad	550-56	Kenya
550-77	Chile	550-81	Korea, North
550-60	China	550-41	Korea, South
550-26	Colombia	550-58	Laos
550-33	Commonwealth Caribbean, Islands of the	550-24	Lebanon
550-91	Congo	550-38	Liberia
550-90	Costa Rica	550-85	Libya
550-69	Côte d'Ivoire (Ivory Coast)	550-172	Malawi
550-152	Cuba	550-45	Malaysia
550-22	Cyprus	550-161	Mauritania
550-158	Czechoslovakia	550-79	Mexico
550-36	Dominican Republic/Haiti	550-76	Mongolia
550-52	Ecuador	550-49	Morocco
550-43	Egypt	550-64	Mozambique
550-150	El Salvador	550-88	Nicaragua
550-28	Ethiopia	550-157	Nigeria
550-167	Finland	550-94	Oceania
550-155	Germany, East	550-48	Pakistan
550-173	Germany, Fed. Rep. of	550-46	Panama

550-156	Paraguay	550-89	Tunisia
550-185	Persian Gulf States	550-80	Turkey
550-42	Peru	550-74	Uganda
550-72	Philippines	550-97	Uruguay
550-162	Poland	550-71	Venezuela
550-181	Portugal	550-32	Vietnam
550-160	Romania	550-183	Yemens, The
550-51	Saudi Arabia	550-99	Yugloslavia
550-70	Senegal	550-67	Zaire
550-180	Sierra Leone	550-75	Zambia
550-184	Singapore	550-171	Zimbabwe
550-86	Somalia		
550-93	South Africa		
550-95	Soviet Union		
550-179	Spain		
500-96	Sri Lanka		
550-27	Sudan		
550-47	Syria		
550-62	Tanzania		
550-53	Thailand		

☆U.S. GOVERNMENT PRINTING OFFICE: 1989 -0- 242-444 (00014)

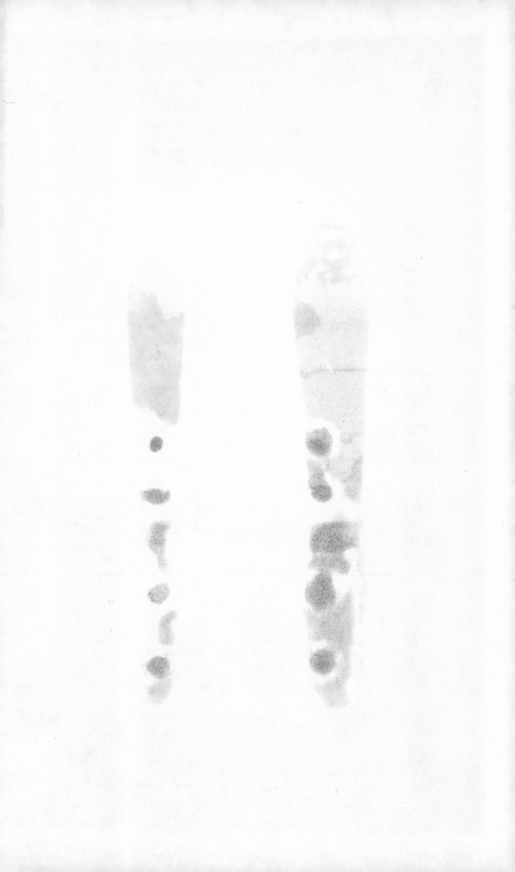